David R. Grant was born and brought up in Edinburgh. His varied career has included being a crofter, fisherman, jackaroo, sheep-shearer, member of a film crew, expeditions leader and ecologist/wildlife manager. He has made excursions to the remoter Scottish islands, to Arctic Scandinavia and most of the western Sahara Desert, been a hostage of the Popular Front for the Liberation of Palestine and for a number of years owned his own horse. His trip round the world in a horse-drawn caravan was the first of its kind, and earned him and his family an entry in the *Guinness Book of Records*.

THE SEVEN YEAR HITCH
A FAMILY ODYSSEY

DAVID R. GRANT

POCKET
BOOKS

LONDON · SYDNEY · NEW YORK · TOKYO · SINGAPORE · TORONTO

First published in Great Britain by Simon & Schuster UK Ltd, 1999
This edition first published by Pocket Books, 2000
An imprint of Simon & Schuster UK Ltd
A Viacom Company

1 3 5 7 9 10 8 6 4 2

Simon & Schuster UK Ltd
Africa House
64–78 Kingsway
London WC2B 6AH

Simon & Schuster Australia
Sydney

The author has used his best efforts to clear all quotations. He would
be glad to hear from any copyright holders not contacted.

A CIP catalogue record for this book is available
from the British Library

ISBN 0-671-02211-3

Typeset in Sabon by SX Composing DTP, Rayleigh, Essex
Printed and bound in Great Britain by
Cox and Wyman Ltd, Reading, Berkshire

INSPIRATION

Exploration is the physical expression of the Intellectual Passion. And I tell you, if you have the desire for knowledge and the power to give it physical expression, go out and explore. If you are a brave man you will do nothing: if you are fearful you may do much, for none but cowards have need to prove their bravery. Some will tell you that you are mad, and nearly all will say, 'What is the use?' For we are a nation of shopkeepers, and no shopkeeper will look at research which does not promise him a financial return within a year. And so you will sledge nearly alone, but those with whom you sledge will not be shopkeepers: that is worth a good deal. If you march your Winter Journeys you will have your reward, so long as all you want is a penguin's egg.

Apsley Cherry-Garrard,
The Worst Journey in the World

CONTENTS

Author's preface   ix
Introduction   xi
Map   xxvi

1. The Netherlands   The Paper of the Dog OK   1
2. Belgium and France   Early Days in Europe   17
3. Southern France   First Winter, Second Horse   37
4. Italy   Pasta and Pain   48
5. Austria to Slovenia   Sauerkraut and *Slivovka*   67
6. Slovenia   Illness, Independence – and War   76
7. Slovenia Again   Slovenia *Moj Drugi Dom*   94
8. Hungary   Goulash and Bull's Blood   105
9. The Ukraine
     'To a Hungry Man There is No Bad Bread'   124
10. Russia   Crayfish and Champagne   157
11. Kazakhstan   Steppe and Snow   173
12. Russia Again   Almaty to the Altai   217
13. Mongolia   The Land of Genghis Khan   234
14. Ulaanbaatar   Mongolian Circus   259
15. China   Chucked out of China   278
16. Japan   Japanese Pizza   299
17. The USA (1)   Boogie-Boards and Beaver   312
18. The USA (2)   Sitting Bull and Snow   345
19. Canada   Halifax – and Home   358

Afterword   377
Acknowledgements   380
Further reading   383
Index   385

AUTHOR'S PREFACE

This book is the story of some of the adventures which befell us during our seven years' travelling around the world with our horses and caravan.

The journey was a private venture, undertaken for no great cause or deserving charity. It did, however, have a purpose. We wanted to give our children a wide look at the world they will inherit, in the hope that experience of different places, peoples and cultures will enable them to become more understanding, caring, tolerant and wiser citizens of it than if they had simply slogged through the National Curriculum. Our secondary purpose was to be first around the world by horse-drawn caravan. We know we succeeded with the second and, as far as may be judged at this point, I think we have probably achieved the first too.

We discovered that the world is full of a truly remarkable number of kind, warm-hearted and decent people. Yet nearly all of them – not excluding ourselves – come equipped with a baggage of in-built preconceptions, misconceptions and frequently prejudices. In dedicating this book to my family, our three gallant horses and the three dogs, I hope that in a small way, which is the only way possible for most people, we did something towards breaking down those barriers and increasing understanding and harmony.

The earth is but one country and mankind its citizens.
Bahá'u'lláh

INTRODUCTION

Envy those colourful travellers
Roaming the rainbows of Ireland
Laden with nothing but freedom
Always travelling but forever home.

Our friends thought we were quite mad. Except for a very few. I suppose it was not surprising, really. For anyone used to the daily round of what passes for normal life among the majority, what we were proposing to do *was* mad. We were about to set off for China in a horse-drawn caravan, taking our three young children with us. From China we hoped to go on across the Pacific to the US and Canada, then finally home across the Atlantic. 'First Round the World by Horse-drawn Caravan' was our proud slogan. Time – and at this point we did not have any sure idea of how long it would take – would tell.

It was not quite as daft as it sounds. We were not doing this on a moment's whim but after a lot of research into horses, horse-caravans, routes, home education and a million and one other things that seemed to flourish like spring growth from the stem of the idea.

Kate and I had been married since 1978. We had met on the Isle of Skye, which everyone thinks is very romantic but that November it had rained every single one of the thirty days, so forget your Bonnie Prince Charlies. I was a crofter and fisherman, spending days tossing about in the Minch on a 26-foot boat hauling prawn creels, which is about as romantic as life on a sewage farm. But I loved it. The snag was, it didn't pay. Kate and I had met at a mutual friend's house one evening and before long had hitched up. There followed a time of fun and hard work, but the fishing went to blazes when the Spanish closed their prawn market for months and inevitably the boat went too. Torcuil had just been born so it was a schizophrenic period of bliss and desperation. I got a job, running the government Job Creation Scheme, and soon after that Eilidh appeared.

We might still have been living in north Skye but for unfortunate circumstances I won't go into. Suffice it to say that to reach our croft meant passing through that of the neighbours. When they sold theirs to incomers from Norfolk, who amongst other delights used to let their large Alsatian terrorise Torcuil on his way home from school, it was time either to smoke them out or to move. By this time we had wee Fionn as well, decided to move – and it was a disaster.

Neither of us had ever run a village shop before but we bought one nevertheless, in Ballantrae, in south-west Scotland. Kate's father's people came from those parts, it was by the sea and we thought the shop would make us a reasonable living. Now, I have nothing against Baptists or bankers, particularly, and in the main for what followed we had only ourselves to blame – and me more than Kate. The young couple from whom we bought the shop were keen members of the Baptist church and wanted to go back to the east coast where their church was. I think her father was ill, too, or something like that. They were extremely helpful, gave us recipes for the home-baking side, showed us all their suppliers and answered all the questions we threw at them.

The place was doing well, they said, promising accounts would be produced before the sale to us was finalised.

Now the stupid bit, the really idiotic part, was that to buy the shop, we needed to sell our house on Skye – but it was still unsold. We did not want to lose the chance of the shop because we liked the locality. We were under a bit of pressure, too, from the situation next door, which maybe clouded our judgement. Anyhow, off I went to the Clydesdale Bank in Portree to see whether a bridging loan would be possible. And it was. But where the bank was wrong was giving us the loan before ever seeing the shop accounts, to make sure we would be in a position to pay the interest until the Skye house sold. Nor did the bank or ourselves *ever* see the accounts and it was not long before we discovered why, for the shop was not making anywhere near the sum we had been told. We were to struggle like slaves for three years just to keep it solvent. Kate bore the brunt of that, especially in the end when I took a job in Lancaster with the ill-fated 'Africar' company, to earn desperately needed extra cash and she ran the shop alone.

Now if you think I have stravaiged far from horse-drawn caravans and world journeys, you would be wrong, because it was around the fire in our wee sitting room in Ballantrae the notion was conceived. If you are unfamiliar with the old Scottish stone house, you probably never sat at a fire, your front frying and your back freezing, trying to get a heat, while the wind howls around outside, the rain blatters against the window-panes and every now and then a roiling cloud of sooty smoke blows back down the chimney at you, causing you to half choke and probably inducing a dose of bronchitis if not lung-cancer as well. On a really wild night you think your dream of a magic carpet has come true because you find you are airborne – but it is only the draught under the door lifting it.

No wonder we used to have these fantasies, Kate and I, as we sat by our fire after the children were abed, enjoying the only quiet time we had to ourselves in the day. We had both travelled a lot. Kate had been to America as an au pair, to South Africa, and various places in Europe. I had been jackarooing in Australia, led off-road Land Rover trips all over West Africa and the Sahara Desert and visited a number of European countries. Together we had been to the eastern Ténéré Desert as part of an expedition assessing a new nature reserve in the Aïr Mountains. Crucially, I had also ridden a lot and at one time had my own horse, but I'm getting ahead of myself a little.

So, where would we go? It would have to be off the beaten track. Popular tourist spots with crowded beaches, where the only locals to be seen would be hotel staff and touts, held no attraction whatsoever. For how long? At least six months, perhaps a year or more. How would we get there? Much thought about transport would be needed. How would we pay for it? We could try for sponsorship – but that would mean doing something unusual. Well . . . why not?

The shop had to go, that was clear. The Skye house had sold at last but ten thousand pounds was owing to the bank because the interest had mounted up. To bring that down, I began selling things I had inherited from my parents. They included a grandfather clock, a painting by Sir William MacTaggart and even my Meccano, Dinky Toys and collection of natural history books. It hurt like hell, but there was nothing else for it. Uncle Willie's picture saved the day. He was not really my uncle, just an adopted one, but it fetched a good sum, which together with the rest was almost enough.

We were making progress. All we had to do now was persuade someone, *with* our accounts, that the shop was a going concern and had potential. Not easy, to be honest. Ballantrae was a queer sort of a place too. Robert Louis Stevenson's book *The Master of Ballantrae* has nothing to do with it, so I always wondered why he gave that title to his anti-hero, after whom the book is named. Then I read that Stevenson had once visited Ballantrae – and been stoned out of it, because of his outlandish dress. His revenge was to give its name to a villain. It was wonderfully appropriate for, with all respect to the nice people who live there (and there are many), the village hasn't changed a jot since.

The shop was 'papered' and we had some replies to our advertisements. Some folk came to have a look and we waited anxiously for a binding offer. In the end we got one, only one, though for much less than we paid. We accepted at once, fearful lest something go wrong. Meanwhile, we had firmed up ideas for our extended trip. The children were too small for a walking or cycling tour; Kate, daughter of a master mariner, a retired Union Castle Line captain, gets violently seasick and neither of us had done much sailing. Besides, keeping small children amused during days and weeks in the Doldrums might have proved difficult. I began investigating buses suitable for conversion, but did not fancy being tagged with the label New Age Hippie Traveller, convoys of whom were committing mayhem around Stonehenge and other parts of southern England at about this time. Nevertheless, as we were not in the market for a brand new Winnebago specially shipped from the States, a bus seemed the best bet. I didn't know the difference between a Leyland Leopard, a Bristol and an AEC but I found a man who did and he gave me great help and excellent advice. Then, one day, I opened a magazine and saw a photograph of a skewbald horse pulling a bow-top gypsy-style caravan in Ireland. There followed a feature about how to rent such a caravan for a holiday tour by the day, week or more. Self-drive too; full instruction given.

Archimedes leaping out of his bath got no bigger thrill than I did when I saw that magazine piece. Buses were forgotten. I wrote immediately to all three of the proprietors mentioned, not to book a holiday but to pick their brains on caravan construction. Only David Slattery, of Slattery's Travel, Tralee, County Kerry, replied. He was courteous and helpful, and we exchanged letters. Then he astonished me by inviting us over to try one of his caravans for a week or so. 'I also own a bus company,' he wrote. 'Let me know when you want to come and I'll send you the tickets.'

While waiting to sell the house, we decided we should have to rent a place for six months while we prepared whatever vehicle we bought for our trip. To this end we had advertised in the *Lady* and *Private Eye*, among other journals. Only a reply to the latter sounded remotely suitable. The place was up on Orkney, though, about as far from the Continent as one could get. Had we not felt exhausted and jaded by the strains of the shop we might have hesitated, but the idea of a long weekend away, up in Orkney *en famille,* held great appeal. So we rang the people there to invite ourselves, bought a family railcard and set off. We debouched at Wick, took a bus to John o'Groat's and the passenger ferry from there to Burwick in South Ronaldsay. It was a lovely crossing, the Pentland Firth calm, puffins, guillemots and razorbills flying hither and yon, seals now and then poking their heads up. As we approached Burwick pier, Kate and I were discussing the place we were going to see, which had sounded ideal, with the people seeming pleasant over the telephone. Then Kate had one of her prescient moments. 'I'll bet it's a tip,' she said.

Jack – we'll call him – was there to meet us and turned out to be a big, burly, black-avised fellow with a beard, not

Orcadian at all but English. It was almost fifty miles to The House, across the famous wartime Churchill Barriers, erected between the islands at the entrance to Scapa Flow after Kapitan Prien's daring submarine escapade had sunk the *Royal Oak*, and on across Mainland. The House was huge, an old greystone place not untypical of lairds' houses of bygone times. And – it *was* a tip. The exterior was unkempt, the interior filthy. One room was full of Edwardian clothing, another of books, and there were piles of magazines and bric-à-brac everywhere.

We were welcomed, though, and as it was about as warm as it ever gets on Orkney, sat outside to have a drink. The children were soon off exploring. Pat, Jack's wife, told us she had just come back from hospital where she had been having breast enlargement. 'Go on, let them see,' said Jack, whereupon Pat lifted up her top to reveal what silicone can do for a girl. And her nipples were pierced. Our jaws hit the ground with a crack and I could almost hear Kate's brain working on the same track as mine. What on Earth had we got into? Pat explained she used to be a professional exotic dancer but now had a job with the DHSS – which shows how little you know about what lurks beneath the modest exterior of the girls behind the desk when you go to sign on social security. Jack had been in the antiques business in the south, was a trained watch- and clock-maker and earned his living from that and from driving a taxi in Kirkwall. Another profitable income, it transpired, was Pat's 'modelling'. Most of the magazines were porn. Not a few featured the charms of our hostess . . . Fortunately the children were too young to realise all this.

We were taken round and shown the sights. At Jack's insistence one day, we went with him to the hamlet of Evie, at the north of Mainland. He was going to look at a freezer a woman was selling before she moved house. 'You must see

Shortie Cottage,' he said. 'It's for sale and has a fabulous view.' The house indeed had a fabulous view. The vet who owned it had already bought another in her native Derbyshire, had a bridging loan and was desperate to sell. She offered it to us for what it had cost her. We made a snap decision and bought it on the spot. During the two years we lived there we never regretted it.

That is how we found a place to prepare for our departure on a round-the-world voyage in a horse-drawn caravan. Destiny played its part for sure: the six months originally envisaged would never have been enough time to complete our preparations. In retrospect, the children would have been too young truly to have enjoyed and benefited from the trip and, vitally, as it turned out, the money from the eventual sale of our beloved Shortie was nearly double what we should otherwise have started off with.

At the end of 1989 we were able to take up David Slattery's generous invitation at last. Getting from Orkney to Leeds, the nearest point his buses ran from, was an expedition in itself. However it also enabled us to meet Mick Brown, who builds carriages in Ossett, close to Leeds. I had been corresponding with him about building our chassis and running gear; now he met us and we had a detailed discussion with him before he took us to Slattery's bus.

After the long overnight drive to Holyhead, a delayed ferry departure (technical trouble, they said) for Dublin and the even longer drive across Ireland, we arrived in Tralee. We were all in, barely able to think, when we got off the bus. David Slattery met us and his wife laid on a reviving spread for us. Then we went out to the yard where the caravans were and soon after that we were in 'our' caravan, asleep.

Next morning was different. We were in Ireland, where the Little People really do still exist and where the sun was shining. We were refreshed from a sound sleep and about to begin an adventure and if this is reminiscent of Enid Blyton's Famous Five stories, why shouldn't it be, for that is what it seemed like. David Slattery came to see us and we talked about the route we should take. It was the end of September and of the tourist season. Only three caravans remained out, the rest were in store. Nearly all the horses, too, were in winter quarters. We opted to head out round the Dingle Peninsula and should be driving Bob, an experienced skewbald Irish draught.

The caravans, all thirty-two of them, were built to a pattern modelled on the traditional gypsy bow-top wagon. However instead of canvas they were covered with light fibreboard over which was a layer of roofing felt. The lower body was wooden, mounted on a light frame chassis. Shafts were of metal piping and the wheels standard car-type with inflatable tyres. Three strakes protected the sides of the caravan from the inept driving to be expected from novices. The interior was simple but well fitted out with bench beds, under which was storage space, and there was a gas cooker and small sink.

Bob was harnessed and put to the shafts. In some trepidation I mounted up, took the reins and – we were off. It did not take long to master the art of driving Bob, who knew his job far better than I did and well before our first stop I felt like a veteran. Even the slightly tricky task of getting out of Tralee proved easier than expected. Nor did a fall follow this quiet pride and soon we could all drive, though at five Fionn could not be expected to have road sense when it came to traffic and we kept a close eye on him.

Slattery's had a network of stopping-places at just the right distance for a day's drive, where at least basic facilities were available. On our first evening we drew into the field at the back of Ashe's pub. It was the perfect place to begin, for after seeing the children safely, if excitedly, tucked into their sleeping-bags, Kate and I went to slake our thirsts with – what else? – pints of Guinness. To complete the harmony, some musicians came in and a few tunes on fiddle and pipe soon had everyone's feet tapping.

The whole eight days were like that. Pure magic. By Brandon Bay we went and over the Stradbally mountains, to Liaspol and Slea Head, whose very names were as great a delight as the scenery. At Slea Head we looked across to the Blasket Islands and the far off Skellig Michael, where early Christian monks dwelt in little stone cells shaped like bee skeps, then back by Ballyferriter and the Gallerus Oratory and Ogham Stones and Inch, to Dingle itself and its beautiful bay, then over Slieve Mish . . . and suddenly we were on a bus and speeding away for Dublin and the long road home.

It had been a wonderful trip, a complete change, and if it seemed almost like a holiday, well, that was all right too because we had learned a lot and I was now quite confident that we not only *could* travel this way but *should*. It would be hard to express adequate gratitude to David Slattery, for had it not been for his generosity, that he did not think we were mad, or not completely, then getting our real journey under way would have been much harder. He had provided the spur, which ensured we should start.

Unnoticed by me, Kate was beginning to have reservations but she did not say anything. She did not want to be the wet blanket who spoiled the fun. She had enjoyed Ireland as much as anyone but I think she foresaw, even then, that a prolonged sojourn in the confines of a caravan might not suit her. In her words, 'I really did have doubts about David and me travelling in such close confinement.

The children I didn't doubt at all. Children are very adaptable, curious about new ideas and concepts. But I thought it was a trifle unfair to expect them at ages five, seven and nine to appreciate what our proposed wee doddle round the world would really mean.' I was in no mood or state to notice. Fired by all I had learned during our travels and from Mick Brown, I was as eager to go as a horse in a starting-stall. And now we had a piece of luck. I read in a newspaper there was a fellow in Crieff who built horse-buses. Crieff was a lot nearer home than Leeds. If he could build a bus he could build a caravan. I determined to go and see for myself.

George Gauld had been an undertaker to trade, had become filled with enthusiasm for horses and horse-transport and had converted his box-making skills to the job. He employed an excellent joiner, Iain King, and a good blacksmith for the metal work. I liked the rugged solidity of the vehicles I saw. I liked the price even better. I could have a caravan built for the cost Mick Brown had quoted for the chassis alone. We did a deal: George would build a van to an outline design I would send him, incorporating as little weight and as much space as possible. I would organise delivery of a small wood-burning stove, gas-rings and water-filter, to be fitted by his team. Work would begin as soon as I sent the first instalment. But I could not do that till we sold our house . . .

Meantime, progress was made with the mass of other vital preparations. These included agonising over essential equipment – such as sleeping-bags and horse-harness – and contacting suppliers to try to obtain it free or at a discount in return for publicity. This was, after all, going to be the FIRST circumnavigation of the globe by horse-drawn caravan. Carriage-driving experts were consulted about what sort of horse to buy and where to get it. We researched how to home-educate children and joined that wonderfully supportive organisation Education Otherwise. Most important of all, we tried to plan our route. Our 1-horse-power vehicle meant we must choose the flattest way we could. Another constraint was imposed by ailments, such as African horse sickness, which ruled out visiting countries where it was endemic. The Berlin Wall had fallen six months before but we should not be ready in time to avoid winter, which excluded a northerly route through East Germany. In the end, we were advised to buy our horse in the Netherlands, from where it would make sense to head south into France for our first winter stop. After that we should go east, probably across the north of Italy. We could certainly go as far as the Hungarian–Soviet border. We thought a route across the southern Soviet republics to enter China via Xinjiang Province and the old Silk Road would be feasible. However, the vital permission to enter the USSR proved elusive, nor was it obtained before we left. While we planned the direction we intended to follow, our exact route would depend on conditions we met along the way.

Back on Orkney, life proceeded normally, Kate managing a bygones shop in Kirkwall, the children at Evie primary school, me working part-time for Ancient Monuments as custodian for the Broch of Gurness, but concentrating on acquiring equipment, free or otherwise, from manufacturers. The expeditions market was over-subscribed and firms were reluctant to help unknown, wildcatting freelancers. Over five hundred letters elicited positive replies only from Grant's of Dalvey and the group managing director of J. J. Lees plc, makers of bakery confections, including that childhood treat, gooey marsh-mallow snowballs. I also had a positive response from David Martin, then head of features at BBC TV Scotland.

In the end, Lees failed us: the firm was taken over and the group managing director sacked. The BBC featured us on *The Garden Party*, live from the botanical gardens in Glasgow. It was great fun to do, despite the organisational nightmare of getting the not-quite-finished caravan, George Gauld's horse and ourselves all there at the same time on the same day. We gave presenter Paul Coia some exercise when, turning a corner just before coming into camera shot, the caravan wheel stuck on a stone; he had to rush off and cover for us until, working frantically, we freed it and arrived where we were meant to have been a minute earlier. Grant's of Dalvey delivered as promised, and remained our main supporters throughout the trip, while several firms gave us generous discounts.

Shortie sold on 30 June, and as soon as the money came through, work began on the caravan. It went well but the schedule was so tight the paint was only just dry and final fitting-out of the interior incomplete when it was delivered to us on Neill & Brown's low-loader at the King George Dock in Hull. In the interim, we had packed up, auctioned off all but our most treasured possessions, visited friends, motored to Southampton and spent a week with Kate's father and step-mother, had a day at Peter Ingram's marvellous Gypsy Museum and *vardo* restoration workshop in Selbourne and, finally, driven back up to spend our last days in the UK with Ian and Juliet Macdonald of Sleat at Thorpe Hall, north of Hull, before embarking on North Sea Ferries' *Norsea*.

In best expeditionary tradition, there was a last-minute hitch. The caravan was aboard, our papers were in order – but our Staffordshire bull terrier Lady's weren't. I had overlooked the fact she needed a Certificate of Health. I played the daft laddie and in the end all was well, I was given temporary papers, and she was allowed to come.

Taking a dog *out* of Britain, not hedged with anti-rabies regulations, is relatively simple. We boarded.

It then took two hours before we left, because some wretched tanker was stuck in the lock.

The children were used to the notorious Pentland Firth crossing to Orkney, from Scrabster to Stromness on the *St Ola* but they had never slept aboard a ship before. There was great grabbing and sorting and giggling as they decided who would have the top bunks and who could shower first, explored the fittings and asked why the bunks had such high sides and what *were* those funny paper bags for? The tiny cabin was meant for four but Fionn 'topped and tailed' with Kate and was not charged for, which was decent of the ferry company. Then Kate took them off to eat so we could get them to bed early: it had been a long day and their small springs were run down. The ship was superbly clean and service excellent, the crossing so smooth that, soundly asleep in our comfy bunks, we never knew it blew a gale all night.

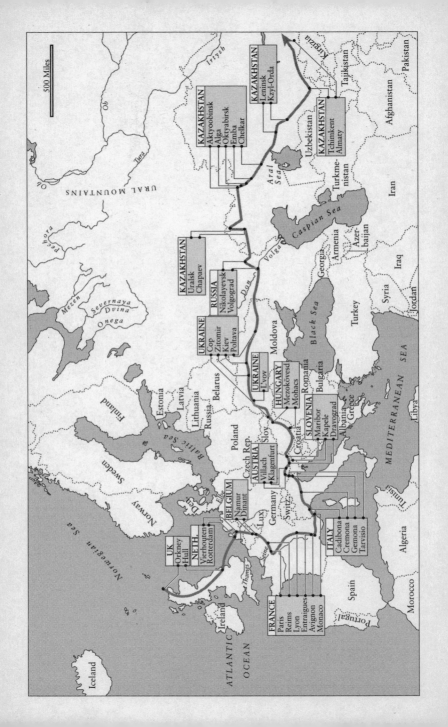

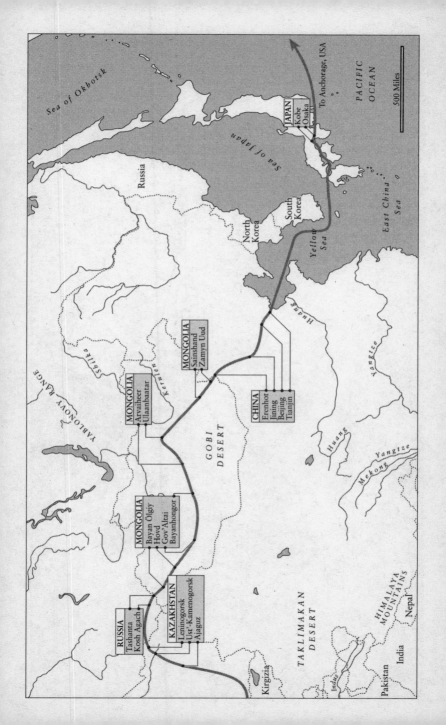

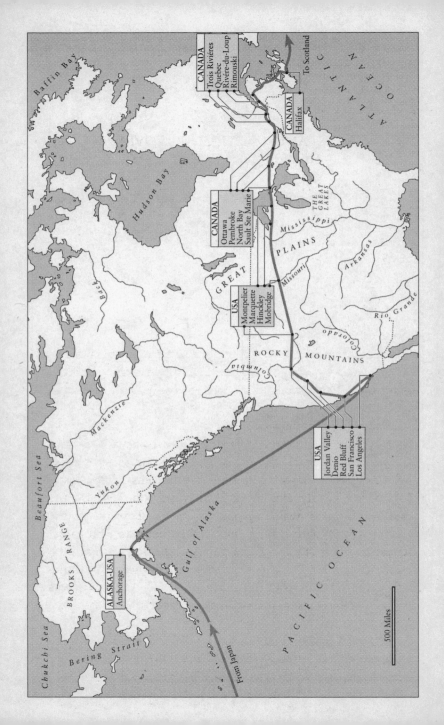

CHAPTER ONE

~~~~o/o~~~~

THE NETHERLANDS: SEPTEMBER–NOVEMBER 1990
THE PAPER OF THE DOG OK

Think more, learn more, you can do anything you want.

<div align="right">

Lu Ban

</div>

Rotterdam on a grey September morning was about as cheerful as Glasgow and not half as welcoming. Excitement was high among the children, for it was their first foreign country: the Netherlands.

We were to be met by Nella van Dishoeck, sister of my friend Willem Dudok van Heel, whose parents had been friends of my parents. We were an hour late docking because of the delay leaving Hull but customs and passport formalities hardly existed and we were soon out on the quayside. There was no sign of Nella. I went to the Customs shed with Lady's papers then back aboard to get her, with a chit that read 'The paper of the dog OK'. Still no Nella when I returned, so we went to the rather clinical tile-and-glass waiting room. And waited. The caravan was offloaded and taken to the Customs shed. And still we waited.

After an endless-seeming hour, Nella arrived and there were greetings all round in the formal Dutch way. She had been stuck in a traffic jam. We were delighted to see her, especially the children, who had explored all there was to see of the docks and were restless. A low-loader was coming for the caravan and I went to see Customs, to make sure it would be all right to take it when the low-loader arrived. They started to be stuffy, said there might be duty to pay and it probably wasn't road legal . . . but it was lunchtime and would I please come back in the afternoon. Shades of Africa! I held my tongue, was very polite and said yes of course.

When afternoon had arrived but the low-loader had not, I suggested we really must go and sort out Customs. I had a Royal Netherlands Embassy letter, which stated bringing our horse-drawn caravan into the Netherlands would pose no problem, and showed it to them. In the end there was no problem: some miserable little jobsworth had been wanting to show how powerful he was.

Outside, Dries Verhoef, his mate and the low-loader had at last arrived. It was a neat vehicle, a mini car-transporter with space for two cars, already occupied. The caravan was to go on a trailer behind. Easy – but as it was winched on, the rear wheels were found to be two inches wider than the trailer. A guttural Dutch huddle ensued. A fork-lift was summoned, planks inserted and lashed down. Then our precious caravan, containing all our worldly goods and hopes, was forked bodily on to the trailer. One rear wheel now hung out, resting only on the plank. I was having litters of small cats, but there was nothing I could say: Dries didn't understand English. Nella expressed reassuring confidence in the proceedings and I became happier when I saw heavy-duty nylon strapping produced, the kind truckers use, with a ratchet tightening system. The caravan was secured as well as could be, and if I was nervous, tough luck.

A car-load of zombies would have been better conver-sationalists than the Grant family. I was not sure about the others but after the ugly, traffic-ridden outskirts of Rotterdam I snored till we arrived at Nella's house at Vierhouten. Our arrangement with her was that we would park alongside her house, use some facilities but be basically self-supporting. However, that first night she took pity and not only offered beds but fed us.

About 6 p.m. the caravan arrived and we trooped over to Dries's for the unloading. As soon as we got there the children insisted I unstrapped the two brand-new Muddy Fox mountain bikes, which were on the rack at the back of the caravan and which they had been longing to try out ever since they had first seen them. As to the caravan, the old barrel, plank and jack now fetched would have given me palpitations if I had not been converted to belief in Dries's competence. A neat, efficient job ensued and our home was soon resting on its own wheels. Coffee next. Then a small tractor towed the caravan the kilometre or so to Nella's and promptly bogged in soft sand, trying to reach the grassy patch it was supposed to go on. We parked at the back of the house instead.

The next five weeks were seemingly never-ending. We had to find a horse. I had to fit out the caravan. Kate had to see to the domestic side and ensure she had all she needed, keep the children amused, buy them clothes . . . all that stuff. But first came the unpacking.

Everything in the caravan was in labelled numbered boxes. These had to be taken out, checked, redistributed as needed and re-stowed. There was work unfinished too: laying linoleum on the floor, fitting kitchen shelves and bookshelves and the three small lights to be powered by the Wincharger aerogenerator, of which I had great hopes. We needed to buy horse-rugs, a couple of haynets and a chain and picket. No one was short of a job for long, but if they were, there were Nella's two horses to muck out or ride, her barn to paint or grass to cut; our rent, as it were, for being there.

Buying a horse proved difficult. With hindsight, we should have gone to France for the type of heavy horse we needed but we found and bought a 16-hand, part-Belgian chestnut gelding, nine years old, with flaxen mane and tail. We had him for a week's trial, during which he was marched up and down the many sandy roads through the pinewoods around Vierhouten, ridden through them and finally hitched to the caravan with our brand-new leather-and-nylon harness and driven through them.

He behaved well outside and was a comfortable ride. In his box, he would try to bite passers-by, viciously not playfully. However, as we should have no box, this was a minor matter. More seriously, the caravan proved to be a heavier drag than I had expected. The problem was two-fold. First, although 'double the diameter half the draught' is a good rule of thumb when assessing the relationship between wheel-size and drag, it did not take into account that our large-diameter, traditionally shaped and hence narrow solid-rubber-tyred steel wheels would sink into any remotely soft surface. Second, we had fitted rubber torsion suspension, which utilises a stub axle embedded in a block of extremely hard rubber instead of a metal spring. The leverage exerted by the large-diameter wheels on the stub axles encased in their rubber blocks was too great, causing the wheels to 'toe out' at rest and flex through a figure-of-eight pattern as they turned. It was no good and something would have to be done. I began stripping off as much weight as I dared from the caravan.

We took the horse to Dr Offereins in Utrecht to be vetted. He was *the* expert, everyone told us, and he certainly made a thorough job, at the end of which he said there was nothing to prevent the horse from doing all we required of him. His hind feet, quite worn as a consequence of not being shod, had worried me, and might need corrective shoes at first but would grow. We had a horse. But a nameless horse, so Kate decided that we should call him Offereins after the vet. He quickly became Offy for short. We telephoned Herr Kroos, his owner, agreed to rendezvous with him and pay for Offy at the meet of the local drag-hunt, which fortuitously was to be at Vierhouten the forthcoming Saturday.

A stiff breeze from the west and clear skies promised a fine day for the meet. A concourse of horse trailers and boxes was already assembled opposite Vierhouten inn when we got there. 'We going for drink. *Kom!*' boomed a voice behind us. It was Kroos. Not the scruffy farmer we had met previously but one immaculately attired for the chase. We followed him into the pub, which was already filled with a hubbub of noisy voices and crisply clothed men in whiter-than-white breeches, gleaming top-boots, yellow waistcoats and flawless hound's-tooth hacking jackets. They were accompanied by an equal number of women, just as smartly turned out, highly made-up, with hairstyling that probably cost as much as their coats. A few, obviously not riders, were even more heavily into powder and paint, perhaps pursuing their own, older version of venery.

After about an hour, the hunters emerged and exchanged their hacking jackets for even more exquisite pink coats. The men donned quaint half-height top hats and the women bowlers. Grooms assisted them to mount their pristine steeds. Even the nineteen couple of mostly black-and-tan hounds looked well brushed as everyone trotted out of the village to heathery moorland. The horn was winded and away streamed hounds, huntsman, master and field, soon lost to view in the rolling ground.

Kate took the kids to Amsterdam where they avoided falling into canals, being abducted for use in paedophile videos or learning to smoke hashish, but did see the Van Gogh exhibition and came back suitably impressed. Another time we all went with Nella and her sister Rosemary to see the Hidden Village. Deep in the forest, this had been a hideaway for about a hundred people during the Second World War, including members of the Resistance, Allied airmen and Jews. The Germans only discovered it because two officers out shooting saw some children where they knew none should be. The children, knowing they had been seen, hastily alerted the camp and most, if not all, the inhabitants were able to escape the inevitable search and raid. Only shallow depressions in the ground now mark where these subterranean dwellings were, except one, which has been reconstructed.

One day Torcuil came tearing round the side of the house to where I was working in the caravan. 'Daddy, Daddy, Fionn's been run over!' I was out and round to Nella's kitchen faster than Carl Lewis to find Kate standing by a tear-streaked and pale Fionn sitting on a chair – apparently perfectly all right. Two women in a car, he said, had knocked him off his bike, and the car went over his arm. The women had got out to see if he was OK then driven off. We doubted the bit about being run over till Kate rolled up his sleeve – revealing a tyre-mark imprinted across the inside of the elbow joint on his little white arm, and some nasty raw grazing below. By some miracle, damage was limited to grazing and contusion. No broken bones.

Everyone was becoming niggly: Kate and I snarled at each other; Nella was obviously wondering if we were ever going to leave; Nella's daughter Caroline emitted silent wrath whenever she found us in the house. We could not blame the van Dishoecks. They had done much to help us but no one, least of all I, had foreseen that it would take so long to prepare. But at last the caravan was finished. The wind-generator worked. The local press had interviewed us. Only the problem of the suspension remained.

Dries Verhoef solved that, by bypassing the torsion suspension altogether, removing our splendid spoked wheels and replacing them with 14-inch car-wheels fitted with oversize tyres. He incorporated the original hubs, which was good because the cost of his labour, plus the ex-Audi wheels he found to fit the hubs, came to a considerable sum. We had already spent more than anticipated on living, on small items for the caravan, and on clothes for the children and had yet to move a yard on our journey. Finally, though, on 24 October 1990, far later than intended, late in the year for good weather, everything was ready. But were we?

I lay abed, running through everything accomplished so far, wondering what might have been forgotten. I also pondered on a potentially more serious problem. Instead of settling into a harmonious working pattern Kate and I had been arguing, to the point where we seemed to conflict over everything. The tension imposed by living cheek-by-jowl with the van Dishoecks for longer than planned was part of the trouble but not all – and was probably nothing compared with the stresses to come. Here, we had had access to bath, washing-machine, loo and sometimes their kitchen. Tomorrow we no longer would. Everything we had was committed to the trip, we had told people we were going to do it, had accepted Dalvey's sponsorship and a lot of discounts in good faith. To quit now would be to fail before we had begun and I did not seriously contemplate it. About the children I had no doubts: they were lapping everything up, including home education. Kate, though, was different. Over the years our relationship had often been stormy, though we had had good times too. Was I wrong in believing her spirit of adventure would predominate over her love of home comforts; that lack of a daily bath, not being able to wash her hair when she wanted, would weigh more heavily than the excitement of the journey? I didn't think so and I hoped it would all work out, once we were on the road.

October 25, 1990, dawned warm and overcast with no wind. Offy, smartly brushed, hoofs gleamingly oiled, looked a picture standing quietly between the caravan's shafts. Hay had been loaded beneath the bikes on the rack. Dries had presented us with a spare wheel. Thanks had been given and goodbyes said. Everyone was aboard. It was 11.15 a.m. I collected the reins, flicked them gently, Offy leaned into his harness and we were off. Off on a journey round the world, longer than Nansen's three-year drift in the Arctic ice, longer than any of Captain Cook's voyages, or the Second World War – longer than Fionn had already lived.

Beside me on the box, what was Kate thinking, and Torcuil, Eilidh and Fionn, aged ten, nine and six? Kate wasn't saying much, but a fine day, release from the constraints of the past weeks and the excitement of starting must have laid her misgivings to rest, for the moment. The children had Offy and Lady, bikes, new things to see and do, and built into it all a sense that they were embarking on a great adventure. Besides, children who are loved and cared for by their parents tend to accept what is happening. Certainly ours did.

After Elspeet, we passed a vast enclosure which, according to a signboard, contained Przewalski's horses, descendants of the true wild horses of Mongolia, but we saw no sign of them. Through Uddel, under the A1 motorway and to Kooterwijk we went, to stop for our first night.

We had asked a boy on a bike if he knew anywhere we

might pull in and he had obtained permission from his grandfather for us to park in some woods. Offy was in a field two hundred yards away. It rained and I worried about him, though he was well wrapped up in his New Zealand rug. Eilidh and I cleaned tack and hung it in a nearby barn where we had already put the bikes and hay, while Kate produced a filling spaghetti Bolognese for supper. With the fire going, the van was cosy, but everything seemed to have taken an age to do and the rain had dampened our spirits. I had a last look at Offy before going to bed and found him grazing contentedly.

The cast-iron Diamond Esse wood-burning cooking stove we had installed gave out plenty of heat. At this early stage, Kate was still experimenting with it. Its one drawback was a rather small firebox, and for cooking, good heat depended on the quality of wood burned. Because it took about an hour to reach working temperature, it was normally used only in the evenings. Breakfast was usually a brew of tea and some toast, and for that we had a gas-burning Optimus double-ring and grill unit. The Optimus was also used for evening meals in summer, when lighting the stove would have broiled us, never mind the food. Kate – and occasionally I – was able to make excellent meals, stove-top space, time and inclination being the only real barriers to culinary art. We almost never cooked outside because in winter it would have been miserable, in summer often a fire risk and, believe it or not, we had nowhere to stow soot-blackened pans.

Offy was glad to see me at 7 a.m. next morning, gladder still to get his feed. There was a Porta Potti in a cramped corner of the caravan, concession to domesticity, but I hated its cold plastic feel and chemical stink, so went outside and contemplated a field of fine cabbages instead. The temptation to take one was enormous but we were far from the point where stealing cabbages was necessary to sustain life, so I resisted.

We travelled by back roads, through mixed woodland then more open farmland. At lunchtime we stopped and unhitched Offy, letting him graze the 'long acre', the roadside verge. Soon after we restarted, a car pulled up, the driver handed Kate a fistful of florins, wished us good luck and drove off. This astonishing performance baffled and might have embarrassed us, had it not happened so fast. Had he mistaken us for gypsies and wished to gain luck from crossing our palms with silver? Or had he read about us in a newspaper and just wanted to express his approval?

We entered the attractive small town of Lunteren behind a superbly turned-out white carriage and pair carrying a wedding party, who waved heartily to us. It began to pour and we were soon soaked. We needed shelter and a stopping-place. Jan and Ancka Fliert kindly let us pull in under an enormous tree near their house at Jagersfeld BV Kuickenbroederij, a huge chicken hatchery they owned. We sorted ourselves out, fed Offy, got the fire going and had the Flierts over for coffee. It faired up and the children played outside with Chris, Willi, Wynanda and their cousin Elska. Jan asked if we'd like to have a look at the hatchery. At any one time, there are half a million eggs in the oscillating trays, which turn them, and hatching baskets. The day-old chicks are graded, five employees processing 30,000 per hour – 100 a minute each. Most of the production goes to the Middle East but a 23 per cent stake in a Kuwaiti operation had just been lost because of that country's invasion by Iraq and the ensuing Gulf crisis.

Later, Kate, the children and I had a discussion about factory farming and what this implied for the animals involved. There was general agreement that it must be nicer for a chicken to be brought up under mother hen's wings, scratching in the farmyard – notwithstanding the chance of a fly fox coming by some day. How far man has come from his roots.

We took only nine days to travel through the Netherlands. In that time the pattern of our daily lives for the journey was formed, though it underwent modifications later as we became more experienced or circumstances demanded. It went like this: feed Offy about 7 a.m., have breakfast, harness up and set off, shop if necessary, lunch stop, travel some more, find a place to park for the night. We often paused to see to things, collect wood or fetch water, take photographs and talk to passers-by.

Those first days in the Netherlands taught us a lot. Duties seemed to fall naturally into an order of their own. Kate tackled the bulk of the children's education, either walking along outside or sometimes at the table inside; she also had the all-important task of knocking at doors and asking permission to stay a night as we approached stopping time. This was not always pleasant, though most people were not unfriendly. I nearly always drove. I enjoyed it, and Kate did not greatly care for long spells at the reins. The children took turns but their ages inevitably meant they found it uninteresting after a time – there was always a frog or a moth or a caterpillar to see, a tree to climb or a bicycle to ride. Torcuil had the surprisingly onerous task of ensuring we had adequate wood and water supplies, with power to deputise any of us to help him. Eilidh's rapport with horses – indeed, all animals – was employed fully, though in these early days her physical limitations meant I had to do the heavier tasks and the saddling-up. Fionn, at six, had no fixed job of his own so he helped where he could. We tried not to impose on them too much. Travel brought its own restrictions and our children, still very young, needed time to play and do their own things.

At the end of our third day we came to the Rhine, approaching along the top of a high bank, with ponds full of duck and cormorants on either side. Fallow deer occupied a field in front of a disused brick factory. Close to the river, and the little Nederrijn ferry we had to cross next morning, we stopped. Anton and Digena Donner, who lived in the converted-brickworks stables and workshop close by, good-naturedly invited Offy to stay in their field and us to tea and cakes with them and their children.

Kate, suddenly remembering next day was Sunday and shops would be closed, decided she had better buy some food. This entailed an excursion across the river to Opheusden. Eilidh went with her while Torcuil, Fionn and I saw to Offy, who had dried off. He was always sweaty, sometimes wet from rain as well. We brushed him, put on his heavy-duty New Zealand rug and gave him a feed of oats. He had oats at lunchtime, too, to build him up: there was no surety of stabling at night and the uncertain weather was getting colder. His comfort and well-being were always a priority.

A humdinger of a gale blew all that night, but morning dawned fair, with wild grey clouds dancing reels across the sky. The Donners came to see us go, bringing eggs, leeks, lettuce and a cabbage from their garden. By the time we had Offy tacked up it was raining, so it was on with his rain-sheet and off to the ferry. He walked on to it as though it was just another bit of road, giving the lie to my fears he might refuse. Barges plied the river but the small yachts seen the evening before had wisely stayed in shelter. The friendly ferryman was concerned Offy would find the cobbled bank on the far side too steep but he managed it easily – though not before leaving a steaming calling-card on the ferry deck.

Opheusden at 10.30 a.m. on a wet Sunday would have made Stornoway seem lively. By the time we had passed

through, the wind was rising fast. Only a bedraggled
buzzard, flapping soggily over the rooftops, provided
momentary diversion from the misery of the increasingly
heavy rain.

In the drab, industrial town of Dodewaard, all works-
units and factories, a sodden football game was in progress
in the park. I wondered whether it was they or we who were
the more lunatic, especially when at the far side of the town
we came to a short but very steep hill. Offy struggled
bravely but it was too much for him. I swung him on to the
grass beside the road. This gave better grip but also greater
drag, being softer. We pushed. Offy pulled. A woman and
her daughter came and pushed and then a man stopped his
car and rushed to help. Offy heaved ... and heaved and
heaved, and we all shoved and shoved – and suddenly we
were up on top of the Waaldijk. Amazing horse, what a
great heart he had.

The Waal water was high, turbid, brown and full of
huge barges. The upriver ones chugged and slugged against
the racing current, while the downriver ones slammed past
at terrific speed. The family retreated inside as the wind rose
still further. Rain battered me as I sat on the exposed driving
seat. We passed a factory with a high chimney and below
me, on a narrow track, two German-registered cars were
parked. Their occupants were down at the river – fishing.
The reins were blown sideways, taut and thrumming in the
wind. Ahead now and ever nearer was the high bridge
spanning the Waal, carrying the A50 trunk road. The
Waaldijk was totally exposed, the rain horizontal and the
wind screaming. Offy thought I was trying to turn him left
but it was only the pressure of the wind on the reins, tugging
at his mouth.

It would be madness to attempt the bridge in such a gale.
Shelter was imperative. Kate braved the elements to ask at a

prosperous-looking farm whether we might stay the night, but was rebuffed. At another place, with horses and jumps in a field, we were welcomed with coffee and biscuits, a stable for Offy and the drying-room for jackets, leggings and horse-rugs, even TV for the children to watch. Jan and Wis Peelen's hospitality to complete strangers, arriving unannounced and looking like scruffs, was not untypical of the Netherlands.

In clear sun next day the view from the bridge was tremendous. In such flat country, you could see a lot from 150 feet up. The slow lane was on the outside, with only modest railings between us and the long drop to the Waal below. Offy was less nervous about it than I, plodding across with great unconcern, despite it being slightly uphill and into the still-considerable wind. After that it was flat, with wooded patches, lines of pollard willows, hectares of grass and more of beet. A few straggling untamed corners had been left here and there as habitat for wild things. The odd swan or buzzard drifted by. We reached and crossed the Maas, our third major river in two days, more pleasant than the grubby, industrious Waal, with fewer, smaller barges.

Theo van Summeren was a charming little gnome of a man, spoke no English and lived in an old-style, immaculate house-cum-byre at Heuvel. He had a terriery sort of a dog called Foxy, a small black cat and two young bullocks, which lived in the byre. He could not do enough for us. Offy was put in a lush grass field, where Theo took him water before bringing some to us. He gave us all the wood we could use and showed the *Vrouw,* Madam, the loo. We discovered he was unmarried and did all his own building and animal work. He said that way it was *sikker,* sure, one of many words that Scots shares with Dutch.

Just before we left, Theo presented us with a bone-dry box of wood and stood watching and waving as we went, after another wet night. How conscious we nomads became of weather. Kate shopped for essentials in the nearby small town of Schaijk, and as we were on our way out, Theo came puffing up on his bicycle, brandishing a small piece of paper. On it was his address. It was somehow very touching he should want us to write to him.

Zeeland was a pretty town with a windmill in the middle. A political battle raged within its seemingly peaceful boundaries, many houses displaying 'Zeeland Zelfstandig' posters. The 'Zeeland gem Uden' town sign we passed coming in had the 'gem Uden' scored out – with archetypal Dutch neatness, by two perfectly ruled parallel lines.

When we stopped for lunch two children of about eight and seven came to visit: Wouter, who had curly hair and glasses, and his sister Jannecke, who was fair and neat. Wouter disappeared for a while, then returned proudly bearing a picture he had gone to draw of the caravan and us, with *Goede Reis,* good journey, on it in bold letters. The two of them – and Otto, who was presumably, from his writing, a still younger brother – had signed it. We still have the picture.

We nudged our way slowly south.

One day I became hopelessly lost. The road out of Bakel for Asten was the Deurne road, but we should have been on the one for Helmond. Two kilometres later, leaving Bakel for the second time, now in driving rain, every passing lorry threw up spray, drenching Offy and me. Visibility was dangerously bad so I took to the *fietspad,* the cycle path, which was illegal but much safer. Four sloshingly wet kilometres more and we turned left for Asten on to a major road where none should have been. The map was useless. We ploughed through ghetto-like housing schemes for aeons. Much bad temper and extra distance later, having stopped a dozen times to ask directions from people who always seemed to be strangers to the area or spoke no known language, we emerged on the road to Ommel and better things.

Our last night in the Netherlands was spent on our own, in a deserted forest clearing, after yet another wet and windy day. Offy was clad in three layers: sweat-rug, towelling rug and New Zealand rug. Fifteen years of riding experience, owning my own horse for part of that time, did not mean that I knew everything about how to care for a light draught-horse, working daily and living out at night, so I was still feeling my way with his regimen. His daily ration had been increased to 12 kilos of hard feed, mostly *paard broeck,* horse-nuts, plus lunchtime snack and grass or hay. On this he was expected to travel about fifteen miles a day. Except when a stable or field was available, he was attached to a picket and chain for the night.

Kate cursed the lack of space and dangling wet clothes inside the caravan, as she wrestled with a reluctant wood-stove and tried to cook curry. The children curled up with volumes of *World Book Encyclopaedia*, donated by the publisher, or its junior version *Childcraft* and wished it would stop raining so they could go out and play on their bikes, kick a ball about or play hide and seek.

Next day we should be in Belgium.

CHAPTER TWO

—◆◆◆—

BELGIUM AND FRANCE:
NOVEMBER–DECEMBER 1990
EARLY DAYS IN EUROPE

*If there's ever going to be a change in human nature,
you've got to get to the kids.*

Orson Bean

A line on a map. A border is often not much more, yet
how marked can be the difference within yards of
leaving one country and entering another. The Dutch–
Belgian border crossing we used was not even manned, the
Benelux countries having done away with frontier
formalities. Only an aggrandised barber's pole, pointing
heavenwards from beside an abandoned cream-coloured
pill-box, denoted where once passports were demanded and
baggage checked. But gone were Kate's 'little Lego villages',
the trim Dutch dwellings surrounded by mown grass,
clipped hedges and litter-free streets. In their stead was a
faint air of indefinable unkemptness, as though next weekend would do for cutting the hedge, the grass was a fraction
overdue a mow and the dustcart had broken down.

The café-bar in Hamont was warm and welcoming,
made great coffee, gave the children biscuits, let us fill our
water-jerries and cashed a Eurocheque. It was grand to
warm up after another miserable wet start, though it had
cleared to a cool, pallid grey.

In Peer Kate stocked up on supplies. During the hour she and Eilidh were away, the boys and I found Offy a patch of scruffy grass to amuse him, a man brought him water and we filled our jerries. Torcuil had a long spell driving on a quiet back road in the afternoon, doing very well, and we stopped for the night beside a rustic football pitch. The country was as flat as it had been in the Netherlands and the skies leaden but the bushy hedges, small fields and little farms were pretty. Another day, at Sonnis, a man waved us over and told us to put Offy in his rich grassy field while we had our lunch. We much appreciated these little Belgian generosities, finding the country more relaxed than the Netherlands.

It became hillier as we progressed through Sonnis, Zolder and Helchteren. Offy amazed us all one day when, coming to a short sharp hill, he first trotted, then cantered up it. He was obviously used to doing this but, in my ignorance of driving techniques (and long years of being warned not to ''ammer, 'ammer, 'ammer on the 'ard 'igh road' because it did terrible things to horses' legs), I was dumbfounded. But it is actually far easier for a horse to take a run at a steep gradient. I was less amused when he tried the same game heading downhill and restrained him firmly. One and a quarter tons of out-of-control wagon had potential for disaster.

There were plenty of woods and copses in the rolling approaches to the Ardennes. The shooting season had opened and at weekends birds, small and large, were at risk but, despite the slaughter, plenty of small birds remained. To a lesser extent we were also at risk, the presence of gunners close to the road unnerving, though we were never peppered.

The children had been doing a lot of drawing. Torcuil designed a wonderful bicycle for snowy terrain and all three had sketched horses of remarkable quality. Eilidh, idly playing with candlewax, decided to model with it and made a very passable elephant. Music, alas, was limited. I had my bagpipes. We had each been given a Jew's harp before we left, Fionn had a mouth-organ and later we acquired a recorder but we were never able to offer the children music lessons.

In Geetbets, a decidedly lively Appaloosa stallion, barely under control, came charging out of a side road with thundering hoofs, ridden by a pony-tail with large moustache. This was Dane Raymaekers, come cordially to invite us to stay the night at his place. Architectural draughtsman by profession, equestrian by passion, he, his wife Ria and son Mathias made us feel very much at home on their tiny two-acre plot. To Kate's joy, Ria offered use of her washing-machine. We smelt distinctly sweeter when we left next morning – in fog.

It was the first and only time we travelled in fog. The road was a quiet country one but the experience of moving along at four miles an hour with less than fifty yards visibility was scary. At any time some speeding car might have come hurtling up behind, braked too late and embedded itself in the caravan. Fortunately it did not happen, the sun soon burned off the vapour, and when it did, before us were hedgeless tracts of tillage. We passed over the E40 motorway, then under a railway by a narrow arch, unwittingly crossing a divide greater than that between the Netherlands and Belgium. Before entering the archway we were in Flanders among Flemings, but emerged within the Francophone land of Walloons, in Brabant. Street names, shop names and road signs were now in French. The first person we asked about a stopping spot told us to follow her. This was Isobel de Visscher. She was a fine-arts graduate, her husband Eric a composer, and we spent a congenial evening with them and their children, while Offy ate their lawn.

Dr Offereins had not produced a Certificate of Health for Offy and I, foolishly, had not asked for one. We had not been required to produce one so far but would need one to cross into France, as well as a blood-test. Eric de Visscher had introduced us to Vincent Beckers, the vet at nearby Hedange. He confirmed Offy would need a Coggins test for equine infectious anaemia, though not one for equine viral arthritis. The blood sample he sent off would take a week to be analysed but he would forward the result to me *poste restante* at the frontier town of Dinant. He also prepared a descriptive 'passport' for Offy.

When I got back from Hedange I discovered that Offy had been allowed to roll with his harness on and one of the terrets, which carry the reins, was broken. Luckily it was a screw-fit and I had a spare. But I was cross, as only the day before I had warned everybody never to let this happen. Harness was expensive and damage from rolling entirely preventable.

I was worried Kate still hadn't adapted to life on the road, and I knew she was unhappy. She felt the deprivation of familiar domestic surroundings acutely. Certainly, we had come up against unaccustomed physical and mental strains during the first weeks of the trip, which involved a new and strange way of life, a lot of learning processes and a surprising amount of tiredness. Nevertheless I wished she could laugh about it sometimes.

We found Belgium scenically attractive, with warm, friendly, helpful people. Harlue, Eghezée, Cortil-Wodon, Noville-les-Bois, Sart d'Avril, Franc-Waret, Marchovelette and Gelbrussée – we passed through these small villages on 7 November but it could have been any half-dozen others on any day. Dots on a map, unknown to the wider world, but with their own characters and we enjoyed them greatly. The one jarring note was widespread pollution. Roadside ditches were thick with stinking, iridescent green slime; a river by a quarry was a soup of brown dust, and once we camped close to a stream that smelt strongly of diesel – which, according to a local resident, was exactly what was being dumped in it.

The caravan was sturdy but a number of faults had developed or were inherent in the design. Most were minor, such as the chronic tendency of the front storage box to leak, which persisted throughout the journey. Worst was the braking system. It was dangerously inadequate. A hand lever at the front operated car-type drum-brakes on the rear wheels; the wire cable was forever stretching and could never be tightened sufficiently. The effect on steep descents was occasionally heart-stopping. We also found the interior layout too finicky and cramped. I had designed it with the intention of creating a personal space for everyone, but the dimensions were insufficiently large for this and the concept actually reduced usable space. I was constantly thinking of how to remedy this as we jogged along through the rich woods of Belgium.

Offy had developed terrific back muscles and pulled well, though sometimes we all had to push the caravan up the hills. I had not yet discovered one could drive from the ground as well as from the box, often helping the horse at the same time by giving some pull, so still sat aboard even on uphill stretches. I tried to ensure we took the flattest routes but found car-drivers have no conception of what constitutes 'steep'. The end of one particular day saw us having to tackle a mile-long horror of sweat, shove and tears: copious sweat from horse and humans; the tears my own, invisible ones of frustration and misery because I had been told the hill was not steep and had subjected Offy to its rigours. But we made it in the end and were rewarded by finding a splendid place to stop.

This was on the Dewez family's farm at Assesse. A pleasant woman answered our knock and said she was sure we could stay but she would have to ask her brother Joseph, who would soon be home. Poor Joseph. It transpired he was a widower, his wife having died suddenly in April of a brain haemorrhage, leaving him to bring up eleven-year-old Claire and six-year-old Guillaume. The small dairy farm, with twenty-odd Blue-Blonde Belgian cows, only just supported them. Joseph's wife had been a teacher, and her salary had formed a good portion of the family income. Nevertheless, we were heartily welcomed and that evening a crowd gathered: Joseph's family, his cousin's family of five from across the road, and his brother's family of four. I think our arrival gave them a chance to turn away from their sadness. We had a grand merry evening, with ten children including Claire and Guillaume, their Burlet cousins Anne-Astrid, Muriel and Jean-Marc from across the road, their Dewez cousins Thomas and Matthieu, and our lot.

Ready to roll in the morning, about to tack up, I picked up Offy's feet to clean them and saw that his front shoes were almost worn through at the tip. It was bad horse-management not to have discovered this the evening before, when I should have checked his feet. We could not continue until the shoes had been replaced. *Maréchals-ferrants* were thin on the ground in this part of the country but Joseph said he would see what he could do.

Meanwhile, the crowd that had gathered to watch us go watched us preparing to stay instead, including Catherine de Thine, a journalist with the national paper *Soir*. Everyone was milling around, Offy was unharnessed and rugged up and I was in the throes of being interviewed in French by

Catherine. Suddenly from the tail of my eye, I saw Offy fling up his heels and take off down the field – *felling one of the twins as he did so*. How quickly bliss turns bitter. I raced to the fallen twin, thinking, hoping, he had been hit on the shoulder but not sure. Mathieu, for it was he, said indeed it was his shoulder, but there was blood on his lip and ear too. His parents, with almost palpable anxiety, fled with him to the nearest hospital.

The next hours were not comfortable. No matter that the boys should not have been behind the horse. I am fanatical about safety, but this time, distracted by everything else going on, I had not been alert to the situation. I had allowed the children to lead Offy away. He, freed for the day and seeing the grey mare which lived in the next field, had simply given a buck of joy and torn off to greet her. It was fortunate that the consequences were nothing worse than a lightly bruised shoulder.

We were having lunch with the Burlet family when a blacksmith arrived. Stockily powerful and swarthy, Alain van der Schueren was contemptuous of the metal in the shoes the excellent Jan de Zwaan had made for us in Vierhouten. When he was told Offy was nine, he snorted, looked at his teeth and said scoffingly he was nineteen or twenty. Having rudely stamped his mark on the proceedings, he announced he could either tack on a couple of shoes cold immediately or come back on Sunday and put on a complete new set, hot. 'My shoes will last for six weeks at least,' he vaunted. As Joseph was agreeable to our staying, I said we would wait till Sunday.

The children were delighted. They had made friends with Joseph's two, and Eilidh and Fionn were tearing around on bicycles with them. Torcuil and Jean-Marc Burlet found mutual interests, and it was a relaxing time for all of us, able to do nothing, apart from chores, for the first time since we left. Kate and I had a quiet, unpressurised talk. She told me she felt almost claustrophobic in the van and that her unhappiness stemmed mainly from that. She also blamed herself for making the rest of us unhappy, which was simply not true. There was no doubt she felt the cramped conditions far more than the rest of us: she found cooking in our little galley difficult, not to mention clothes-and personal washing. Laundry was certainly a problem, for the children got grubby, and it was often hard to find time and space to do it.

She wrote about how she felt at this time: 'After Scotland I found the Netherlands and Belgium rather bland; I love the hills and sea and both were non-existent where we were. I thought I should slim my fleshy thighs walking every day and did up to a point. But PMT seemed to take over and depression set in at times. I wondered what I was doing here. I guess I just found it hard adapting.'

Monday was a glorious morning to be taking the road. We said goodbye and offered inadequate thanks for free grazing, free washing, fresh milk and piles of *pommes frites*. On Sunday, van der Schueren had come, had been rough, pricked Offy once, boasted his shoes were good for 500 kilometres and that he would rectify free any trouble we had before the border. Now we were running down into Crupet, past a small fairy-story castle in a lake, alongside a stream with a dipper, a yellow wagtail, lots of mallard and a couple of herons living by it, through Yvoir to Houx, where we reached the river Meuse and stopped for lunch. It was beautiful, with great cliffs of limestone behind the remark-ably clean river, an occasional barge passing down and houses, a railway and roads all squeezed into the tube of the valley somehow without either ugliness or the appearance of crowding.

We reached Dinant that evening and had great difficulty

finding a place to park. We settled for a grassless patch near Walsort on the southern side of the town, where there was at least good spring water and plenty of wood nearby. Didier de Daele, a retired Belgian civil servant, with twenty-seven years' service in the Congo and an African wife, lived close by and invited us to tea. We had some target practice with his bow and arrows, which was fun. It was already our last night in Belgium – assuming that the Coggins result awaited collection at *poste restante* in the morning. And that it was negative.

Looking across the river, the twinkling lights of many houses, racked in tiers on the hillside, gave a fairyland effect to the darkening day.

Next morning I was outside the post office before it opened. When it did the joy of finding Becker's note safely arrived and the Coggins result negative was short-lived. His note stated we needed to obtain a *papier d'inspection* from a Dr Dufey, the ministry vet in Dinant. I rang him.

'Avez-vous le test Coggins?' asked Dr Dufey.

'Oui,' I replied.

'Et pour l'artérite virale?'

'Non.'

'Ah. Il y a besoin de ça . . .'

Catch 22. Vincent Beckers, regional ministerial vet, had told me we required only Coggins. A viral arthritis test would require another blood sample – and another week for the analysis to be done. Dr Dufey suggested I ring Paris, to ask for a *dérogation*. I did. No one was at the Service Vétérinaire until 11.30 a.m. I telephoned Vincent Beckers to tell him what had happened and he in turn called Dr Dufey to see if he could help, but that rock was adamantine.

I cycled back to tell the others and found Didier de Daele with them. He ran me back to town to call Paris. Three 220-

Belgian-franc telephone cards later, most of which was spent listening to recorded jingle, I had not only failed to get a *dérogation* but added a test for *morve* (whatever that was) to the requirements. Didier rang Dr Dufey but he had gone out. However, his deputy gave a number in Namur we could call – and a loophole appeared. For an *exportation* of not more than ten days, they said, only Coggins and a vet's description of the horse was required – and the official in Namur could accept the latter over the telephone. The papers would be ready for collection in five minutes.

I was pondering how to reach Namur when Didier offered to take me there. It was as well, for the veterinary office was several kilometres out, in Erpent, and I should never have found it before closing time. So after all that telephoning, a lot of Didier's time and petrol, for which two coffees in Namur seemed scant return, we were equipped with the relevant papers. Or so I believed. In the past twelve hours, four different officials had told me four different requirements. That they did not know the basic veterinary requirements for border-crossings by horses beggared belief.

As if to echo the shambles we had encountered among European officials, that night on BBC World Service we heard Sir Geoffrey Howe make his astounding resignation speech, in which he lambasted Prime Minister Thatcher for her position on Europe and her style in cabinet. It was staggering to hear a one-time chancellor of the exchequer, foreign secretary and deputy prime minister turn on his former chief in such brutal fashion. Kate and I were convinced it must soon destroy her.

A week later we reached Charleville-Mezières.

The crossing into France on 14 November had been anti-climactic, our papers barely glanced at by indifferent

Customs men. The passage alongside the Meuse had been attractive but hard for Offy and, at times, for us. Unfortunately the almost level *halage*, the old towpath, had been allowed to fall into disrepair and most of it was impassable. We had had to take roads instead, which often involved steep sections. In Laifour, Torcuil, Eilidh and I went to telephone our friend Paule Person in Orsay, south of Paris, where we planned to stay a few days. Mail already awaited us and Paule and her family were looking forward to our arrival. I bought a bottle of wine and hastened happily back to the caravan for a celebration of this news, which I thought would delight Kate – and ran smack into a telling off for not having done any shopping. I had not known we needed any. I was shocked and hurt and there was a row. 'I was feeling particularly low,' Kate noted, 'and felt, however irrationally and unfairly, that David should have known we needed things. I suppose it was an accumulation of many things, the weather, harder-than-expected walking, lack of facilities.'

Later that evening, when I looked to see why the brakes had been less efficacious than ever, I was appalled to discover damage of a different kind. The frame bracing the brake-cable and pulley inside the front box had come adrift at the rear. The strain exerted when braking had caused the inadequate small screws to split the wood and pull free. Scared sideways at what I had found, I effected a repair of muscular proportions. Had this piece of construction failed on a descent, it could have killed us.

Gradually we wore south and now left the attractive Meuse valley for the terrible desolation of northern France. Cold rain slashed us. Flatly uniform low grey cloud pressed down on the landscape and upon the soul. The excitement and hurly-burly of our departure was already far behind us as we trudged through monocultural desert. Nothing relieved the monotonous ugliness of the prospect before, behind and all around us. Grey mud, grey road, an occasional grey house. Even the vestigial roadside grass was grey-green. On a distant slope, tractors slithered their way through the glaur, harvesting fodder beet for cattle: invisible cattle, in grey pens in grey barns. The roadside ditches gurgled, filled with fast-flowing grey water.

Our bright red caravan with its green trim, its colours heightened and glossy in the wet, was garishly out of place, a *faux pas*, laughter at a funeral, a fart at a formal dinner. Poor bedraggled Offy plodded on, his hoofs making a soggy sploshing sound. Waterproof clothing was a relative term, as penetrating rivulets trickled their chill paths down my neck and up my sleeves. Inside the caravan, the children at least were dry. Kate, miserable, trudged some distance behind. What were we doing here?

Rain or shine, driving Offy along quiet country roads at three or four miles an hour gave me plenty of time for thought. Sometimes, on a sunny day, the sheer beauty of the scenery, the joy in a bird's song, the glory of a carpet of autumn leaves or the splash of a rising fish in a pond was enough to occupy my mind. Or we would talk. Or the road might demand concentration. But not today, not in this bleakness, this scene of old clashes of arms in the war to end all wars. I could almost hear the boom and roar of howitzers, rattle of machine-guns, crack of rifles, screams of ghostly pain as phantom troops charged across the battlefield to be savagely cut down by withering enemy fire, bodies torn to bits, red in the toneless grey.

My mind slipped from the trenches of France to the trenches of Gallipoli and memories of my father. He had never spoken much about it but after he died I had found his diaries. Those poor trusting lads of the 4th/5th Royal Scots, Queen's Edinburgh Rifles, off to the Big Adventure by train and troopship. On 28 June 1915, only weeks after landing, they went over the top, uphill, against the well dug-in Turks, for the first and last time. Only one man in my father's company survived unscathed; some were wounded, including Lieutenant L. R. Grant, full of shrapnel and minus his right thumb. Most died. I loved and admired my father, though we were never as close as either of us wished, being perhaps too akin. I wondered what he must be thinking now, if he could see us. Would he approve? His sense of adventure would have been tickled – he was invariably supportive of his children's efforts. I could almost see his gentle smile, especially for his three grandchildren whom, sadly, he never knew.

Was it madness to have set off into the unknown with a young family? Not a geographical unknown, of course – nowhere on Earth is any more – but a spiritual unknown and an uncertain future. Many people we knew had been horrified when they learned of our plans. Most thought we were daft. But the few whose opinions really mattered had said, 'Do it.'

'You'll regret it for the rest of your life if you don't go.'

'Wonderful education for the kids.'

So here we were. Are. In the pouring rain. The miserable grey pouring rain in miserable grey northern France. Why, then, was I singing?

Suddenly a huge oncoming lorry, laden with beets, spraying sheets of water from its wheels, seemed to block the whole road ahead. There was just room to pass but the driver gave no quarter. I took the brunt of the spray full in the face as I desperately pulled Offy on to the verge. *Et ta grandmère!* I swore futilely and sent up a fervent prayer of thanks to whoever had trained Offy. He was bomb-proof.

Already we faced problems. The immediate one was, where in this grassless mud wilderness were we going to stop for the night? More serious was Kate's mood. She was dejected and depressed. To me, the caravan had already become home, a place to eat, to read, to sleep; to be warm and dry. If I wanted more space, there was the whole world outside. But Kate, walking in the rain behind, was wrapped in a cocoon of gloom. Whatever had happened to the girl who had once agreed we should go to Callanish and sleep inside the prehistoric ring of stones? The girl who walked happily over the wind-torn moors of Skye? Who had travelled and worked abroad in as many countries as I had? Now we had the chance to make a new beginning, with multiple challenges to face, but it seemed as if she almost hated the prospect. I had to believe that when the weather improved she would be happier.

The children had taken to our gypsy lifestyle with gusto. I had been worried that Fionn, at six, would get bored but he was contentedly ensconced aboard with a pile of Lego. Torcuil and Eilidh had their noses in books and their feet tucked warmly into sleeping-bags. On this flat terrain, their weight imposed negligible added burden on Offy, so they could play or study as we went, in our gently shoogling mobile home.

Next morning, as Eilidh and I were saddling Offy, the rain began again. We slung the rain-rug over him, put to and swung on to the road for Reims. It continued wet all day. The road was as dull as the previous days' had been: ploughed fields, beets and intermittent strips of thin woodland. Not far north of the town we came to a military airfield. The road ran close to the end of the runway and the two-seater jets taking off and landing were passing low over it. The boys especially enjoyed this, whooping with excitement as each aircraft roared over. I had qualms about their effect on Offy but he paid them no heed – till one almost singed his ears. The aircraft landed but Offy took off at a fast trot. Anything was an improvement on beets.

The road took us straight into the centre of town, where we parked right in front of the vast bulk of the cathedral of Our Lady of Reims. There has been a cathedral on this site since AD 401. Clovis, the first Christian king of France, was baptised here in 496. The present one, constructed during the thirteenth century, is the third. In 1429 Joan of Arc attended King Charles VII's coronation in it. Severely damaged by bombing and burning during the First World War, it was restored and reopened in 1937. The interior is most noted for the magnificent stained-glass windows by Chagall and for a statue of St Joan. The united Grant family view was that, mighty though it was, 'our' eleventh-century St Magnus Cathedral on Orkney surpassed it both for beauty and interest. However, only Reims had a jackdaw with the temerity to steal a cardinal's ring.

The old tale about this wretched bird, put into verse by the Reverend Barham, had long been a favourite with us. Jackdaws, of course, are notorious for their love of shiny objects and this one had been in a league of his own as a successful thief. However, he overreached himself when, tempted by the sight of a huge ring lying on a cushion awaiting presentation to the cardinal, he made off with it. Unfortunately for the jackdaw, a curse was put upon whoever had stolen the ring, with the result that most of his feathers fell out and he was revealed as the thief. Suitably contrite and penitent, he was forgiven and lived happily ever after, as did everyone else involved. It brought the story vividly to life to be visiting the scene of the crime. But we didn't see a single jackdaw.

We wandered round the cavernous interior of the cathedral, lit candles and had a quiet moment in the Lady Chapel. We always lit candles when visiting churches, for though not Catholics, it seemed a nice thing to do, a little act of reverence to whoever was watching over us. Back outside, looked down on by a motley collection of grinning gargoyles and fantastical carved-stone beasts, we ate the tasty sandwiches Kate had made. Some passing American tourists took photographs of us, probably thinking we were an authentic Romany family. A mother and her wee boy brought some hay and a stale loaf for Offy. The rain rained on.

South of Reims the landscape changed abruptly to steeper, rolling slopes covered in vines. We were entering champagne country. Horses do not eat grapes and the task of finding grass to make night-stops on became even more difficult.

One morning as she clambered back into the caravan after giving the horse his breakfast, Eilidh asked me, in a nonchalant sort of way, 'Have you looked at Offy this morning?' Peering out of the window I saw what appeared to be a life-size clay model of a horse. He had been having a fine time rolling and was plastered from the tips of his ears to his fetlocks in gelatinous mud. His rug and the picket-chain were similarly coated.

Leaving Kate to ready the inside of the caravan for travelling, which meant stowing everything liable to fall and break, the children and I went out to clean our darling horse. It was fortunate we had stopped close to a stream. His head, neck, backside and belly were dry so Eilidh and I brushed and brushed, raising clouds of fine, choking dust. Gradually patches of chestnut began to appear. When we came to his legs we sloshed bucket after bucket of water over them till they were more or less clean. Meanwhile the boys were doing great work scrubbing the New Zealand rug. The worst task of all was washing the encrusted links of the picket-chain in the icy waters of the stream. It took an hour to get the mud off horse and tack, by which time a fair proportion of it had been transferred to us . . .

Near Chambercy we saw a First World War cemetery – those tragic rows of little white crosses that bestrew this part of the world, reminders of and tributes to individual sacrifice, and the political and administrative madness that squandered so many precious lives for so little. And Offy cast a front shoe. Van der Schueren's pride had been vain and I had perforce to tackle my first blacksmithing. Offy stood like a post. 'Nippers. Rasp. Nails. Hammer.' Sounding like a surgeon in theatre, I rapped out my requirements to Eilidh. It seemed to take for ever, but at last, minor triumph, I had finished trimming bits of broken-away hoof and renailed the shoe. Though it did not look very pretty, it was tight – but, oh, my aching back!

As the end of that cold, and often wet, November came near, things began to go wrong. Our game horse became unwell, scouring a lot and in poor form for several days. Eilidh lost a small multi-tool and got a row for her carelessness, then the caravan ran over her foot, bruising it, as we moved off after a brief stop. The day we crossed the Marne, Margaret Thatcher resigned and Kate bought a bottle of champagne from one of the many producers we passed to celebrate. We neared the environs of Paris. Traffic increased.

It would have been great to have gone into Paris and done a couple of circuits of the Arc de Triomphe. Prudence, however, and Offy's continuing diarrhoea, decreed that we must reach Orsay as soon as possible. Descending to cross the Seine, I found with the brakes fully on I could not hold the caravan. Only Offy, sitting hard back into the breeching strap, kept us easing down gently. Then he had to pull back up the other side, through thick traffic, round the perimeter of Orly airport. 'How're ye doin', pal? Aw'right?' came a cheery shout from a passing Glasgow lorry driver, as we struggled uphill.

Offy desperately needed time off, to sort out his innards and rest. We drove on through a built-up area, noisy, fume-filled and dull, and again had to climb – hard, hard going for Offy – to Ville-Juste, before we attained a plateau. It was the ugliest plateau on Earth, unrelieved ploughland criss-crossed with a forest of electricity pylons set against a backdrop of billowing clouds of steam and foul industrial smoke, and we had to plod four kilometres across it before, at long long last, we came to Orsay.

Number 41*bis* rue de la Ferme proved mercifully simple to find. A knock on the door produced a smiling Paule to greet us. She guided us a short distance further, to the Poney Club des Ulis where, with relief, we installed the brave, weary Offy in a well-bedded box with plenty of water, hay and feed.

Much as we loved and admired Offy, it was evident that we needed an altogether bigger horse. He was stout-hearted and willing, had delivered his very best effort and brought us safely to Orsay, but it had taken a lot out of him. It was not our intention to emulate Genghis Khan's couriers, racing in two weeks from Mongolia to the Polish border, wearing out horses, or the Pony Express hustling across the USA. We had been travelling on good roads in relatively flat country but harder conditions awaited further along our way.

With Paule's help we arranged with Jean-Michel Sullam, of the Poney Club des Ulis, that he would take Offy. He would be well cared for and Paule, who kept her own horse there, could keep an eye on him. We were satisfied to have found such a good home for him so easily. Finding a suitable successor would be harder.

During our ten-day pause in Orsay the children were taken to Versailles, to the Louvre, round the Arc de

Triomphe and down the Champs-Élysées, and Torcuil and I took the glass-fronted lift to the top of the Eiffel Tower. They soaked up this whirlwind dose of culture like sponges, though we were careful not to overdo it and put them off for life.

I spent several days revamping the caravan interior. Everything was readied and soon only a draught-horse was missing. Then a man rang up from an obscure village near Avignon. He had heard we were looking for a big horse and had a six-year-old, 900-kilo, cross-Percheron gelding for sale, which he thought might suit us. Was I interested? Avignon was almost eight hundred kilometres south. Monsieur Joël Moyne wanted five thousand francs to bring the horse to Orsay. For half that sum we could transport the caravan to the horse. We were losing enough from changing horses, so any saving we *could* make we *had* to make.

The journey south at the beginning of December was uneventful, apart from the lorry-driver falling asleep at the wheel. Premonition had prompted me to leave the bunk at the back of the cab and sit in front just before he did, or I should not have seen what had happened, yelled and woken him up. The story of this journey would have ended then as just another frightful autoroute fatality.

Domaine de 'Saint Sauveur' was not far from the industrial town of Entraigues-sur-Sorgues, ten kilometres from Avignon. The truck was too big to negotiate the narrow right-angle over the bridge at the end of the track, so we had to unload there. Shortly afterwards we were greeted by a man on a bicycle, Monsieur Moyne himself. He said he would send Sylvie with Petite to fetch us.

Petite was an enormous grey Percheron mare, with a back on her like a helipad. Sylvie was a slip of a lass of about sixteen. She helped us put the mare into our nearly-too-tight shafts. I expected her to hop aboard and drive: she, after all, knew the animal. But she indicated that I must drive. Me, drive this monstrous horse? This moreover *totally unknown* horse? The caravan was not even facing the right way and would first have to be turned, then manoeuvred across the little bridge and immediately swung through ninety degrees to the right. The scope for falling into ditches on either side was not only great, it seemed inevitable. However, Sylvie simply stood there, expressionless, so there was nothing for it.

Driving Petite after Offy was like conning the *QE2* would be after paddling a canoe. She just walked off, as though nothing was attached to her, obviously used to idiots at the other end of the reins. She turned just where I asked and, as we came back at the bridge, slowed, went across gently and far enough beyond so that the inside rear wheel of the caravan did not clip the corner and foul the ditch as we swung. It was an easy short mile to the farm thereafter, a thoroughly enjoyable drive along the typical Provençal avenue of plane trees.

This was our introduction to the eccentric world of 'Saint Sauveur,' its twenty-one heavy horses and assorted collection of other creatures. It was to be our home for the next two months.

CHAPTER THREE

When it is not necessary to change, it is necessary not to change.

Lord Falkland

The mistral whined viciously through the plane trees. Further north, the worst early snow for decades blanketed France, and Lyons was cut off. The BBC said that Britain was 'white from Shetland to Cornwall'. We had taken a wiser decision than we knew in coming south.

Our expedition had had a difficult start, with unexpectedly long preparations followed by some hard and uncomfortable travelling. Entraigues was different. Memories are of happy times there, the children immensely enjoying riding all the horses, trips out with Traceur, who would be ours if we liked him, and evenings with Joël and Christiane Moyne over a *coup de rouge*. Seeing little Fionn perched atop gigantic Napoleon, totally confident, watching Eilidh galloping the nippy Barb, Amaran, or jumping Vitesse as though born to it, having Torcuil accompany me on long tours through the Provençal countryside with Traceur, hauling one of Joël's many carts or genuine French gypsy caravans, these indeed were times of bliss. Even Kate was more relaxed, had found a friend in Christiane, but remained introspective.

Joël had inherited a canning factory from his father when he was just twenty, sold out six years later, invested the money unwisely and spent most of it on high living. Now impoverished, with demand for his horse-drawn caravans in decline (he once owned thirty, now had four), he continued to maintain an *élan,* breakfasting over his newspaper each morning in a café in Entraigues, buying a dozen oysters or a bottle of fine wine now and then and occasionally entertaining in style. The farm-house was splendid and old and a little decrepit, sitting in twenty hectares of land. It was good land but periodically flooded when the Sorgue penetrated the none-too-well-maintained banking and sometimes invaded the house. Horses were his life's passion, as classical dancing was Christiane's, and he adored them all from Ker, the Comtois stallion, through a motley range of fine draughts to Quicko, the Arabian stallion, and little Amaran, who was into his twenties, had melanoma but was fit as a flea. The property produced enough hay to feed them, but it was heavy work humping the bales about, and grain had to be bought in.

One day, hearing yells from out along the track, I hastened to see what was afoot, for I knew the children had taken Traceur out for a spin. And there indeed was Traceur, hitched to the small, lightweight, red-topped cart, galloping, galloping, galloping, a white-faced Torcuil at the reins, unable to stop or even slow him. He was hanging in there like Ben Hur, steering, while Fionn, standing on the ledge at the back of the cart, clung tightly on. Of Eilidh there was no sign. The cart thundered by me spattering mud, past the front of the house to disappear from sight round the far end. I sprinted after it, expecting a complete wreck. However, Traceur, arriving home, had stopped and – bad luck for him – Joël happened to be working behind the house at the time. What a walloping he got! After that, for both their sakes, I made Torcuil take him back out to the end of the track and come home at a sedate pace, which they successfully accomplished. We never had any bother of the sort from Traceur again. As for Eilidh, she had not been pitched out and impaled on a fence-post or smashed into a wall but had been walking alongside and left standing when the horse took off.

Next to take off was Kate. She had been brooding about something and now revealed she had decided to go home to Britain, to her father's at West End, near Southampton. To me, though, home now was where we happened to be: 'Home is where our horse is.' Kate had hinted at the possibility when we had talked, but now it was almost Christmas. Terrible days of tears followed as the children were told, decisions made, changed and remade about who might go with Mummy and who might stay. Eventually Torcuil and Fionn decided they wanted to go on travelling; Eilidh, to my surprise because she was our equestrienne, said she wanted to go with Mummy. I was not happy Kate was going, but devastated about splitting up our little family. They were such a strong trio, in spite of inevitable childish squabbles, with Eilidh balancing the two boys well. Now we should be two lamed units, heading off into the unknown, divided, weakened and very, very sad.

Kate wrote of this time: 'After the first few weeks, a time of great expectation, getting used to the children being always around and trying to adapt to a new way of life – our jaunt in Ireland was idyllic in comparison with the reality of doing it full time – the weather deteriorated. By the time we reached north France life wasn't too funny, with much rain, hills to push the caravan up and not too friendly French folk who, on seeing the caravan, often shunned me when asking for a place to stop for the night. We had reached our goal for the winter in southern France and I felt I could no longer stand it. How wimpish of me, but I was probably making life hell for David and the children and I was going mad. I didn't want to spoil the trip for the others when it had only just begun.'

At this point, Joël developed an inguinal hernia and had to go immediately to hospital. After the operation, he was forbidden to lift heavy weights. Who would feed the animals? Of course we volunteered. It was a practical way to recompense the Moynes for their manifold kindnesses. Whether this influenced Eilidh I never discovered, but on my way back from Entraigues, whither Torcuil and I had cycled one morning to buy him some fishing hooks, I was met by Kate who told me that Eilidh had opted to stay. I was overjoyed, though I tried to conceal the fact. Eilidh's departure would have been a desolation. But poor Kate. Now she had no babies to go with her; yet I believed she would be the better for it. She needed time to assess her life, without the complications posed by having even the ever-sensible Eilidh about her.

Kate's departure from Avignon station on 20 December was surgically swift. The TGV glided up to the platform, Kate boarded, became immediately invisible behind the tinted glass, the doors closed and the train vanished as smoothly and silently as it had arrived. No chance for a last hug, kiss, wave, or even a tear. Perhaps it was as well. To dispel the immediate gloom we trooped off to explore the Pope's Palace. The magnificent frescoes, the Gobelin tapestries and the many artefacts uncovered during excavations provided the required distraction. Then we met Christiane for a lift back to 'Saint Sauveur'.

Meanwhile, speeding away, Kate understandably felt 'much unhappiness at leaving my wee ones to go and stay with my father. On arriving back in the UK I wondered why I was there.'

At Entraigues there was a lot to be done: preparations for Christmas, feeding the horses, mucking out the indoor ones, mating mares, and working on the caravan interior to make it more comfortable. Traceur required daily exercise, our route over the Alps remained undecided – and I had to make our meals and wash our clothes. I kept the children busy making decorations or tackling their lessons when not helping out on the farm. Shopping, which we had to do by bicycle, was another chore. Money, as ever, was a nuisance, taking ages to come through or a bank refusing to cash Eurocheques. It never seemed possible to make a straight-forward transaction.

Offy's harness was too small for Traceur but I was able to buy a new set from Monsieur Paul Coeur, Joël's harness-maker, who supplied all but a collar. I got a 'Harnatel' collar from Normandy, which was rugged, though heavy, looked traditional but was adjustable for size. We also changed the curious box-section shafts fitted by George Gauld for round ones. This was done by another character to whom Joël introduced us, Monsieur Podzolli, who was that rare craftsman, a wheelwright. This all took time and money and was not completed until well into the New Year.

Christmas was almost upon us. One day Lady disgraced herself by chasing and murdering the little bantam hen, Wet-Wet-Wet, while we were away in Avignon buying festive supplies. I finished making a table for the caravan, then carried out much-needed repairs to the Moynes' shower and the saddle-room door.

On Christmas Eve, which was as crisp and cold as tradition demands, we walked into Entraigues to attend midnight mass. Some carols we knew, but the congregation left most of the singing to the choir and the service was too long for the children, who could understand even less of it than I did. We were given tasty *fougasse* bread at the end, which sustained us on the walk home.

Mother or no mother, Christmas was Christmas, and between the Moynes and myself the children had plenty to enjoy. Torcuil received a small pair of binoculars and an Opinel knife; Eilidh, water-colours and sketching paper; Fionn, Lego and coloured pens. In addition they all got cash and mounds of sweets. The Moynes surprised and delighted us by inviting us over early and presenting us all with gifts, then at lunchtime they came to the caravan with champagne. Kate rang and we all talked to her and to Grandpa, and then it was time to enjoy Christmas dinner, not turkey but a succulent guinea-fowl, stuffed then roasted in our wood-stove oven, served with Brussels sprouts and baked potatoes. Fruit salad followed, more appreciated than plum-duff would have been. Feeling bloated we tackled chores and fed the animals, before a light supper, a bedtime tale and a slightly subdued early bed.

On 2 January we took the train to Switzerland, where we had been invited to spend a few days by old friends Christine and Stephen Little, at their house south of the mediaeval town of Fribourg. New Year's Day had been an absolute cracker of a morning, clear and blue and with a light drying wind. Kate had called – and astonished me by saying she was thinking of coming back. Caught unawares, I did not know what to think. I had become used to doing her share of the work, ably helped by all the children but especially Torcuil, who was a tower of solid strength. Kate was sure she wanted to give it another go and we should meet on neutral ground in Switzerland, which might help but I was concerned that she would find the caravan no less claustrophobic than before.

The complete break, the taste of Alpine air, cheese

fondues, fiercely fought carambol* contests and walks in the snow-girt forests did us all good. Kate flew in to Zurich, still ambivalent about caravan life, but we decided to try again.

It felt very much like being home when we got back to 'Saint Sauveur', as we greeted not only the horses but Zablor, the moth-eaten mongrel, the tame bantam cock Type, and his ladies Très Gentil and Calline, Moi-même the cat and even the bedraggled pigeon, known for some obscure reason as Cuckoo. The whirl of work began again immediately, because we wanted to move on as soon as possible. In the outside world, war between Iraq and the UN was now certain. It was only surprising that it took until 17 January to begin. We saw some news reports on the Moynes' TV, and once a squadron of nine B-52 bombers came flying high down the Rhône valley, polluting the sky with their trails and sending a frisson through me, knowing their mission was spreading death and destruction. Desert Storm had no effect on our preparations, however. Traceur was now nearly fit. I approached the horse-driving magazine *In memoriam Achenbach* about writing articles for them and they agreed to take a quarterly piece. Our route had been decided and maps had to be bought. We were going by the coast, which meant we had to cross built-up Nice and Monaco to reach Italy but also that we would avoid big mountains.

Sadly Kate was still wretchedly torn between wanting to be with the children and almost hating caravan life. If I had believed giving up the expedition and returning to Britain would have made the difference between harmonious

---

*Also known as carom, it is played on a board about a yard square with counters and resembles billiards. By flicking the master counter with one finger, the object is to cannon one's own counters into any of four corner pockets.

relations and a split, I should have done so. But it was not like that. On 30 January, she went into Avignon to buy a train ticket back to Zurich, from where she would use the return portion of her air ticket. It was a sad rerun of her pre-Christmas departure. 'I again felt my staying wasn't working, so again heartache and the decision to go back, work in the UK and return at a later date. I knew I had to see it through this time and make the best of it, but I felt awful guilt at not being with my family, missed them and yet felt I was a chain around their ankles. Looking back, I was perhaps too hard on myself: the caravan was small, especially after leaving a four-bedroomed house on Orkney. I found it claustrophobic, to the point that it was like a prison sometimes,' she wrote.

Just before Kate left we had had to endure another sad parting. Lady died from an infected wound sustained in a fight with a visiting Alsatian. This, and the death and destruction that was continuing in the Gulf, combined to make us all very gloomy, for a while.

Last time I had been glad Kate was going, for we had needed time apart to try to regain balance in our relationship. This time, although it made all sorts of sense and although we knew that the parting was to be temporary, I did not want her to leave.

By 7 February we were ready to go. Traceur was shod and blanket-clipped to prevent him sweating too much while working or feeling overly cold at rest. I'd bought a portable electric fence in preference to the picket and chain, the new shafts had been fitted and everything in the caravan was well arranged. We showered and went early to bed in preparation for a smart start next morning.

We awoke to find the world turned white.

It was snowing hard. It made no sense to start our first day back on the road with a new horse under such conditions. Instead we got the fire going, soon had a good fug up and devoted the day to reading, painting, writing and snoozing.

Next morning was crisply frosty, no more snow had fallen and a watery sun was trying to break through. About mid-day, Traceur having been put to, the harness adjusted and with Joël fussing around like a broody hen to cover being upset at seeing Traceur go, we pulled away from 'Saint Sauveur' through crunchy frozen slush.

We soon settled back into a comfortable routine as we plodded through Taillades and other small villages to Mallemort, where we turned up the valley of the Durance. The brakes seemed to be binding and causing extra work for Traceur but I checked them and they weren't. I then tried inflating the tyres very hard, which made pulling much easier. People were usually helpful and Traceur was much admired as we wended our way among the small Provençal towns and villages.

Visions of a hospitable bowl of soup with the monks at the twelfth-century Abbaye de Silvicane were dashed when we found it was a ruin. After Jouques it became hilly but by then Traceur was well muscled and we encountered nothing steeper than he could manage. Rians was a spectacular small town, situated on a high mound. A church on the summit dominated it, the third to have been built there, although the original tenth-century clock-tower remained. The children were helping all they could, and we still had time for fun after chores were done. One day, turning a corner too sharply in Varrages on a nasty steep tug up to the old village, I hit a house. The house was undamaged but the caravan's right-hand strake was bent in, though easily repaired. We were making progress towards Callian, where we intended to have a few days' rest. Travelling in this region was often hard work, shoving up hills, shopping, trying to keep the children doing basic lessons, finding a suitable stopover each night and looking after Traceur. We were surprised by how tired we became, and how ready for bed at the end of every day.

Callian is a *village perché*, sitting high on an escarpment. Our destination was Julia Arbuthnot's house at Ferme St Jean even further up. I would never attempt it today, but at that point we were still learning so Traceur began to climb. And climb. We all shoved and were joined by a dreadlocked jogger, a Parisian African, without whose help we should have ground to an early halt. Perhaps it would have been better if we had. It was not the gradient that was murderous but the unending length of it. We inched upwards at a pace that would have bored a snail and had almost arrived when out of a car in front of us stepped Julia and her partner, retired doctor David Clough. We all helped the fast-flagging Traceur over the last yards, then parked the caravan and gave him a well-earned rest.

In retrospect it was astonishing that Traceur suffered no ill-effects from this experience. It was a ridiculous thing to have asked him to do and only his youth, strength and mighty legs enabled him to bounce back to fresh vigour within a few days. During our stay, Eilidh had Julia's horses to help with and ride, and Fionn joined her pack of Staffordshire bull terriers and other assorted canines as a fully paid-up member (at least one of them spent more than one night in his sleeping-bag). As children always will in the right circumstances, all three mucked in and helped Julia, and were taken swimming and to the grottoes at St Cézaire in return.

I had been interviewed for the local English-language radio station, Radio Riviera, and had appealed for someone to take me on a route reconnaissance into Italy, expecting to hear nothing. But half an hour after the programme ended,

Gemma Cunningham telephoned. She had use of a car and free petrol. Her offer was a godsend. We *had* to cross the tail of the Alps but I still had not ascertained the best way over. We drove as far as Savona and checked out the Cadibona Pass. Its 413 metres was not too high, the approach from Savona not too steep. It would do.

It was late when I got back to the caravan and Torcuil burst into floods of tears. He *said* it was because he had had trouble getting the fire to go and was missing Mummy but that, I was sure, was compounded by my being overdue. Old Ginger-top felt things so much that sometimes his sensitivity worried me. And Kate, whom we telephoned regularly, was undoubtedly missing us all.

We had made excursions to the Alpes Maritimes and to the sea at St Tropez; feed and hay had been bought and loaded, Traceur had been reshod and a tractor tow arranged to bring us down from Callian to the flatter ground below. It was time and past time to move on. We had been in France long enough. Italy would be a pleasant change.

CHAPTER FOUR

~≈≈≈~

ITALY: MARCH–MAY 1991
PASTA AND PAIN

Travel is necessary to understand man.

Freya Stark

Italian Customs waved us through almost peremptorily and we headed for the first *galleria*, or tunnel. There are many on the coast road but all are short and were not dangerous for Traceur.

Ho! Hey! Hoi! Was someone shouting at us? Up alongside came a breathless Customs man. *Prego* (pant, pant), would we (pant, pant) come back? Apparently we needed a cachet from their vet on our papers. As law-abiding, cooperative folk, we wheeled round, back to the *dogana*. Though officially out of France, it seemed we were not yet officially into Italy. It had been difficult enough getting this close.

From Callian, we had taken the D562 through Montauroux for Grasse, famous for its scent but to us a traffic-clogged hilly nightmare and extremely dangerous. The caravan was towed through, Eilidh rode Traceur and I walked behind to keep thoughtless drivers from hitting them. One car actually struck the bridle I was carrying on my outstretched arm.

The descent through Roquefort-les-Pins to Villeneuve-Loubet was pleasant. A Range Rover pulled up beside us and the driver got out. 'Ah,' he said, 'you are Scottish. I play the bagpipes.' Thinking to call his bluff, I produced mine and handed them to him, whereupon Jean-Pierre Boucan played some very fine music – Breton music. This led to our staying at the extremely smart Centre Hippique St Georges, where he was under-manager and where 250 horses stood at livery. We were there for five days because of another foul-up over border requirements. Having been assured that a health certificate was all Traceur needed, we discovered at the last minute that a Coggins test would be required too. However, the children had a splendid time with the Boucan trio, riding ponies and their mini-motorbike, and Eilidh met Princess Caroline of Monaco, who kept a horse at the Centre.

Traceur's papers had to be stamped in Antibes after which they were valid for only twenty-four hours. There was no way we could make it from there to the frontier in a day. Again Gemma Cunningham came to the rescue. She would collect the papers and bring them to a rendezvous near the French exit post.

Driving the caravan from the Centre through Cagnes-sur-Mer, Nice and Villefranche was ghastly, with congested roads and a mishmash of ugly buildings, though the Mediterranean glowed appropriately azure on our right. On our left towered phalanx after phalanx of high-rise apartments, although occasionally a beautiful old building that had escaped improvers and property speculators survived among them, a reminder of past splendours. We braved the traffic along the famous Promenade des Anglais, where people waved and called greetings to us. Traceur's eyes came out on stalks at his first sight of the sea. We then slogged up to the Bas Corniche, pulling off for the night at the worst place we ever had to stop at: Traceur was on the pavement chained to some railings, the caravan tucked into a small bay at a viewpoint overlooking exclusive Cap Ferrat while vehicles raced past us all day and all night. Why we were not moved on I do not know.

At the border between Monaco and France was a sign showing a car towing a caravan – with a big red cross through them and *Interdit* printed below. Traceur being a horse not a car, we carried on; in a kilometre we had entered Monte Carlo and were flagged down by a polite *flic*. I decided I knew no French. A crowd gathered. Much muttering on police radio. Then we were allowed to go, by the route along the sea-front. As we pulled away, the crowd broke into applause. The Boulevard de Princesse Grace had a hellish climb out at the eastern end but an enormous tipper-truck towed us up. Wickedly we enjoyed the further traffic chaos we caused in this Mecca of the rich and famous while we rehitched Traceur at the top. In Menton, reliable Gemma, to whom we were much indebted, turned up smack on time with our papers and stayed for a valedictory mug of tea.

I went to the *dogana* cubicle with Traceur's papers to have them stamped. After an hour of farce, during which I was asked for a carnet,* then asked to return to France and go to one of the higher border posts, which I refused to do, it was too late to go on. I agreed to go into Ventimiglia in the morning with the police to an Italian vet, who would examine Traceur and stamp the papers. Eilidh cooked us a great supper of mince and tatties, Torcuil and Fionn having found wood by the shore.

---

*Carnet: a Customs permit allowing a motor vehicle to be taken across a frontier for a limited period.

A small old Mercedes van, driven by a slightly sleazy youth, was being searched when I strolled over to Customs at 8.30 next morning, and excitement increased as a siren-sounding, light-flashing blue police van raced up and disgorged two Alsatian sniffer-dogs. They sniffed in vain, and the youth was allowed to go.

So, unexpectedly, were we. All the silly kerfuffle of the previous day was dropped, they wished us well and waved us away. This time we made it into the short tunnel and all the way to Ventimiglia. There were narrow streets and traffic in town but people called out, '*Bel cavallo, bel cavallo,*' which Traceur must have understood, for he was ever so well behaved and sensible as we negotiated our way through this friendly town. We bought fruit, vegetables, bread and meat, and headed for Ospedaletti, where I had spotted a suitably grassy patch on which to stop, when motoring through on the way to Savona. But disappointment: there was no way over or under the railway to reach it. Pressing on, to my consternation we reached San Remo. It had not been part of the plan to tackle a city traverse last thing in the day. A snooty creature, who owned a rather nice-looking camp-site looked down her considerable beak of a nose, said they did not allow animals and suggested a place next door, which did. All I could see was a well-filled lorry park. I walked round for a look, though, and found beyond it a fine place used by motor homes – and it was free. Best of all, there was a splendid patch of lush grass for Traceur.

There was a group of gypsies there and the younger ones immediately crowded around us. They were nosy and a bit pushy but amiable, and later we had a guitar and bagpipe session. We traded paperback books with an Australian couple next to us: fresh reading material was always welcome because we could carry so little and were always running out.

San Remo took an hour to pass through. The Italian drivers were much more patient than the French when, inevitably sometimes, we held them up. It made life more relaxing to have someone call, 'Buon giorno,' instead of giving a blast on their horn as we clopped past. East of town traffic was heavy, due to the imminent arrival of a cycle race, and we had a long pull up to the lighthouse on Cape Verde. We decided to have a half-day and stopped in Arma di Taggia on some grass by the sea. As so often happened, this seemed to have been determined by Fate. Eilidh took Traceur for his first-ever swim in the sea, which he adored almost as much as the prolonged roll in the sand he had afterwards. We had just returned from the beach when an Englishwoman, who lived in Arma, came up to tell us about Bussana Vecchia. This village in the hills behind, destroyed by earthquake in 1887, now housed a thriving artists' colony and was worth visiting, she said.

We left Traceur in his temporary paddock beside the caravan and set off. It was a steep climb but worth it for the view alone. The old village was extraordinary, parts of it unstable and dangerous, especially near the top, but much of it still intact. Imagination easily filled the narrow cobbled streets with the bustle and noise of daily living, all reduced to ruin on the instant when the earthquake struck. Now new life existed among the old stones. Wherever rooms had survived, in nooks and corners, dwelt artists: painters and sculptors, weavers and basket-makers, leatherworkers and woodworkers. Some of the inhabitants had gardens, and shops sold the art- and craftwork.

The Ligurian coast provided fine views. The undulating road was not too hard, though there was a tough hill after splendidly named Imperia, which dominated its surroundings from its perch on a promontory. Stopping-places were sometimes awkward to find because there was no open country, and prices were high because the pound was weak. We swam. We made Easter cards to send Mummy. And reached Savona.

There was industrial sprawl at the edge of the town and we had to plod past that and go quite a long way in before turning north on the Turin road, which for us meant the Cadibona Pass, Acqui Terme, Alessandria and the Po valley. When we stopped to give Traceur a snack, we bought much-needed paraffin for our lamps. As the wind-generator was unable to store enough power to sustain even modest lighting requirements when coupled to only one battery, we had left it in Orsay. Our lamps and candles proved adequate and were less trouble.

That night we parked by the roadside at the beginning of the ascent to Cadibona. The country had changed from sand and sea to mixed woodland, trees already well budded, full of spring birdsong and with rushing streams gurgling their way to the valley bottom. And we had our first puncture. Stupidly, I had left behind the spare wheel at Entraigues to save weight – and we didn't have a jack. One of those practical little three-wheeler trucks you see all over Italy pulled up. John, an American of Italian descent, offered to drive me to a garage to have the tyre repaired . . .

We worked away at the ascent to Cadibona next morning. The road ascended in a series of steps, giving Traceur an ease between pulls. We took it slowly, had a long breakfast stop, and in two hours were at Cadibona village, three kilometres from the summit. A lady gave the children small Easter eggs. The local priest helped me find hay and pointed out a house in which Napoleon had stayed.

There was a single-lane *galleria*, controlled by traffic-lights, above Cadibona – and not a chance that we could get through during a single green phase. Traceur set off smartly when the lights turned green but half-way through we met oncoming traffic. However, there was plenty room and we emerged safely.

We spent Easter weekend as guests of a wild and hospitable crowd of horsemen at Centro Ippico La Marcella, near Ferrania. Sabine, the German groom, soon had Eilidh, Torcuil and Fionn fixed up with horses to ride. She, with Carla and Caterina, who cooked, bottle-washed and tended the bar, also washed our pile of indescribably filthy clothes and produced a great meal for us. We were not allowed to do anything or pay for anything. Twelve or fourteen club members came to dine. Afterwards they sang, I played the pipes and endeavoured to teach them the Highland Fling. As we were with Italians, the children were not left out of the gaiety and we managed to ring Kate. Eilidh rode again next day and jumped super little Belinda, who was the perfect sized pony for her. Then she took Traceur out and jumped him. It was a sight to see our muckle lad popping over the poles.

Sabine, and her daughter Jasmine, mounted on Giarry, an Argentinian Criollo, escorted us the first part of our way when we left. Later, travelling through the strange unstable tufa country around Piana Crixia, a family stopped and gave us a bale of lucerne hay, and yet again we were astonished by the generosity of strangers towards us. That same day, we had more brake trouble: the wire cable had frayed, with only three strands remaining. As soon as possible, a redesigned system would have to be fitted. I was thankful we were leaving hilly country for the flats of the Po valley.

Fionn had a bleak miserable spell one evening, and I resolved to make more time for him. He never said much, never complained and, in fact, we had had a grand walk that day through the tufa. It was not always easy to know what his six-year-old mind made of what we were doing. He seemed to enjoy most of it, though at times he missed his mother.

The Bormida River was full and rushing down the valley to the plains. As we reached the flat land short of Alessandria, a man stopped us and asked if he could book our act. He became quite angry when I told him we didn't have one. Contemplating the idea of becoming strolling players or wandering minstrels, we took a byway for Castelceriolo but couldn't find anywhere suitable to stop. The track I took became rough and rather heavy going in places but there was nowhere to turn. It led by a back entrance to Azienda Agricola Santa Maria, a dairy farm. I asked where we might find a place to stay and they said, 'Here!' Traceur was accommodated in a shady, open-sided implement shed, with masses of hay and a deep straw bed. We were given stacks of firewood and so many eggs that a massive scramble became the menu for supper. Having hung up wet horse-rugs and put the saddlery out to dry we walked to Marengo.

The battle of Marengo, fought in 1800 after Napoleon had crossed the Alps, ended in the decisive defeat and capture of the Austrian army, which allowed France to regain control of Italy. I had not realised we were so close to the site until our host, Giovanni Ottocello, told us about the bayonets, lances and bones they sometimes ploughed up. A good chance for an enjoyable history lesson was lost when we found the museum shut and the whole area pretty unkempt. Instead we turned to biology – swallows nesting in the byre – and agriculture. The farm was new, built from scratch six years ago by Giovanni and his three sons. They ran 250 cattle, milking about a hundred in the huge computerised byre, grew their own maize and hay but bought in feed, all on about 150 acres. It was agribusiness, impressive, and dispelled lingering images of idle Italians dozing under olive trees. Northern Italy was up-to-date, clean and with a go-ahead air about it.

Our route took us across the wide river Po, through little farming villages, past thousands of hectares of ploughed land and very little grass, through the Parco d'Adda nature reserve and on to Cremona, where Stradivarius was born, and where violins are still crafted. We mostly made progress and lived harmoniously. Occasionally I would lose my temper, usually with one or other of the boys over some silliness, often because I was strained and tired rather than because they deserved it. There were moments when I missed adult company and there were things the children simply could not do but I loved travelling with them. They were great companions and willing helpers.

The name Scotti, common in the region, derives from the Scottish Border name Scott. Bearers of it, returning from the Crusades, having sampled the delights offered by local lasses, apparently never made it home. Our stop east of the town was on a huge triangle of grass bordered by two motorway access roads. It was a bit noisy but the grass was good. Fionn helped me prepare a huge vegetable curry for supper.

In the morning, Traceur refused to pull the van up the short slope on to the road. Several attempts failed and eventually we hitched him with a rope to the back of the van, pulled it clear then rehitched. This time I swung round in a wide circle, building up momentum before aiming at the bank. As we charged forward we hit two appalling bumps and became airborne at both. I nearly fell off, but we got on to the road. A quick survey revealed no apparent damage inside or out, except Torcuil's prized tumbler with his name engraved on it, which was cracked. I was exasperated with Traceur because there had been no need for this perform-ance, so trotted him all the way to Malagnino. There, a man in a flat cap, sports jacket and red waistcoat flagged us down. 'Ah, you are Scottish,' he said, in fair English, 'I drive horses too. Come to lonch.' It was only 10.30 in the morning, the place we had to go to was five kilometres off the road and normally I should never have accepted. What prompted me to do so could only have been the benison of Providence.

Traceur would not respond properly when I tried to turn him, though the reins were not snagged and his harness was attached and fastened correctly. He was worse on the road, refusing to turn left. A very thorough look underneath the caravan revealed a badly bent turntable, which was fouling the chassis. Poor horse, no wonder he was not turning properly: it was impossible. We limped into Giovanni Massera's yard at via Garibaldi 32, in the small town of Sospiro. There he introduced us to his vivacious wife, Anna, and elegant daughter, Sabrina. We were given the promised, most delicious 'lonch' of pasta with a rich sauce, fresh fruit and new-ground coffee.

Giovanni was an expert amateur saddler and coach restorer, with a marvellous workshop. Our turntable was beyond him, though, so he summoned Ferdi Mainardi, neighbour and farmer, to tow the caravan to an agricultural blacksmith nearby. Two hefty men de-mounted the front chassis. With a few deft blows of a colossal hammer, one straightened the lower turntable ring. His mate knocked the kinks out of the upper ring and welded on new cross members to reinforce it. It was a great piece of work, for which they flatly refused any payment. We parked in Ferdi's farmyard that night, for it was too late to go on.

Torcuil had begun a fever and was quite flushed, with a pain in his midriff, which I was sure was appendicitis. He failed to appreciate the soup, chicken and cheese Anna gave us for supper. Pills brought down the fever but the pain remained. The next morning he was still feverish so I took him to Dottor Fausto Garini's surgery. He confirmed what I thought and gave us a note for Cremona hospital. Anna drove us in. Fionn wanted to come too, so I left Eilidh in charge. At ten, she was more reliable and more capable than many an adult.

The hospital was huge and pleasantly cool inside, but a bewildering maze. We reported to Casualty and were directed to the children's department. A probationer who spoke English interpreted while Torcuil was examined. The doctor sent him to Male Surgical for a second opinion. They confirmed it was appendicitis and he was assigned to bed number 8 in a small ward for six people. Having seen him settled, I went with Anna to the admissions office to submit Form E111, the form governing reciprocal arrangements whereby UK citizens are covered under the National Health Service while in other EEC countries. It meant there would be nothing to pay.

I snatched a bite of lunch in Sospiro, snatched up things for Torcuil, saw that Eilidh and Fionn were all right then went back to Cremona with Sabrina, who worked there, to be with Torcuil until evening.

He was miserable and rather dopey, had had a blood sample taken, his blood-pressure read, been given an ECG and also an antibiotic injection. He was ravenous but forbidden to eat until after his operation, scheduled for 10 a.m. the next day. In mid-afternoon I went to buy him a respectable pair of pyjamas but mostly we sat in companionable silence. He had been carted off once more while I was out, this time for a chest X-ray. They were certainly thorough. As I was leaving for the night, Torcuil's firm control ebbed and two great buckets of tears rolled down his hot cheeks. No wonder. I should not have been half so brave aged eleven, about to be left on my own, hungry, sore, unable to communicate and surely a little scared about the forthcoming operation. And miles away from Mummy.

Eilidh was in the middle of making supper when I got back. She and Fionn had done all the chores and the farrier had been. Some children they had been playing with had brought eggs and mineral water – kindness and help showered upon us again.

Leaving them totally in charge next morning placed a heavy burden on the two younger ones but Torcuil's need was greater. He was subdued when I arrived, not least because of the agony of another antibiotic jag in his skinny wee bum. They *hurt*. Mid-morning came and went but there was no mention of his operation. When I enquired they said the theatre was very busy and the op had been put back till 4 or 5 p.m. The long day dragged on. Torcuil dozed and I caught up on my correspondence. By 5.30 p.m., with still no call for Torcuil, I again enquired and was told he would definitely be going into theatre at 6.30. At 7 p.m. he was carted off on a trolley. Then I was summoned to the pre-theatre anteroom to sit with him as there was a further delay. After ten minutes a doctor came out and explained in English to Torcuil what they were about to do to him and showed him an appendix! It was decent of him, especially as there had already been six operations in that theatre that day and he must have been weary. At last Torcuil was wheeled away and I had just time to dash down and tell Sabrina I would have to stay on. We arranged that I should telephone when ready and someone would fetch me.

Half an hour later, Torcuil was rolled into his room, zapped out and with a drip in his arm. The nurses lifted him gently to his bed, transferred the drip-bottle to a stand and told me to hold his hand to stop him tearing the needle out. His eyes flicked open and shut now and then, and he complained his ribs were sore. The nurses gave him a pain-killing suppository and an ice-pack over his wound. 'Sore, sore,' he said, and I am sure it was but he was wandering in a miasma of anaesthetic fog and making little sense. I telephoned Giovanni and agreed to wait outside for him at 9 p.m. On the way home, he said he had a surprise for me, but refused to say what.

Anna fed me. Given the rain, the cold and a certain infirmary-induced fatigue, this was the greatest kindness she could possibly have rendered. Then Giovanni sprang his surprise: he had had two springs made to give the caravan front suspension again, which it had lacked since its enforced removal during the last-minute wheel-changes before we left Vierhouten. For once I was speechless.

The children had been in the house and the caravan fire was unlit, so it was cold. Diving into chilly sleeping-bags, Eilidh, Fionn and I curled up on the double bed together like pilchards in a tin and soon slept.

Torcuil made rapid progress after the first day. On 22 April, six days after his operation, his stitches were removed. The same day Eilidh, Fionn and I ascended the 552 steps of Cremona Cathedral *torrazzo*, the highest bell-tower in Italy. The view from the top was terrific but it was too hazy to glimpse Monte Bianco. We did some shopping and I bought Fionn a much-needed pair of new trainers.

The courtyard at Ferdi Mainardi's *cascina,* where the caravan was parked, was surrounded by traditional old-style farm-buildings, with only a gate at one corner for access. They housed everything: animals, hay, grain, implements and people. In their heyday, the biggest would have held between 100 and 120 resident farm-workers and their families. Now only Ferdi and an old couple, the Andrusinis, lived in his. We had many visitors, who always brought something for us, eggs, wood, cakes or whatever, and several times we were invited out to eat – by local chemist

Emilio Beduschi, by Ferdi and often by the Masseras.

I was sitting beside a fully dressed Torcuil on his bed on
23 April, waiting for Emilio to collect us when the nice
English-speaking nurse whom we had met when Torcuil
was admitted came into the ward. 'Meestair Grant, there ees
a problem.' I must have looked startled but then she added,
'Your daughter Eyelid is in Pronto Soccorso and-a she has-
a broken ankle.'

I don't recall racing down the stairs to Casualty. I just
remember being there, with a pallid Eilidh sitting in front of
me with her legs up on a bench. Dried tear-streaks belied her
offhand air of bravado. She had fallen off Traceur and it
was sheer bad luck that one of his soup-plates had come
down on her dainty size two. There was a deep, contused
wound on the inside of her left foot behind and below the
ankle. The X-ray showed a hairline crack in a foot bone.
Plaster for ten days. And crutches.

Kate had been kept fully briefed: 'I was not there for
the children and felt awful. I remember speaking to Torcuil
just after his operation and hearing his muffled sobs. I
wanted to be there but David said there was no point in my
returning . . .' I wholly understood Kate's maternal instinct
but leaving her job and incurring considerable expense
simply to satisfy it made no sense. An appendectomy was
not much worse than a tooth extraction. It would have been
different had Torcuil been gravely ill.

In three more days the work on the new caravan suspension was completed. What a difference! The shuddering
and banging we had felt when hitting potholes and bumps
was now absorbed by the new springs.

Eilidh was charging around on her crutches as though
fully fit, but Torcuil, his middle still tender, moved carefully.
Nevertheless, we were ready to go. Just before we did, il
Sindaco del Comune di Sospiro, the Mayor of the

Community of Sospiro, presented us with an engraved plaque and a testimonial letter in our honour. We were greatly flattered but thought in truth we should have been honouring Sospiro for the tremendous help and kindness we had received there. Waving to the Masseras, Ferdi and the Andrusinis from the farm, we pulled away. 'Lonch' had lasted eleven days.

The via Postumia runs straight as an arrow across north Italy, carrying traffic today that would be more foreign to its Roman engineers than spaceships are to us. We followed much of its length, through a multitude of little villages, staying on hospitable farms or by the banks of creeks, being visited by the Masseras and friends and moving steadily eastwards. Close to Pelegrina, one wet afternoon, I answered a knock on our door to find a pistol pointing at my stomach. Three very young *carabinieri* stood outside with drawn weapons. Apparently a policeman had been shot in a fracas with gypsies, miles away near Bologna, and these lads were taking no chances. Passports, *prego*.

We reached Cologna in a downpour and parked near the hospital. There, Eilidh's plaster was removed. '*Cammina!*' commanded the doctor. She walked – but with much pain. New X-rays were ordered. Waiting in the hot, stuffy, crowded foyer for the lift to Radiology, Eilidh suddenly said, 'My head feels funny' – and went out like a light. The male nurse accompanying us caught her before she hit the floor. He then fetched a trolley to wheel her the rest of the way. The end result: twelve more days in plaster.

Another few days and we were into Carmignano di Brenta and turning into the farm at via Prominente 35, home of Terese and Ivo Baldisseri, friends of Giovanni Massera. From Carmignano we were going to take a train – to Venice. It was exciting getting up early to catch the 8.16

train for Vicenza. We had to change there, from the sleepy local train to the Intercity, and it was only 9.50 when we drew into Venice station. The day was effervescent, sunny and clear, and the first thing we did was buy all-day runabout tickets for the *vaporetti*: Eilidh could hurtle about like a missile on her crutches but not all day long. Besides, at their age I thought it would be more fun for the children to spend time on the water rather than surfeit on sightseeing. We puttered off down the Grand Canal.

Our first stop was completely unplanned and unexpected. The Palazzo Grassi was advertising the I Celti exhibition, probably the biggest assemblage of Celtic artefacts ever seen in one place and an irresistible opportunity to show the children something of their heritage – though ironic to be doing so in Venice, so full of its own treasures. We battled through hordes of schoolchildren and other visitors but it was worth it. Some of the best and most famous Celtic works of art, jewellery, weapons and utensils, were on display, including the famous Brecbennoch of St Columba from Scotland, the bronze Battersea Shield from England and the Ardagh Chalice from Ireland. There were Czech, Spanish, Scandinavian and French items, too, and from Denmark something I had yearned to see: the unique magnificence of the huge engraved silver Gundestrup Cauldron. To look properly at the many lovely animal figurines, beads, brooches and earrings, torcs, carriages and carved stone figures needed more time – a lifetime, perhaps – but we had come to see Venice, the incomparable. On to San Marco! And pizzas and sandwiches for lunch.

Mindful of Eilidh's foot – or hands, really, because they took her weight and were in danger of blistering – we took ship for the Lido and cruised gently out and back, soaking up sun and scenery, watching the busy, waterborne life of Venice. Back at the landing stage by San Marco, we boarded a Linea 5 boat for a sail past the Arsenal and Cimitero di San Michele to Murano, to see the glass-blowers. We ate *gelati*, too, for it was pleasantly hot and no one in the world makes better ice-cream than the Italians. At the Piazzale Roma we changed boats and went down to the Rialto. Gondolas plied their trade, and crowds thronged. Finally we made our way through back alleys, through domestic Venice with not a tourist in sight, to the station. It had been a day out of time.

Before leaving the Baldisseris the following morning, Ivo showed us his collection of horse-drawn coaches, carriages and sleighs. He had over thirty, all in top condition, lovingly restored reminders of a graceful, quieter and less polluting age.

In a few more days we arrived at Gemona-del-Friuli and drove directly to the hospital: Eilidh's plaster was overdue for removal. The bone had healed but the deep wound on her ankle looked unhealthy. The doctors cut away a lot of necrotic tissue and bandaged it but it suppurated for a week, requiring frequent dressing. However, nothing could dampen Eilidh's joy at being crutchless again after twenty-two days.

It was getting late by this time and, in lieu of anywhere better, the deputy administrative doctor said we could spend the night in the hospital grounds. Couldn't quite see that happening at Bart's, St Thomas', or Edinburgh Royal Infirmary . . . Late that evening, Elisabeta Serafini from the admin office, who spoke English, came to say she had found a place for Traceur and that we could park the caravan in their yard. Her husband Armando was a radiologist, as was her brother Stefano. Stefano played folk music in a group, which included a Celtic harpist and a Friulan bagpiper. Eilidh and ten-year-old Rebecca rapidly became good friends.

Our time at Gemona flew by, for we were busy during all of it. The town itself occupied a day, seeing its fine church, with its interesting stone carvings of Celtic origin. Somehow it had survived almost undamaged in 1976, when over a thousand people were killed and the town was flattened by an earthquake. We learned about the invasions of the Longobardi and the continuing Celtic influence, as well as the Friulan language, which is very much alive: one of Europe's many less-known minority languages, it is related to the Swiss Romansch tongue. We collected mail. The anticipated Easter eggs, broken into bite-sized pieces, at last arrived, and a lot else besides. Michele Cuttini, a photographer we had met, took us to see the workshop of his uncle, Roberto Milan, who was an excellent sculptor, and some splendid pieces adorned the workshop walls. Torcuil and I walked up Monte Quarnan, which at 4435 feet was 29 feet higher than Ben Nevis, though a mere pimple beside its craggy, unstable neighbour, Mount Cjampon. We had a great day among the alpine flowers and birds, which included alpine choughs flocking noisily around the top, chiffchaffs calling, a soaring buzzard and a sparrowhawk dashing after prey. From the summit we could see Monte Cania on the Yugoslav border. Later, Armando took me on a recce some way up the Tarvisio road.

The north road up the narrow Tagliamento valley was beautiful. At our first stop we had a surprise when Michele arrived. He presented me with a bronze replica of a huge wooden sculpture of Longobardi horsemen by his uncle, which I had admired, rendering me wordless with astonishment and gratitude. Then he took a lot of photographs of Eilidh riding Traceur into the river. There, we shoved a car belonging to a couple of East German lads out of soft sand where they had stuck. They had pale pinched faces and wary eyes, unable yet to believe freedom was for real. Before he left, Michele promised he would visit us again.

In two days, on 29 May, we were at the frontier town of Tarvisio. It had proved impossible to discover what papers we needed for Traceur, opinion varying from full health certificate and Coggins – twenty days for analysis here – to a simple form sent to me by Austrian officialdom.

In a few miles, we should find out.

CHAPTER FIVE

———◆◆◆———

AUSTRIA TO SLOVENIA: JUNE 1991
SAUERKRAUT AND SLIVOVKA

Do stop telling me what to do! Right, what do I do?
Kate Grant

Fears about the Austrian border had been engendered by
Tim Severin's account, in his book *Crusader*, of bureaucratic problems and delays encountered there when riding
to Jerusalem. Before we essayed it, however, we ran into
other difficulties.

The road from Tarvisio to Austria is busy and runs
through a long, ill-lit, narrow tunnel with fast traffic. I had
asked the *carabinieri* for an escort but they said we could
take the back road. I had already been told it was steep in
places but they assured me it was not . . . First came a short
horror Traceur just managed to struggle up, with us shoving
like the Scots pack against the English at Murrayfield on a
good day: on this beautiful but quiet little road, there was
no vehicle to tow us. There was worse to come. First a sharp
descent on which only Traceur, not I on the brake, held the
van. There followed another descent, vertiginously steep,
again short but with a right-hand bend over a bridge at the
bottom. Failure to take the bend would end in destruction
in the gorge below. Had we had good brakes, it would not

have been a problem. Tying a stout rope to the back rack of the van, to which Torcuil, Eilidh and Fionn were ordered to cling as living anchors, I climbed gingerly to my seat on the box. Adjusting the brake tension to maximum, I yelled to the children that we were about to go and almost whispered to Traceur to move off. The combination of brake, horse and three pairs of dragging feet held down speed famously and we arrived safely at the bottom, the sole damage being to – well, soles!

At the Austrian *Zoll* I flourished the form I had been sent and had completed, which they took into a building, along with our passports. A Customs man waved us across to a parking place and, in good English, told us we might have to wait a little because he had had to telephone for the vet to come. He apologised for this but said it would not be long. I went to cash a Eurocheque and change my remaining lire. The children were ahead of me, having already changed their money, and headed for the shop. The *Tierarzt* soon arrived, a pleasant, courtly, oldish man. He looked at Traceur, then took a closer look at his eyes, filled up a paper and stamped it. The hardest part was shelling out 130 schillings for the fee.

Approaching Arnoldstein, a small industrial town, an hour later, a man on a tractor waved to us. I thought little of it and not much more when, a few minutes later, he overtook us. Then he made distinct 'follow me' gestures. I did not connect this with having asked one of the Customs men if he knew a place where we might park for the night. We followed anyway and shortly drew up outside Gasthaus Satz. Herr Satz, for it was he, climbed down from his tractor. He conveyed that his son-in-law worked at the frontier post – at which point rusty cogs whirred in my brain – and had telephoned him. He would be delighted to accommodate us. The caravan was parked close by and

Traceur made comfortable in a fine stall next to Joseph's Noriker mare, Gretel, and opposite three milk-cows. Joseph was the current Satz of six generations who had owned the 300-year-old inn. We were taken in, given soup and bread.

Joseph was sixty-six, had fought in Yugoslavia with the Wehrmacht for three years and been wounded. He had an artificial lower-right leg, from a horse accident in 1965. His wife Agathe, who had served us, was a pale shadow of her solid husband. They had five children, including Bernhard, who lived at home, Sep, the Customs officer, and Karl, who lived nearby with his family.

In the afternoon, Gretel was harnessed to a flat cart and we went to a meadow, towing a motor-scythe, to cut grass for the cows and horses. Eilidh and Fionn sat on Gretel, Sep drove and the rest of us piled on to the cart. Bernhard cut swathes of grass, everyone else helped rake up and load, then back we went to feed the animals. We were fed again, too. The meal, served on round wooden trenchers, with large knives, consisted of hunks of *Speck* (bacon fat), cheese, *Hauswurst* (home-made sausage), gherkins, rye bread and butter, washed down with Gösser beer for the adults, fizz for the children. It was a complete contrast to the pastas and sauces of Italy but the children liked it and delved in with gusto.

Kate telephoned. After four months on her own she was coming back for another go. We agreed a rendezvous at the station in Villach, a day and a half's drive away. Accompanied by a crowd, and enough bread, beer and *Speck* to make Traceur groan at the extra weight, we departed.

The children had been continuing lessons all the while and excitement at Kate's impending arrival was not dampened when I gave them stories to write. Torcuil had to describe being Eilidh driving Traceur for a day, Eilidh to describe being Traceur for that day and Fionn had to describe being his pencil for a day. Fionn's tale was most imaginative. They appeared to be losing nothing academically because of their unusual lifestyle.

We found a space for ourselves in Villach not far from the station. The children were all on the platform, bursting with excitement, when the 12.49 clattered in on time. I raced up breathless in the nick of time having rushed from the Konsum supermarket where I'd been shopping.

Kate was not on it.

Had she missed her connection at Munich or had a last-minute change of mind? It would be strange to be five again but I was looking forward to seeing her. After twelve years of marriage, her absence had left a void.

The 13.43 clunked up to the platform as punctually as its predecessor. For a moment I thought Kate was not on it, either. Then there she was, striding down the platform in a bright multicoloured wool coat and black knee-boots, recent hair-do and looking stunning. There was rush and babble as the children squeezed their mother half to death and a commotion getting from platform to caravan with a mountain of luggage – luckily for Traceur, a relatively small mountain. Kate seemed radiantly happy and obviously overjoyed to be reunited with the family.

The Ostachersee was a tourist trap with ribbons of hotels and houses flaunting *Zimmer frei* signs. We needed grass not rooms but we had to go twenty kilometres before we found a field. It rained that night and more during the following days. We wended our way wetly towards Klagenfurt. Kate bore up well and it was good to have her back. Perhaps, I noted in my diary, we had needed the four-month break to appreciate each other.

The valley floors in southern Austria were flat and broad, our road level, most of the time. I had hoped to go round Klagenfurt but the chosen bypass became too steep and we reversed our course. It was needless to subject Traceur to hills for the sake of avoiding traffic: he moved effortlessly among streams of cars. However, as we were drawing up at a red light in Klagenfurt, a car cut in front of us from the wrong side, leaving Traceur insufficient stopping distance. We hit it and broke some plastic. The driver jumped out but, in the face of our anger, retreated rapidly. The light turned green and he drove off at furious speed. On the whole, drivers were, if not always thoughtful, at least respectful of our size.

One morning Kate jumped off the moving caravan, slipped and fell. She hit her head hard on the road and was nearly run over by a passing car. She was badly shaken and the incident underlined once more the need for care. The next morning she jumped off while we were still parked and wrenched her ankle so badly that she could barely walk for several days. She wrote, 'David shouted some command, giving me such a fright I fell – what an idiot. Next day another shout, "Jump!" This time it was my ankle which gave way.' Nor was I immune to accidents. On leaving the field we were in that second morning, I cut the exit too fine, collected the gatepost with the caravan and scrunched up some planks on the side. I was *not* pleased with my handiwork.

These awkward incidents faded from my mind as we passed through lovely country beside the river Drau. Bird-life was prolific, spring flowers a colourful array along the verges. A short hill required a tow but there was a tractor at the bottom just when we needed it and the driver happily agreed to tug us to the top. We crossed a bridge over the Drau, its still, deep, muddy waters surging powerfully below. The road on the far side rose extremely steeply to the top of a low escarpment, which necessitated another short tug. These little hills were impossible for Traceur but were infrequent and did not justify having a second horse. In Kühnsdorf, Eilidh and I bought shoes and materials to patch the planks I had damaged. We had no idea how easy it would be to find necessities in either Yugoslavia or Hungary, so we stocked up.

The road away from our most recent overnight stop, in bonny woods near Aich, was cut into the side of the hill running along the south bank of the Drau, through sometimes dense woodland. It was early June, everything was growing in lushest profusion, birds were flying into every bush with food for their young, bees and other insects hummed and buzzed. The rich, unstoppable forces of life thrived in the humid heat that engulfed the land. We dropped lower, through slightly more open country with patchworks of grass and cultivation, and entered the small frontier town of Lavamünd.

There, we found a BP garage, with a field behind containing a mare and foal, some deer, a hare and some fowl. Traceur needed fresh papers for entering Yugoslavia. Surely these people would know where to find a vet. They did, and kindly telephoned Dr Melitta Pogner. She came, looked Traceur over, drove me to her surgery, filled out a paper and ran me back, all for the princely sum of 100 schillings and a beer. Meantime Kate had accepted an impromptu invitation to lunch from Anita and Gernot Pucher at their nearby house. Then Michele Cuttini appeared, as he had promised he would, so he was invited too. While we ate, Traceur grazed contentedly under a shady tree by the garage.

When the day had cooled a little, we put to, crossed by the bridge in the centre of Lavamünd to the north bank of the Drau once more and sweated the five kilometres to the border. I was very tense: this frontier represented transition from the known culture and customs of Western Europe, where whatever country we were in felt secure and relatively familiar, to the beginnings of the unknown East. Tito's unorthodox form of Communism had been more open, but it had still been Communism. I had been to Yugoslavia in 1967, my sister had lived there when her Canadian diplomat husband had been posted to Belgrade, and millions of Western European tourists flocked every year to the Dalmatian coast. I had been assured before we left by the Yugoslav Embassy in London that there would be no difficulty. Nevertheless, rolling up to the border I speculated on what sort of reception we would be given.

Short of Austrian Customs we said farewell to Michele and I got out the paperwork. The Austrians let us through swiftly. We covered the few hundred metres from the exit point and pulled up smartly at the glass cubicle on the Yugoslav side. Speculation and worry ended as, with grins, we were directed to park a few yards away. Our papers and passports were looked at, stamped, and we were in! – into the province of Slovenia. We changed money and filled the water-jerries. Unlike most other countries, the Yugoslav exchange accepted small coins in any currency, so the children delightedly cashed in their accumulations for dinars. We quickly learned our first Slovenian words, *prosim* and *hvala,* please and thank you, and with a big *hvala* to the still-smiling border guards, we were waved on our way.

To our right the road ran just a field away from the river, no longer the Drau but the Drava. Immediately to our left was sharply rising ground. On the far side of the river were trees and behind them partly wooded hillside. The verges were a long profusion of flowers. Between Austria and here, a difference existed similar to that between the Netherlands and Belgium, an absence of rigid neatness and order, hard to define but unmistakable. There were small farms, with wooden houses, maize fields and cows, one or two ponies and fertile vegetable plots. We rounded a gentle curve and saw ahead a church with a small, onion-domed spire, western sentinel of the town of Dravograd. As we entered, Traceur tiring, more than ready ourselves to stop, someone told us there was a horse-club just across the river. We continued past extensive allotments, where beans grew luxuriantly up a forest of poles, came to the main street with shops all closed, for it was Saturday evening, and at the end turned right over a bridge.

After a further half-mile, which included a hill, there was still no sign of the horse-club. I felt we must stop, so pulled on to some grass well behind what appeared to be a fuel dump. We had the electric fence up, Traceur installed, the fire going and supper cooking when, simultaneously, a man from the fuel depot came to tell us we could not stay there and a man from the horse-club arrived. The latter introduced himself as Otokar Praper, told us that we could stay at the horse-club, that it was not far and he would help us move. We had been only a few hundred yards from Konjeniski Klub Dravograd. Traceur was resettled and fed. Otokar invited us to his house, which we could see just across the river and after we finished supper he came back for us in a rubber dinghy. All four Praper brothers were there: Otokar, who was in the *milica* (more than police but less than army), Peter, a psychology lecturer, Joc, who taught gymnastics, and Hari, headmaster of a school in Kamnik, along with sons, daughters, cousins and friends. The evening developed into a party. The brothers sang traditional songs in four-part harmony, Peter played guitar, and there was even a guitar and bagpipe duet. Plentiful libations of good local wine and *slivovka,* plum brandy, were consumed. At some point the children had been put into beds and around 2 a.m. Kate and I were poured back across the river, ending a long day and a memorable introduction to Slovenia and the Slovenians.

The fourteen-day run down the Drava to Hungary would be enjoyable if everyone was this friendly – and our livers could stand it.

How little did we know what Fate had in store.

CHAPTER SIX

Learning rules is useful but it isn't education. Education is thinking, and thinking is looking for yourself.

Alice Middleton

Traceur was ill. I awoke groggily, on our first morning in Dravograd, to find him walking round and round his paddock, not having eaten his feed. It looked like colic, but wasn't. At lunchtime we sent for a vet. Traceur's temperature was high, his pulse rapid and weak. Because he had just crossed the frontier, regulations stipulated that a government vet had to be summoned before he was given any medication. Neither vet could offer a definite diagnosis but his yellowish eyelid linings and lips suggested liver infection. He was a very sick horse.

The next days were anxious ones. Penicillin injections and a charcoal-bismuth oral dose were administered to Traceur, and he was wormed. There had been *Gastrophilus* larvae in his droppings – horse-bots, a parasite, which can cause internal damage. I was horrified, because I had been punctilious about regular worming. His temperature crept down but remained too high, hovering at about 40°C. He was given streptomycin and a liver-protecting injection, and soon became more alert and began to eat a little.

Otokar Praper had taken us to nearby Črneče to buy supplies and later to Dravograd, where I bought a Slovene dictionary. The children were finding plenty to do, riding at the club, ragging with some of the local boys there and canoeing on the Drava. I dug latrines for us in the bushes and Kate tackled a clothes-wash. Rado Krpač, another horse-club member, brought us logs and excellent home-brewed cider and delighted Kate especially when he offered us baths at his house.

Another afternoon Otokar took Torcuil and me to meet seventy-two-year old Anton Konečnik, who owned and bred Slovenski Hlvadnokrvni, Slovenian Coldbloods, light but powerful draught-horses, weighing about 650 kilos. Stocky, intelligent beasts, they are now rare. Beside the stallion's quarters, I noticed a barn door with thirty-two little wooden crosses on it. Traditionally in spring, a bouquet is made from branches of the first-flowering tree, usually willow, and afterwards a small cross is fashioned from the wood and nailed to the door. The custom probably pre-dates Christianity, perhaps having Celtic origins. The stallion was magnificent and there was no need to be an expert on the breed to perceive his quality. The mares, too, looked good, especially in traditional harness.

After four days, Mariana the vet reached the limit of her resources and arranged for Traceur to go to the clinic in Maribor, sixty kilometres east. Rado lent us his Lada Niva jeep, borrowed a horse trailer from someone else and Otokar drove Traceur and me to Maribor at five the next morning to avoid the heat.

The road to Maribor was beautiful, following the Drava all the way. Traceur travelled well on the hour-long journey in cool air. The clinic was small and we had to wait before unloading him while a Caesarian section was performed on a cow. Dr Borut Trapečar, who would be treating Traceur, gave him a thorough going-over and drew a blood sample. His temperature was down. Though installed in a light, airy box he looked thin, sad and wabbit. It was a wrench leaving him and I wondered gloomily if we should ever see him again.

On the way home we visited Maribor horse-club, an impressive place with a trotting track in a lovely setting. Back at the caravan, we collected the rest of the family, drove into Dravograd for a beer at a local café, with ice-cream for the children, then went to Otokar's. He showed us some of his hunting trophies, and he and I embarked on a long conversation about shooting and conservation management in Slovenia. It is strictly organised on an ecological basis, far ahead of most countries.

We settled in for a stay of several weeks. I noted in my diary: 'I must say I like the Slovenians. They are a hardy lot, with a practical approach to life and exceptionally kind and generous.' That opinion was enhanced many times in the days, weeks and months that followed.

Before we had committed ourselves to a route through northern Yugoslavia, I had been aware from press reports that armed disturbances had been taking place, albeit infrequently. Kate and I had discussed it and agreed the risk to us was minimal because none had occurred anywhere near our proposed road along Drava-side to Hungary. Now we learned what it was all about. Tito died leaving no power-structure behind him. Yugoslavia had since been lurching along under a Council of Ministers from the six provinces, with a rotating presidency, dominated by Serbia. Slovenia and Croatia were the most economically advanced provinces and generated most of the country's wealth, which was expended largely in the south, a cause of great frustration. These two provinces had been attempting to loosen the federation sufficiently to allow them greater control over expenditure of the revenue they were contributing but in vain. Underlying Croatia's case were old wounds and scores dating from the Second World War, while added to the brew were strong stirrings of Serb nationalism.

The clashes we had read about had been between Croats and ethnic Serbs in Croatian villages, where both had cohabited peacefully for years. Now, dark elements were trying to reawaken old fears and set people at each other's throats to serve ancient dreams of power. In Slovenia, with its different language, its population almost all ethnic Slovene, its culture in some respects more akin to neighbouring Austria than the rest of Yugoslavia, it was an entirely economic matter. The situation having reached impasse, Slovenia had announced it would separate unilaterally from Yugoslavia, unless compromise was reached. Croatia had followed suit. The Slovenian ultimatum would expire on 25 June . . .

News from Maribor was good. Traceur's temperature was normal. The problem was his liver, but definite diagnosis awaited results of blood-tests.

Even without Traceur to see to we were kept fully occupied. The horse-club held an open day for 150 pre-school children and parents at which we assisted. Club member Boris Kolenbrand invited us to a barbecue at his weekend house in the hills. It was a spectacular ride up and a great feast. Rado, who was a forestry officer, took Torcuil and me to visit some of the farmer–foresters in the hills behind Dravograd. Typically, he and the farmer would select and mark trees to be felled, choosing carefully, allowing young trees room to grow, taking out appropriate numbers of mature ones. This system of management resulted in beautiful uneven-aged forest, a joy to look at, ecologically balanced yet the source of a steady commercial crop. It contrasted starkly with the devastation caused by clear-felling, and demonstrated how land *can* be managed constructively if the will to do so is there. We learned that farm income not generated by timber came mostly from cattle, enough maize and hay being grown to feed them. Some sheep, a pig and hens were usually kept as well.

We were beginning to feel we had lived in Dravograd all our lives. Kate had become friendly with Moica Cehner, a primary-school teacher who spoke English and lived in Črneče. I had been into the alpine forest with Rado on a number of occasions, which always entailed eating some gorgeous home-cured ham, or sausage, or cheese, with salad and home-baked bread, drinking *slivovka*, home-distilled plum brandy, or *mošt*, home-brewed cider, sometimes both. Time of day and place were irrelevant to drinking in Slovenia – I had had *slivovka* for breakfast, a glass of wine in a draper's shop, a dram in a library, beer in a police station – yet it was rare to see anyone drunk. Life for the farmer-foresters in their traditional houses – whether a 300-year-old wooden one or traditionally shaped and brand new – followed an ancient pattern. They worked hard but lived well, on food so deliciously tasty no supermarket shopper would believe it. Our children had been doing plenty of lessons but played hard too, helping with the club horses, riding, walking and kayaking. It was midsummer and very hot and humid. On occasions powerful thunderstorms built in the west, then advanced down the valley from Austria, tongues of forked lightning spurting from clouds dark as octopus ink, sheets of icy rain following. Brief and spectacular, these storms would clear the air for a while, lowering the temperature to more comfortable levels.

Rado, Eilidh and I went to fetch Traceur early on

22 June. He was standing on bare wet concrete munching hay, his neck swollen from many injections, looking thin and unhappy. When he heard us he lifted his head and a light came into his eyes. He was overjoyed to see us, and for all his scraggy appearance, he was better, though we never did discover precisely what had ailed him – only that it was a liver infection.

Traceur had been put on a low-protein diet for three weeks to protect his still-recovering liver. Oats, barley and grass were forbidden. Finding old hay was difficult but some was eventually located. We had a terrible task forking it out of the hot, dusty, stuffy barn it was stored in, behind a load of new hay which had to be moved first. Organising this had been hard on *my* liver, entailing a beer with Rado, a beer with a friend of his in Črneče, a *mošt* and a beer at the hayshed and another beer on return. Slovenia, I thought, would cease to function without Laško Pivo. But Traceur really appreciated the hay when we finally got a big bundle to him that evening.

Our stay had already lasted three weeks and was going to be at least three more. Berta Poberžnik, a teacher from Ravne na Koroškem, invited us to visit her school. I played the bagpipes and Torcuil bravely demonstrated his skill on the Jew's harp in front of the whole school. We visited classrooms and were given lunch. Our impression was of a happy school, run on dated lines with limited funds. Berta brought us home over a mountain road, across superb alpine meadows richly carpeted with flowers.

These patterns became our normal life. There was always talk about the political situation but it did not dominate. Unable to read Slovenian newspapers, we relied heavily on the BBC for information. Yugoslavia was never mentioned. On the night of 24 June, however, the World Service mentioned that the then President of Yugoslavia,

Ante Markovič, a Croatian, had appealed to Slovenia and Croatia not to declare independence. This was surely in vain, we thought, because both provinces were saying too little was being offered too late. Slovenia requested its 4000 national servicemen to come home, saying it would protect them from charges of desertion. There was scare-talk from the President about civil war but one could only hope it was brinkmanship. We knew very well Slovenia was going to declare independence: the federal government's views and position had not altered since Slovenia announced its intention months before.

The imminence of independence was sharply brought home next day. We had been invited to share Ojstrica primary school's end-of-term barbecue. The school lay high above Dravograd on Rado's forestry patch and we had called there several times for coffee with the teachers, hence the current invitation. Now, soldiers from the Slovenian reserve force, dozing or playing football, occupied the school. Nevertheless a sizzling pile of sausages accompanied by tomatoes, onions and bread awaited us. There was *pivo* for the adults and soft drinks for the children. After a tune on the pipes, we roared down to Dravograd in Rado's red Niva, had another beer and I cashed a Eurocheque in case the banks closed precipitately. Radio Slovenj Gradec had interviewed me that morning but I could not interest the BBC in an item about a Scots family in Slovenia on the eve of independence.

I went with Rado to cut grass for horses but first we had a bowl of soup at his house. While we ate a Mig-21 fighter–bomber overflew Dravograd. Then, fortified, we did cut grass and returned to the club to feed the horses. Another Mig flew over, very high. There were a lot of soldiers and *milica* about. They had removed their federal-style hats and donned Slovenian ones instead. On Rado's television we watched Milan Kučan, president of Slovenia, addressing parliament. His speech, implementing the independence laws, to take effect next day, seemed well received. It was a momentous moment for the Slovenes. How it would affect us, we did not know.

Slovenian Independence Day dawned jungle-humid with the temperature soaring towards 32°C/90°F. A thunderstorm and heavy overnight rain had provided an appropriate symbolic baptism for the baby state.

Just after breakfast Rado brought two journalists to see us, one from Radio Slovenija, the other from *Večer*, a Maribor-based newspaper. We were interviewed at length about the trip and I was prevailed on to play my pipes. I hoped desperately there were no competent pipers within miles to hear my tyro performance. When we harnessed Traceur for a photograph, I realised how thin he still was.

Kate and I went with Rado to Črneče, to see a farmer and drink two glasses of *mošt*, then down the Maribor road to a tree nursery. Here we collected a small *lipa*, lime, the national tree of Slovenia, to be planted at the independence ceremonies that night. Kate did some shopping, Rado and I sat at a pavement café and drank *pivo*. The deputy mayor came by. On a whim he presented me with a small brass badge in the shape of a lime-tree leaf which he took from his lapel. 'Samostojna Slovenija', Independent Slovenia, was engraved on it. Posters and slogans were appearing everywhere. An atmosphere of expectancy was building but there was underlying tension, too. Rado told me he had been up all the previous night. There had been a confrontation at the frontier. The federal authorities had sent troops from the south, without informing the local federal CO. Forty *milica* from Dravograd had jailed the southern soldiers.

We delivered the *lipa* tree, then Rado dropped us off at

the horse-club and departed on other business. The children were highly indignant we had been gone so long without telling them. In the afternoon Kate's friend Moica's brother-in-law, Max, drove his tractor and trailer over with the last of the horse-club hay and we helped fork it into the barn. I became almost liquid with the effort in the sticky heat.

About 6 p.m., while we were dressing in our best gear to attend the independence ceremonies, a fast pass by a Mig-21 was a reminder that forces opposed to Slovenia waited in the wings.

Rado, whose kindness and attention was beyond adequate thanks, collected us about seven. We went first to his house and saw on TV that four policemen had been killed in eastern Croatia. This was the old trouble, which had been going on for months. Everywhere else seemed calm. The government in Belgrade claimed federal troops controlled all Slovenia's borders. This was untrue. Control, at the Vič border post at least, was in Slovenian hands.

In the street a crowd was gathering. The new Slovenian flag, a white blue and red horizontal tricolour with a shield in the upper left corner, bearing three gold stars and a symbolic representation of the triple-peaked mountain Triglav, hung bravely from the Občina, the town hall. Traffic had stopped. A hole had been dug for planting the *lipa*; microphones and a small dais were in place in front of the thirteenth-century church in the centre of town. An armoured car bearing federal insignia raced by, heading for the frontier, and shortly after raced back, greeted with a low hiss of dissent. Soon a brass band could be heard. It came up the street, preceded by a red fire patrol car, blue lights flashing brightly in the deepening dusk. Behind the marching brass was a fire engine, its lights also blazing, succeeded by a cavalcade of horses and farm carts. The band marched up and wheeled into place beside the dais, still playing, as dignitaries took their stand on the platform.

Abruptly the music ceased. A carillon rang out from the church tower. To the accompaniment of a ragged but loud series of reports booming out from the hills, a banner in the blue, red and white colours of Slovenia was slowly unfurled from the top of the tower. Finally came the singing of the national anthem. Dravograd, too, was in independent Slovenia. Seven minutes late.

The Mayor planted the lime tree and a priest blessed it with holy water. Lightning flashed far off to the west. A choir sang 'Naša Lipa', 'Our Lime', the song of the lime. Then it was time for 'our Scottish friend' to pipe a welcome to the new republic and squeakily, rather out of tune, I did.

The ceremonies concluded, bars and cafés opened and people went to toast their newly emerged country, as yet barely out of the chrysalis, wings wet, unrecognised by any other state. The long-threatened rainstorm burst, and signs of the developing party were quashed. People still in the street fled for shelter, some to bars or under awnings to sink *pivo* or sip a *žganje*, brandy. Many went home. A massive triple bonfire had been lit on open ground near the fire-station, big enough to defy the rain. National songs and folk-songs played over loudspeakers but the festivities were damp now and subdued, perhaps appropriately with the future so uncertain. Would the federal army attempt to crush the upstart state? Tomorrow was full of uncertainty. Back at the caravan door, under turbulent skies, I uttered a silent 'Good luck' to the new nation. *Srečno Slovenija!*

Tanks surrounded Ljubljana airport. Federal forces had orders to take over all frontier posts. Force would be used if necessary. So said the radio next morning. But Traceur and the club horses had to be fed and the citizens of Dravograd appeared to be going about their normal daily rounds.

Torcuil and I cycled to Vič, the frontier post we had come in at. Both Slovene and federal Yugoslav troops were there but traffic flowed as usual. We went into the café for a cool lemonade before biking back, getting the messages for Kate in Dravograd on the way. Slovene soldiers were grouped by the town hall. The lieutenant hailed us and we wished them good luck, as we headed across the river, back to the caravan. No one came near the club. An unnatural quiet and lack of movement descended on Dravograd.

It was unsatisfactory having to rely on the BBC for news. Their inevitably out-of-date reports were confined to Ljubljana and environs. Frustrated by not knowing what was going on, in the afternoon Torcuil and I took another tour towards town. The situation had deteriorated. A small federal helicopter was buzzing about overhead. In front of *Milica* HQ, at the south end of the bridge, a lot of men were donning flak-jackets and driving away. The railway and road had been blocked against tanks from Maribor and the road to Slovenj Gradec, ten kilometres away, was blocked as well.

Late in the afternoon, Gagi, Miro and Marco, the three lads who were the backbone of the daily duties at the horse-club, came over the river by canoe and began the work of evening stables. All at once the beat of heavy aero-engines was heard. Low through the Mislinja valley from the direction of Slovenj Gradec lumbered two huge helicopters, hefty Russian-built Mil-8s. They were incredibly noisy as they came almost up to us, veered across the river and put down on the football field just out of our sight. The boys gave a yell and rushed for the canoes. Our three raced after them and I tore after *them*, to stop them going too. Then the Mils lifted off and flew slap over us. I shook my fist and roared invective at the pilots. Pointlessly, of course. We learned later they had disgorged fifteen special-forces police from Belgrade, who were promptly captured by the alert Slovenians.

The children and I finished feeding the horses. Cyrilla and Vanč Čeruh, and Rado's daughter Maja arrived. Then Rado rolled in with Boris Kolenbrand. They had spent the day building four massive road-blocks between Dravograd and Muta on the Maribor road.

The situation had become serious.

It must seem strange, reading about this, that we identified so completely with the Slovenians after only a few weeks in their land. This was undoubtedly due in large measure to the enormous support and help we had been given when, as total strangers, and after less than a day, Traceur had fallen ill. But it was more than that. We had genuinely fallen in love with the country, the way of life and the character of the people. I think, too, it had a lot to do with our Scots natures. Coming from a small nation ourselves, frequently chafing at being the junior partner in three hundred years of union with England, it was easy to identify with the Slovenes' desire to run their own country. Above all, these people were our friends, their aspirations just. We would help if we could.

BBC News, 1800 hrs GMT, 27 June: 'British nationals have been advised by the government not to travel to Yugoslavia.'

What a joke. But we were wondering what to do for the best. So far the conflict had been confined to fencing and probing by the federal forces. If it blew up into full-scale war, we should not only be at risk but would probably be a burden to our friends. The only place we could go was back into Austria. However, Traceur, still far from fit, could not yet pull the caravan. Four kilometres might as well be four hundred.

*

It was plain from BBC broadcasts that the British politicians had not the faintest idea how Slovenians felt. Their pronouncements about 'need for moderation', 'rejoining Yugoslavia' and 'solving Yugoslavia's problems by discussion' were not only far too late but totally irrelevant. The situation, both politically and on the ground, had passed beyond all that. I wondered what we had an embassy for if our rulers could not be kept better informed – or perhaps they just did not listen. After a mere month, we knew more than they did.

In the early cool next morning, a barrage of shooting broke out over by the hill east of Dravograd. It sounded as though it came from the area of the barricades, towards the federally occupied barracks on the south side of the river. It was all small-arms fire, some automatic, and went on all day, interspersed with long periods of silence. Once or twice there were heavy explosions, perhaps mortars or dynamite. The barricades held as far as we knew. A goods train had been drawn across the Slovenj Gradec road to block it more effectively.

We looked after the horses as best we could, and did not venture far. Late in the morning, Gagi and co. came over the river to see how we were faring. To our sorrow, they told us Otokar had been badly wounded that morning while in charge of the defence of Holmec frontier post. Men had died in desperate battle there; some reports said as many as thirty-four.

Slovenia, three days old, was fighting for her life.

In the afternoon, I determined to try to go into town to fax an article I had written about the situation to the *Scotsman*. I crossed the Drava with Torcuil, in the canoe we had been left for this purpose, and went to Otokar's house. Paula, his wife, was pale with worry but had no fresh news. I left Torcuil there with the boys. Strung up and tense, not helped by being told a sniper was overlooking the town from the hills, I crept cautiously forward to survey the street from the cover of the church wall. Nothing moved. Then an old man came walking up and I noticed a young woman standing nearby. If it was safe for them, it was safe for me. I set off. The short walk seemed inordinately long. Contrary to rumour, I noticed the little lime tree was in its place by the old church and had not been torn out. Nearer the shops, little knots of people huddled here and there, close to walls or under cover of café awnings. I was stopped by the guard at the Občina but they knew me and let me pass. No one answered my knock at Rado's. As I turned to leave, his mother, who had survived the Nazi concentration camp at Ravensbrück, came out from her house next door. Rado had taken his wife and children up into the hills for greater safety so I asked her to pass on the article for faxing when he returned.

The walk back was less eerie, perhaps because it was less tense – until a young woman came up to me. 'They're coming to bomb Dravograd! They're coming to bomb Dravograd!' she blurted. I asked how she knew. 'It was on the radio,' was her bizarre reply. She seemed frightened and an outburst of distant firing sent her scurrying away to shelter. Further on, the owner of the Ham Ham café had boldly hung a banner outside his premises proclaiming, 'JLA OKUPATOR'.* As I reached the fire-station beyond, opposite the allotments, I heard aircraft . . .

Gazing into the bright sky, I could not at first see anything, then spotted them at about three thousand feet, heading in a wide circle round the hill at the back of

*The JLA, Jugoslavanska Ljudska Armada, or Yugoslav People's Army. The Serbs, and most press and other outside agencies, referred to it as the JNA, Jugoslavanska Narodna Armada, or Yugoslav National Army.

Dravograd to the north. Mig-21s. Two of them. They swept round clockwise – and suddenly the leading one was much lower, skidding round, diving in a tight, banking turn to the right, lining up in the direction of the bridge, making a low pass, very fast, vanishing down the river valley. His number two, remaining at high cover, followed. Half a minute later they came again. This time the leader lined himself up first, then made a fast, diving run. BANG BANG! In a plume of fire and smoke, two rockets left his wings. And the aircraft were gone.

The firemen, rapt as I had been in the air display, suddenly remembering they were supposed to sound air-raid warnings, belatedly cranked up the old hand-powered siren.

I had been beside myself with fury as I watched the attack, literally dancing with rage, shaking my fists and yelling at the aircraft. I was boiling with anger at these people coming here, perhaps to kill or maim our friends. I could see, from my own pilot experience, with Aberdeen University Air Squadron and later as a private pilot, I was not in the target area but was glad all the same that Torcuil had stayed at the Prapers'. Kate, peacefully engaged at the wash-tub, had had the Daz, Tide and Surf scared out of her as the jets came screaming low over the caravan.

I was practising my pipes later, when two more Migs came howling down the Mislinja valley, banked sharply and roared over the town. They made two more runs but did not attack. The Slovenians had no anti-aircraft weapons so the federal air force flew where it liked. Unlike the army, however, the air force had many Slovene officers among its pilots. Its overall loyalty to Belgrade had to be in doubt and its apparent unwillingness to use its massive power fully probably stemmed from this. Črneče was the home village of the commander of the Western Air Force, which may be why Dravograd remained unscathed from the air – though the narrow valleys and uncertain updraughts also made low-flying there particularly hazardous. That one attack on the bridge missed, the rockets falling harmlessly into the river.

In the absence of everyone else, we tried to scythe grass for the horses. The old couple in the flat above the stables, appalled at our ineptitude, helped. Abruptly a huge pall of dense black smoke moiled upwards from beyond Dravograd to the east, soon covering half the sky. It smelt awful. When we retired to bed that night a good deal of shooting was still going on. Internationally, the EEC had brokered a ceasefire, news that had obviously not reached the troops.

By 4.45 next morning the dawn chorus was in full swing. To my astonishment I saw that the mortar battery, which had been encamped well up the hillside opposite us, had gone. At 8 a.m. we were taking breakfast, when Rado and Ivan Čeruh suddenly arrived. There really was a ceasefire.

That 29 June ceasefire did not hold if, indeed, it had ever been universal. In the early hours of the thirtieth, sleepless, I decided we ought to go back to Austria while we could. I sought out Rado and told him. He concurred, and said the frontiers at both Vič and Libeliče were safely in Slovenian hands. We used the back road along the south bank of the Drava, through Libeliče – a crossing normally permitted for Yugoslav and Austrian nationals only – because it was shorter and avoided going through Dravograd. The decision to go was, we knew, right, but I felt like a rat leaving our friends in peril and was almost in tears. Young Borut Praper had seen our movements and paddled over to say goodbye. Max Cehner towed the caravan and Eilidh rode Traceur to the border, from where it was downhill to Lavamünd. As before we stopped at the BP garage and had lunch with the Puchers. The same afternoon we found a rambling old farmhouse out on the Dravograd road, owned by Dieter Winkler, with a few acres where we could stay.

The Austrian army presence at both frontiers was massive, with constant air activity along the border. We saw more troops and aircraft while waiting out the war in Austria than we ever did in Slovenia. The Vič frontier remained open every day except one. That day, Tuesday 2 July, I noted in my diary, 'I cycled past seven tanks to the border. It was closed. Many loud explosions from Dravograd direction and the noise of jets.' Gazing into Slovenia, hearing the fury of battle raging, I prayed for the safety of the people of Dravograd. On other days one or other of us usually cycled over to see friends. On one visit I went by car with Peter Praper to Slovenj Gradec hospital to see Otokar. He had sustained twenty-two wounds in his back from a phosphorus shell. Lying prone trying to shoot a sniper, it had burst above him, igniting the fire that destroyed the Holmec frontier post at the same time. One fragment had exposed a lung but he was recovering well. We were having a good talk – when eeow-eeow-eeow-eeow-eeow! It was the dreadful din of the air-raid siren. Everyone began shoving the beds of those unable to walk along to the lifts. Only one worked. 'Because they're made in Serbia,' laughed a nurse. Fortunately it was a false alarm.

Slovenia's war lasted ten days and cost sixty-nine Slovenian lives. We fretted in Lavamünd, not only anxious about our Dravograd friends but also about the wider implications for our journey. There was no road out for us except through Slovenia, the alternatives being impossibly steep. In a sense Traceur's convalescence helped: it com-pelled us to stay in Lavamünd for two weeks instead of impatiently seeking costly transport to take us over the mountains. Our time there was memorable mainly for Kate's fortieth birthday party, attended by many Prapers, the Winklers and by Sissy and Hannes Frkowitsch, local residents with whom we had become good friends.

'I adored Slovenia and its people,' wrote Kate, 'but my greatest friends of the trip were Sissy and Hannes. Sissy and I clicked immediately, and though my German was non-existent she talked English. She was a treasure, and both she and Hannes incredibly kind. They arrived on my birthday with a present and wine only a few days after we'd met. They often visited us later, usually with food and wine and lots of laughter.'

By 12 July Traceur's convalescence was over. So was the war in Slovenia. Gaily we set off again for the familiar frontier, left Austria and pulled up on the Slovenian side.

And they refused to let us in.

CHAPTER SEVEN

—◦◦◦—

SLOVENIA AGAIN: JULY 1991–AUGUST 1992
SLOVENIA *MOI DRUGI DOM*

I hear a voice you cannot hear
Which says I must not stay,
I see a hand you cannot see
Which beckons me away.
Thomas Tickell

Inspector Žjelko Kljajič slammed down the telephone in fury, wrenched Tito's picture from his office wall in Dravograd's *milica* headquarters and threw it on top of a cupboard. That moment marked the end of the old era for him. I had sought his help, after long and fruitless argument at the border. Now, disgusted by four hours of bureaucratic wrangling, he had finally obtained permission for us to return to Slovenia.

At the horse-club we settled into our familiar routine as though we had never left.

I am not sure when the idea of spending the winter in Slovenia came to me. Traceur was still not fully fit when we returned to the Konjeniški Klub but it was only mid-July and Hungary quite within reach even if we did not start until August. Perhaps it was visiting Raduha with Rado Krpač, high in the mountains above Črna, or our day in the magical karst caves at Postojna, where you travel on a little open train into a vast network of limestone caverns, all carved out by the river Pivka, which is also home to a unique, blind, amphibious fish, *Proteus anguinus*. You then walk back through a labyrinth of stalactites and stalagmites and beautifully lit grottoes to the entrance. Or it could have been seeing the ruined remains of the Holmec border post where Otokar's men had fought so fiercely. Maybe it just grew. Kate was in love with the country, too, but we still prepared for departure. Traceur had been shod, we had begun to say our farewells – had even held a party. Then we were interviewed for *Zdravo!*, Hello!, a very popular TV programme, by presenter Barbara Jerman. We told her how much we enjoyed Slovenia and I made some remark about wishing we could stay for the winter.

The programme was broadcast and, as a result, offers of help to enable us to do so came in. Kate undertook to give English lessons, I was commissioned to draw up a management plan for a proposed local nature reserve – and the children were enrolled for two terms at Osnovna Šola Dravograd, Dravograd primary school. Our wages took the form of a free flat in one of Dravograd's two high-rise apartment blocks, plus a token sum in cash. Many people went out of their way to arrange this for us. We were amazed and grateful. The concept of our journey seemed to have struck a chord with the Slovenians. Our strong support for Slovenian independence, the *Scotsman* having published my feature–article and reports about the war I had sent them possibly helped. Whatever the reason, Slovene–Scottish relations were firmly cemented.

The children settled in remarkably well at school. Eilidh, Fionn and Torcuil fast became proficient Slovene speakers. Kate gave conversation classes at Ravne school for Berta Poberžnik and held a class of her own in Dravograd. As well as working on the Upper Drava River project, I continued to practise my bagpipes, which led to an interesting invitation.

Jože Galič, his wife Cita and four others formed the

traditional music group Ansambel Slovenija. He now approached me and asked if I would go with them to a gig and play in the interval. Nothing loath, if somewhat nervous, I said yes. This led to lots of gigs, was good fun, a great way to see much of Slovenia and I was paid too, which was gilt on gingerbread indeed. I often referred to Slovenia as my second home and Jože wrote a song about that and our journey. We eventually recorded a cassette, entitled *Moj Drugi Dom*, My Second Home, after the title song. It featured a few bars of piping and a comic picture of Jože and me on the cover. Fame at last. It was fun to make and I learned much about the production of recordings at RTV's Studio 14 in Ljubljana. The children, as part of home education, came to see how it was done.

Croatia was attacked before the ink was dry on the Slovenian peace accord. Nightly reports were screened on TV, including scenes of appalling bloody butchery perpetrated by the Četniks, a group of horror merchants revived from the Second World War. A Yorkshireman in the Croatian army was interviewed on television and said landmines and capture alive by Četniks were the only things he and his comrades feared. EEC monitors buzzed about Slovenia in white helicopters, making sure that everyone was behaving according to treaty terms.

The August 1991 Kremlin coup ousted Gorbachev from the Russian presidency; Boris Yeltsin made his courageous speech from a tank turret; and shortly afterwards the plotters were foiled. How this affected the USSR was well publicised but we speculated how it might affect our entry to that country. The parts of the world we were in, or wanted to be in, all seemed to be in ferment.

In September Fionn fell off Traceur and a hoof tipped him on the head as he landed. He became dizzy and sick and was taken to Slovenj Gradec hospital for X-ray as a precaution. They kept him for two days, though there was no fracture. He returned in time to open his seventh birthday presents. Later in the month Kate and I went to Budapest for a weekend, with Miran Švarc, on reconnaissance. In persistent rain, Hungary looked drab and poor, but the roads were mostly flat so would not be hard for Traceur.

In October Slovenia introduced temporary tolar banknotes. Inflation lowered their value fast, though nothing like so fast as the Yugoslav dinar they replaced. We discovered another Scot in Slovenia. Donald Urquhart, an artist, was holding a one-man exhibition in Ljubljana and invited me to pipe for the opening. The children went to a traditional autumn chestnut picnic organised by the school, with roast chestnuts, pancakes, lemonade and musical entertainment. Eilidh turned eleven and after visiting Ravne with Kate, ostensibly to help with the English conversation class, came back with her ears pierced. The Frkowitsch family visited and Kate frequently cycled to Lavamünd to see Sissy, remembering 'days in summer sitting in the garden talking and drinking wine'. And on 25 October we celebrated our first anniversary on the road. Vierhouten seemed worlds away, Scotland another planet.

Winter was disappointingly mild, with little snow and never colder than −15°C/5°F. Torcuil learned to ski on a school trip and later demonstrated his prowess to the rest of the family. He and Eilidh went skating for the first time too, on the frozen Drava lake. Fionn made a magnificent mask for Hallowe'en and we learned about the 'Day of the Dead' on 1 November, when Slovenians visit family graves to lay flowers. Those of the men so recently killed in the war made it especially poignant.

In Croatia war continued and world outrage was expressed when the Serbs shelled historic Dubrovnik, but no global cry of agony rang out for a small town in eastern

Slavonia. Reduced to rubble, it fell on 17 November after heroic defence against the full might of Milošovič's rampaging Serb forces. Its name was Vukovar.

The American Secretary of State James Baker said the USA 'would never recognise Slovenia and Croatia' but in November Germany announced it intended to recognise Slovenia. The House of Commons passed an early-day motion voicing its wish that the British government would do the same. On 12 December the Ukraine *did* recognise Slovenia, the first nation to do so. On 7 January a Serb Mig-21 shot down an unarmed EEC monitor helicopter, killing three Italians and a Frenchman; crocodile tears were shed and an apology made by Milošovič. No country appeared willing to stand up to the bully and every day he grew stronger.

At New Year, Traceur was hitched to a rustic open carriage to pull Dedek Mraz and his acolytes, two brown bears, round Dravograd. This traditional winter figure, Grandfather Cold, fulfills a similar function to that of Father Christmas. No one would have recognised Rado, Gagi and Lampi as we circled the school. Also traditional in Dravograd was a Planinski Izlet, a hill walk on 2 January up to Košenjak summit (1577 metres/4977 feet) on the Austrian border. Eilidh accompanied me – and forty others – through the snow. It was a crisp, clear day and the views from the top were superb. In August Torcuil had tackled the much harder ascent of Skuta (2533 metres/8310 feet), entailing vertiginous scrambling. I had quit ignominiously half-way, singularly unhappy on the narrow paths with precipitous drops.

Regular duties included looking after and exercising Traceur, which Eilidh undertook for the most part, often assisted by Fionn or by her friends, and I worked on the Upper Drava River project. We were frequently entertained or entertaining, usually on a casual drop-in basis. Rok Skrap, Otokar's son-in-law, took us to see the famous stud at Lipica, original home of all Lipizzaner horses. It was wonderful to see them but Rok, who used to ride there, was in despair at the dilapidated state of the magnificent buildings.

I continued to play slots with Ansambel Slovenija and had also been invited on my own account. Once, at a charity show and concert in Slovenj Gradec to raise money for paraplegics, several government ministers had participated in a five-a-side indoor football match. Going to my allotted changing room after my own appearance, I opened the door – and beheld half the Slovenian cabinet naked in the shower. Wrong room.

On 16 March 1992 we prepared to depart. We had held a farewell concert of our own in aid of cerebral-palsy sufferers, had had the caravan fitted, at long last, with efficient disc brakes and toured beautiful Lake Bled with the Galičs. Eilidh's entire class came to see us leave, along with Rado, our neighbours the Štajmec family, the apartment caretaker, the shopkeepers from Mini-market next door and lots more. I lost count. We were given cakes and meat – and booze. There were bottles all over the caravan, so many that we could have stayed put and opened as a *gostilna*. Poor Traceur had to pull it all as we drew out of Dravograd, heading for Maribor and points east.

Until our journey restarted none of us had realised how well known we had become in Slovenia. Not a day went by without an invitation to coffee or a meal, or a gift of cakes or *slivovka*. Traceur was going well on the flat road and I was careful not to overdo the miles to begin with. It was frosty, and we had the fire on at night.

Travelling via Maribor and Gorna Radgona, we reached the village of Beltinci, in Prekmurje, 'land across the Mura', flat and fertile, part of the great Pannonian Plain. It was the hometown of Beltinška Banda, who had performed at our concert in Dravograd. The average age of this unique group of traditional musicians was seventy-five. Miško Baranja, who played the *cimbalom*, a very large form of hammer dulcimer, owned Gostilna Baranja, a restaurant and bar near Murska Sobota. We went there to eat. Miško's niece Smilja, a presenter with Radio Murski Val, arrived, armed with microphone and tape-recorder, and Vlado Kreslin, Slovenia's biggest singing star, whom we knew, was there too. The feast began with a goulash and ended with *palačinka,* pancakes, and coffee. Then we did a long radio interview, during which Smilja had Eilidh interviewing Fionn *in Slovenian*! The hilarious result was duly broadcast and a copy of it is one of my favourite souvenirs.

Prekmurje was gently rolling or flat, altogether different from the mountainous Koroška region. The grapes for Ljutomer Riesling grow there, as does a great deal of maize. To our delight we found white storks nesting in almost every village, sometimes several pairs. Small farms abounded, though large acreages of maize dominated the level country.

In foul weather, cold and wet, reminiscent of northern France, we reached Dobrovnik v Prekmurje. Igor Šetinc, a vet, his wife Irena and daughters Nina and Katja, had met us on the road east of Maribor and invited us to stay. It was to be our last stop before the Hungarian frontier. The border area was an ethnic mix of Hungarians, Slovenes and considerable numbers of gypsies, though we did not meet any of the latter at this time. Road signs were bilingual and some schools too. The Šetinc family looked after us well. Katja and Eilidh became close friends. We swam at nearby Moravske Toplice thermal baths. The caravan was checked and moving parts greased. Harness was oiled.

On 7 April, the USA, *pace* James Baker, belatedly recognised Slovenia, Croatia and Bosnia-Herzegovina as well. Two days later the Conservatives, against all predictions, won the UK general election. Alarmingly, the situation inside Russia looked increasingly volatile. Reports about conditions in the Ukraine were not encouraging either. I began to think we should hold on a while longer in Slovenia, which we liked, where we knew people and a bit of the language, especially as we had been offered use of a house for the summer.

Nevertheless on 14 April we drove through Lendova to the Hungarian border. To our astonishment and joy, a familiar red Niva rolled up and out got Rado, Otokar, Jože Muc and Vili Vravnik. They had come to say a final farewell and to present us with honorary membership of Konjeniški Klub Dravograd. Igor Šetinc went to see the Hungarians, to make sure we had all the right papers. He returned and said he would have to nip back to his office in Lendova and type up a paper for us. 'Don't bother, we're not going,' I said. He thought I was joking and went anyway. I wasn't. I think if we had been able to go straight through the formalities on arrival we should have done so but the wait had reinforced my instinct, which was screaming at me not to go.

Only Torcuil was upset when I turned Traceur about and headed back into Slovenia.

We had had a pleasant, uneventful seven-day journey south from Dobrovnik to the village of Kapele. The former priest's house we were being lent was four hundred years old, huge, bare and lacking in all facilities except a cold tap. This was the proverbial last straw for Kate. Visions of hot baths and a loo vanished in the reality of the enormous house, which had been empty for nine years. The loo was a disaster area, the electricity had been disconnected and there was no hot water. Perversely, I rather liked the place. Local women had cleaned it, there was a good paddock for Traceur, a barn for hay and a stable, which would be fine once cleared of junk. There was plenty of garden and lots of cupboard space. Unlimited scope for initiative and imagination, after a few days' effort. By the following evening the electricity was on, I had planted lettuce, radishes, onion sets, beetroot and carrots, the boys were eagerly anticipating the arrival of pet rabbits. Kate, though, was miserable.

'People often asked about our caravan washing arrangements,' she remembers. ' I always said if the three Fs were clean – face, fanny and feet – the rest didn't matter too much. We washed in a bowl, one after the other, with water heated in a large pan on the stove. Privacy was ensured by hanging a towel to conceal all but head and feet. As for the other, though David pointed out that squatting was the natural way and most of the world did so, we weren't most of the world and what came naturally to *me* was sitting in a private spot, not worrying if someone would appear at an inappropriate moment. I had so looked forward to being in a house. Finding it lacked all the facilities was the absolute last straw . . . Matters had come to a head. I felt undermined much of the time and by July it seemed only fair I should go. Fionn wanted to come with me, his own decision entirely . . .'

This time, the parting looked like being permanent. With heavy hearts, Torcuil, Eilidh and I turned away from watching the car bear Kate and Fionn off to the station. The second half of the summer stretched ahead, almost unbearably long.

The corner of Slovenia around Kapele was rich in wildlife. The flat meadows below the village were carpeted with wild flowers: gentians, ragged robin, forget-me-nots, buttercups, clovers, *phragmites* and many more. Two pairs of buzzards lived in trees close by while in a clump of dense bushes red-backed shrikes nested. There were stonechats, too, and ponds with muskrats and lots of small bright green frogs with brown legs. Clouds of butterflies of at least ten species flittered everywhere like coloured snowflakes, and little lizards scurried about on boulders. The vegetation was profuse and luxuriant in the humid heat, the scene one of peace and rich beauty.

However, the more than usually wrenching parting had soured Kapele for us. Torcuil, Eilidh and I stayed on for a short time but when the opportunity arose of taking a house not far from the Šetinc family, in Mala Polana, we trekked north again.

Emotional disturbances apart, it was a good summer. Torcuil and Eilidh each went for a fortnight, with different Slovenian friends, to the Croatian coast. I had the chance to fulfil an ambition and climb Triglav (2864 metres/9396 feet), Slovenia's highest peak. We all took part in a gymkhana at Velika Polana. Torcuil and I went to a microlight air-show at Lendava and were taken up in a motorised hang-glider. There was never any shortage of things to do or people to visit, especially our lovely next-door neighbours, the Čeh family.

Kate and Fionn came back in mid-August. 'I had spent a miserable five weeks missing the children and unsure of my decision. Letters from David said how much he missed us both, which touched my soft heart,' she wrote.

I had set 20 August as the date for departure, and we set off as planned, spending our last night in Slovenia near the hamlet of Mostje. That evening Eilidh and I cycled to Lendava to spend our remaining tolar and visit Nađa and Muris Bešlagič two Bosnian children from Doboj, sister and brother, aged fifteen and twelve, whom we had met at the

Šetinci. They had become separated from their parents and did not know if they were still alive. With sixty-two others, forty of whom were children, the rest mostly women, they were accommodated at the Lendova refugee centre in a tiny bedroom sleeping nine, four in each of two big double beds. Only Muris, as a boy, had a bed to himself. Nađa and Muris were surprised and delighted to see us and we took them and Nađa's friend Cristina for ice-creams. It didn't seem much to be offering.*

The twenty-first was baking hot. We started early and reached the border at 7.30 a.m. Unlike last time, we did not see any of the appalling double-decker horse-lorries, taking redundant workhorses from Poland to Italy for slaughter. During the four-day journey they were neither fed nor watered and often suffered physical injury. Apart from the morality of it, transporting horses this way within the EEC was illegal, a law Italy plainly flouted. We have been leery of eating salami ever since.

There was no waiting this time. The Slovenians glanced at our passports so quickly that we hardly stopped and the Hungarians were almost as fast. I had to seek out the vet, still in his pyjamas, who stamped Traceur's papers. I then changed money into forint and that was it.

Into Hungary at last.

---

*Their tale ended happily. An uncle in Germany took them in. Their parents had survived and were reunited with them there. Doboj, however, remains in Serbian hands.

CHAPTER EIGHT

～๛～

HUNGARY: AUGUST 1992–MARCH 1993
GOULASH AND BULL'S BLOOD

The spirit of liberty is the spirit that is not too sure that it is right.

Judge Learned Hand

Hungary was dilapidated. This was apparent even before we reached Rédics, four miles from the border. It was barely more than a village, plaster was peeling off house walls, the streets were bumpy and grass-grown, and its people looked poor.

I took a pleasant wooded side road but it deteriorated fast, culminating in a sandy track rising steeply up a ridge. Locals had tried to tell us this, but we had not understood. We had to backtrack – which I hated doing but in this case it had dual benefits: we avoided the hill and found an excellent stopping spot in young forest, close to a fire dam. It was scorching, we were dripping like oven-roasted chickens by the time everything was set up and a plunge into the dam's cool water was complete bliss.

The Hungarian border with Ukraine lies in the north-east. Our intention was to cross it as early as possible in 1993, after wintering somewhere close by. Kate and I had travelled on both sides of Lake Balaton on our earlier recce with Miran Švarc. Its attractive shores were infested with hotels, boarding-houses and tourist facilities. The roads would be filled with summer traffic now and stopping-places few. We had time to spare and headed in a wide, southerly arc. Later we should curl north, cross the Danube and make for the frontier.

Vast acres of stubble, grass, plough and maize stretched as far as the horizon in huge, unfenced fields, interspersed with large deciduous woods and vineyards. The scale of arable farming here dwarfed anything in Western Europe. Once we stopped for water at a colossal state farm, which covered 22,000 hectares (53,000 acres) and employed three thousand people. The most striking feature of the country-side was the absence of houses. Rural Hungarians lived in walled villages like fortresses, their houses also had high walls around them, iron gates and sometimes a fierce dog too. It is perhaps not surprising that Hungary and its citizens developed a siege mentality: the country has been so frequently fought over throughout history,

Traceur went lame our second day in Hungary. I was certain this was caused by bad shoeing, done shortly before we left Mala Polana. In the small town of Letenye, the first thing we encountered was a fine pair of bays hauling a heavily built cart in the opposite direction. There would surely be a smith here.

A long, heavy afternoon loomed at Tibor the black-smith's. It was extremely hot and humid and Traceur liked to lean on whoever was holding his feet. But Tibor's nephew took over and, for once, I only watched. Meanwhile his wife served us wine, fruit, cheese scones very like Scottish ones and coffee. The shoes came off, were repaired, restudded and replaced. In poor countries maximum use is made of everything. In Western Europe, these shoes, though still having plenty of wear left, would have been discarded.

The people in this very different land were friendly

although we understood nothing of their chirrupy language. Food was plentiful but they were materially poor. Most days someone would give us a bag of peppers or tomatoes and usually maize or hay for Traceur. We were short of space and keeping weight to a minimum was a constant battle, so we carried very little we could give in exchange, except postcards depicting us on the road and, for a few special people, expedition T-shirts; both were always well received. We travelled parallel to the river Mura, the border with Croatia, where many villages were bilingually signed. The road was potholed and bumpy but traffic light: East German Trabants, Wartburgs and IFA trucks were reminders of how recently Hungary had been a Soviet satellite and part of the eastern bloc. Old people appeared to have little, other than a small house, a bike and a vegetable plot. Litter was everywhere, including unsightly dumps in woods and odd corners. On a hot day nothing was more refreshing than a juicy watermelon bought at a roadside stall.

It was steamingly hot. We travelled early, which helped Traceur, and often found places to swim where we stopped. One of the best was a lake near Háromfa, which had a controlled outflow, the building for which provided a fine diving platform. Its cool water was balm to our hot, sticky bodies. That evening, a family of gypsies from the village brought a guitar and accordion and we had music and song till twilight.

At Drávafok, Jenő Gál stopped and invited us to his farm. It was a small dairy with twelve milkers, calves, two pigs, hens and an orphan lamb. And Jenő's pride and joy, Babi, a good-looking pedigree roan Belgian mare. The vegetable garden was full of peppers, cabbages and lashings of plums, the yard was gravelled with broken roofing tiles and water was drawn from a traditional sweep well.

Traceur, stabled next to Babi, was given mountains of maize flour mixed with oats, and plenty of lucerne. Mrs Gál fed us mountains of food too, starting with stuffed cabbage leaves containing a peppery mixture of meat and rice, followed by deep-fried veal and chicken pieces. It was tasty fare, accompanied by several glasses of wine.

In the afternoon we rode on a cart behind Babi to a field at the far side of Drávafok to cut and bring back a load of maize for the cattle. The maize stalks and attached cobs were put through a chopper before being fed to them. Three electric-powered portable machines were used for milking. Afterwards Jenő took the milk to a central reception point, where the amount was recorded, the milk checked for quality, then poured into a big holding tank, along with the production from other small farms, to await collection. I hoped this excellent system of small farming could survive the Common Agricultural Policy, if Hungary eventually joined the European Union.

Despite our protests the Gáls insisted we sleep in the house. I never liked being in a house, preferring my cosy caravan bed, but refusal would have given offence. I put my foot down next morning, though, when offered a large pre-breakfast glass of plum brandy. We gave what thanks the almost total language barrier allowed, and then, loaded with bags of oats and maize flour, tomatoes and paprika, we left.

At Harkány we had to park near the town dump, where legions of brown rats thrived on raw sewage. In the bustling town of Siklós we went shopping and visited the castle, dating from 1294 but modified hideously in the eighteenth century. Torcuil spent an afternoon lying down feeling unwell, Kate and Traceur were weary. After weeks of hot, hard travel we needed a day off.

The hill of Sársomlói stood conspicuous in the flat land

near Villány. We halted close by at a vineyard. Opposite, in a large old quarry was the Villány International Sculpture Park. Englishman Colin Foster had been involved in its creation and the exhibits included items by Mary Kenny. The tactile nature of some exhibits was irresistible and clearly not only to us: 'feely bits' were highly polished from the touch of many hands.

Fionn and I climbed Sársomlói. The views were superb: east to Mohács, north to Pécs and west and south over vast acres of ploughed land to our old friend the Drava. Deep blue Croatian hills lay faint on the horizon. Fionn, who would be eight next day, was saluted by eight buzzards, wheeling and soaring in the updraughts. A female sparrow-hawk joined them briefly, then peeled off and dropped like a stone into the dwarf oak and ash wood that covered the hillside. Red admiral and swallowtail butterflies fluttered in profusion, and countless small lizards scurried about the rocks. I saw a snake and Fionn found a complete sloughed skin.

Our descent to the caravan was rapid and we supped on grapes, paprika-flavoured sausage and sour cream. Delicious.

We reached the Danube close to the city of Mohács. Five kilometres south lay the site of the battle of Mohács in 1526. Here the Turks, under Suleiman I 'The Magnificent', had routed the forces of Louis II of Hungary, leading to 150 years of Turkish occupation of eastern Hungary, while Austria grabbed the west. In 1979, the 450th anniversary of the battle had been marked by the creation of a memorial park, the Mohácsi Történelmi Emlékhely. We arrived on a Monday – and it was shut. Fortunately the children discovered a huge gap in the chain-link fence, so we wandered at leisure among the remarkable wooden carvings representing the opposing forces of men and horses.

That evening we parked at the back of an extensive

maizefield close to the Danube. Badly polluted, dammed and abused though it is, in the gloaming, with small fish jumping, sandpipers piping, ducks drifting on the current and a large bat flitting overhead, the river retained all its fabled romance.

Next morning TRACEUR HAD DISAPPEARED.

There was no sign of him, bar the flattened electric fence and some tracks in and out of the maize. Binoculars showed nothing in any direction. A man on a moped said that he was not on the road we had come in by. Another man in a car, going fishing, said in broken German, 'Go to the police. There are a lot of gypsies here.' I disliked his implication, though I had begun to fear Traceur might have been stolen. The *rendőrség* station in Mohács was not hard to find. I produced photographs of Traceur. 'Moment,' said the man at the desk. Another policeman appeared, made signs that I should follow and led me to a patrol car. I assumed we were going to the caravan, then realised that the police did not know where it was. After a short drive we pulled up outside No. 23/B Hungyadi tér. 'Kiss, Péter; Fakitermelő' read a sign on the wall. Inside, in a bit of garden at the back, tied by strong string to a rose bush, stood Traceur. All we ever learned about how he came to be there was that he had been discovered at about 5 a.m. By whom and where and how he came to be at Kiss, Péter's (if indeed it was he) remains for ever a mystery.

It was still only 9.30 a.m. when we put our runaway to and headed for Mohács. It was a pretty town with a lovely square, a beautiful modern votive church built to reflect the shape of a mosque, some fine statues and a Peruvian Indian band busking in the street. The Danube had to be crossed by ferry. The slope down to it was very steep but we had good brakes now and descended safely. Traceur walked on to the boat with nonchalance. The crossing was short, the east bank sloped gently and we had no trouble in getting up it.

The Great Plains now stretched before us, vast and flat, almost entirely given up to arable farming.

We had an introduction to Lajos and Éva Szerdahelyi, owners of Maxima Mink Farm at Vaskút. The caravan and Traceur shared space with seven thousand-odd mink, several hundred polecats and dozens of silver, blue, red and shadow foxes. Here, we learned how Hungarians love to eat. At a name-day feast for one of the Maxima workers, we were served soup, huge bowls of chicken goulash with a side salad, macaroni, dumplings and vats of beer, brandy and wine. It was very good – but we demurred when offered chicken's feet and cockscombs. Next day the Szerdahelyis gave a feast for us. A large red rooster, living free in the woods, was required for goulash and six of us sallied forth to trap the flying fowl. Actually, he couldn't fly but had Olympic ambitions as a sprinter. After half an hour a heroic flying tackle brought down the unfortunate bird. Comb, gonads, gizzard, heart, lungs, kidneys, liver and feet, all went into the pot. Hungarians waste nothing remotely edible. A bigger pot bubbled for *bogrács*, a mutton stew. Our education in Magyar cuisine was completed on Sunday when we ate pikeperch with pepper and cabbage salad, followed by four varieties of strudel, washed down with gallons of gorgeous wine.

Travelling through Baja on Monday, suffering from what can only be described as gross bloat, we admired Deri, the central square, surrounded by magnificent 150-year-old buildings. In the Russian cemetery, many tombstones had been desecrated in 1956, during Hungary's bid to loosen its Soviet ties. Symbolic of Hungary's recent return to democracy, many street names were new, the old Communist ones crossed out neatly in appropriate red. Most interesting to us was the statue to Andris Jelky, 1738–83. This man, a tailor, had walked around the world and visited, among other places, Madagascar, Algeria, Holland, Germany, India and the USA. An astonishing feat for his time.

Just before Nemesnádudvar a street stall was selling jeans. They were labelled with well-known brand-names but although the suspiciously poor-quality jeans were new, the labels were plainly not . . .

Nemesnádudvar, a village comprised of wine-cellars, is unique. The cellar we visited was double, a concealed rear section having been added as a bolt-hole during the Second World War. It was over two hundred years old, with written records from 1797. The grape harvest was in full swing and roads were busy with tractors and carts.

The area around Bugac is known for its extensive grass-land, the famous *puszta,* much of which has been conserved within the Kiskunsági National Park. Our contact there was Imre Abonyi, a former world champion carriage-driver. We stayed at Garzó Tanya, a small riding school, owned and run by György 'Georgie' Garzó. It was the perfect place for us: Georgie's ex-husband was British, she and her thirteen-year-old son Orvil both spoke fluent English and we were made most welcome.

Traceur needed shoeing again but his feet were so hard from travelling on tarmac that farrier Tarjányi said they must be softened before he could tackle them. A mixture of sloppy cow-dung and chopped straw was plastered on to and into the soles of his feet twice daily for three days – a treatment frequently used in the sandy Bugac area. While the cow-pats were doing their best, we went to see the highly skilled display of horsemanship demonstrated by the *puszta* riders. Their horses were trained to sit and lie down on command but the most spectacular feat was five horses galloping, driven by one man standing with a foot on the back of each of the two rearmost ones.

Georgie took us to the splendid virgin juniper forest in the national park where we also saw unique old domestic breeds, Magyar Szürke cattle, Backa sheep and the extraordinary curly-haired Mangalica pigs. The finale was taking part in Szüreti Felvonulás, the Bugac wine festival, parading up and down the streets of the town in carts, finishing with a feast and dance in the evening. Eilidh and Traceur were decked out in finery and acted as outriders, along with the wild display riders cracking their long stockwhips.

Before we left, Klára Pólik, a relation of Imre Abonyi, offered to find us winter accommodation in Mezőkövesd, where she lived. It was about a week's drive from the Ukraine and two hours by train from Budapest, where we should have to go for visas. It was a wonderful offer, accepted with alacrity.

Overnight parking anywhere near the ugly industrial town of Szolnok was impossible. In desperation, I asked two men at a smallholding if they would allow us to stay a night. I did not take to them and one looked like a heavy drinker, but they said yes and told us to help ourselves to hay. The boys went fishing while Eilidh and I spent hours untwisting the electrified tape for Traceur's fence. It was dark when we finished. Arriving back at the caravan we were met by one of our 'hosts', roarin' fu' and cursing us for filthy *cigan*, gypsies. He had pestered Kate for whisky and now ordered us off, pulling up the electric-fence poles, hurling them at us and raising his fists. Threatened with the sharp-pointed end of a pole he backed off, but all we could do was leave. Fast. We travelled a potentially hazardous mile, ill-lit by our two paraffin lamps, to a grassy corner, the only time we ever moved after dark.

In big fields adjoining the road grew more sunflowers than Van Gogh could have painted in a lifetime. One day out of the blue came a white BMW, hooting at us. 'It's Giovanni!' yelled Eilidh. 'Giovanni and Anna!' The Masseras were in Hungary on business and had tracked us down. What a wonderful surprise!

We made a detour of several days to see Hortobagy National Park, world famous for its bird-life and were hugely disappointed. The time of year was wrong and to see the many lagoons and ponds properly would have required days wandering afoot. We saw quite a lot of duck and a beautiful lesser grey shrike, hawking for insects, near Ohat, and the trumpeting song of cranes became a feature of daily life as they began their migration.

After much meandering, several ferry crossings of the river Tisza, and a backtrack through Tiszafüred because one ferry was high and dry for repairs, we reached Mezőkövesd on 12 October. Klara had found us a house and, not far from it, a stable for Traceur. That night we had the first frost of winter. Our arrival was timely.

Winter stops formed a significant aspect of our journey. They allowed our horse and ourselves time to recharge our batteries for the next stage and gave us the chance to know people and places in greater depth than was possible while we were on the move.

Mezőkövesd was an old, not very large town. It was bypassed, so traffic was light. Mátyás Király út, the main street, had a church, a central plaza and a few big shops. Residential streets meandered pleasantly but their surfaces were bad, seldom tarred and often just mud after it had rained. A junction near our house was christened the Swamp, so atrocious did it become. Houses were plaster-rendered with red-tiled roofs; a few were thatched. About a fifth of the inhabitants were gypsies. The Magyars, the Hungarians, seemed genuinely afraid of them. 'Don't go there, that's where the gypsies live,' they told us. 'You'll be stabbed.' Nonsense, of course, and we always found them friendly and polite. Kate later took some surplus clothes to one family, who were surprised and overjoyed. These people have a hard time, are at the bottom of the employment stakes and subject to long-standing racial prejudice. Kate remembers it well: 'We had been given boxes of clothes, far more than we could use. Eilidh, Fionn and I took most of them to the gypsy family that lived round the corner. Not speaking Magyar, I proffered the box to the lady of the house. She comprehended at once and ushered us into her small but neat and clean house, insisting I stay for coffee and a brandy. We sat and looked at each other, understanding each other's frustration with no common language but she understood my clumsy gesticulations. After coffee we took out the clothes, laughing at some, they were so obviously unsuitable. We often saw the family afterwards and the children always called hello. They were just people, trying to live in hard times.'

We had rented János útca 11 from Mátyás Hajdú. It was a substantial bungalow with garden in a quiet tree-lined road, split into two halves, for summer letting usually. It was adequately furnished and our rent included a weekly change of bed-linen. We rented a stable nearby for Traceur from burly József 'Csöpi' Nyeste and his cheery wife Manci. Klára Pólik was manageress of the Mezőkövesd bureau of Borsod Turist, the Hungarian state tourist agency. Not content with having procured us a most acceptable house and stable, she used her good offices to cajole free passes for us to the two local swimming pools and some for the local bus service too.

Although the house was fine, we arrived earlier and with

less warning than expected, giving the Hajdús no time to prepare, so at first Kate was disappointed. 'I had been looking forward to being settled again and was horrified to find that the house was dirty and cold, though at least there was plenty of room for us all. The kitchen area was something else. All I could see was a sink, cupboards and a table. I wondered where the cooker was, then opened a door and found a tiny separate room. There, in isolated splendour, was the cooker. The cook was to be banished, it seemed.' Once the airlocked heating system had been coaxed to work and hot water became abundant, life took on a warmer hue.

Hungary could not be regarded as expensive but I had become alarmed at the plunging pound and tumbling UK bank rate. When we left Britain, it was at 15 per cent, now it was 6 per cent and slipping. The pound, never officially devalued, crashed by about 18 per cent when Chancellor Norman Lamont pulled the country out of the European monetary 'snake'. I had intended to use only interest from the invested sale-price of our house to finance our journey, plus whatever we might earn on the way, but now we should have to dig into capital.

Mária Kovaćs, English teacher at St Istvan primary school, was a fluent Russian speaker and we arranged to have a weekly family lesson with her. If nothing else, we needed to know Cyrillic to read road signs. She told us a US Peace Corps girl was teaching at her school and it was not long before we met Amy Thomas, who lived in a tiny flat not far from us. She may go down in history as the person who introduced the festival of Hallowe'en to Hungary. She certainly introduced it to St Istvan school and we attended, suitably attired. Eilidh was the most bewitching witch imaginable, Torcuil wore a mask, Kate painted feline whiskers on her face and would have graced the cast of *Cats*, while Fionn, after endless hours and many rolls of aluminium foil, metamorphosed into a dashing Roman legionnaire. I was in plain dress, wielding a camera.

The Peace Corps had a widespread presence in Hungary, and at the end of November we were invited to join several other Americans for that quintessential American feast, Thanksgiving, in the large, industrial city of Miskolc. As always with Americans, the hospitality was wonderful, with a selection of tasty foods such as we had not seen for many months.

It had been a lovely evening. However, Kate and I were both struck by how insular and lacking in zest many of these kind folk were. Bearing in mind the role of the USA in the world today and that all of them were well travelled, we found that depressing and alarming.

I had made my first trip to Budapest four days after we stopped. It was essential to begin the business of obtaining visas for the Ukraine and Russia as soon as possible in case of protracted difficulties. We also wanted to transfer the children from our passports to ones of their own. It was a fifteen-minute walk to the station, where I caught the 7 a.m. train for the two-hour ride to the capital. It was on time, the coaches Spartan but adequately clean and moderately full. On arrival, I followed my nose to the underground railway and emerged at Deák tér, where a short walk led me to the Union Flag and massed Range Rovers of the British Embassy.

The unreal world intruded: I was metal-detected and bag-searched by a security guard on the way in. The children's passports could not be issued that day, nor would the embassy post them out, not trusting the mail service. No matter, we should be in Budapest again. I resisted the temptation to pinch the sole copy of *New Scientist* from the waiting room and tramped off to the Ukrainian Embassy, a two-kilometre walk away on the other side of the Danube.

I crossed by the splendid lion-guarded Chain Bridge, designed by Scotsman Adam Clark and, ignoring the 'Tunnel Polluted, Pedestrians Not Advised' sign at the far side, kept on till I reached Nagrad út 8. There was no mistaking the big crisp blue and yellow flag flying outside the newly painted white walls. The door was invitingly open. No security barrier here. No information either. I walked upstairs and found myself in a short queue of ten or so. They all appeared to be Ukrainians, mostly men, dressed drably in grey or black. After ten minutes, nothing had happened. When a girl emerged from a back room I waylaid her. By good fortune she spoke English and told me visas could be obtained on the spot. All that was required was a photograph, twelve dollars and a filled form. Easy!

My next call was at the Russian embassy. It was shut. Mondays, Wednesdays and Fridays, 1000 to 1300 only . . . Footsore, I limped back to the station in heavy rain, caught a packed train and had to stand, next to a happy gypsy family and three chain-smoking national servicemen, all the way to Mezőkövesd. To my surprise and delight Torcuil and Eilidh had braved the unpleasant drizzle to meet me.

A cinema in town often showed English-language films with Hungarian subtitles but mostly entertainment was home-made. Bravely fought board-game battles raged within the walls of János út 11, at which Fionn trounced his father at 'Cats and Dogs', Torcuil became expert at 'Vulgar Bulgars' and Eilidh frequently defeated Kate at 'Nine Men's Morris'. We rarely watched the ancient black-and-white TV.

Every Thursday there was a huge open-air market in town. The produce and hardware stalls in the centre were mainly Hungarian. Encircling them were stalls manned by an ethnic mix of East Europeans. Ukrainians predominated, but there were Russians, Poles, Lithuanians, Romanians and the odd Latvian too. Much of what they sold was poor-quality stuff but one could find almost anything, from Russian model-aeroplane kits to Ukrainian toffee, felt boots to Lada car parts, clothes, shoes, electrical goods, fruit and vegetables, hot meat snacks, pirate cassettes and videos. I enjoyed walking around soaking up the atmosphere, the chatter in many tongues, the smell of cooking, the differences in dress. The Ukrainians were friendly and sure we should be made welcome in their country, despite the prevailing poverty.

We did not have to travel to find poverty, though: it was on our doorstep. It was not unusual to see elderly people, usually women, raking in dustbins and refuse skips. They might claim to be seeking scraps for their hens but in reality they wanted bones to make soup for themselves. Zsuzsana Nyéki and her father were a bleak example of the thin line between existence and starvation. Kate met Zsuzsana in town one day and we were invited to visit. She was seventy, a retired teacher. She had had a fiancée in America but he had died and she had returned to look after her father, now ninety-two. They lived in a minuscule traditional house, in one room for warmth. Their water pump was frozen and the nearest standpipe did not work. Zsuzsana used precious forint to pay a boy to carry a bucket from quarter of a mile away because she had not strength to do it herself. Meat was seldom on the table. Nevertheless, there was a bottle of wine to welcome us and Zsuzsana chattered away in an amazing but fluent mixture of English and German. Father was a little deaf and asthmatic and spoke only Magyar, but he could still sing well.

Klara told me the state pension was 7500 forint per month (about sixty pounds). As manageress of the Borsod office she earned seventy-five pounds a month while her dentist husband István made two hundred. With prices approaching those of Western Europe such amounts did not go far. The insistence by the International Monetary Fund that former Communist countries transform themselves overnight into free-market capitalist economies as the price for obtaining loans did, and continues to do, untold damage to ordinary people. The pronouncements of faceless, grey-suited bankers and bureaucrats in distant offices have reduced many to penury. The cruellest and most destructive element has been the time-scale. This more than anything has precipitated the descent into hardship and poverty. Only sharp operators and Mafiosi have thrived.

Boldog új évet! Happy New Year!

Nineteen ninety-three started with Eilidh being arrested. Two policemen knocked on our door. 'Passports!' They selected Eilidh's and mine and made it clear that I should accompany them. 'Accident?' I must have looked worried, for they grinned reassuringly and shook their heads. When we turned on to the Szentistván road out of town, I clicked. The airfield. The enormous grassy sward of what had recently been the largest Russian military aerodrome in Eastern Europe was unused and a tempting prospect for a gallop. Only a token detachment of soldiers was billeted there but apparently it was *not* open to small foreign girls to gallop heavy horses on. Once it was established she was not a vedette from some new Mongol horde, Eilidh was released without more ado. Everyone thought it a huge joke – except, perhaps, the Commandant and the prisoner.

We made many excursions, including to the historic town of Eger. In the eleventh century it had become a bishop's see. In 1241 invading Mongols annihilated town and people. By 1553 it was strong enough to inflict the first defeat on the Turks, but in 1568 they took the castle and occupied it for the next 101 years. Their mosque was demolished in 1840, though the minaret still stands. Today it is a thriving town, with a university, its nineteenth-century cathedral and its famous heavy red wine Bull's Blood of Eger. We sampled many local wines and found them excellent.

István Galambos, who was our farrier and was also fitting rear springs to the caravan, took us on two outings. The first was to Parád, in hill country beyond Eger, where there is a marvellous coaching museum housed in a magnificent nineteenth-century building. The second was to Szilvásvárad, to Bükki Ménes, the Hungarian Lippizaner stud. The buildings were in good condition and there were more horses than at Lipica, but the Hungarians had let Roman noses creep into their breeding and in my view the Slovenian horses were better-looking. Mezőkövesd had an excellent agricultural museum – and the many long-eared owls living in the pines there were a big attraction for Torcuil and me.

The time for departure approached. After a fruitless day, I recorded, 'I am thoroughly depressed, really down. If ever we were to give up it crossed my mind it could be now. Nothing is going right, the horse, the weather, bureaucracy, all ganging up on us, not to mention the plummeting pound and nagging doubts and fears about what to expect in the Ukraine and points east . . .' We had all had bouts of flu and heavy colds. Traceur had a swelling on his left knee. It was cold: fresh snow had fallen and the procurement of visas for Russia seemed as far off as ever.

Gradually, though, things came together and by mid-March we were ready. István Pólik had examined and treated our teeth. Traceur had been vetted and a fresh Coggins test carried out. Galambos had fitted Russian UAZ jeep springs to the caravan. My sister had sent out a new New Zealand rug for Traceur. We had Ukrainian visas. Our list of helpers was longer than ever, especially the incredibly kind Póliks, and thanking them enough was impossible, though we tried our inadequate best.

I thought it essential to have a guard-dog where we were going and we had bought a Hungarian Komondor. They were bred to guard cattle on the *puszta* and, with their incredible thick white curly coats – dreadlocks any Rasta would envy – could live outside. Kate had selected the four-month-old puppy. We called him by his most apt pedigree name: Tsar. 'He looked like a sheep, with a big cuddly teddy-bear head and, like me, wasn't cut out for expeditioneering,' recalls Kate. 'He had no road sense and took off if allowed to run loose, so he had to be tied on behind most of the time. Eilidh, Fionn and I had a particular affection for the Woolly Maggot – the nickname derived from an infested cut he once had – and we had some laughs with him. David maintained he had wool for brains as well.'

Five skeins of northbound geese flew over Mezőkövesd on 10 March. Next day we continued our own migration. It took two weeks to reach the border because I was not prepared to chance Traceur's knee flaring up again by pushing miles at the start. Tsar, still young, could not be overtaxed and had to learn our road routine.

On our last night in Hungary I lay in my sleeping-bag reflecting on what we had seen. Much of the country was flat, dirty and scenically dull, though Parád and Szilvásvárad had given glimpses of the beautiful hilly parts, Mohacs and Bugac were lovely and Budapest endlessly fascinating. The environmental degradation, infrastructure problems and inherited difficulties of collective agriculture formed a depressing picture. 'Though many were wonderful to us, I felt the Hungarians were a sad people,' Kate felt, and I agreed. Recent history alone would account for that. I recalled reading harrowing accounts in the newspapers of the 1956 uprising: Russian tanks rolling in, the heroism of the people as they fought for their freedom street by street, that bright beacon Imre Nagy, so swiftly and inevitably extinguished.

We had enjoyed Hungary, but I looked forward with eager anticipation to our next country, our first in the ex-USSR. The Ukraine.

CHAPTER NINE

~∽∽∽~

THE UKRAINE: MARCH–JUNE 1993
'TO A HUNGRY MAN THERE IS NO BAD BREAD'

He who travels much, doubts many things.
                                        African saying

It took an hour and a half to clear Hungarian passport control and Customs at Záhony. Our passports were stamped in no time but Traceur and Tsar required exit examinations by the local vet. Záhony was the only place we encountered this.

The bridge over the river Tisza was old, narrow, single-lane and busy. Most of the traffic consisted of westbound trucks. We rolled gently across to the Ukrainian side and were stopped by two young soldiers. Nonplussed by our appearance but friendly, they telephoned for instructions. An electrified barbed-wire fence, red with rust, stretched along the bank, with a thirty-yard cleared space between it and a second parallel fence.

We were waved on and joined a queue of cars, only to be directed to the lorry park. None of the officials could believe what they were seeing and all the staff came out to look. Most were soldiers. An officer with a wide grin on his face took our passports. A young lad had a look inside the van, prodded the beds, glanced around but did no real searching. A stout civilian came and took the animal papers. After a short time I was summoned to his office. He stamped every piece of paper there was, including the outdated French, Italian and Austrian documents, for which service he politely charged eight dollars. The cheerful officer came in. Could they have a souvenir?

'What?' I asked.

'*Cassetta?*'

This gave me an idea and I fetched each of them a *Moj Drugi Dom* tape. Instant success – but when they saw the bagpipes on the cover photo, they insisted I demonstrate the real thing.

A lass from the visa section took me over to currency exchange. Her English was flawless and she told me the dollar rate was 2000 *coupon* for a dollar. I had been going to cash fifty but decided that ten would be plenty – at that, I was cashing almost the equivalent of her month's salary. In February she had received sixteen thousand coupons, this month twenty-nine thousand – and was considered well paid.

It was after 1 p.m. when we moved off, past an endless line of articulated lorries, to Čop. At the poor end of town, mainly gypsy, you could almost reach out and feel the poverty of the ragged people in their tumbledown houses. The road became cobbled and very rough. Lenin still stood in the town centre, while all he believed in crumbled about him. People here were open, waved and talked, an instant contrast with Hungary. 'Slavic people generally were vivacious, kind, flamboyant at times, easy to like, interesting and interested,' observed Kate acutely. Through the centre and on to unmade road, with lidless manholes, terrifying yawning chasms. I missed the first one by luck. Traceur would have smashed a leg had he gone in. We made it on to potholed tar to find we had taken a back road needlessly – and the road out of Čop was fine.

A rubicund peasant lady let us take water from her well. A small boy with a sweet face, clutching an 8-inch diameter ninja death-star, drew it for us. The distant snow-capped Carpathians rose forbiddingly across our path from the plain. The landscape was flat and grassy with villages scattered over it. A keen wind blew through to our bones. Traffic was light. A Mig-29 performed aerobatics in the distant sky, and a small helicopter flitted about. People in passing cars and lorries waved. But where were we to stop? Deep ditches alongside the road prevented us pulling off. Just before Kisdobron we found an adequate place. Its Hungarian name reflected the fact that 200,000 ethnic Hungarians live in the Ukraine, the area we were in once having been part of Austro-Hungary.

Local schoolteacher Paul Balog interrupted our chat with a small crowd of courteous but curious bystanders. In excellent English, he invited us to his home to meet his family. The house, which he had built, was lovely, finished in wood, with tiled bathroom and kitchen, nice carpets and some attractive oils painted by a cousin. We stayed till past midnight. Paul's salary was the equivalent of eight dollars a month. His wife, Miraslava, on maternity leave, got four dollars, which was why Paul, like many others, crossed to Hungary every weekend to trade in the markets, boosting his income by a hundred dollars a month. Using the cheapest vacuum cleaner as an example – 4800 coupons two months ago, currently 55,000 – he said that hyper-inflation would now make building a house impossible.

Before we left next morning, Paul advised us to stay close to villages at night, as lawlessness was on the increase. The Balogs brought us firewood, eggs and paraffin, a lovely small embroidery Mira had made, a map of the Carpathians and photographs of them all. They said we would find nothing in the shops.

I was beginning to get the feel of this immense country. We saw a number of horses, smallish but in good condition, except one, which had bad feet. They were mostly hitched in pairs, using breast-harness, to heavily engineered wooden carts of which there appeared to be two or three per village. A brooding dark wall of hills fronted the still-distant 6000-foot Carpathians. Everything else was flat as a table, with tree plantations the size of mini-forests. Villages had a Hungarian aspect but were neater and tidier. The same was not true of the many lorries, some in the last stages of dilapidation. Motorcycles built like tanks with hefty side-cars were common. A distant goods train pulled sixty-four trucks. Then a prosperous-looking young gypsy in a Mazda waved us down. He greatly admired Traceur and wanted to swap his car for him on the spot!

Again we had trouble finding a pull-off but in Veliki Lučki we were directed to what looked like a disused works. As we turned in, hordes of women appeared from long sheds. It was a potato-grading station and at one time had been a much bigger centre of agricultural operations. Some horses occupied an old barn, there was a huge polythene-covered greenhouse and a selection of ramshackle sheds, grass for Traceur and hard-standing for the caravan.

We had not long been stopped when maize was brought for Traceur, then potatoes and milk for us. Someone brought hay. Three men and an oldish woman, dressed in clothes no self-respecting scarecrow would wear, lit a fire nearby and began to cook *salno* (salted pork fat) and very fatty sausages. One of the men had brought a half-sack of potatoes. He took out a few to bake in the coals and gave the rest to us. 'Take them,' was the message. 'There is nothing over the other side of the Carpathians.' They invited us to join them for supper and we dripped the fat from the *salno* and sausages on to chunks of coarse bread, then ate it with onion and home-pickled gherkins. The potatoes were extracted from the embers, rocked vigorously in a sack to clean them and eaten with a little salt and oil. A bottle of light wine was passed round.

Our benefactors were Yuri and Nora and Ivan No. 1, who were pensioners, while Ivan No. 2 was a mechanic for the co-operative we were on; his pay was eight thousand coupons a month – four dollars. These incredibly poor people willingly shared what they had with us and repulsed all our efforts to contribute to the feast. We were guests. Never rich, the demise of Communism had led to their destitution. Yet they lived beside fertile, productive land, which should have provided them with much more.

In the morning, Ivan (No. 1) Ivanovitch, aged seventy-eight, who had one and a half teeth on his upper denture and had regaled us with song round the fire, came to give us his address. A lady appeared with bread, another with milk and a third with more eggs. Wonderful, kind people, they would not let us go hungry while we were visitors in their country. We overflowed with eggs and the milk was gorgeously creamy.

A huge castle on a knoll dominated Mykačevo, the first town of size we had come to. It was pretty, with the river Platica running through it, but the cobbled streets were uneven and full of holes, giving Traceur and the caravan a hard time. The shops really were empty. Many were closed and long queues had formed for what little bread and fruit there was. From our point of view queuing was the worst part, because we did not have time to spend hours stopped. The van attracted a crowd and a policeman moved us on. I noticed some people with loaves, one or two with celery, and there was a stall selling gherkins and insipid-looking oranges. The reality was: little quantity and no choice. There did not seem to be any real starvation – though who could tell about the hidden corners – and backyard farming undoubtedly formed the mainstay that prevented it.

On the way to Chinodyevo two men stopped us. Did we have oats? Hay? Would I like some? They were from the Chinodyevo Ko-operativ and would see us when we got there. When we reached the village they were waiting by the roadside with an enormous sack of oats and a bale of good-quality hay. What touched me greatly was that they had thoughtfully waylaid the local farrier, in case we needed him. So Traceur had his shoes tightened, which was no bad thing, given the mountains ahead. I tried – I always did – to pay for all this but could not prevail against the three of them.

Shortly after, a man came from his house to invite us for coffee. He was an engine-driver on the Moscow to Slovakia railway. His father, a retired policeman, and his mother, wife and daughter were all present. A friend, Latsi Odyoot, came in and said we must go to his place for the night. He had a place for the horse, he said, and somewhere we could park the caravan.

Fionn, who had been left to mind Traceur because it was his turn, had had a nasty experience. A man, probably drunk, had come up to him and asked to see our map, which I always kept out on the box while travelling. He had then calmly pocketed it. Fionn well knew how precious our maps were. I asked him what he had done. 'I kicked him,' said my bold lad. The man had eventually dropped the map but not before Fionn's hand had been scratched in the affray.

Latsi Odyoot's 'place for a horse' was a garage, full of things on which Traceur would certainly have cut himself. Neither did we fancy being parked outside a huge apart-ment block so we moved to a field a bit further on. Determined to offer hospitality, he and his wife Nina then brought *shashlik*, kebabs, to us, which Latsi barbecued outside in the bitter north wind. He served them in the caravan with bread, *klačinka* – meat loaf – and wine. Latsi was an electrician, Nina a professional pianist and accordion player. They had three children. Latsi's pay was fourteen thousand coupons a month. On this they ran an old Lada, had two TV sets and lived reasonably well, thanks to home produce, especially the all-essential pig. Asked about Gorbachev and *perestroika* their answer was a snort, but they were none too keen on the incumbent Ukrainian president, Leonid Kravchuk, either. We had a great evening, despite language limitations. It was oiled by *spirt*, which one diluted 50 per cent with water. I believe it was nearly pure alcohol. On parting we were given home-made jam, four loaves, a pile of wood and apple-juice concentrate for the children. In return, and with difficulty, we persuaded them to accept our remaining forint.

The Latica river flowed green and fast, flushed with snowmelt. Cone-shaped Mount Smoj (1677 metres/5502 feet) was a distinctive landmark. A man stopped his car, jumped out, thrust a bottle into my hands, yelled, 'Presyent!' and shot off. Our road, the M17, skirted industrial Svalyava and we stopped for a break at a lay-by overlooking it. Some wee kids scrambled up the bank to ask for food. Looking down below us we saw where they had come from: a shanty-town of collapsing houses. No hens, goats or pigs there, only hopeless, grinding poverty. Further on we met a gypsy woman and her son searching for wild food in the hedgerow and gave them a loaf. It was so little, after all we had been given, but we couldn't feed the world or even Svalyava.

It snowed during the night, then turned to sleet and rain. The 'Mactack' New Zealand rug kept Trass dry. Kate and I had each had to make nocturnal excursions with the runs. I was still queasy by morning, when we set off into the cold north wind. Sleet slashed at us, bedraggled Tsar trotted along gamely and Traceur, ears back, was miserable. We plodded steadily uphill, past wooded hillsides, with the Latica rushing south beside us. Passing a derelict shack, the roof of which had collapsed in the middle, I was astounded when an old woman in a bright blue smock came out to wave to us. Although becoming used to the terrible conditions some people had to live in, we were still far from inured to it.

Gankovica lay well into the hills, just off the road. We parked in glutinous mud at a co-operative dairy. Traceur was housed in a huge empty byre with all the hay he could want, and Tsar and a pathetically thin little two-year-old chestnut for company. The next shed was full of good-looking, well-fed small cattle. The brother of a man who had given us hay the night before appeared in a large, old, yellow Mercedes. He worked at the Customs at Čop, wanted to see Traceur – and gave us three jars of caviar.

Some very nice boys, Pavel, Tolya and Sasha, had helped us find our accommodation and in the afternoon took Eilidh, Fionn and me on a tour of their village. There was a church, primary and secondary schools and an odd mixture of houses from new bungalows to forlorn but still pretty wooden houses. People not employed by the co-operative farm worked in Svalyava. Everyone reared hens, ducks and pigs. Some had a cow and several had horses. Pavel's family had two rather unkempt horses in their barn, a pregnant four-year-old mare and a gelding of ten. The cow, goat and kid beside them were in much better order. A wooden sledge and heavy cart stood outside.

We crossed the Latica on a rickety suspension foot-bridge, walked through the village and on to the hill, joined by Tolya's brothers and nine-year-old Nella, who was shy and pretty. These children knew their wildlife and told us that badgers, foxes, two or three species of deer, moles and something fierce, which inhabited small burrows (martens?) lived nearby, while bears, wolves and lynx were found further away. They also knew about the curative properties of sphagnum moss and how nuts are used to flavour tea.

The co-op chief brought us a slab of his home-cured *salno* and half a bucket of still-warm milk. His fat and not very polite wife and small son Oleg came with him to see the caravan and Traceur. I discovered the evening-shift cattle-man was paid the equivalent of five dollars a month and the four dairymaids, who hand-milked as there were no machines, got half that . . .

It was snowing steadily as we pulled out of the muddy yard next morning. The road was busy with lorries and once a convoy of twenty or thirty brand-new, bright yellow, Hungarian-built Ikarus buses passed us. The woods and hills were beautiful and even the stink, noise and occasional douche of muddy water flung up by the traffic could not detract from that. Houses in this region were wooden, many with designs painted on their soffit-boards and around windows. As we came to the village of Podpolozya and passed its small well-preserved church we saw people carrying loaves of bread. This was so rare that I urged Traceur on to reach the shop quickly before it ran out.

The queue at the *magazine* was only ten or twelve long so Eilidh and I joined it while Torcuil went to fetch water. I took out my camera and all the people said, 'Take a picture of the empty shelves,' so I did. We had a good laugh about it and what *perestroika* had not done for them. A few boxes of biscuits, sweets, matches, jars of gherkins, vodka and tinned tomato ketchup seemed to be the total stock – apart from the excellent bread. Three loaves, a poke of sweeties and five boxes of matches cost 348 coupons, or 12p.

We parked on a small common at the far end of the

village, got the fire going and had lunch. We were millionaires, dining on caviar with fresh brown bread, pickled shredded vegetables, eggs and bottled fruit. Afterwards the children and I walked a mile or so up the road we would take next day, through tall pines by a rushing stream. We saw a lot of goldfinches, chaffinches and fieldfares. There was also a First World War memorial to about a hundred Hungarian soldiers, with a new bow in Hungarian colours tied to it. Somebody still cared.

With snow beginning to fall once more, we were glad to return to the caravan and climb in. Hardly had we done so when we felt the van shake a little. When it happened again, I went to the door. A small crowd had gathered, and eggs, jam and milk had been put on the front box. Then a young man brought five bottles of beer, plus a packet of cigarettes for Kate. On leaving he handed me his address in Užgorod *and ten thousand coupons.* I was horrified, this represented so much, but he was adamant, saying he just wanted to sponsor us a little. Another man brought a pot of home-made honey, a bag of apples and some biscuits. Trying to pay these good people was futile and they became quite offended when I persisted. 'I found this hard to take,' said Kate, 'as by comparison we were so rich.' We had an excess of glass jars and later I took these to a couple who lived in a picturesque old farmhouse just across the Latica. The farmer showed me his beautiful traditional byre, which contained two fine cows and their month-old calves. Inside, their house was unbelievably bare, except the best sitting room. It had chairs and a sofa, with two beautifully embroidered cushions, worked by the farmer's wife. Her tablecloth, lovingly unrolled from its double covering of newspaper and cellophane, was a work of art, revealing intricate floral designs hand-stitched on a white ground. I returned to the caravan burdened with yet more milk and a net of hay.

The snow became so thick as we climbed towards the top of the 839-metre/2753-foot pass that we stopped to give Trass a feed, have lunch and think about it. I was reluctant to stop before we reached the summit in case the road became blocked overnight, so we went on. It became steep and slippery. A lorry pulled up in front of us. Would they tow us up, I wondered, Of course. The two men and I rigged a hitch because they had no tow-hook, and the van was driven carefully up, passing Eilidh on Traceur before we reached the vehicle park just over the top. My offer of payment was refused and my attempt to put money in the door pocket of the lorry thwarted. Ukrainians! Impossible to give them anything.

In driving snow, we put Traceur, wearing three rugs, into a wooden half-shelter that had once been a picnic place, and the children built Tsar a snug, windproof igloo against the caravan. By the time we had finished Kate had the fire going and the caravan warm, which was good because we all had wet feet and jackets. It had been a hard day. Normally, when she was with us, Kate cooked, though occasionally I did. This evening, to celebrate reaching the top and everyone having done so well, we decided to eat in the nearby restaurant, which, surprisingly, was open. The building was better than the food, although the loos were atrocious and the heating marginal. Torcuil and Kate opted for 'beefstake [sic] with egg' and fried potatoes, tough and tepid. (Kate had two helpings!) Eilidh just had soup and Fionn and I the very tasty fresh-caught trout. Including 'fruity juice' and one coffee, the cost was 4763 coupons, expensive for here but at approximately £1.60 even our bank balance hardly noticed the outlay – though for a dairymaid, it represented a month's pay.

We had cracked the Carpathian barrier. I was in daft enough mood to stand outside, windless now but with snow still gently falling, and give a blast on the pipes before joining the children and Kate in the fuggy caravan to play quiz games. Name twenty colours, six makes of film, thirty African capitals. I was pleased with progress to date. But I was worried about Kate, whose dislike of our way of life was not lessening. Nor did I know how I could help.

Next day I ran over something sharp in the snow, punctured a tyre and ripped a slit in the outer cover, which gave much trouble in the days ahead.

Near Kozova two little chestnut horses were hauling logs in a porridge of snow and mud. The children and I went to visit them and talk to the foresters. We were invited into their hut, where I was given the inevitable large vodka. A mini-mountain of hay stood on a big sled outside. The horses were hard worked but well fed, and looked well cared-for.

This winter travel was tough on us all. One day in early April I noted '. . . Our latish lunch consisted of Hungarian packet soup, some of the excellent Gankovica smoked *salno*, a slice of brown bread and two very stale rolls. "To a hungry man there is no bad bread" (French proverb). Too true.'

White storks and one rare black stork heralded spring. In Verchne Siniovedne we had showers in the electricity sub-station workers' washroom. Eighteen-year-old English students Lilja and Galya brought us doughnuts and jam. What about the economy? 'We have everything,' Lilja said, 'we grow it ourselves.' While this was true, a piglet cost anything up to twenty thousand coupons, so there must have been people who were excluded from the back-garden economy. The girls returned later with onions, candles and a big bag of flour, which they knew we needed. They said that in spite of present hardships and disappointment that so little had been done to make things better, they, and the

Ukraine, would not want to return to pre-1989 times.

'Stryi 16; Lvov 85; Kiev 616.' I stopped to photograph the sign, hard evidence of where we were. *Sssssssss* from the badly split tyre. Oh, no, not again. But it was. The umpteenth puncture.

Approaching Stryi, the driver of one of the little yellow and blue milk tankers stopped and gave us milk. On the outskirts of town a man waved us down and offered us hay and water. His wife was an English teacher so we could chat while admiring their pigs, goats, hens, cats and dog. A chap with a camera, who had earlier photographed us, erstwhile ship's doctor turned journalist Lev Rishko, asked if he might ride through town with us. We moved off, having meantime been given a cake, a jar of bottled strawberries, two bottles of vodka and a bottle of champagne. We crossed a railway and were stopped again by another man who thrust an enormous bag up to us. It contained fresh tomatoes, two jars of bottled ones, a big bag of grain to make some sort of porridge and about five kilos of sugar. This town of seventy thousand inhabitants had neat, tidy houses, many decorated with picturesque traditional patterns, either painted on, or made with mirrored glass. Some had wall plaques depicting historic scenes, of a kind we had noticed in villages previously.

Police stopped us in Pisochka but only out of curiosity. We crossed the river Dnestr, to find that Micholayev had a shop selling meringues but no bread — and a bus depot where at last I had the troublesome tyre gaitered. Next day a couple of men got out of their car and handed us a copy of the newspaper containing Lev Rishko's piece about us. We plodded up some long hills through dense forest, emerged to pass some allotments and half-completed housing schemes and unexpectedly found ourselves on the L'vov ring-road. By luck we were in the right place.

'Hippodrome,' announced a big red sign over some buildings. The racecourse. We had an introduction to the
director, Wyacheslav Stashensky, and he was happy to let us
stay. The course vet examined Traceur's papers and we
were directed to the stables, on the opposite side of the track
from the offices and grandstand. A few days' rest were going
to be welcome.

I have deliberately described our first weeks in the
Ukraine at some length. We had experienced the end of
Titoist Communism in Slovenia and seen the ravages inflicted
on Hungary as a none-too-compliant Soviet satellite, but this
was our first experience of the former USSR, a place still
relatively little visited by Westerners, whose trips are usually
confined to Kiev and a few tourist spots. 'The West has *no
idea* what it was and is like for most Ukrainians. Even more
appalling, there isn't too much hope left there either,' wrote
Kate. Our view was unique, travelling slowly along, living
alongside ordinary people, talking to them, seeing cameos of
their daily lives at a turning-point in history.

L'vov, L'viv in Ukrainian, had been Lwow under Polish rule
and Lemburg when Austrian. A typical old European-style
city, with beautiful stone buildings, parks and trees and
thoughtfully laid out centre, it was sadly run-down. From
the Hippodrome, going into town meant boarding a No. 5
trolley bus after a muddy kilometre walk. We had a contact,
Dr Oleg Katchmar, a senior physician specialising in treatment of cerebral palsy. He and another doctor, Andrew
Tooziak, met us and they showed us around. As it was
Easter, the baroque Catholic church was full. The university
quarter had fine architecture, notably the veterinary school.
Near the centre of town, we saw the quaint chemist's shop,
reputedly the oldest pharmacy in the world. Shops were
reasonably stocked, though expensive for Ukrainians. At a

piece of wasteground in the suburbs, where car parts could sometimes be bought, I had no luck in obtaining a tyre. However, a man sold me a pump and tyre-lever for two dollars. He just took them off his lorry. No doubt he would report them lost or stolen to his boss. On the way back Oleg pointed out the ex-NKVD, ex-Gestapo, ex-KGB, current security headquarters building. *Plus ça change*, indeed.

Food was readily available in L'vov and we were able to buy good-quality fresh fruit and vegetables, bread and meat. The massive department store had vast stocks but little variety. It sold loo-rolls, which we needed, and imported Austrian ice-cream at huge prices, but neither a tyre nor paraffin could be found. A shirt might cost half a doctor's monthly salary, but at least in large towns you could get one. In the country, such things were not available. On the overcrowded rickety old sardine-can buses, official seating capacity was thirty-five and standing fifty-eight, but many more squeezed in, at great risk of bruised ribs from the sharp elbows of the *babushkas*, dumpy old ladies with headscarves who gave way to nobody. One had to buy a ticket, then validate it by punch-stamping it in one of several machines in the vehicle. Once I forgot and was fined 250 coupons on the spot by an inspector, a dragon lady of great bulk in a blue wool coat. The children enjoyed the novelty of exploring the urban environment and were small enough to wriggle into gaps on the buses.

Traceur had been shod, oats procured at around fifteen dollars for three probably purloined bags, and tack cleaned. On 10 April, in a bitter north-west wind and flurries of snow, accompanied by Andrew Tooziak, who had brought Kate a bunch of traditional Easter catkins, we headed east.

Shortly after, pulling on to the verge at the little village of Zoubra to say goodbye to Andrew, Traceur collapsed. I thought he had had a heart-attack, so suddenly did he go down. We rapidly stripped the harness off his inert form. To my astonishment he then got up unaided, quite unhurt. He had simply stumbled in a pothole I had not seen. The shafts had been severely bent but willing onlookers lent muscle and they were soon made serviceable, if not quite as straight as before. How vulnerable we are, I thought, recovering from my very real shock.

Kate had had a bout of sickness while we were in L'vov and was still feeling rotten. Once again she had contemplated going back to the UK but decided to carry on. The sight of many storks on their nests meant spring was on its way. Perhaps it would help both her health and her mood.

Daily life east of the Carpathians meant undulating roads, passing through villages, searching for food in often empty shops, finding somewhere to fill the water-jerries, obtaining feed and hay for Traceur when required and almost invariably attracting visitors when we stopped for the night. The country was agricultural, mostly under the plough, with platoons of crawler-tractors in echelon formation harrowing the broad acres. However, such was the scale of the terrain that hedges, marshes, streams, woods and copses had not been ruthlessly removed, drained or diverted as in Western Europe, so most days we saw a great variety of birds, smaller mammals and butterflies. Hardly a day passed without someone giving us something, usually food or wine or hay.

On 12 and 13 April the Serbs poured shells into Srebrenica. The UNHCR's Larry Hollingworth stated on BBC World Service he hoped the generals who ordered it would burn in the hottest corner of hell and the soldiers who loaded the guns would have nightmares for the rest of their lives. We thought many of the procrastinating politicians should suffer a similar fate. The war in the Balkans still seemed close to us.

On the outskirts of Olyesko people were tapping birch trees for sap with which they made a cordial. Half a mile away, on a mound that rose in a lump from the plain, stood a massive castle, begun in the thirteenth century but mostly dating from the sixteenth and seventeenth. The man in charge of restoration, who spoke fluent French, showed us around. In a few rooms there were ikons, tapestries and religious figurines carved in wood. The rest was empty. Below the castle, in the oldest Capuchin monastery in Europe, three thousand sculptures were stored awaiting display.

Each village or town held something different. In Yaseniv we shared the village green with a flock of geese. My memory of the town of Brody is of two twelve-year-old boys having great fun playing ping-pong outside on a makeshift table with a line of bricks for a net. In the village of Radiviliv it seemed as if the whole population was lying in wait to give us traditional Easter loaves: two-tiered, round and high, the children called them 'chimney-stack bread'. The potholes were bone-jarring. Basharivka had startling cobalt-blue silver-domed churches. Pochaev lay dwarfed in the shadow of a huge green-roofed, golden-domed monastery of impressive grandeur. Dunaev was a veritable Mecca for horses and carts; good-looking horses from the local *kooperativ*, well fed and shiny. While we were admiring them, a high-sided Gaz truck went by, laden with brand-new cart-wheels. Kremenec had a fort built originally by the Turks and a steep hill whose glass-slippery tarred surface necessitated a tow. At the top, a lady gave us a pail heaped with apples. In the birchwoods before Plochke there was nowhere to stop and after we had passed through all we could see was plough. Daunted, we pressed on, eventually finding a fine grass field.

Just before Jampol thirty cranes flew over, but the western entry to the town was disgusting. Overflow from a big cattle complex had covered about three acres in stinking brownish slurry. Orthodox Easter holidays meant that most shops were shut, and at first Kate failed to find bread. There was bread – it just took a bit of a search, finding a *babushka* to ask where to go. They always knew.

Four men in a white Lada Niva stopped and wanted me to go for a drink with them. I was reluctant but they turned out to be some of the nicest people we'd met. They worked at the local co-operative farm, where they drove tractors and lorries. They were not working because it was Easter. We all marched off behind the hedge with a pint of 45 per cent proof home-brew, *klachinka*, bread and eggs. Ukrainians and Russians always eat something when they drink, which probably saves their guts from dissolving and certainly helps damp the fires of often rough neat spirits. A standard 100-gram shot of vodka is no mean dram on its own – though it seldom is on its own. Our new chums were Anatoly, Sasha, Peotr and Franz, whom the others said was Polish. Only Eilidh, Fionn and I joined the party. Torcuil was feeling queasy and Kate rarely socialised. The children started a fire with help from Franz. Anatoly and Sasha went to fetch Anatoly's mother, another pint of paint-stripper, bread, milk, a sausage and a dozen painted Easter eggs. There was also a bag for us: potatoes and carrots – rare carrots! Mother, who was sixty-two but looked older, had been taken to Dachau aged twelve in 1943. The rest of her family's fate was unknown. She showed us the number tattooed on her arm. Perhaps Eilidh and Fionn will remember seeing that, in years to come, when all the concentration-camp survivors are dead.

This had been a typical, though particularly pleasant, encounter. Verbal communication was often minimal but it was amazing how much could be conveyed using limited language, signs and drawings.

Driving through Chudniv we were imperiously waved to a halt by some bystanders. A funeral procession was approaching. I hauled Traceur and the caravan to the side of the narrow road as best I could and stopped. First came a group carrying a portrait of the deceased, then people bearing wreaths, then a long box covered with a white sheet, bearing a big loaf of bread on top. Behind this came a lorry with the coffin on it – open. Poor fellow, he looked much better in his portrait. A brass band and crowd of mourners brought up the rear. It was an interesting sight, though the children were startled to see the corpse.

The day before we reached Zhitomir we stopped at an abandoned camp-site. Red squirrels and birds were its sole occupants, apart from some workmen who said it would be all right to stay. They gave us some desperately needed paraffin for our lamps, too.

After lunch we went down to the sandy riverbank, where people were sunbathing and swimming, though it was only late April. Eilidh took Traceur right in, feet off the bottom, then boldly stood up and dived off his back. Startled, Traceur came racing to shore, up the bank and on to the grass where he rolled, grazed, and had a lovely time. A Ukrainian lad took the children out fishing in a rowing-boat, without success. I sat with the binoculars for a while and saw more than a dozen species of birds, including many herons, motionless fishermen, along the banks of the lake.

Zhitomir had a beautiful, wide, spacious square, with well-established trees growing round it. Although it was completely modern and built entirely in concrete, it was well proportioned and pleasing to the eye. Kate and Torcuil went to a *Produktia* to buy food, while I tackled the bank. I was directed up several floors in a lift and got out at an anteroom where two men and a policeman sat watching TV. A fourth man showed me into a shoe-box of an office. My ten one-dollar notes were scanned for forgery. Two copies of something were made out, one of which I had to sign. Then it was off to the *Kassa*, where the teller started counting out 5000-coupon notes. '*Nyet, nyet,*' I said, '*Dva tisoc illi adeen tisoc, pazhalsta.*' She understood, and gave me ones of a lower denomination. The rate was 3000 to the dollar now. It was twenty minutes before I returned to the caravan, where Kate and Torcuil were loading bread, milk and pasta. No butter, though. If your name was not on the list, you were not allowed to buy it. To the post office next, with a letter to Kiev and twenty-one postcards for abroad. The girl at the counter stamped everything with an oblong rubber stamp, then *wrote the value of the postage* in a space provided. Then she went through the whole lot again, franking them. Inflation was rising so fast postage stamps were no longer issued. We ourselves were living on less than two dollars a day, including major expenses.

Banging through potholes and squeezed by trolley-buses, we made our way out of town. A stretch of six-lane highway reverted to two-way traffic after a short distance and we were in countryside once more, where lots of horses and carts were taking people to the fields to plant potatoes.

As we neared Kiev, the castellated outline of the city loomed like some futuristic fortress. Close to, the ramparts dissolved into serried rows of multistorey flats, concrete warrens for massed humanity. We battled round the long, busy orb of the ring-road to the race-course. This time we had no introduction but after discussion with the director we were permitted to stay. It was a trotting stadium, with 340 stables but we declined the offer of one and kept Trass outside.

The blacksmith came, took off Traceur's shoes, then guided Torcuil and me to the city centre – a fifteen-minute bus ride followed by a short run on the clean, efficient metro. There was mail for us at the British Council, including a copy of a Ukrainian newspaper article about us translated and forwarded by Andrew Tooziak. Meanwhile, Kate and Fionn had been able to buy bread, meat and margarine but no milk or vegetables. More serious than the vagaries of post-Communist shopping, Tsar was ill, resulting from a massive tick infestation picked up in pinewoods on the previous night.

Kiev was beautiful, with plenty to see, but during five days in the capital, most of our time was taken up with arranging necessities, and very little spent sightseeing, which was a pity. The acquisition of Russian visas was vital. Things had changed since we left Hungary and it was now a matter of applying and paying. I went to the consulate at 8 byl. Kutuzava and received a nasty shock: half the population of Africa and most of the Pacific Rim was milling about in the street outside in total disorder and confusion. This was the queue. It would take a week to get in. A sympathetic Ukrainian soldier on guard at the door suggested the best thing I could do would be to telephone, or get help from our embassy. There was certainly no chance of getting in that day.

The British Embassy was not long established and had just moved from rooms in the Zhouteva Hotel to temporary quarters at 9 Desyatinna Street. The receptionist sat amid piled-up packing cases and boxes of Russian champagne. I had a long chat with first secretary Bill Somerset about our journey, and before I left he furnished me with a letter of introduction to the Russian consul, whom he had also telephoned. The visas would be no problem, he said, but he could not help me with getting into the building.

Two days later, hoping that the queue would have diminished, I arrived early at Kutuzava Street – but nothing had changed. I went up the steps and showed the two guards my letter addressed to Consul Gruchkov. Instant admission. My name was noted in a ledger and I began to fill up a form in Cyrillic. Then the man on the desk, a caricature massive blocky Russian security gorilla, spiky crew-cut and all, came over, said I was jumping the queue and must go out. '*Ne panemayoo, ne panemayoo*,' I yelped. 'I don't understand.' All seemed to be well as I stood in line for the consul's office, but then the gorilla came back with the two Ukrainian guards. 'I've been outside for two days,' I protested, stretching the truth. 'We leave Kiev tomorrow.' Some Pakistani and Indian students sided with me but one of the guards was getting heavy and about to eject me by force. Then the other one, who spoke some English, and whom I had never seen before, *confirmed my story*. I flicked a look of enormous gratitude to him, hoping it conveyed at least half of what I felt. All really was well then. The gorilla even apologised.

Twenty minutes later I met Mr Gruchkov, who was charming, very interested in what we were doing, and gave us visas valid until 1 April 1994. They were good for Kazakhstan, too, as Russia was still handling Kazakh consular affairs. I learned later the crowds of Africans and Asians were students requiring transit visas for their already-booked homeward flights via Moscow. The visa system had just been introduced so perhaps there was some excuse for the delay, though at fifty dollars per skull, the Russians were doing well out of it.

Tsar was given antibiotics but remained ill, though I had managed to find a tick collar for him to prevent future problems. Traceur had been shod, another set of shoes reinforced and a bag of horseshoe nails bought. Our gas cylinder had been refilled for ten dollars – exorbitant, but all fuel in the Ukraine except coal was imported from Russia. The large indoor produce market in town was too expensive for most Ukrainians but beef at 50p per pound was cheap for us and the good fruit a luxury. We even found Colgate toothpaste and good-quality tea in the imported-goods shop. With the caravan restocked, we were ready to leave.

Kate, swithering whether or not to go home, had been to airline offices and found she could take a flight out on 8 May. It looked as though we had again come to the parting of the ways. I was on the point of setting off for round two at the Russian consulate on the seventh when, in the throes of being sick from a tummy upset, she said, 'You'd better take my passport too.' I was glad, hoping her decision might mark a turning-point and that her spirits would lift.

With only glimpses of St Sophia's, the Dnepr and the grand architecture of central Kiev as souvenirs, we were almost ready to roll early on 8 May. Then Fionn, packing up the electric fence, discovered the pulse-unit was missing, probably stolen for the batteries. This was a minor disaster. Neither had a new inner-tube been delivered as promised. I'd paid for it, too, which had been a mistake. Nothing could be done on either count, so with thanks to the race-course director and the farrier, we left to rejoin the ring-road eastbound.

We followed the Dnepr southerly, through lovely rolling green country at the height of spring, seeing chiffchaffs, black redstarts, sand martins, yellow wagtails, little ringed plover, a hoopoe and a peregrine falcon on the way. The beauty of traditional wooden houses continued to delight us. Near Kanev we swam in the Dnepr. Sixty miles north of Kiev was Chernobyl. As Kanev was only a further fifty miles south I wondered whether we should glow in the dark that evening, and was thankful we had no Geiger counter. It would have spoilt the pleasure of the afternoon to have registered rocketing rads or burgeoning bequerels. We bought some lovely fresh goat's milk from a woman whose animals had been grazing near us.

The road over the Dnepr ran across the top of a big hydro dam and shipping locks, then took us off into beautiful pinewoods, with a scattering of birch and some sandy clearings. After that we came to a more open area of mainly scrub birch and willow. A track led to a quiet, shady spot fifty yards from the shore of the massive lake formed by the dam. Tsar, fully fit again, was taken for a bath, which he hated, and Traceur for a paddle, which he enjoyed. We all swam. After lunch the children built sandcastles and plashed about in the water. The reed-beds were full of the sizzling songs of great reed warblers and grasshopper warblers, the croaking of big green frogs and the buzzy clatter of dragonflies' wings. It was idyllic and for once not a visitor came near.

As we jogged along, it occurred to me that things of interest to us earlier were now so familiar they went unrecorded – for example, the state of the roads was largely good but had patches of bad potholes and in one area fresh tar, undusted with chippings, had formed a viscous surface, which clogged hoofs, tyres and shoes with sticky black goo. Town roads were often far rougher than country ones. There was marked variation from *oblast* to *oblast* and even *rajon* to *rajon.** All food shops were virtually empty. Display of goods to enhance sales was unknown. If you wanted something they had, fine, but there was no attempt

*An *oblast* is an administrative region; a *rajon* an administrative district.

at promotion. To us, not being bombarded with advertising was a welcome change. There was no street advertising either, except for *oblast, rajon* and *kolektiv* or *kooperativ* signs. In towns there were sometimes large posters, exhortations to produce more or praising the workers or the army; relics of Communism, most were torn and decaying. The commonest vehicles were Volga, Moskvitch and Lada saloons, Lada Niva and Uaz jeeps, Latvia vans, Zil, Gaz and Kamaz medium-size lorries and large Kamaz and Kraz trucks. Foreign cars were rare even in cities, an Audi, Mercedes or Peugeot remarkable. Aircraft were frequent, mostly twin-prop feeder airliners. We saw military fighters occasionally but fuel shortages kept them grounded for much of the time. In Kiev we had seen police helicopters and at the inner airport we saw row upon row of AN-2 biplanes. Visible pollution was minimal, apart from some dumping and a number of filthy streams. Empty vodka bottles formed the bulk of roadside rubbish. Around towns, if a building site was needed, it was carved out, heedless of aesthetics or wildlife. After the Carpathians, we saw no truly wild country and no local reserves or parks. Ammonium nitrate appeared to be the fertiliser of choice, sprayed on in liquid form. Agricultural machinery was parked centrally, fields full of combine harvesters, huge four-wheel drive tractors and many small ones, often rusting to pieces. Big brick-built, animal-housing units, roofed with asbestos sheeting, seemed to be standard. Many were in dire need of maintenance. The few industrial areas we saw were mostly old, worn and polluting.

An invitation from Paulov Gregorovich Petrovich and his wife Ljuba to stay at their house in Perevica meant a diversion but we thought it would be interesting to see village life at first hand. We manoeuvred the van into their yard with difficulty and squeezed rain-soaked Traceur into the byre beside a calf and a pig. Later, dry, he was moved to a small, locked paddock at the local co-op because the calf's mother needed her stall. We were fed thick soup, followed by small fish and plates of what I can only describe as mashed meat. There was sour cream, honey and bread too. Kate helped wash the dishes after, *sans* hot water or washing-up liquid, using cold tea as a rinse ... great for greasy plates. There was no running water. The outside loo was a clean squat 'n' drop. Most houses in the country were like this. Not surprisingly, people reeked of sweat. Dentistry may not have been confined to gold and silver capping, but the number of rotting teeth was legion. Experiencing someone's force-ten halitosis was a hazard, particularly of bus travel. Breakfast consisted of more soup followed by a heap of greasy pancakes, good with sour cream, plus honey, bread and black tea.

We took Paulov's recommended scenic route cross-country, which would have been fine had it not recently rained. First, we mired to the axles in a short stretch of oleaginous black mud, requiring a crawler tractor to pull us out. The driver assured us the track to Bela-usovka was *harasho*, all right. It probably would have been, but half-way there a ten-minute thunder-plump turned the surface to mud the consistency of thick semolina. Poor Trass had a terrible time. I had never seen him puff and blow so much as when dragging us to the end of that track. Or almost to the end. The last few hundred yards were a quagmire. We stopped another tractor and persuaded the driver to unhitch his trailer and tug us out. Wheels spinning, slithering and skidding ferociously, jarring the caravan badly in ruts and potholes, he finally made it and we reached tarmac with nothing broken.

We travelled sixteen kilometres that day to make seven. A long, long slog of digging, heaving, sweating and driving

Traceur on, half covered in rich, fertile, Ukrainian glaur. No wonder whole armies foundered in it. Finding a shop selling butter, seeing a great grey shrike feeding young and hearing corncrakes and quail calling at dusk were consolations. But I vowed never again to trust advice from people unfamiliar with the capabilities of our rig.

One night by the river Sula a young drunk kept us awake for ages, refusing to go. When at last he did, it was only to return with several comrades on mopeds. They made a lot of noise revving their engines and Tsar made a lot of noise barking but they did not stay long. Much later Tsar's barking again woke me. Traceur was out! Our inebriated friends had stolen three of the electric-fence poles. They had probably thrown them in the river. Anyway, they were gone. So was sleep for that night, and an invasion of mosquitoes meant everyone was lumpy as well as grumpy by morning.

I cycled back to Lukimya to ask help from the local *kooperativ*, because loss of three out of eight poles seriously reduced the size of Traceur's paddock. I was ushered in to meet the director and the president. They were interested to hear at first hand about our journey, having seen us on TV. 'Do you have some time?' they asked. We talked as best we could for fifteen minutes over coffee in the wood-panelled office. Then a man entered bearing four metal electric-fence poles with insulators of the standard type often used in farming. Heavy, but most acceptable. '*Spasiba!* Thank you. Very much.' Carefully carrying a bunch of tulips they had given me for Kate, plus the unwieldy poles, I recrossed the Sula, where exquisite white-winged black terns wheeled over the water, and caught up with the caravan.

We came to Horol, where the Germans machine-gunned a hundred thousand civilians during the Second World War. The quiet sleepy town yielded bread, milk, wine, liver for

Tsar, imported Italian spaghetti – and Vassily Cherenko. He was a part-time blacksmith, and during a busy afternoon and evening we reshod Traceur as well as going for a swim and helping cut grass for his beasts. I had a chance to examine the Russian harness system, too, so different from ours with its wooden hoop over the shafts to which the collar is rigidly attached, leaving the horse free to move.

The terrain was gradually changing. There were more woods and grass, less arable land. We saw exotic-looking birds: gaudy golden orioles, brilliantly coloured bee-eaters and an almost equally colourful roller. The latter, a foot long, vivid blue, chestnut and black, pounce on insects from their perches, often on telegraph wire. And they really do roll sometimes! One day eight Iranian trucks passed us, drivers waving. On 21 May the Ukrainian prime minister walked out because hard-liners wouldn't support his reforms. On the twenty-third, the BBC reported a fire and explosion at the Zaporozhe nuclear plant. Hydrogen gas had leaked and met a welder's torch, killing him. The reactor, thank goodness, was decommissioned.

Batteries were scarcer than hens' teeth. Our Sony radio required six, so we confined our listening to news reports. However, though playing cassettes gobbled batteries, there had been grumbling in the ranks that we never played any. To counter the impending rebellion, once a week one of us would choose one side of a cassette to play. For fun, the others voted on this, giving it points out of five. Any choice scoring less than ten out of a possible twenty was banned from being replayed. Eilidh's choice, Boney M and Erasure, scraped through with eleven, mine, *Play Gaelic* by Run Rig, fared little better, and Kate's Queen tape eventually topped the list.

The left-hand rear tyre seemed very soft when I looked at it one morning. Closer examination revealed catastrophe.

The whole wheel was collapsing, rusted through. I managed with difficulty to get the worn wheel-nuts off and the spare wheel – I'd got another at a Hungarian scrap-yard – on. Two hours later, the gaitered 'Carpathian cut' finally went again. A lorry-driver and his mate from a nearby *kolektiv* stopped to help. They took both wheels and returned that evening with a neat weld done on one wheel and a huge plug in the other. But tyre trouble continued to dog us until, much further on, I was able to buy new ones.

One of the most important battles in European history took place at Poltava. The total defeat of the Swedish forces under Charles XII in 1709 by Tsar Peter the Great was of enormous significance. It marked the end of Scandinavian expansion, the loss of all Swedish territories in the east and, ten years later, in 1719, led to the Russian invasion of Sweden. Only British and French interest in maintaining the balance of power prevented a complete dissolution of Swedish possessions. A monument to the battle stood in the large, wooded, circular park in the centre of the city. Before visiting it we had parked Traceur on the outskirts, taken a trolley-bus into town, changed money, posted letters and sent a fax. Renewing visas for another month took longer but cost only 60p equivalent for two whereas in Budapest they were fifteen dollars each: I suspected that in Poltava they had never before had to issue visas to foreigners.

Saturday 29 May's diary: 'Cheese. CHEESE! In Lannaya, in the shop. This was like finding gold in the Ukraine. We bought a kilo for 27p.' Our daily menu was dictated by the availability of food, which meant village shops that might or might not have what we happened to need. It was a lottery. Kate 'had dreams of food. Toast with butter and jam, tea with milk, basic stuff.' We always carried reserves, though these could be pasta one week and potatoes the next. Most days we found or were given milk. Treats like cheese or chocolate were rare. Somehow we maintained a balanced if eccentric diet. Water was also a constant concern. It's heavy and it was never easy to make the choice between not carrying enough and having to pass a good pull-off, or asking Traceur to haul two or three hundred pounds extra weight for hours. Our maximum capacity was 200 litres, a hefty 440 pounds. Traceur, of course, drank most of it.

At the beginning of June, I had to face shoeing Traceur myself. Having watched over a dozen smiths at work, I knew in theory what to do. Practice was different and it took me an hour to remove a shoe, trim the hoof, then replace it. Though the job looked rough, I had not pricked his foot, the shoe stayed on and Traceur remained sound. I was relieved and rather pleased.

We seldom knew in advance where we should spend the night. We tried to achieve a daily distance of ten to twelve miles but sometimes lack of a suitable pitch forced us to go on a bit. Only exceptionally did we stop short, because it was essential to cover ground during the travelling season. In 1993 especially, we needed to keep moving to reach our target winter destination, distant Alma-Ata, capital of newly independent Kazakhstan, where I hoped to obtain visas to cross China.

One morning I was rolling up the electric-fence wire when there was a yell from Eilidh. She was lying on the ground by the shafts, having slipped getting off the caravan. When, unusually, the yelling continued, I sprinted across to her. She got up as I arrived, said, 'It's my wrist,' and fainted. I managed to catch her and between us Torcuil, Kate and I lifted her back into the caravan and on to her bunk. Kate bound her wrist and arm and I finished getting ready for the road.

That night, stopped just short of Izjum, she was still in pain and was no better next morning. We headed into the town, to the hospital, which fortunately was on our road. I parked at the entrance while Kate took Eilidh in. After an hour, out came the patient, chanting 'It's broken,' and brandishing her newly plastered arm. She had a hairline crack in her right ulna. As with her leg, she didn't let it stop her from being active. Her treatment was free – some aspects of socialism were very civilised.

We went through pinewoods to Borova, where we stocked up, or I thought we had, for the two days' travel to the next village. Two jerries developed pinhole leaks but silicone was effective as a plug. A stop at a *kolektiv* failed to produce any oats or barley. At this point I was furious to discover how little potted meat and other stores we had. Torcuil offered to bike back and see what he could get. Seven kilometres out from Borova a *moloko* lorry stopped and asked if we would like some milk. *Da, pazhalsta,* yes, please! Shortly afterwards Torcuil caught up. He had bought bread, a tin of fish and two jars of potted meat. He wanted to cycle on, so I suggested he find us a pleasant pull-off.

After he had gone, a white Lada Niva 1600 stopped in front of us. Out of it emerged a very large stomach in a suit, Anatoly Krivoruchko, director of *kolhoz* – collective farm – Novi Shlyach. Did we need anything? Well, as it happens . . . would it be possible to buy a sack or two of oats? Of course. See you shortly. We camped three kilometres short of the *kolhoz*, where another Lada, driven by the farm's agronomist, arrived to fetch us. Eilidh and I went, expecting to be back soon. However, we were first taken to the *kantora*, the office, to see Krivoruchko and be shown his astonishing collection of over eight hundred pens. At the grain store we were given two well-filled sacks of barley, then continued to another store. There, we saw a stack of items I had thought unobtainable in the Ukraine, notably quantities of welly-boots and heavy-duty work clothes, which explained where most country-dwellers got their clothing from. We were given rice, eight enormous pork chops and potatoes in exchange for a couple of pens for the collection and a T-shirt for the agronomist.

There were some large and extensive animal burrows at this stop. We saw one of the inhabitants, which resembled a fur-covered tube. Peachy-beige in colour, with a small black nose, tiny limbs and no visible eyes or ears, we deduced that this extraordinary creature must be a mole-rat.

Traceur at last discovered there was no electric current in the fence so we had had to revert to picketing him. We also had to fly-rug him to deter squadrons of enormous horse-flies, with appetites for blood that made Dracula seem anorexic. A third jerry, of a different type, was breaking up, the plastic decayed by sunlight. Our water had recently been tasting like the bottom of a pond, so I stripped the Whale Mark IV pump – and found it full of rotting flowerheads and small leaves. A piece of nylon mosquito netting over the intake solved that problem.

As part of our education and for entertainment, we agreed that each of us would prepare a short talk. Torcuil had given a most creditable account of the space-shuttle. Now, appropriately, as we had seen a number of terrapins and I had just finished removing primal ooze from the pump, Fionn delivered a masterly dissertation on turtles. Home education was proving highly successful.

Belovodsk, the last town we visited in the Ukraine, nestled at the foot of a spur of chalky marl. I cashed a few dollars and found the rate had jumped to 3300 coupons, a terrifying 65 per cent devaluation in three months. Ilya, a four-star policeman, invited us to lunch. His wife served radishes in cream with dill, spring onion tops with tomatoes in oil, fried scrambled eggs – this is not a misprint! – and bread and strawberries. We drank wine that turned out to be cherry brandy, and home-distilled hooch. Ilya had twenty years' police service behind him and was sneering of independence, Kravchuk, Gorbachev and Yeltsin, lamenting that his brothers now lived in foreign countries – Belarus and Russia. Tongue in cheek I said, 'What about Stalin?' and got an enthusiastic thumbs-up.

Our last night in the Ukraine was appropriately spent at the Horse Factory at Novostoilivka. The stud had been founded in 1805 and the magnificent stables, dating from 1881, were undergoing much-needed restoration. There were 240 horses, plus 500 cattle, 7000 sheep and 2000 pigs on the farm. We were looked after in customary Ukrainian fashion, Traceur shod by the farrier, sacks of oats loaded on to the van.

At five o'clock next morning Tsar woke me, barking at a woman milking a goat. I rose, fed Trass, enjoyed the fresh morning air and listened to BBC news. Just after eight we left, waving farewell to head vet Vladimir Kolibenko and his family, who had come to see us off.

A thirteen-kilometre up-and-down slog to Melovoe in the heat was uneventful, and happily we could bypass the grimy industrial town. North of it, a frontier control and Customs post had only three weeks earlier been set up in a shed by the roadside. What a good thing we had bought Russian visas and not relied on using Ukrainian ones, as had been suggested in Budapest. The officer in charge said ours were the first British passports he had seen. A young soldier took them and jotted details. They apologised for keeping us – all of ten minutes – posed for a photograph and waved us on.

We were out of the Ukraine.

CHAPTER TEN

RUSSIA: JULY AND AUGUST 1993
CRAYFISH AND CHAMPAGNE

In the process of learning another culture, you learn just as much about yourself and how you are part of your culture.

A. C. 'Chuck' Ross

Entering Russia was an important milestone on our road but it was more than that. We, an ordinary Western family, were travelling into the land Kate and I had been told all our lives was our enemy, Ronald Reagan's 'evil empire', which might at any time have unleashed a nuclear attack upon us. The Ukraine had been part of the USSR, but this was Mother Russia herself. When we pulled up at the border post, I could scarcely believe it was not a dream.

A smartly turned-out captain was in charge and a goofy-looking private toted a sub-machine-gun. Their uniforms were the same as those of the Ukrainians with different badges. A tall man in a dark blue uniform with a Russian tricolour on the shoulder had 'Customs' in English over his breast pocket. Recovering rapidly from their surprise at our appearance – we were the first Westerners they'd seen – our passport details were recorded in long-hand in a ledger. During this lengthy process I examined their 1:750,000 wall map of Rostov *oblast*, because our own maps were inadequate. Clerking completed and handshakes all round, we were in. *In Russia!* It was 19 June 1993.

In the short distance between the border and the village of Chertkovo we were passed by a wildly waving wedding party and stopped by a couple who insisted we drink a beer with them. *Na zdrovya!* Welcome to Russia!

The village shops had full shelves: bread, butter, wine and tinned meat. Luckily we had some roubles, as neither the border nor Chertkovo had exchange facilities. Loaded with these luxuries and water, we went on a few kilometres to a little lake, where we swam, washed clothes and the animals, and joined a Russian family for a picnic. A great introduction to the country and a peaceful place to have stopped but I should never have remarked, 'There'll probably be an all-night party here.'

There was.

Late next morning we dawdled to Stari Mankovo, chatting to folk on the way, feeling decidedly jaded after the noisy night. Traceur was off-colour too, with diarrhoea. It was Sunday but shops and market stalls were open. We bought ice-cream and I changed money with a stall-holder at a thousand roubles for a dollar.

A man and his companions stopped us on the road. 'Do you speak English?' he asked.

'Yes.'

'How nice of you to come to our country.'

On our second night, parked a little off the road on good grass, I was in the throes of making a risotto when a Gaz truck stopped. The driver handed us a bottle of Russian champagne. 'Welcome to Russia!' he said, and drove off. Then a Latvia van pulled up, three lads and a lass in it and a bulging wet sackful of something in the back. Would we like some *rak,* crabs? And filled our biggest pot with live crayfish. 'Welcome to Russia,' they called cheerily, driving away. *Salt mines?* We were more likely to succumb to gastro-enteritis and gout.

Next day we crossed the M4 Moscow–Rostov road, narrow, busy with fast-moving truck traffic, glad we were not on it. In Alekseivo-Lozovskoe we bought cabbage, tea, spring onions and gherkins before starting to climb a hill. Half-way up was what we thought was an abandoned factory – but half a dozen people came rushing out to look at us. At the top we stopped Trass for a blow and a bite of grass and heard a whistle. Two men from the factory were trudging up the hill, each carrying a pail. One contained mixed grain for Traceur, the other sunflower oil for us, produce of the factory, gift of the workers.

Wildlife was prodigious, with lots of birds and butterflies and masses of marmots. They were hilarious, tubby fellows, whistling to each other from the entrances of their burrows. At each whistle, their heads jerked forward and their little flat tails flicked upwards in comical fashion. If we came too close they dived underground, where we could hear them grunting to each other inside their holes.

Anatoly Borovitskiyi was chief engineer at the Setraki *kolhoz*. He and his family invited us for a bite of lunch. The bite included all the contents of a 20-litre vat of crisp home-brewed sparkling white wine and was followed in due time by a swim in the nearby lake. It was so hot even Eilidh went in, plastered arm wrapped in a plastic bag. Anatoly took me to see a route he had suggested – and we learned how to catch crayfish.

For twenty minutes Torcuil and I bumped and bounced cross-country in the sidecar of Anatoly's seventeen-year-old Ural motorcycle-combination to a lake. We had borrowed a net, a mini-trawl. At the top was a four-foot wooden bar, to each end of which was attached a two-foot metal rod with a skid at the foot. Along the bottom was a lead-weighted lead-rope. The net was about eight feet long. Anatoly jumped into the water and proceeded to drag it back and forth. In two hours we had a sackful of fat green crayfish. What a feast we had. The children, theirs and ours, had a great time and elected to sleep in the hay barn that night.

It was late June and boiling hot. Anatoly's route, a firm, macadamised track, took us across lovely rolling grassland with some woods and fields. One morning what appeared to be a collection of huts resolved into several lorry-trailers, each loaded with fifty or sixty beehives. One had a little shack at one end with a bed and stove in it. The hives, tended by two old men, were painted in different colours, some prettily decorated. They told us that sixty hives would produce about two tons of honey. They insisted we stay to breakfast and we were served with great plates of honey, accompanied by brown bread. There was *salo* too, fried with potatoes. Yummy. Even the mandatory dram of vodka went down well and we resumed our journey laden with jars of honey, good potatoes and some extra water. It was sweltering and we flowed along, sweaty spots trickling down the landscape.

Two days later we reached the junction marked with a tank on the sketch-map Anatoly had drawn for us. A T-34 was mounted on a plinth as a memorial to the 3rd Guards. We turned right for the Chyr valley, through mixed woods, crops and the extensive grassy plains of the famous Cossack country. The Cossacks, fearless and highly accomplished horsemen, once virtually ruled this area and their descendants still live there. Straight on led to Veshenskaya, where Sholokov, author of the classic novel of Cossack life *And Quiet Flows the Don*, had lived.

The bounty of our first days was replaced by scarcity worse than in the Ukraine. In smaller villages, shops were either empty or shut. Even seeking supplies door to door was fruitless and we were glad of our reserves.

An hour spent birding by the banks of the Chyr produced magpies, wood pigeons, a green woodpecker and a great reed warbler, swallows, sand martins, a yellowhammer and a yellow wagtail to add to recent sightings of woodlark, buzzard and red-backed shrikes. There were many varieties of butterfly and wild flowers and swirls from fish in the river.

Nearing Bokovskaya some gypsies stopped to admire Traceur. They were a handsome family, brightly dressed and prosperous-looking, quite at variance with those we had known in Hungary and the Ukraine. They said we should find food in town and we did. The shop stocked bread, eggs, margarine, cherries and *kasha*. This last, a mixture of barley with a little meat in kilo-sized jars, became a staple throughout our Russian journey.

We sustained our progress and, thanks to many people, fed better than we might have done but for some things selfhelp was the only way. Eilidh's sandal-straps had torn but the soles were good. With no likelihood of finding replacements, I cut inner-tubing to the pattern of the old straps, effecting a passable repair. How ingenious one becomes when needs must.

Eilidh's other broken item, her arm, was due to have its plaster removed. There was a hospital in Sovyetskaya, the centre of a collective farm, a kilometre off the road. We were directed down a muddy track with potholes like lakes to the town centre. There were several shops and as usual Trass and the van attracted a crowd. Hearing we needed to go to the hospital, a lady who worked there said it would open in an hour, at eleven o'clock. We also needed to change money, having depended on shopkeepers and passers-by till now, so Fionn and I sought out the bank.

It was festooned with buckets, because the roof leaked

in several places and steady drips plopped from the ceiling. And – crisis! In April the law had been altered and small banks were no longer permitted to exchange foreign money. I should have to go to the nearest big town, Rostov, miles and weeks away in the wrong direction. We were taken to the manager's office and given seats. 'Something must be going to happen,' I said to Fionn. Sure enough, several people arrived, filling the little office, among them the manager, the mayor and a man from the bottled gas depot. After discussion, the problem was solved. *I* told *them* the rates – 1200 in Moscow but 1000 on the street – and four crisp 5000-rouble notes were produced from a cupboard in exchange for my twenty dollars. No paperwork was involved . . .

The mayor took us back to the caravan in his twenty-nine-year-old Gaz jeep to collect our gas bottle. Russian bottled-gas fittings were different from ours but the gas-depot chief managed to fill it using a complicated array of interconnecting rubber tubing. We were given warm crusty loaves at the bakery and taken for a tour of the town. Meantime, Eilidh had been to the hospital – by ambulance! – and relieved of her plaster cast. The shopping had been done, the jerries filled. Even by Russian standards the hospitable people in Sovyetskaya were exceptionally good to us, notably its young and enthusiastic mayor.

Day followed day and every evening another small line was drawn on the map to mark our advance. Everyone was becoming tired from the oppressive heat and the long spell of uninterrupted travelling. We had been going steadily for four months, most of the time on a limited, uncertain, though usually adequate diet. Kate and I bickered, mostly over her lack of enthusiasm. She was also frustrated by the lack of available provisions. Only listening to commentary on the Wimbledon tennis seemed to afford her any pleasure.

There were lighter moments, of course. Kate recalls one which, in view of the over-protective hygiene regulations imposed in the UK, serves to highlight what our food was sometimes like: 'I was overjoyed to find a woman selling mince at a roadside stall and had visions of the lovely shepherd's pie I should be able to make. The mince was just there in a bowl and the woman weighed out a portion for me. The temperature was not particularly hot but I put the meat in our cool-box – for which we had no ice but which still acted as insulation. When I took it out next day to cook, it had gone green! It had begun to whing a bit too but none of the others was around so I just washed it, squeezed it out and cooked it very thoroughly. No one noticed and it tasted fine.'

'Today should have been cancelled,' reads my diary for Monday 5 July. 'Overnight rain turned the track we were on into a bog and we had to be towed on to the road by a colossal Kraz truck. Two successive villages had no shops open. The road was a switchback. Heat and humidity were high. Water was low and limited. Traceur almost cast a shoe. While I was tightening it, rain poured down and I got soaked. We pulled off into woods, where there was good grazing, hit a short stretch of soft sand and sank to the springs. A huge Ural mobile crane pulled us out, bending our towbar in the process. The driver took me to the local *rajon* maintenance yard to have it straightened and welded. When I got back, Eilidh asked, "Where did you put the picket?" It was in the ground where I'd left it – thirty kilometres back.'

There were redeeming features. We had crossed the magnificent river Don that day. On the east bank we had found market stalls, selling fish, sausages, radishes, bread and matches. Eilidh cycled into Kalach-na-Donu and added tomatoes, margarine, condensed milk, potted meat and loo-rolls to the list. These gourmet stores lasted many days.

I walked to the permanent *gai* (police) post on the road east of the river. Situated at strategic points, with heavy gates barring the road, these posts monitored all traffic and stopped anyone they chose. Under Communism, an internal passport was required to go anywhere and control had been almost total. The *gai* flagged down a rattly Gaz and asked the driver to lift me back to where I had left the picket. I found it easily and the driver decently stopped another truck, a more comfortable Kamaz, to take me back. A chivalry now unknown in the West still existed among travellers on the roads of the former Soviet Union.

Traceur compounded the previous day's miseries by breaking his tether in the night. He was returned by a goat-keeper, who had been putting out his animals. His freedom must have done him good, for he was on top form. Kate, seeking milk, had some squirted into a pail on the spot for her. The entrance to that day's stopping-place was via a short but very steep bank. As I drove down it, Tsar jumped or fell off the caravan, breaking his lead and disappearing beneath the wheel. There was a horrid thud and terrible screams from Kate. I thought I'd killed him, stopped the horse and leaped off, to see Tsar hurtling away up the road-side, apparently unharmed. He did not go far and the only damage was a strip of missing hair on one leg and some bruising. The shock did not stop him from eating, drinking – or barking.

East of the Don the country was flatter, mostly grass-land. We passed a military airfield, then a tented camp with lots of troops beside a gunnery range. The road ran close to the railway for a while and lengthy trains of up to a hundred trucks would go snorting and snurfing by, belching dense clouds of black smoke.

At a tranquil stop near Prudboi a large ship hove in

sight, apparently sailing over the steppe. It was neither mirage nor vodka-induced delirium: the Volga–Don canal was behind and above us. Its high banks concealed it from view, creating this illusion. The canal was clean and we swam in it.

If food has featured large, it is because the uncertainty of finding any preoccupied us. The plenty we had come upon near the border had long since petered out and except in larger towns food was hard to find. Distances between towns were so enormous that it was difficult to carry enough to last. The problem was only mitigated by unsought largesse.

On 9 July we reached Volgograd. The sign at the boundary showed a nice sense of history, giving all three names by which the city had been known: Volgograd was writ large at the top, then Stalingrad in smaller letters and at the bottom Tsarytsyn. It was another major milestone and we seemed to have come a great distance, though geographically still in Europe.

The battle of Stalingrad was arguably the most important of all Second World War battles. The might of the German army and air force had swept through Eastern Europe, apparently unstoppable as it thundered in a great wave towards the Volga. It smashed down on Stalingrad in September 1942, a rock which by February 1943 had broken it. The eventual defeat of this onslaught greatly weakened Hitler's power both militarily and psychologically, marking the beginning of his end. But it was achieved at a cost almost inconceivable. Ninety per cent of the city was reduced to rubble. One and a half million Russian troops and a further half-million civilians died in its defence, while a million Germans also perished.

Today Volgograd is a beautiful city. No expense was spared in its reconstruction at the end of the war and the result is a spaciously laid out metropolis with pleasing neo-classical buildings, wide streets and leafy avenues. Its situation on the banks of the vast Volga river enhances its beauty. On the site of the fiercest fighting, on Mamayev Kurgan, is a poignant war memorial, constructed on a grand scale with huge heroic sculptures. Dominating this, and the skyline for many miles distant, is a colossus, the finely proportioned 52-metre/170-foot-high statue of Mother Russia, brandishing a sword. We were awed by what had been accomplished here. Just below, in a rotunda, is the Hall of Valour. Arranged around its walls are thirty-four lowered banners of red smalt, on which are incised seven thousand names, a tiny proportion of those who died. An eternal flame is held in an upraised hand and Schumann's 'Reverie' plays quietly in the background. Four soldiers, rigidly at attention with bayonets fixed, waxwork-like in their stillness, mount a poignant guard. It was easy to weep in that place.

Nowhere in the city is far from where the battle raged. Plaques and sometimes tank turrets commemorate points where the fight was most significant. Outside the Stalingrad tractor factory, which famously switched to the production of T-34 tanks, one tank stands sentinel. Near the centre of town is an excellent and comprehensive museum. At the top of it, a 360-degree panorama depicts the combat's last days and with imagination adding sound and smell, one can visualise a little of the horror and privation endured through that ghastly winter. Inside were many detailed exhibits; outside, tanks, artillery pieces and aircraft were displayed. Volgograd is appropriately twinned with another allied city which suffered hideous destruction in the war: Coventry.

Mail was always anticipated with eagerness. Among that received in Volgograd was bad news. Kate's stepmother Janet had died a month before. We were all concerned for

Grandpa, and Kate decided to return to Britain to be with him. Also she had been having dizzy spells, was feeling less and less well and needed a medical check. For four hundred dollars she could take the train, via Moscow, Minsk and Warsaw, to the Hook of Holland, and she left on 14 July.

'I took two suitcases of stuff to lighten the load in the caravan. With heavy heart, I was escorted by Torcuil, Eilidh and Fionn to the station in Volgograd. It was the worst parting in the whole seven years. Watching my three brave young children standing on the platform waving, the boys crying, was heart-rending. I hadn't even realised through my tears that I was to share my compartment for the twenty-two-hour journey with a man.' So began Kate's long journey. Her travelling companion was gallant and she had no problem with him. An English-speaking couple helped her with the transfer between stations in Moscow: 'They insisted on taking me by metro to where I was supposed to pick up my ticket for London, only to be told I had to go to another station. On arrival there, the office was shut for lunch and there was an enormous queue. My two guardian angels waited with me, and then, with Russian words flying in all directions, eventually procured my ticket. Then I was told my dollars were too old! Luckily I had newer ones and at last, clutching the precious ticket in a shaky, sweaty hand, I sat down to await the train.' She eventually arrived, exhausted but safe. We did not see her for seven months.

For five days we camped in a secluded spot north of the city, during which time we managed to restock with almost everything we needed. Urgently required new jerrycans were miraculously found at Univermag department store, 20-litre-capacity aluminium ones. I changed enough dollars to last until Alma-Ata. The risk of carrying so many roubles, albeit in our concealed compartment, had to be offset against not being able to exchange at all in remote areas. We had failed to find better maps; route information gleaned was variable and uncertain. The southerly course by Astrakhan and Guryev was apparently sandy and salty without grazing or good water, which, if true, meant travelling instead by Uralsk and Aktyoobinsk. But no one really knew.

The Volga, like the Dnepr, was crossed by a road running on top of a massive hydro dam. On the far side were the outskirts of dusty industrial Volzhskiyi. A battery of six chimneys fired forth foul fumes, the cooling towers of a power-station emanated slow clouds of vapour and on the horizon gas was flaring. Craters were being excavated alongside the road, at the bottom of which men were welding together sections of pipe. Lorries passed in profusion, kicking up layers of choking dust, and the noise was tremendous.

That evening Eilidh and I were cutting extra grass for Traceur when four Volga saloons drew in and parked nearby. A man came over and invited me to visit. I demurred but thought it best to be polite. The cars were carrying heads of state farms and a more senior supervisor with his son back from a meeting in Volgograd. All had chauffeurs, so were able to indulge in substantial shots of very smooth Rasputin vodka with their sandwiches. I was questioned about our trip, what I thought of Russia, of Gorbachev and Yeltsin, which called for adroit diplomatic answers as I had no idea of *their* views. Viktor Ragosa, director of Sovhoz Veliki Oktyaber in Solodushino, six days' travel away, insisted we must visit him when we got there. Dmitri, the supervisor's son, accompanied me back to the caravan. He had refused to say what he did in front of the others; now he said baldly, 'I'm a racketeer. The criminal police in Volgograd are after me, which is why I must go home with my father.' He had been making a million roubles a month, big money in Russia but not much more than an average wage in the UK. I felt rather sorry for him: he had a wife and daughter, had been tempted and was now one step ahead of paying the penalty.

Solodushino was on the river, about two kilometres off the road down a sandy track. Viktor was away when we arrived but his Kazakh deputy, Ivan, organised lunch for us in the canteen and hay for Traceur. The canteen lady took the children swimming in the Volga and Traceur was allowed to wander free, enjoying the company of the farm horses. It was cruelly hot, with high humidity but this did not deter a crowd of about fifty forming in the evening to view the exotic strangers.

The *sovhoz* had attractive wooden houses with prolific gardens, the central street was tree-lined and the place busy and dusty with an air of working scruffiness. Women were tipping baskets of *vishnya*, cherries, into a milk tanker for transport to Volgograd, to make cherry brandy. Someone hailed me. It was Viktor's wife, Svetlana.

Their cool and airy house was well furnished, with a well-equipped kitchen, and reminded me of the Balogs' house in the Ukraine. The big garden had loads of vegetables growing. Four pigs, some hens and ducks occupied the outbuildings. Fish hung up to dry in a netted cage and the children had a sand-pit to play in. Svetlana's eighty-seven-year-old grandmother lived with them and Viktor's parents were next door. They had two children, five-year-old Masha and three-year-old Dima (Dmitri), who, she told me, was a *hooligan* – a word English apparently shares with Russian. We were invited for supper that evening.

The party consisted of four Ragosas, four Grants, Svetlana's architect and sculptor brother Nikolai, Viktor's parents and deputy manager Ivan. Svetka, as everyone called Svetlana, and Viktor had been Komsomol members, which is how they had met. Viktor said that so far the political changes had not caused him many problems. We had *shashlik,* with new potatoes and salad, followed by tea, with a choice of several jams and honey for stirring into it, a common Russian custom. There was vodka, of course, and by the time a convivial evening ended in the small hours, the adults had averaged a pint apiece, about par for the course.

Viktor had sixteen wheel-nuts made for us, which was great because most of the original ones were burred and hard to turn. Svetka insisted we all came to tea, which meant soup, salad and *blinis* with cream and jam. She was a non-stop hive of energy, drying herbs, making jam, gardening and minding the hooligan and his much quieter sister. We much enjoyed the Ragosas' hospitality but Alma-Ata remained far off and it was time to go.

In Nikolaevsk, we shopped and enjoyed a cool drink of *kvass,* a weak but refreshing beer sold from small tanker-trailers at street corners. The day after we left, two old boys on a motorbike stopped to ask if we knew that Yeltsin had ordered all pre-1993 rouble notes recalled to prevent wholesale forgery. BBC news had mentioned it too. There was a limit of thirty-five thousand roubles on the total that could be exchanged. We had eighty-five thousand in notes dated 1992 from my transaction in Volgograd . . .

I left the children to take the caravan on by themselves next morning and biked back to the bank in Nikolaevsk. I was surprised to find only twenty or thirty people round the door. Then I realised it was *shut.* However, people were at work inside. A quick-witted member of staff, on her way out, learned of my difficulty and took me in to see the director, a hefty lady of middle years, smartly dressed in a hound's-tooth check suit, with a forbidding expression and a shock of red-dyed hair. Behind this grim exterior beat a kind heart. Not only did she agree to change our roubles on the spot but to change them all. In relief, on the way out I spontaneously planted a kiss on each of her cheeks. She was most astonished.

The rest of the town was pretty much closed down, the bazaar reduced to a dribble of stalls and customers, but I saw bread being delivered to the bakery. Terrific, I thought, as I joined the queue. Then the shopkeeper opened the doors, told everyone she had no money for change and closed them again, imprisoning about a thousand lovely fresh loaves unsold within. I caught up with the caravan just in time to help hump water-jerries. Later, stopped and deliberating about a parking-place, a bakery van pulled up. 'Would you like some bread?' asked the driver.

A statue of Pallas, standing by a pack-horse, graced the entrance to the lovely town of Pallasovka. A species of sand-grouse and a warbler both bear the name of this eighteenth-century naturalist. We called Kate, who was fine and glad to hear from us. The Kazakhstan frontier was only forty kilometres away. Flocks of sheep and herds of cattle, tended by mounted men or boys, ranged the flat steppe. Strips of wheat and oats were planted here and there. The roadside was fringed with scrubby trees, providing cover for hoopoes and collared doves.

Marat and Armin Ooteshkalyev, twelve and ten respectively, rode up to visit us on their horse Orlik on our penultimate evening in Russia. They were exceptionally polite and thoughtful by any standards, and Fionn and Eilidh got on especially well with them. I found it interesting to see how selective our children were in choosing others to associate with. Whenever we met nice children there was quick rapport; nationality and language barriers did not seem to affect this instinct. Eilidh and Fionn went off for rides on Orlik, while Marat and Armin came in to see the caravan. We had tea at their house, mutton on a bed of macaroni with a side salad of tomatoes and cucumber, provided by their mother Valya. A serious card-game involving the boys' father and some other men was in progress and Valya told me her husband's gambling was a problem. As a shepherd he received fifteen thousand roubles a month – but the stake was a thousand per game.

Marat came next morning, as arranged, for his lift to the next village. He chatted non-stop and was obviously proud to be sitting on the caravan. Though still just in Russia, the village was typical of many we should see in Kazakhstan: squat mud-brick buildings, dusty streets and lots of people milling about. The shop had nothing in it except salt. Marat helped us fill our water-jerries at the pump, then we said goodbye to him and trundled off down the road. It was August now and already the grass, which stretched to the horizon on all sides, was yellowing.

We were about to turn off the road for the night when the driver of a big blue Zil truck stopped and pointed. 'That's my house over there. You will please be my guests tonight.' So we were. The Baimuradovs were a Chechen family, moved there in 1944 by Stalin, at a time when many minorities he regarded as troublesome were sent away from their homelands. They killed a sheep in our honour and we dined on broiled mutton, traditional bread-cakes called *masli*, *shashlik* and salad. Nor were we let go without breakfast in the morning: more mutton, bread, jam and cream, with copious quantities of tea. The caravan was loaded with two sacks of barley, eggs, cheese, cucumbers, two onions, cream and a loaf before we fetched Traceur.

Thus laden, we put to and headed on down the road, out of Russia.

CHAPTER ELEVEN

KAZAKHSTAN: AUGUST 1993–JANUARY 1994
STEPPE AND SNOW

Very occasionally I would vaguely ask myself what the hell I was doing . . .

Lucy Irvine

A week after entering Kazakhstan everything went wrong. We were miles out on flat, grassy steppe, on gravel track where the map marked tarred road. Fionn had a persistent headache and fluctuating temperature. Torcuil exhibited similar symptoms. And Traceur was lame.

Our first evening we had dined with Dr Amangeldy Ootegenov and his family. He had warned us that a serious water-borne horse disease, *Sibirski yazva*, Siberian ulcer, was prevalent in the region and suggested we call at the next *sovhoz* to have Traceur vaccinated. He also gave us a magazine cutting about two Russians, who were setting off on a voyage round the world with two horses and a small cart. Their route was described: from Ivanovo to Sakhalin, into China, then in a big circle to Archangel. Momentous but hardly round the world. We were still the only expedition attempting that.

Traceur had his vaccination, which entailed a mandatory three-day rest afterwards. We spent it beside a small lake, a chance to wash clothes and tackle harness repairs.

We encountered our first Bactrian camels and nearly cap-
sized the caravan on a rough, sloping track to a well at
Sovhoz T. Zharokova. The Kazakhs were friendly but
incredibly nosy. On one occasion two women climbed into
the caravan and demanded our autographs without so much
as by-your-leave.

In the middle of the night Torcuil was violently sick. He
had a splitting headache as well. I put this down to too
much sun as it had been fiercely hot and he had spent a lot
of time swimming the previous day. However, by morning
he still had a headache and Fionn, who had had one off and
on for three days, said his was worse. There were no
symptoms of meningitis but analgesics had no effect and I
could give the boys no relief. Both had temperatures and
Fionn began vomiting, so I determined to consult a doctor –
if one could be found.

Eilidh posted off on our remaining Muddy Fox – the
Purple Fox, as we called it to distinguish it from the smaller
yellow one which, outgrown, had been given to friends in
Slovenia – to see what she could root out of the shops and
to ask about doctors. She returned triumphant. She had
arranged for a doctor to call, and bought bread, rice,
macaroni, toffees and three jars of an unheard-of treat. *Jam!*
True, we were occasionally offered jam, to put in tea, when
visiting people, but finding jars of it in shops was most
unusual.

The doctor gave Fionn an injection in his posterior.
Stoically he never squeaked. I had given the doctor one of
our syringes and needles to use, because they were short of
such things and I knew ours were sterile. Probably hers
were, too, but there was no point taking chances. Torcuil's
temperature was down from over 102°F to 100°F (39°C to
38°C) by the evening, but Fionn still had his headache.

Next day was hot and humid, produced a surprise short

shower and went back to being hot again. Despite the boys' headaches and high temperatures, I determined to go on. They were well enough to travel as long as they remained in bed. Between us Eilidh and I managed the work. We stopped at a *tochka*, shepherd's house, to fill the water-jerries. The well had an ingenious motor-driven rotating belt. This brought the water up about eight feet. It clung to the belt by surface tension and was scraped off by a pair of rubber 'lips', to flow down a short pipe into a trough. It was good water, too, which was not always the case.

Traceur adored the fluffy steppe grass but the flies drove him berserk. Small black brutes like quarter-sized house-flies descended on him in clouds and bit and bit, drawing blood. His fly-rug gave only limited protection. He had begun to go worryingly lame behind at times but there was no obvious cause.

The steppe imperceptibly began changing from table-top flatness to gentle undulation. Steppe eagles perched on every other telegraph pole, abundant *suslik*, ground squirrels, providing easy dinners for them. We passed a dry lake and came to another *tochka,* which had stacks of what appeared to be peat drying. It had been dug one spade deep and left to dry *in situ,* before being stacked. I became instantly homesick until I discovered it was not peat but hard-trampled sheep shit, the product of the flock's previous wintering, closely confined in pens. It made excellent fuel, burned with a good heat and left almost no ash. We watered from another belt-pump, bought some mutton and headed off again.

Traceur suddenly became desperately lame. We pulled off and parked immediately, not far from a lake. I could see about twenty white herons, several grey herons, well over a hundred cranes and a number of ducks and geese on or around the water. But bird-watching had to wait. We were far from succour, with limited food supplies, an extremely lame horse and the boys were continuing to manifest wildly fluctuating temperatures and headaches. I had been pressing on to reach a town as fast as possible in case they became worse, or I should have rested Traceur sooner. Now there was no option. I was extremely concerned.

Next morning Traceur's left hind fetlock was hot and swollen. It could only be tendon trouble but I had no means of alleviating it except letting him rest. We needed a doctor, and a vet too. I hitched a lift to *Sovhoz* Terenkul, twelve kilometres away, to seek help.

Bulat Aitmyxanov, the director of the *sovhoz,* could not have done more for us. I was sent back to the caravan with a vet, in a battered old black Volga saloon driven by a delightful, cheery character called Zhenis Gubaev. The vet felt Traceur's legs carefully, said he had inflammation of the tendon sheaths, a common ailment here, and would be all right in a short time. He prescribed two ampoules of camphor oil to be rubbed in twice daily for five days. The *sovhoz* would arrange for a doctor to visit and ensure that we were supplied with food and water while we were stopped. Laws of hospitality applied: we were their guests.

To my astonishment the swelling on Traceur's fetlock was almost gone next morning and he was no longer limping – but I discovered a nasty cut on his coronet on the same leg. That afternoon a high-level delegation, consisting of the *sovhoz* director and vet, with the *rajon* and *oblast* vets, visited him. I was taking photographs when Tsar, barking furiously, suddenly lunged out and his chain snapped. He tore after the *sovhoz* vet and sank his teeth into his calf. Seldom have I felt so embarrassed but the vet was very good about it and doctored himself from his bag. It must have hurt like hell.

Torcuil remained abed, Fionn was still weak and I was

wilting. Even Eilidh's apparently inexhaustible dynamo showed signs of fatigue. I had rarely had more than six hours' straight sleep in the five months since we left Hungary. Our diet remained more or less balanced but was not always adequate, and sometimes the children did not like what we were able to get.

Then I got the bug.

I had never experienced a headache like it. I woke at two o'clock in the morning thinking that someone had cleaved my skull with an axe. My temperature seesawed between 100°F and 102°F, exactly as the boys' had. A doctor eventually came but could not diagnose what we were suffering from. Symptoms resembled brucellosis but she thought that unlikely as cattle hereabouts were free of it. She took a blood sample for analysis but we never did discover what it was we had had.

When at last we were all fit to travel again, and had given presents of Dalvey flasks and expedition T-shirts to the *sovhoz* staff, we continued eastward towards Chapaev and the Ural river. Just after the next town, Kaztalovka, a combination of weakness from fever, accumulated tiredness and being sole adult combined to drive me wild. We had had a successful visit to the town, acquired a new Russian gas cylinder and an abundance of provisions. However, the rough roads had reopened the cut on Traceur's coronet. In treating it things did not go smoothly and all three children did trivially silly things. Something in me snapped. I roared at the kids and reduced even Eilidh to tears. They had been silly – who on Earth would produce an Elastoplast to bandage a horse's foot? – but hardly deserved quite such a bawling out. I felt suddenly totally unsupported, the whole weight of three years travel with all the responsibility pressing on me, far from anywhere, unable to communicate, Traceur apparently groggy again and no one to share the burden with. The latter was the crux: lack of another adult to share it all. The children were so good, so competent and so loyal that I felt guilty at having lashed out at them – no one could have wished for better travelling companions – but they were not adults and could not be expected to comprehend the mental strains, which now and then became too much to bottle up.

A new concern about Traceur arose from head-shaking, an imperfectly understood affliction I had never heard of at that time. It manifested itself in frightening fashion. Without warning he began throwing his head up and down so violently he became uncontrollable. I thought initially he had been bitten or stung. He then snuffled the road with his nose before another bout of wild head-shaking. Later we found putting a rug over his head calmed him and he could even be driven while thus blindfolded. The few times he exhibited this behaviour subsequently was on hot, close, muggy days, often with thunder threatening; the cool of evening always brought an end to it.

The morning after this alarming experience I discovered Traceur's right eye weeping copiously, with an opaque patch over the pupil. He had damaged the cornea, almost certainly when rolling and scratching in the prickly steppe grasses, perhaps piercing it with a thorn. He was not blind: the intricate workings of iris and pupil were unimpaired, and seemed unaffected by what became a permanent opaque spot on the surface of the cornea.

One evening the director of Sovhoz Sarikiylik stopped and invited us to visit. 'When will you be passing?' he asked.

'About nine a.m. tomorrow,' I replied.

'Fine. We shall expect you for breakfast.'

Director Sarsenby awaited us next morning, dressed in a powder-blue suit, dark blue shirt, pale blue tie and immaculate pale blue suede shoes. We filled our jerries and settled Traceur before following him to his wood-panelled office. Before us in the well-appointed room, stood a long table heaped with large bowls full of apples, tomatoes and slices of bread; smaller bowls contained *kurt* – curds – roasted wheat, sliced tomatoes, a type of sweet yoghurt and raisins. Beyond it was a glass-fronted cabinet filled with books, and a substantial desk covered in papers, three telephones and a two-way radio. On the wall hung a portrait of Lenin, while on top of the free-standing TV set was a small cast aluminium bust of him reading a newspaper.

A number of men filed in and it became apparent we were to eat with the *sovhoz* department heads – '*Moj apparat*', as the director called them. A basin, kettle of hot water and towel were brought for us to wash our hands and we were then bidden to table. Plates of cold lamb garnished with tomato and spring onion were served, then plates of hot spaghetti with lamb. Tea was brought. 'Eat! Eat!' they urged. It was very good. I particularly liked the roast wheat, which one dipped into with a teaspoon loaded with thick cream and the fine-ground wheat with sweet yoghurt.

As we ate, first the director, then several of the department heads made informal speeches of welcome. Of course I had to reply, I am sure less than adequately but my words seemed to go down all right. The finance chief, a man we all took to, then presented me with the metal bust of Lenin. There was entertainment too. Two women and a teenage boy in costume played *dombra*s, elegant two-stringed instruments with slender necks and bowl-shaped soundboxes. They sang individually, strange, harsh songs. Were they of war? Love? Beautiful women? Beautiful horses? Or just about meeting this year's production norms? I wished we could have known. After the music everyone went outside to be photographed and to watch an agile youth leap on and off a rather unco-operative horse. The immense trouble

Director Sarsenby and his people had gone to on our behalf had shown us another facet of Kazakhstan and given us a memorable event to add to our experiences.

The road to Chapaev began to seem infinite but with only eighty-nine kilometres to go – only fifty-one to tarred road – the questions were, would Traceur stay fit and would the rain hold off?

The rain didn't hold off. In two hours it turned hard track to glutinous mud. Multiwheel-drive trucks were slithering about and sticking. Traceur had no hope of pulling the caravan through it. We had already lost eleven days we could ill-afford, so rather than wait till the mud dried, I arranged a tractor tow to the start of the tarred road.

Chapaev was pleasant. We got almost all we needed there and telephoned Kate to update her on progress. Eilidh, Fionn and I went to have a look at the ferry across the Ural, to find *it did not exist*. Instead there was a pontoon bridge, with two half-sections missing from the downstream side. Not a happy prospect but I thought we could manage it. We walked across the river, which marks the eastern geographical boundary of Europe, past several fishermen, and set foot in Asia. The road, marked on the map as asphalt, was not even a track, just a sort of sand soup, used by large tractors and 6×6-wheel-drive trucks. We should have to detour 130 kilometres north to Uralsk and back down to reach Dzhambetoo, 100 kilometres east. It would cost five more precious days and already it was 26 August. Alma-Ata was still more than three months away.

The immensity of the steppe: a trite phrase to describe the ocean of grass on which we were embarked. Every day brought something fresh, a new species of bird or mammal, an unusually kind gift or a surprise invitation to someone's house. The long rolling road, adequately surfaced, had a thin but constant stream of traffic along it. Our daily routine varied little, except when Traceur required shoeing or lack of clean clothes enforced a laundry day. August passed into September, and as October approached temperatures were falling fast. Obtaining commodities of every sort, including food, remained chancy, as always, but whenever we despaired of finding a pot of jam, a packet of Elastoplast or shoes for Torcuil, we would come upon somewhere that had them. Tsar's staple diet was tins of *kasha*, augmented when possible by meat, but he was a lean and hungry Komondor at times, for he was a fussy eater. One day Eilidh discovered a lump on his leg, from which I plucked eight fat maggots; goodness knows how he got them but they must have been uncomfortable. Traceur remained sound and, with the advent of cooler weather, ceased to have bouts of head-shaking. Every night, the progress line on our map was extended another centimetre.

I cursed the strips of trees planted along the roadsides as they were scrubby, unattractive and obscured the view. However, I revised my opinion the first time strong winds howled across the steppe. Traceur's life would have been hell without the trees to shelter the road from the worst of the blast. It often rained, especially overnight, and more than once we had to be towed back on to the road from what had been a firm enough place when we had parked on it the night before.

On Fionn's ninth birthday, his presents were the best to be had in Uralsk: a plastic lorry with four interchangeable bodies, a model aircraft kit, a propelling pen, a puzzle book and a Mars bar. Sadly no cake, but we made pancakes, which went down well after a big feed of corned beef – from tins bought in Volgograd – mashed potatoes and tomato sauce.

Scenically, the steppe was monotonous. It was the characters we met every day, who made life interesting. Why should a judge and his advocate wife travel in a battered twenty-six-year-old Gaz jeep – and give us five melons? Was it *really* normal for a couple of militia captains to procure two sacks of barley for visiting foreigners then offer *sto gram* of vodka, which ended in us finishing the bottle? How usual was it for television journalists to invite their interviewees for baths? Did everyone buy their meat from people who carried a pig carcase in the boot of their car?

Our chief difficulty at this time was getting water. Distances between villages were great, rivers and streams few. Once Torcuil and Eilidh, armed with empty jerries, hitched a lift to the nearest well and were away for four hours. Their return was heralded by the roar of engines as two big Kamaz articulated lorries, driven by a couple of nice Russians, thundered up to the caravan. If you throw up your hands in horror at my allowing young children to do this, I can only reply that the risk was minimal. There may have been Mafiosi in Moscow but in rural Kazakhstan there was little danger to a pair of scruffy-looking kids. It might possibly have been different if they had been dressed in brand-new sweaters and trainers but I doubt it. People were intensely curious about us, but while they sometimes disturbed our peace they were not covetous and we never felt threatened.

At Dzhembetoo the post office could not change a 5000-rouble note and the bank was shut but I got change at the chemist's, where I bought French soluble aspirin and some sticking-plaster. The telephone system was Noah's ark but efficient, and after a half-hour wait we were talking loud and clear to a sleepy Kate at 6.30 a.m. UK time. Amazingly the hardware store had a stock of shoes and I bought trainers for Fionn and shoes for myself but there were none in Torcuil's size. On the way out a bunch of twelve-year-old boys pestered us, a couple of whom threw stones. Several times we had had bother from boys of this age – always boys – the worst case being the evening before, when Torcuil, on reconnaissance, had come out of a shop to find the Purple Fox flung into the mud, reflectors, gears and gear-guard damaged. Such nastiness was fortunately not the norm.

The steppe looked empty but there was usually a *tochka* somewhere and always wildlife. An extract from my diary gives a good idea of conditions and the country we were travelling through by mid-September:

Autumn roared down the wind this morning, blasting leaves off trees and bringing portent of winter. Low grey stratus clouds scudded eastward. Yellowing leaves told of summer's end. I slept badly, waking at every blatter of heavy rain on the roof.

We were travelling by 8.30 and soon came to the junction of the road from Komintern, then shortly after to a dramatic change in landform, for abruptly we were on sandy ground. The road remained tarred but we had a change of vegetation from steppe grass to low bushy plants and clumps of willow and other trees. Some south-bound swallows passed, making a circuit or two of us in the hope of finding insects disturbed by our passage. Steppe eagles looked down lugubriously from atop tele-graph poles and sometimes brilliant bee-eaters called and cavorted among the roadside trees. Wherever there was water, a stream, river or lake, there were duck, such as teal, shoveller and mallard. Cattle and a distant *tochka* could be seen and a herdsman came up to have a look at us before cantering back to his beasts.

We came to the river Tamdi and decided to fill jerries

for Traceur there, as it looked reasonable water and we still had plenty aboard for ourselves. This was a good move as it enabled us to take a track off and stop an hour later.

This ground had an extensive flora, including plenty grasses, where we stopped amongst the small trees. We had seen a young hedgehog dead on the road and a spotted a *phyloscopus* warbler but small birds were difficult to identify whilst we were on the move.

Tonight we have a good feed coming up: mutton lightly stewed with fresh aubergine, tomatoes, light-fried onions, using garlic, rosemary and coriander, accompanied by potatoes mashed with cream, butter and milk. Honeydew melon to follow. As the fire is on, I shall make plum jam too, from the rather inedible ones we were given recently. Traceur was fine and did not even sweat under the saddle.

On reflection, this was a rather better day than usual, foodwise, but not untypical.

Stresses occasionally surfaced. For example, Torcuil could be very pernickety about hygiene. One lunchtime one of us jokingly switched my fork for his. He was about to eat off it when he realised what had been done, became extremely upset, and barged out of the caravan in his slippers leaving two fried eggs to go cold. He was away for an hour and it took considerable coaxing to induce him to return and eat. We were all capable of similar tantrums and moods from the strains of the journey but they did not happen often.

There was never any shortage of people to talk to along the way. They included three men from Baikonur, a kind English teacher in Novoalexeyevka, a doctor and a fisheries ecologist. An ex-submariner, who donated oats and a most welcome selection of vegetables, told us he had seen a great deal of the coasts of Sweden and Norway during his three-year service in the Baltic. It was watermelon season and at one point we had ten in the caravan, weighing almost a hundred kilos and taking up a lot of room. Even Fionn's passion for them waned – for a while.

Aktyoobinsk was a large town devoted chiefly to servicing and maintaining aircraft, especially Yak-40s. The unlovely approach took us past a depot piled with innumerable bales of wool, with nine filthy smoking chimneys beyond, two petrol stations, an LPG gas store, blocks of flats and a huge *gai* post, which disgorged a dozen or more curious coppers anxious to see us. In answer to my query they said we might be able to buy horseshoe nails from gypsies to the south of town but to be careful as some were not to be trusted. We passed a park displaying historic aircraft types and in light traffic reached Lenina Prospekt and the head post office. We had expected mail here, including a replacement pulse-unit for the electric fence. There was nothing.

Sunday 26 September: 'Cold enough to snow,' I wrote in my diary. And it did. 'Eeahhh. Bloody hell!' said Fionn. To add to the joys of this untimely and unwelcome change in the weather, Torcuil had been sick in the night and had a slight temperature. Striding along beside Traceur I became chilled, and after Eilidh had made the breakfast toast she took the reins while I dug out winter clothes for everybody and donned thermal underwear.

The outskirts of Alga were like some vision of hell abandoned. A huge derrick dominated an apparently derelict factory shed. Two colossal boilers and a great red-brown gantry lay to one side of it. On the other side, another vast building, equally dilapidated, was covered in what looked like lime or flour. The corrugated sheeting was falling off its sides, windows were missing and two tall chimneys stuck up from the middle with steam rising from them. On the opposite side of the road were bright iridescent green lakes, polluted and sterile, with outflows to a river. This appalling place was a hydrochloric-acid factory.

Wildlife had gone to ground. Temperatures were down to –5°C/23°F. A man in a Moskvitch car stopped and jumped out brandishing a vacuum flask and a bag of buns. The hot, sweet, milky tea was just the thing on a cold morning. Near Oktyabirsk we saw two Berliet trucks belonging to the French Girault company, engaged in oil exploration operations between there and Guryev to the west. In town we met the Adjoint au Responsable Opérations (Temir), Daniel Gaultier de Carville, who kindly agreed to take some films back to France for posting. Kazakh post was unreliable and I never trusted precious film to it.

It warmed up a little. Traceur almost trod on a sleepy snake. Zhurin rhymed with urine, which about summed the village up, for it was a muddy, dirty hole. A strong head-wind blew against the caravan front, making Traceur's job tough but luckily only for a day. We drove a kilometre along a track beside the river Kolbenen-Temir and parked for a much-needed day off, to wash clothes, clean tack, change Traceur's front shoes – and relax, if there was time to, after all that.

Traceur was not in as good condition as I should have liked to withstand the onset of winter. Something among the steppe grasses he was eating caused frequent diarrhoea, though I never pinned it down to a specific plant. I beefed up his feed to about 35 pounds per day, plus hay. This sounds excessive but he worked hard and I suspected the barley or oats we got were often of poor quality. We ourselves were well, apart from an occasional bout of 'runs'.

White wagtails and wheatears accompanied us south-wards, with now and then an eagle or falcon being spotted, but as October advanced it became windy, wet and unsettled and we did not see many birds. One particularly vile day, parked in slight shelter in a dip, Traceur well rugged up, with the fire going and Torcuil's choice of tape playing, a lorry came up and the driver asked if we needed barley. At the moment it was required, we got a sack of excellent grain. This sort of thing happened so frequently, I no longer believed it was coincidence. Someone 'up there' was looking after us.

The outside world rarely impinged but we kept an ear on it through our radio, mostly using BBC World Service. We heard Kevin Connolly describe rioting in Moscow as 'the worst street violence since the Bolshevik revolution' as Rutskoi stirred up demonstrators, Hasbulatov and the old guard challenged Yeltsin yet again and a state of emergency was declared. I thought the effects unlikely to be felt in Kazakhstan, unless the rouble tumbled – or if Yeltsin were deposed. Elsewhere, Georgia appeared to be falling apart as Aphazia split away; Bosnia looked set for further fighting as the Muslims rejected a peace plan unjustly giving Serbs land they had taken by force. In India, ten thousand people died in an earthquake with a final toll of thirty thousand predicted.

It was a pleasure when we came to hills again, albeit only distant 2000 footers, as we descended towards Emba. Occasionally we came to places that seemed entirely negative and Emba was one of these. The approach was through scenes of dereliction along bumpy roads. The town was noisy, smelly and dirty, the people unhelpful. We had difficulty finding a water-pump and when we did, the water tasted strongly of iron. Two women standing beside half a dozen big round bales of hay refused to let Eilidh fill a hay-net. The post office could not produce any of the new 90-rouble airmail envelopes, or stamps to upgrade my 50-rouble ones. I snagged my right welly-boot on barbed wire and tore a hole in it, and on the way out some kids, who were trying to get a ride, had to be yanked off the back of the caravan by Eilidh. The only redeeming feature of the place was a nice lad who got us some hay and his mate who gave us a jar of sour cream.

There were camels about again as we drove southerly, stalking their stately way over the steppe, and quite a lot of migrating birds, including a flock of twenty-odd lapwings. A series of low ridges made a change from the endless flat plain. Missiles were being fired on a distant range west of us, presumably being tracked by the radar stations set back against the hills. The air was crystal clear. Torcuil went on a mammoth forty-four-kilometre round-trip cycle ride to Mugodzharskoe. During the night we were disturbed by a truck stopping and its driver shouting at us, not the first time this had happened. A marble catapulted against the vehicle door usually removed such pests. Visitors in the small hours were unwelcome and unlikely to be friendly and I took no chances, for we were very vulnerable.

In the hills silver birch trees lined the banks of the burns. Larks, chaffinches and wheatears were common, and we found a small pretty falcon of a species new to us dead on the road. The road descended to another, drier plain and ceased to be tarred. An old herder rode up to us on an eighteen-month-old chestnut, which he said cost him twelve thousand roubles – around ten pounds. What price Traceur, I mused, knowing we should never contemplate selling our big pal.

Most Kazakhs were friendly, kind and helpful, but often pestered us with the daftest questions: 'Is this your horse? Is that your dog? Are these your children?' as well as the usual where were we from and where were we going. They almost all had yellow- or brown-stained teeth and never walked if there was a horse, tractor or car to hand. They were generous and as difficult to pay as the Ukrainians and Russians had been. At Kompressornoe we got a bit of beef from three men with blood to their elbows, who were butchering a cow. As we travelled on, the steppe to the east remained pristine, unchanged for millennia, but to the west marched a line of concrete poles carrying electricity wires, and distant caterpillar-like trains crawled along the barely visible track. Genghis Khan would have been astonished – though the trains were probably slower than his famed mounted messengers, who galloped from Mongolia to the Polish border in two weeks, tied into their saddles so they would not fall off when fatigue came upon them and they dozed.

On 11 October we camped within sight of Chelkar. Next morning we had a lot of provisioning to do before tackling the long empty stretch of track down to Aralsk, so we made an early start. The two men who had so kindly given us a sack of barley on that wet evening ten days before, Khambal Zaritov and Rakhim Magdeev, greeted us on the outskirts. They were in a Lada Niva this time, and having ascertained we needed to go to town, Khambal said he would take us in. They were Tatars, friends and business associates, whose families had fled, or been deported, during one of Stalin's periodic purges in Tatarstan. Tatarstan Autonomous Republic lies on the Volga river, centred round its capital, Kazan, and is still populated mainly by Muslim Tatars, descendants of the Mongol horde and the peoples it conquered when it swept westward in the thirteenth century.

With their help we sped through our shopping list with ease. We were talking about our onward travel and I explained we were going to go south via the railway. 'But you can't,' said Rachim. 'There's no road, just twenty kilometres of sand dunes.'

The main road, which ran east to connect with the M32

by Irgiz, was houseless, shopless and, most seriously, waterless, for 300 kilometres. Impossible for us. On the way back to the caravan, through this attractive desert-edge town with its extensive lakes, we discussed what might be done. Irgiz was out. The railway would charge a fortune and anyway, there was no lifting gear in Chelkar to load the caravan. To cross the sand would require a 6×6 tow-truck . . . and a gleam came into Khambal's eye. He went off to do some 'arranging'. I gave him five thousand roubles for petrol for the Niva and another four thousand for a bottle of vodka. The former was a thank-you present; the latter turned out to be the price of 'hiring' an ex-army Ural 6×6 to pull us through the dunes.

So soft was the going that we had to stop and deflate the tyres. The caravan ones had to be done individually but the Ural's monsters could be deflated by a central control. Eilidh had set off ahead on Trass but we overtook her. Midway, we came to a flat place with grass and a thatched mud hut, protected from camels by a thorn hedge. An old woman was drawing water from a well, similarly protected. It was reminiscent of a Saharan Tuareg hut, even to the utensils hanging in the thorn-bushes and pans full of water by the door. We got route directions from the woman's son, siphoned off some diesel for his tractor and were given fermented camel's milk, *kumiss*, in exchange. I rather liked its tangy sour-fresh flavour.

The track became so soft the Ural stuck. The caravan was unhitched, the truck driven to the top of the next ridge and the winch-wire paid out. I hooked the caravan on, it was winched up, then rehitched. We went a little faster after this, to avoid a repeat performance. The track snaked about between the dunes, which were covered sparsely with low, tough, scrubby bushes. Abruptly, we emerged clear of sand and in sight of the railway. Descending to a *tochka*, inhabited by friends of Rachim, we drank more *kumiss*, accompanied by bread, spread with the thickest cream I had ever seen. When Eilidh caught up, Khambal pulled us another kilometre, 'to make sure', but the track was firm. We uncoupled from the massive Ural and said a grateful farewell to the Tatars. They did not ask for payment but this time I insisted. They had saved us at best the need to hire a vehicle to accompany us with water and food to Irgiz; at worst an ignominious retreat to Aktyoobinsk.

The track paralleled the railway and for the next three days we had a peaceful time. If we had not fully realised it before, we were now really in Central Asia. There was not a Caucasian face to be seen, camels stravaiged across the steppe and the few houses were constructed of mud and lath. Small settlements, railway halts, housing invariably friendly track-maintenance men and their families, provided us with water. We waved to passing trains and they whistled back. The going was firm and the grazing good.

Beyond Shilikti, a second, shorter stretch of sand barred our way. This time the local *sovhoz* director provided a Gaz 4×4 to tow us. The vehicle was too light and the driver clumsy, so we stuck a lot. He banged and bumped the caravan mercilessly each time to get going again and I was relieved when we reached firm track with the turntable undamaged.

The country was dry, the temperature averaging 10°C/ 50°F, as we dropped down a series of ridges towards the depression containing what remains of the Aral Sea. We were reduced to lunching on caviar, for which none of us cared much, and using sugar instead of jam, because stocks of nearly everything were low. There had not been a shop since Chelkar – a week and nearly a hundred kilometres ago. Three men brought us some dried meat and told us there were wolves in the area, that a metre of snow was usual in winter and gave us information about watering points on the way to Turkestan.

In Saksaoulskyi the shops were shut – because the shop-keepers were all out looking at us! A minor triumph occurred when at last we found a pair of shoes for Torcuil. Just in time, too, for the soles of his boots were threatening imminently to depart from the uppers. He had to settle for best leather-look black plastic in a grievous style, but at least they were a good fit.

Aralsk was horrible. An old man warned me to watch out for the children in town. '*Hooligani*,' he cautioned. Another man pulled up alongside in his car and said, 'The shops will be shut from twelve till three. Would you come and have lunch at my house?' Our visit to Dr Gabit Nurgalyev's was the sole pleasure we had in that place. Traceur was taken to an enclosed yard, while the caravan, minus removables, was locked and left at the gate. We took off our shoes at the door, as was usual here, and in we went. The first and most surprising thing about a Kazakh house to a Westerner is the total lack of tables and chairs or, indeed, any furniture, other than mats, rugs, cushions and wall-hangings: the lifestyle of nomads transferred to a permanent dwelling. The kitchen did have a table; there was a TV, telephone, coat-stand and a raised bed for the adults. It was stark to our eyes but comfortable enough.

Gabit's daughter Goolya served us side dishes of raisins, dried apricots and fresh pears. The first course was a huge dish of mutton pieces served on flat sheets of pasta, ornamented with tomatoes and carrots and accompanied by a side salad. Buckets of tea with bread and a choice of apricot or strawberry jams followed. Then, when I thought all was done, another enormous platter of mutton and potatoes arrived. Before we left, Gabit's neighbour, a frail old lady with all-gold teeth, provided us with a bale of good hay, a real boon because hay was almost non-existent in the region.

Tsar was cowering under the caravan when we came out. Sweet little boys had been stoning him. There were more nasty brats at the market. Eilidh, Fionn and Goolya, who had come with us, went shopping while Torcuil and I stood guard. A couple of militia stopped their car and advised us not to stay long. *'Mnogi hooligani,'* they warned. I believed them. The place had an unquiet air of petty malevolence about it. The shoppers reappeared and we moved out. A crowd of rough-looking kids trailed us and when Eilidh dropped a thousand-rouble note a boy grabbed it – but a girl made him give it back. One could not blame these children. They were living in one of the most destitute places in a country with a near-bankrupt economy. Once a thriving fishing-port, the diversion of the Syr Darya and Amur Darya rivers for cotton irrigation had not only dried up the Aral, leaving the port of Aralsk fifty miles from the water, it had removed its prosperity, its *raison d'etre* and major source of employment.

Eilidh turned twelve the day we were in Aralsk and had a non-birthday, her presents being three cards, some money and a few trinkets, with soup for birthday supper. Traceur's food had all but run out and he faced the prospect of three days without hard feed. At least water was not a problem. Two hundred metres from the road lay a huge water-pipe running all the way to Kazalinsk. The frequent valves, requiring only a spanner to open a flow of water to a relief pipe, were in cavernous concrete housings, reached by entering a manhole and descending a ladder. We used this system for several days, the fastest jerry filling ever, though it was difficult to avoid a soaking in the process from the gushing high-pressure outlet. Three men from Turkestan gave us a huge bag of meat. It was saiga, a wild bovine which frequents the Steppe, and most welcome, for only two small tins of mutton and some dried salted ribs remained. They also gave us their telephone numbers. In the village of Aralkum we scrounged three buckets of *kombi korm,* mixed meal, for Trassy. Somehow we stayed ahead of hunger.

The day we reached Chumish started cold. I was back into thermal underwear and the children into thick sweaters. We had pulled on to the road, and Traceur was in high spirits after a good night's grazing, only to go lame with a recurrence of tendonitis. Fortunately Chumish station was visible not far ahead and he limped the four kilometres to it.

Chumish was a slightly bigger halt than most. I went to the station office to ask whether we might stay a few days to rest Traceur's leg. One of the officials knew about us, which eased explanation of our difficulty. In the midst of discussion, the bread train arrived. We had wondered how the stations were supplied and here was the answer. I bought five loaves. We were told to park in the lee of a row of wagons awaiting repair and to take coal from the stockpile. We got water from a standpipe across the tracks and there was grazing at hand for Traceur. They also gave us hay. We were lucky to have found such a friendly place to be stuck in, though the feed problem remained and I could have wished we had more camphor oil to rub into the affected leg. Elliman's embrocation made an adequate substitute.

Trouble was not confined to Traceur that day. Torcuil complained of a tummy-ache, Fionn was sick and Eilidh slipped, barked her shin on the shafts and fainted on the footboard climbing into the caravan.

Our prime mentor in Chumish was machinist-in-charge Aleg Ainigazov. Eilidh and I went to fetch a sack of barley from him and were invited for a cup of tea, which always meant a snack as well, in this case salt fish, bread and onion. We were introduced to his wife, Bibi, and their three children, Gala, aged nine, son Toxa, who was seven and wee Gala, three. Their mud-built house was warm and pleasant, with thick carpets on the floor and whitewashed interior walls decorated with hangings. Adding to its charm, nothing about the building was quite straight or level. Outside was a big *serai* for sheep, goats and a calf. Bibi took down the *dombra*, which was hanging on a wall and handed it to Aleg, who played and sang for us. 'Do you know Catherine?' he asked at one point. We didn't, but it transpired a European woman of that name, apparently alone, had passed by some time before, riding a horse.

Profiting from misfortune, I cleaned the filthy tack, the children washed clothes and I repaired the hand-brake cable again. More excitingly, the children had a ride on a fine big pale-coloured male camel. We attended Grandpa Ainigazov's eightieth birthday party and gave Bibi a tube of antibiotic ointment for a painful stye she had in one eye. The boys and I paid an educational visit to the station control office, where radio contact was maintained with other stations and with engine-drivers. I listened to Thoreau's *Walden* being read on World Service. Familiar robins, chaffinches and goldcrests were about and a hundred-odd rooks resided in the trees. Traceur was sound again, but we were still short of food for him.

On the road the following day, Torcuil volunteered to cycle to the next station in search of horse feed. Not five minutes on his way, a lorry stopped and offered to give him a half-sack of *kombi korm*, which Traceur loved. Yet again our needs were fulfilled in unlooked-for fashion.

Sugar-frosted flat steppe stretched cold and empty to every horizon under pewter grey skies. A fanged wind tested every crease and seam in our clothing, penetrating our bodies, sinking its teeth into exposed parts. The caravan looked like some monstrous cake-decoration while Traceur, ageing overnight, had developed a white mane. Behind us the ruined mud-brick mosque in the lee of which we had parked resembled a cream-topped jelly quivering in the blast. It was November, the temperature −4°C/25°F, snow on the ground, a thin west-south-west wind slicing at everything. Weather to expect wolves in.

We had over twelve hundred kilometres still to go – or three months. Winter snapped at our heels but there was nothing we could do except press on. Everyone we met said it would be warmer further south.

The snow remained and the temperature stayed below freezing in the mornings, as we worked our way towards Leninsk. Wildlife was less frequent now for the chill had driven wild things away or to deep cover. One early November morning I looked up just after we set off and said casually, 'Look, there's a wolf crossing the road.' And it was. A cheeky, nonchalant, quite small, sandy wolf, which we had an excellent view of as it strolled away. A dead horse in the ditch had been its breakfast.

The dreary hunt for supplies was a fact of daily life. We always found something but never everything. Occasionally, we encountered hostility. The atmosphere in the village of Toguz had been unfriendly and we were refused hay there. A small horde of aggressive children would have stoned us, had adults not prevented them. On another occasion, a village was apparently deserted. Knocking on house doors to ask for hay produced no response and we found the water-pump padlocked. No one came to assist and in desperation I cut the thin wire securing the padlock, with the intention of starting the pump. Immediately a foul little man appeared, with a crowd in his wake. He berated us and, almost unthinkably in this nomadic culture, refused us water. Another time, Torcuil had a nasty encounter with six men on a tractor and trailer. They threatened to beat him up if he did not hand over his watch and said they would take his bike too, but another vehicle came by and he was able to pedal away unscathed. These exceptions were more than counterbalanced by the kind, thoughtful folk, a legion of mostly anonymous helpers.

The children were stalwart and worked like Trojans. We all had to, just to keep ourselves and Traceur fed and the caravan warm. One morning Eilidh was in a mood, which I found so funny I got the giggles – which made her mad and me laugh more. Her retaliation was to sing over and over again 'There is nothing like a boat ride, there is nothing like a boat ride.' I countered that with 'Lloyd George knew my father, my father knew Lloyd George' equally monotonously. We kept at it for half an hour or more till we both ran out of steam.

Wood for the stove was collected mainly from the roadside and occasional clumps of trees. Coal became a useful addition, because it kept the fire in overnight. We scrounged it from stations and an occasional lorry driver would stop and donate a bucket of *ugl* from his load.

A regular supply of hay was essential but because we could carry so little at a time it was the most difficult commodity to find. This was especially true while we were traversing cotton country from Kyzl-Orda to beyond Turkestan, with snow covering what little grass there was. We were often on the verge of running out, and bundles of reed hay, which Traceur did not much like, were sometimes all we could get. Traceur himself was remarkable. He had become thinner than I cared to see him but was all muscle. A daily distance of about twenty kilometres suited him. Much over that and he began to flag. If the pulling had been hard, we would stop short, sometimes after only twelve kilometres. He was prone to sloppy droppings but given the uncertain quality of his diet we were lucky not to have greater difficulties. His lameness recurred a couple of times but vigorous application of Elliman's and a warm bootee-cum-bandage made from a piece of felt found by the roadside eventually eliminated it. After Leninsk he was never lame again.

We walked or cycled a great portion of the distance and our own health remained good, apart from minor tummy upsets. These could be temporarily debilitating, not to mention hazardous when, as once happened, they caused six nocturnal excursions in a temperature of −14°C. Fionn caused alarm when he had a pain for two days in his appendix region. I did not fancy him going under the knife in Kazakhstan. Then two days before we got to Leninsk, cycling ahead to reconnoitre, he was away for four hours and did not return till after dark. The town was twenty kilometres away, not seven as he had believed. He was pretty well done in and, though he said nothing, had given himself a fright, for traces of tears streaked his flushed face.

That night Radio Alma-Ata's English-language broadcast announced that Kazakhstan would be leaving the rouble zone. By extraordinary coincidence, a feature on Baikonur Cosmodrome and Leninsk followed and finally this message: 'We send greetings to the Grant family, who are travelling by horse-drawn caravan somewhere in Kazakhstan.' I had found the station by chance for the first time. Their greeting was the result of a letter I had sent, asking for the frequency.

For the last four kilometres before we reached Leninsk, rusting metal and vehicles, lumps of broken concrete, shards of glass and pieces of plastic were strewn across the steppe without regard for the environment or aesthetics. It turned out to be a purely military town, with quarters for personnel involved with Baikonur Cosmodrome. Having wandered around fruitlessly for some time achieving nothing, we left, and some distance further on found a quiet corner off the main road to park for the night. Leninsk was also European. We had seen our last Orthodox church months and miles back in Uralsk. Since then, mosques and Muslim shrines had become the norm, while villages and small towns had become more and more Kazakh in style and nature. Now, we abruptly jumped back for a day to an essentially Russian atmosphere, uniquely associated with the existence of the Cosmodrome.

Next morning, when we hitched a lift to Leninsk, Igor Berezin, engineer in charge of constructing rocket-gantries at Baikonur, picked us up. He helped us change money and shop. While he attended to his own business I photographed the replica of the rocket in which Yuri Gagarin made the first manned space flight in April 1961, which was mounted on a plinth on a main street. Nearby was a memorial to three cosmonauts who had died in a launch accident in 1962.

Igor, who lived in Alma-Ata when not at work, had invited us to supper and came to collect us. Baikonur was forty kilometres from Leninsk along a potholed track and it was almost dark when we arrived. Igor's hut was basic, used by ten people on a rota basis. Only one other man was there. We had showers and supper and American Orloff vodka, which was cheaper than Russian brands. I had not realised Igor thought we were going to stay overnight so we could see the Cosmodrome in the morning. Unwilling to leave Traceur unguarded, but not wanting to deprive the children of the chance to view Baikonur, I got him to run me back while they stayed. I left Torcuil my camera.

It was strange, setting off alone the following day under dull grey skies, the temperature just below freezing and a

nippy south-west wind blowing. I had trudged twenty kilometres, seeing only linnets, partridges and a distant flock of
fast-flying duck, before Igor brought the children back.
They had seen all the gantries and launch pads, including
that from which Gagarin had gone up, but unfortunately no
rockets. The monthly unmanned rocket supplying Mir
space-station had been launched the day before –
appropriately 5 November – but from another base forty
miles into the desert. Baikonur, unlike Cape Canaveral, is
largely military, short of cash and sadly run down. There
cannot be many other Scots children who have seen it.

November   7 –1°C; overcast
           8 –1°C; blizzard of wet snow
           9 –9°C; 25 m.p.h. N wind
          10 –7°C; 20 m.p.h. N wind; snowed lightly all
             day
          11 –11°C; strong N wind
          12 –14°C; wind N 10–15 m.p.h.; light snow
          13 –14.5°C; 20 m.p.h. NE wind; sunny but no
             warmth
          14 –12°C; E wind up to 30 m.p.h.; thickening
             visibility; ring around the sun
          15 –10°C, rising to +2°C, falling to –2°C;
             25 m.p.h. SW wind
          16 –10°C rising to –6°C; light SW wind,
             occasional light snow
          17 –18°C rising to -10°C; overcast, little wind

The overnight blizzard on the fourteenth/fifteenth had been
unbelievably ferocious, building steadily all day and
buffeting the caravan. We had had a hard, frustrating day,
in which we passed a butter factory with no butter, milk ran
out just before Torcuil reached the counter after half an

hour's queuing and Traceur's right front shoe cracked and had to be replaced. At stopping time we found a lee in a dip behind some bushes. That night the wind rose and rose, bouncing and buffeting the caravan as though it was a boat ploughing into heavy seas. I had never heard such a gale, not on Skye, not on Orkney, nor even far into the Atlantic on North Rona. It literally roared, deafeningly, out of the east. Then what sounded like a million mice began to tango on the roof. It was ice crystals falling and went on all night. I did not sleep till 2.30 a.m., dozing fitfully thereafter. The others, too, were restless. I thanked Providence the van was behind bushes and Traceur, rugged as always now, well protected by a deep dry ditch.

We were nearing the town of Kyzl-Orda. *Orda* means horde and historically the Kazakhs were organised into the Great, Middle and Small Hordes. The territory by the Syr Darya river had been occupied by the Great Horde. Essentially a nomadic people, the Kazakhs had a formal, complex clan system under a khan, with auls, or migratory units, of up to forty tents. Fine horsemen, they were more pastoralists than warriors and no match for Russian imperialism, which began under Tsar Peter I and continued until the dissolution of the USSR in 1991.*

The road into Kyzl-Orda was glacial. Endeavouring to pull the caravan on to it, Traceur slipped and came down on his face, badly chipping one tooth and cracking another right across. Thereafter, with Eilidh at his head for security, we moved slowly along. In town the ice was so polished that he was in danger at every step. We tried tying sacking round his feet, which helped but wore through almost immediately. After a long, tense struggle we reached the centre. There was more than usual to do, because the

*See Olcott, M. B., *The Kazakhs*, second edition, 1995.

Kazakh government had advanced the date for switching from roubles to tenge. I had to change our roubles, and cash some dollars; we had mail to seek and shopping to fetch.

I found the Alum Bank, where I was quickly able to exchange $160 for 640 tenge. However because I was a foreigner, exchange of our roubles had to be authorised by the Administratsia of the Soviet. I was courteously escorted there and taken to an office where I met a large amused official. Downstairs, in a capacious hall, was a massive queue of more than five hundred people. We marched to the head of it, to grins and mild applause, to a row of tables where I was introduced to another official. A bevy of girls noted my name, passport number, amount of roubles and their tenge equivalent by hand in various ledgers. I was then taken to the head of another queue. A chap standing behind the row of clerks and carrying a sub-machine-gun said he had seen us in Aralsk. The clerks sorted the roubles and handed over my tenge. Transaction completed. It had taken two hours, for only 76 tenge or twenty dollars. On my own, it might have taken two days.

The rest of our time in Kyzl-Orda was equally productive. My kind bank escort guided me to the post office and there took her leave. The head postmaster, resplendent in mid-blue uniform with gold piping and three gold stars on each lapel, had to be rousted out to retrieve our considerable pile of mail. Local TV and newspapers had discovered the caravan in my absence. 'Do you know Catherine?' they asked. They had interviewed her and told us she was Swiss, riding from the Ukraine to China.

It took another chill fifteen days to reach Turkestan,* during which time we left the steppe for cottonfields and all

---

*The town of Turkestan in Kazakhstan should not be confused with the independent ex-Soviet Republic of Turkmenistan.

our effort went into staying warm and fed. And we were given a puppy. Fionn described the occasion: 'After stopping to get water cans filled, a man came running up with a sack in his hand. He thrusted it into Eilidh's hands and when we looked inside we found a cute mongrel puppy that we later decided to call Lenin but Nin for short.' Had I not earlier consumed a generous libation of Kazakh brandy with the governor of Aktyoobinsk, whom we had met by the roadside, I might have refused to accept it. But the children were in favour, so the ten-week-old Kazakh herd-mongrel joined the team. Tsar loved him.

I thought that seventy fast-moving beasts we saw one day were sheep, until till I got a glass on them. They were blue-grey in colour, with white heads and rumps and white legs. We could not identify them at the time, though a lorry-driver called them *durgan* or something like that. They were the only group of large wild mammals we saw before reaching North America and were almost certainly saiga.

Turkestan is famous for the ancient mosque and library complex that houses the jade tomb of the Muslim saint Ahmed Yasawi, who ranks second only to Muhammad in Islam. The vast building was commissioned five hundred years ago by Timur the Lame – or Tamerlane, or Tamburlane, as he is variously known. It was undergoing major restoration, paid for by a Turkish government aid project. Turkey provides a lot of aid to Central Asian countries, recognition of their common Turkic stock as well as for sound commercial reasons. The exterior was superb, with three blue domes, one fluted, and with intricate mosaics on the walls. The high, arched front and carved doorway showed the skill required to build this brick structure. Unfortunately the interior was a latticework of scaffolding. The huge bronze cauldron, cast nearby at Shernak, was still there and Ahmad Yasawi's jade tomb had not been moved, remaining fenced off in a nave as in former times. Patches of paint on the walls indicated traces of past splendours but much work remains to be done before they are restored.

We spent three days in Turkestan, with the Abdurahmanov family, who had given us the *saigak*, saiga meat, weeks before, north of Chumish. They helped us to arrange for a second cracked wheel-rim to be welded, and to buy gas and horse-feed. I washed mountains of filthy clothes in their machine, having been unable to tackle it since the advent of the snow and ice. They gave us some heavy-duty polythene sheet, too, which I cut up to 'double-glaze' the caravan windows, which did much to keep us warmer and combat horrendous condensation problems, which threatened to ruin the contents of the boxes stored beneath the seats.

In twelve more gruelling days we reached Tchimkent.

The penultimate evening before our arrival, we requested water at a *chaban*.* The shepherd and his family were Kurds and invited us to park beside the house and eat with them. We were served flat, round, pancake-like Kurdish bread, mutton from a sheep's head with puréed vegetables and a spiced tomato sauce, followed later by bowls of steaming broth. Fionn and Eilidh helped feed the 850 sheep, twenty-one cows and four horses, then the family and some neighbours put on a display of Kurdish songs and dances for us. I played the pipes for them and we had great fun. Kurds are amongst one of Kazakhstan's reputed two hundred minorities. Thirty-six per cent of the population are Kazakhs, 41 per cent Kazakhstan-born Russians, and 6 per cent each Ukrainians and Germans. The remainder comprises the other 11 per cent. We had already met Tatars, Chechens, Kirghiz, Uzbeks, Turks and now

---

*Another word for *tochka*.

Kurds, and would meet Koreans, Uighurs, Azerbaijanis, Armenians, a Mari and Germans before long.

Saken El Basiev and his wife Zhannat met us near the town of Temirlan and offered us accommodation in Tchimkent. 'Just telephone when you arrive and we'll guide you to our house,' they said. Saken was as good as his word when I called him from Khatyn-Kupr, a Tchimkent suburb. He answered at once and all I said was 'Scots.'

'Where are you? Fine. I'll be there in twenty minutes.'

He arrived in forty and took the children to his house while I followed his brother-in-law three tiring kilometres back the way we had come, then up a slippery side road to where the caravan was to be parked, a fierce dog at either end as protection. Traceur was housed a few doors along, in a reasonable stall. I hated not being with the animals and the caravan but here there was no option.

By the time I arrived at the El Basievs' the children were showered and clean. I proceeded to do the same, washing away exhaustion, frustration and worry along with accumulated grime. I couldn't remember when I had last had a shower. It was often weeks between some kind soul offering one and the next, and always bliss, because our daily body-wash never got us really clean. Then we did what Kazakhs seem to do all the time: ate, and drank tea. Saken and Zhannat, who was pregnant, lived in a large house, with expensive furniture and were undoubtedly rich by any standards, notably so here. During the course of conversation Saken mentioned he had given his relations a car each: fourteen Ladas. Next day I saw the office from which he conducted his affairs, trading in coal, steel and china-clay. It was a small, green-painted room, with two tables arranged in a T-shape, a telephone and a computer. A posse of young men hung around, seemingly doing little, perhaps relatives. I suspected they were 'gofers' for the most part but possibly also protection: at least one was armed.

Our three days were fully occupied with the usual round. We collected a lot of mail, including a parcel of horseshoe nails and worm-doses sent long ago to a contact in Karaganda and which had failed to catch up with us in Aktyoobinsk or since. We should never have coped with the form-filling that had to be done to collect a parcel, or acquired many other things we needed, had not Saken's younger brother Abai been with us. The huge Tchimkent market had permanent covered stalls and seemed well stocked but on closer inspection many stalls sold the same things. I remember it because we got gloves for Eilidh and Fionn and a cheap penknife for me to replace the superb one I had lost months before – but chiefly because of the lavatory, which must be the worst in the world. On the principle of 'going when you can and not when you must', I followed Abai into the large, gloomy loo. The urinals were all broken, many hanging half off the wall, so I performed against the wall like everyone else. Sounds of groaning and grunting emanated from behind me and I looked round. There, in the semi-dark, was a row of stalls, with dividing walls no more than waist high and no doors . . .

Two days before our arrival, Traceur had begun to slobber. Drool hung constantly from his lips and he seemed to have trouble eating, especially hay. A *vyetvrach*, a person qualified in veterinary skills but below full vet status, was summoned. The palate behind Traceur's teeth was soft and swollen. He heated an awl to sterilise it, then proceeded to pierce a series of holes in the palate to let blood and rubbed salt into it. I was aghast at this primitive, barbaric-seeming treatment but, knowing nothing whatever about what was afflicting Trass, could only watch and hope it worked. Traceur, remarkably, had stood calmly throughout. Saken later told me the problem was common but I could not make out what caused it, only that it was connected with water. By the time we left, two days later, Traceur was cured.

After many weeks of moving south-east, our direction from Tchimkent was at last due east again and the land became hillier. The double-glazed caravan was warm and we bore the warmth of the El Basievs' hospitality in our hearts, but the seven hundred kilometres to Alma-Ata were colder than ever. Nice though it was to stop, I was always happiest when on the road, even in these conditions. The icy unsalted asphalt was often dangerous for Traceur, but though he came down once or twice he did no further injury to himself and his damaged teeth did not seem to cause him discomfort or stop him eating easily. South of us, the foothills of the Tien Shan range stood up high, clear and pristine white. To the north and east were more mountains.

One evening the children, who had done all the routine jobs associated with stopping for the night literally hundreds of times, behaved in such a daft way I decided I had had enough and went on strike. From now on they were in charge, I told them. The experiment worked well. They did everything competently, even their studies (as I knew they could) and giving them a bit more of the daily onus kept them up to the mark. It was good experience for them and more relaxing for me. There was always the possibility that I might in future be so ill or so badly injured they would *have* to cope.

We began to see horses pulling sledges but fortunately the road remained clear of snow. The weather was bright and, on one memorable day, the temperature rose above freezing. An Uzbek couple with whom we spent a night fed us traditional Uzbek *plof*, similar to risotto, and the next morning donated hay and *kombi korm*, tins of meat, bottled fruit, a jar of honey and a fresh-killed cockerel. On Christmas Eve an Uaz jeep stopped and disgorged three slightly drunk Russian army officers, a colonel, a major and a lieutenant. They insisted I drink a toast with them, then gave me a brass horse-whip with a knife concealed in the handle and a pair of gloves. Merry Christmas! *Dosvidanya!*

That night we parked on a snow-strewn field with a view south to the majestic Tien Shan. We decorated the caravan with a fir branch in lieu of a tree and covered it in tinsel, stars, balls, glitter and little wooden Czech gnomes brought from home. Cards from Kate and each other adorned the walls. After the children slept I delved deep in the Christmas box to find trinkets for stockings so that they would have something to unwrap in the morning.

Wispy cloud wrapped the hills on Christmas Day. Father Christmas had visited, leaving apples, walnuts, a Snickers bar each and some little packets with paper-clips and matches in. Eilidh remarked that Traceur's eyes looked dull but he went off all right. A kilometre took us to the Kooyook Pass, in reality the top of an escarpment, where there was a *gai* post and we were given two fresh loaves by the police. To our surprise the steep six-kilometre long descent took us below the snow-line.

Traceur had been behaving in a most unusual and contrary fashion as we came down. We stopped near the bottom to fill jerries with water piped from a spring and I took off his bridle and gave him some hay to keep him amused. I also gave him a precautionary 50cc anti-colic injection. A Lada stopped ahead to look at us – and bridleless Traceur, quite uncontrollable, took off. *'Davai! Davai!'* 'Go! Go!' I yelled frantically at the driver, as Trass headed straight for the car's back-end. By some miracle we missed it. The driver just sat gawping at us as though we were nuts. Torcuil, who had courageously scrambled on to the footboard, eventually did what I was shouting at him to do and stood on the footbrake instead of using his hand, which slowed the rig enough to let Eilidh get to Traceur's head and stop him.

As Eilidh had noticed, Traceur's eyes were dull and now half shut. He lurched and I thought he would fall. We took him out of the shafts with difficulty, because he did not want to move. We untacked him and put on his rug. He was gaga, lurching, nearly falling, eyes almost closed. I yelled into his ear but got no reaction. Somehow we got him tied to a roadside tree and manoeuvred the caravan on to the shoulder by hand. Eilidh and I hitched a lift twenty kilometres to the nearest farm, a *kolhoz*, as it happened. The vet was out but the director promised to send him to us when he returned and provided a truck to take us back. When we arrived, Traceur was no worse, though Fionn said he had been down on his knees at one point. There was nothing more to do but get on with making Christmas dinner.

I had plucked cocky as we travelled, and while he was roasting, we lit up the candle-powered Swedish chimes and opened our presents, with Ansambel Slovenija's Christmas tape playing in the background. Model aeroplanes for the boys, some tenge for everyone and various nonsense presents. Fionn surprised us all, having made presents and cards for each of us. There was a festive air in the caravan, greatly enhanced when we looked out of the window at Traceur and saw him grazing and definitely better. There was no sign of the promised vet, though.

Christmas Dinner Menu
Smoked fish 'Doroga'
Roast Cockerel 'Boornoya Oktyaber'
Roast and Boiled Potatoes
Carrots and Cabbage
Sweetmeats 'Shili'
Coffee

Not bad fare for weary travellers stuck on the shoulder of the M39 in the middle of the worst winter in Kazakhstan for thirty years. We all had a glass of sparkling Russian wine and for me there was a dram of Dalmore malt to finish with. The best present of all was Traceur's recovery. By evening he was eating and drinking almost normally. I began to think he must have eaten something poisonous, perhaps in hay, as there was little grazing now.

Next day, with Traceur 98 per cent fit, I decided we must move. We were unrugging him when the vet arrived – he had not been told about us until that morning. I felt a bit of a fraud, with the horse seemingly well. The vet found nothing wrong with him but told us to call when we reach the *kolhoz*. The director met us on the road and gave us a note saying we could take hay from a stack and promised us barley next day. It was easy downhill travel, under a hard grey sky with a black mass of cloud on the horizon ahead. We made fifteen kilometres and stopped short of the *kolhoz* on a grass strip. Soon after, Traceur went gaga again. He circled round and round on his picket chain, apparently seeing and hearing nothing, quite goofy, with sweats. He was not as bad as he had been on the previous day, however, and by nightfall was calmer.

In the morning a pale blue Izh van brought six bundles of best lucerne hay, two sacks of barley, potatoes, masses of sugar, tea and several kilos of meat, a gift from the *kolhoz*. There was so much that we had a struggle to stow it. As it was winter the meat would stay fresh – or even freeze. The vet came again but Traceur, though not right, was much better and there was little he could do. We had a day off to see how Traceur behaved. I replaced his shoes with heavily cleated winter ones. He leaned hard on me and was very wooden when asked to move.

Eilidh and I hitched into Dzhamboul in the afternoon,

on a railway workers' bus, to check for mail, make a quick call to Kate and visit the bazaar. Dzhamboul had nice old buildings and the bazaar supplied all we wanted, including a huge Chinese firework for New Year. When we got back Traceur had finished his feed and was brighter eyed. I hoped whatever was affecting his system would be flushed out quickly.

Not a trace of deranged behaviour remained by morning. I was more certain than ever a toxin in his hay had caused the alarming problem. We skirted Dzhamboul, passing through a noisome coal-mining and industrial area and headed out to open country with the Arataou mountains visible south of us. Some lorry-drivers on their way back from Urumchi in China told us the roads there were good, food plentiful and the people friendly. The temperature rose to an astonishing 8°C/46°F, with warm sunshine, and Traceur sweated profusely under his woolly winter coat. Then it began to rain. It was Hogmanay and New Year looked set to be wet.

The rain turned to snow. We uncorked a bottle of Soviet champagne – labelling had not caught up with events – to bring in 1994. Although 1993 had been physically tough and not uneventful it might have been much worse. Good fortune had favoured us and we had received help and generosity from countless strangers along our way. We toasted Kate and Grandpa, then went outside to light sparklers and the Chinese cracker. It was a splendid cracker, sending about twenty little coloured balls, one after the other, high into the air. When it finished we sang 'Auld Lang Syne' and 'Flower of Scotland'. It was still softly snowing when we went to bed.

On 4 January we arrived at Konj Zavod 97. This 'horse factory', situated idyllically on flat ground against a backdrop of mountains, was the Kazakh national stud. There were plenty of horses to see, including Thoroughbreds, Arabians and Tikinets, better known as Akhal-Teké, tough little beasts from Turkmenistan. Only the poor saddlery testified to the present harsh economic climate. The famous 'Absent', Olympic dressage champion at Mexico, Tokyo and Munich, had lived here and was commemorated by a statue. Horse factories are also farms, and this one covered 84,000 hectares (207,560 acres), with 34,000 sheep, 1700 horses and a herd of fifty pedigree Finnish cattle. There was arable, too, and I counted forty Niva combine-harvesters lined up in the machine park. One of the best things for us was finding the shoemaker, who turned out fur-lined boots for us all at less than ten pounds a pair. It was wonderful to have warm feet at last.

Two days later we stopped at the flour-mill in Kulan. Our map called it Lugovo, the Russian name, but such changes were frequent in newly independent Kazakhstan. The mill-owner, Ruslan Edelbiyev, turned out to be Chechen, whose family came originally from Grozny. His recently retired advocate father, Shervenye, invited us to their house for the night. After hot showers, plates piled with steaming *plof* and gallons of *tshai,* tea, life looked rosy. Ruslan and Natasha had three lovely but noisy girls, Janeta, aged five, Mareta, four, and Alyeta, who was two. Ruslan was going to Bishkek, once Frunze, in Kyrghyzstan, two days hence and I asked if I could go with him, for that road was shorter, might suit us better and, to quote the late, great and irascible General Patton, 'Time spent on reconnaissance is never wasted.'

Before we left in the morning, Ruslan took us to the market in his Ford Granada 2.3-litre saloon. I remarked on the huge butcher's knife by his seat and the West German gas-pistol in the glove compartment. He said that the flour-mill was a cash business and sometimes he carried considerable sums. The weapons were a form of insurance. Our talk

The family on the caravan in 1990: Fionn, Lady, Kate, Eilidh and Torcuil.

Offy pulling the caravan, Eilidh driving, Torcuil aboard. Belgium.

The caravan beside the Meuse, with barge (and train) passing. France.

Torcuil and Eilidh mounted on Vitesse and Valentine at Domaine de St Sauveur, France.

Eilidh swimming Traceur, Spotorno, Ligurian Coast. Italy.

Torcuil looking out over the Tagliamento Valley from Mt Quarnan, above Gemona. Italy.

Dravograd from 'sniper's rock'. Slovenia.

Torcuil and Fionn, with Borut Praper, on turret of tank destroyed in the war. Slovenia.

We talk to Gara School about the trip.
Hungary.

Torcuil washing dishes in the caravan.

Empty shelves in a Ukrainian shop.

A roadside encounter near Darnadezhda, Ukraine. (Note the Russian system of harness.)

Mrs Petrovitch dishing out our supper. Ukraine.

Playing handball with locals near Starobjelsk, Ukraine.
(Note Eilidh's arm in plaster.)

Kazakh herd boys on the steppe near Aralsk, Kazakhstan

(*Left*) Meeting the locals, Konir, Kazakhstan.

Replica of the rocket in which Yuri Gagarin made the first manned space flight at Leninsk, Kazakhstan.

Eilidh, Traceur, Tsar and 'Nin in a blizzard near Kzyl-Orda, Kazakhstan.

(*Right*) Traceur's icicle-encrusted nose.

The author, Torcuil, Eilidh and Fionn at the tomb of Ahmad Yasawi, Turkestan. Kazakhstan.

Kazakh shepherd and family at their yurt, with Kate,
Torcuil and Eilidh. Kazakhstan.

Kate with the never-ending washing, somewhere in Kazakhstan.

The caravan and our escort of cavalry. Western Mongolia.

Catching Chessy, Eilidh's and Fionn's birthday present, the Mongol way.
Bulgan, Mongolia.

Typical Mongolian valley scene – green hills, gers and animals.
Bayan-Olgiy, Mongolia.

Sometimes Torcuil had a hard time fetching water.
Near Arvaiheer, Mongolia.

Home-schooling could be done almost anywhere . . . Plains, mid-Mongolia.

Ox-rider, Mongolia.

Second-hand bookstall, Ulaanbaatar, Mongolia.

Torcuil and Fionn walking down a
street in Ikoma, Japan.

Roadside serenade: women playing
the dombra with children in national
dress. Kazakhstan.

Vegetable market in Saihan, China.

(*Above left*) Fionn buying the *Rapid City Journal* in Belle Fourche, South Dakota, USA. We were featured on the front page.

(*Above right*) The wide open spaces at Echo Canyon, Nevada. USA.

(*Opposite top left*) The International Bridge Walk from Sault Ste Marie, USA to Sault Ste Marie, Canada.

(*Opposite top right*) Indian prayer offerings at Mahto Tipi, Wyoming, USA.

(*Opposite bottom right*) A bit of flooding near Roslyn, South Dakota, USA.

Traceur.

Bertha and Kate in the Matapedia Valley, Quebec. Canada.

Joe Miller and Nick leading us the very last mile through foggy Halifax, Nova Scotia. Canada.

drifted to weapons in general. I had read many accounts of the easy availability of almost any sort of arms as the Soviet Union imploded. A pistol? I asked. Very easy. What about a Kalashnikov? Easy too. Well, a tank? Yes, but ... *that* might take a little longer! Loaded with fresh stores from the market, plus a huge slab of butter, some rice and other gifts from Natasha, it was time to go. The entire extended family all helped shove the caravan out of the yard. 'We don't really need a horse,' I joked, as we set off, 'just lots of Chechens pushing.'

Three kilometres down the road the following day Ruslan caught up. Leaving Torcuil in charge, not without inward trepidation, I transferred to the Granada. There was fog, so no view, and the Ford had a fuel problem, which necessitated the fuel lines being laboriously blown down with air every so often. The border crossing into Kyrghyzstan was a formality. The way to Bishkek lay through fifty miles of ribbon development, with almost nowhere we could have stopped at night. It would have been disastrous for us to come this way. Food was abundant but petrol extremely scarce, sold from jerry-cans, and even a petrol-tanker, by the roadside.

On the return journey, as we approached the pre-arranged spot where the children should be, I spotted the lights of the caravan glinting through trees even before the excellent sign Torcuil had erected to show where they had turned off. We were three hours later than expected and I was glad to find the gang well, cheerful and warm, despite a damp day's travel in fog on their own. Ruslan came in for ten minutes, then we bade him farewell. The Edelbiyevs had family still in Grozny and I have often wondered how they fared during the uprising in Chechnya.

In mid-January the temperature dropped to −28°C/ −18°F. Fortunately it warmed a mite during the day and there was little wind, but travelling had become much harder. Our gas froze. We had long been keeping filled water-jerries inside, a confounded nuisance but it stopped them freezing and perhaps splitting. Now the water in them turned to slush-ice. The outlet-pipe from the sink froze constantly and had to be thawed before water would drain away. The horse-rugs were kept supple when on Traceur by his body-heat but snow and ice built up into big chunks on the soles of his feet overnight and had to be knocked off with a hammer. The harness was stiff to handle in the mornings. Worst of all, many jobs were difficult or impossible to do with gloves on. Everything took so long to accomplish that we never set off before ten o'clock.

It was strange listening to news of the rest of the world under these circumstances. I felt like an alien, eavesdropping on another civilisation, an inept, barbaric one. Fighting had flared in Afghanistan. The approaching Russian elections had brought the crypto-fascist Zherenovski out of the woodwork to spread his poison. NATO was once more timorously thinking of air-strikes to stop Serbian aggression in Bosnia, while Sarajevo continued to be pounded into ruin. At home John Major's back-to-basics policy of a return to high moral standards in public life was being daily riven, as one Tory Minister or MP after another resigned for reasons of impropriety. An estimated one-fifth to one-third of the damage to the ozone layer is being caused by emissions from cars but the UK was embarking on a £23 billion road programme – yet for lack of a measly $1.5 million was dropping out of the European Space Agency project to design a new shuttle. Madness – and all far removed from our daily battle with the elements. It was easier to relate to reports of temperatures of –40°F in the eastern USA.

The cold brought compensations. Trees were indescribably beautiful in thick coatings of ice and the Tien Shan, the

Heavenly Mountains, soared magnificently, a solid, stark white rampart to the south. Our bird list had been growing too, with the advent of more trees. Great tits, greenfinches, linnets, lots more fieldfares, blackbirds, buzzards and rough-legged buzzards, a kestrel or two, tree sparrows, a couple of great grey shrikes, a treeful of long-eared owls and a waxwing were some of the more recent sightings. In the Khoordayisky Pass, Torcuil had seen another wolf. *Susliks* remained abundant, though less frequently seen.

We visited the village of Stepnoe, a little enclave just inside the Kyrghyzstan border. There were slight differences in house decoration and less litter. The shops had more variety but would not take our tenge and we had no Khirgizian soum. Visions of sweets, tomato paste, biscuits and honey evaporated. We did get our hay-nets filled, though. A couple of likely lads took them, later galloping back on their horses to deliver them. Tiny flakes of crystalline snow were floating down and when the sun broke through they glittered and twinkled to earth like myriad diamond chips.

In the main street of the village of Risorb a man tried to sell me hashish. Igor Berezin had warned us the town of Chu was 'the grass capital of Kazakhstan' and to be careful, because the police had a habit of planting it on unsuspecting travellers, then stopping them a few miles down the road, confiscating the grass and fining the unfortunate victim. (Or worse. Someone told us a dreadful story about illegal immigrants having their passports confiscated by criminal gangs and being forced to work as slaves in the hemp fields – but I have no idea if it is true.) Ruslan Edelbiyev had confirmed Igor's warning. Needless to say, I did not buy the marijuana.

Eilidh, always lucky, looked down as she walked along the roadside one day and spotted a 3-tenge note – under which were ninety-nine more! Someone had dropped a bank bundle. We debated handing it in but decided the police would only pocket it as it represented two months' wages.

On 25 January I recorded, 'We are out of all vegetables except three small onions and dried peas; no biscuits or sweets; no fruit. There is meat, rice and bad pasta, a tin of disgusting fish, a small jar of tomato paste and little else. Ironically with under 100 km to go to Alma-Ata we have seldom had so little provender on board.' Luckily, soon after that we found bread and from then on things got better again. Traceur was certainly fitter and fatter than when we left Tchimkent, because of the availability of better feed.

On a calm, overcast day, with a pall of brown smoke hanging in the air, we entered Alma-Ata. At a large round-about, we took the road signed 'Hippodrome', crossed the Big Almaty river, passed ramshackle houses, an industrial area and more houses. We came to a long stone wall and the gates of the Hippodrome. The director of Konj Zavod 97 had warned them to expect us. The gates swung back and we drove in.

Traceur, the children and I had covered 3465 miles in the 326 days since leaving Mezökövesd on 11 March 1993, traversed the former Soviet Union mostly on foot, endured privation, storms and bitter cold. It had been a grand journey but we, and especially Traceur, were more than ready for a wee bit of rest.

It was 30 January 1994.

CHAPTER TWELVE

Altai. Group of mountains where the borders of China, Russia and Mongolia meet. It stretches a thousand miles from Siberia to the Gobi Desert . . .
Guide to Places of the World

Alma-Ata. As a child, when I used to pore over maps and imagine where I should go, it was one of the romantic places. The reality was a city with brown smoke continually hanging over it from the emissions of its power-station's twin chimneys; muddy residential streets full of rotting refuse; piles of rubbish remaining uncollected for weeks; steam pouring out of manholes from defective district heating systems; men with mink hats; decaying buildings; kiosks selling Snickers, Mars and whisky; people begging in the streets; Kazakhs who stared, Russians who did not; an old woman spreading salt on the pavement from a bucket she carried, using her bare hands. And the Kazakh government had changed its name, to Almaty. Yet it had taken much striving to reach and still retained a tarnished aura of romance.

At the Hippodrome, Traceur was ensconced in a stable-block leased to Irina Tchainikova, who trained dressage horses for export. We met Director Dosaev and his deputy, Mrs Galena Gorchkova. A kindly Russian who had been there for twenty years, *gospozha* Gorchkova offered us use of a flat. It was bliss to have somewhere to bath and wash clothes, though it was inconveniently far from the stables to move into.

I aimed to leave in early April, which allowed two months to carry out repairs and refurbishment and acquire visas for crossing China. Anna and Igor Berezin's flat became our home from home. Visits to town entailed half an hour of purgatory on one of the ancient yellow Liaz buses. So old were they that when full and turning corners they would roll hard over like an ill-ballasted ship and only slowly came upright again on the straight.

The British Embassy shared a building with the French and the Germans in an expression of European unity – or to save money. The ambassador's personal secretary, Margaret Stoves, agreed to give my films to the next person leaving for them to post in Europe. Then a security officer decided they must not give my films to anyone to post as they might be pornographic. He should have been with us on the road in –28°C to see all the stripping we did. It was suggested I go to the Dostyk Hotel and search for a British passport-holder to ask. The desk girl there gave me the room number of the first on the pile – and I woke Steven McTiernan, managing director of Chase Manhattan Bank's London-based energy group, from jet-lagged sleep. He was very good about it and agreed to take my film with him. Four days later, Simon Jackson and Annie McMahon, in Almaty to set up a joint venture between Chase and the Kazakh government, rolled up at the caravan, embarrassed and most apologetic, carrying my films. McTiernan had been told by the embassy not to take the films, lest Kazakh officials delayed his departure from the airport – suspicious that state secrets might be being breached! I cursed the embassy officials whom I had told about the films and who must have passed on the information. Two good things came from all this. Simon and Annie, the most relaxed and humane of bankers, helped us immeasurably with communications and became firm friends, and the Kazakhstan International Bank footed the expense of sending home my pornographic state secrets by courier.

Penetrating the newly established Chinese Embassy was a minor miracle and took several attempts. Once in I managed to make an appointment and eventually had a short meeting with Consul Dzha, who was rude and unhelpful. Separately from and nothing to do with the Chinese Embassy, I had faxed the China International Sports Travel Co. in Beijing. Their reply, which I had in my pocket, stated that foreigners were not allowed to drive in China now, except with a guide. At $250 per day for the three hundred days we should need, a guide would cost us seventy-five thousand dollars! Not for the first time, the Chinese had changed their rules. Footsore and heartsick, in a vile mood with all bureaucrats who impede free travel by honest people, I tramped to the Berezins' in Kozhamkulov Street, where Anna produced that remedy for all ills, a good cup of tea.

If we stayed to fight for permission, we risked losing a travelling season, still without getting into China. We decided to cut our losses and detour 1,600 kilometres north, via Russia to Mongolia, which also kept open the option of going to North America via Vladivostok. We still needed visas. At the Mongolian Embassy I was met with courtesy and charm by the ambassador, who had at one time studied in Leeds. 'Do you know Catherine?' he asked. In a week we had entry visas. The Russian consul, fascinated by what we were doing, gladly renewed our Russian ones, which we should need for passing through the Altai.

Throughout the long, difficult days I spent slogging

round offices the children were marvellous. Eilidh or Torcuil would have supper ready; they tackled chores unbidden, even lessons. Torcuil, newly turned fourteen, had fallen under the spell of Dina, a beautiful half-Uighur half-Russian girl who worked at another stable – and he suddenly took up riding. Simon and Annie fed us at their flat, an enclave of Britishness. Agronomist Daulet Chunkunov invited us to his eighth-floor apartment for lunch, where his family welcomed us. The table was covered with many traditional Kazakh dishes, salads and plates of meat. All the meat was horse . . . And Catherine found us. Swiss, mid-forties, five-foot nothing with a ready laugh and permanently perched behind a cigarette, she also was wintering in Almaty, also getting nowhere with the Chinese. For her, refusal was serious because, courageously riding alone in the tracks of William of Rubruck, a monk sent to the Mongol court from the Crimea in 1253, part of his route had gone through Xingiang.

On 3 March we welcomed Kate back, burdened with supplies, staggering sleepily off a Transaero Ilyushin IL-28 inbound from Moscow. Communication had often been difficult during the preceding months. Quoting Kate: 'Receiving mail from them was wonderful and I lived for these letters arriving. Christmas came and went and I felt torn in half being away from them. Then the terrific high and excitement of the approaching reunion.' Torcuil and I were late meeting the flight and '. . . I finally arrived only to find no one at the airport. Eventually David and Torcuil arrived. I clutched Torcuil, tears filling my eyes, unable to control them any more. To be . . . with my family again was almost too much. They all looked thin.'

Spring took a holiday and it snowed on 1 April. After an unusually hectic last-minute rush, farewells and grateful thanks had been said to Irina, and the directorate and veterinary staff at the Hippodrome. Waved away by the staunch and unbelievably kind Berezins, Traceur hauled us through the gates and headed north.

Eastern Kazakhstan was steppe, but more undulating than before. Clear to our east, the Hrebet Dzhungarski Arataou mountains frustratingly delineated the border with China. Traceur, fatter and fitter after two months' rest, was pulling excellently. Kate, though, was not well. The travel had again upset her digestive system.

South of Sariozek, we were expertly towed up a steep hill by a Kamaz truck. The driver and his companions were brothers, Tatars from Karabulak. We had put to and were setting off when the brothers returned. Would we stay with them in Karabulak? It would mean a detour but we liked them and said yes. It was a decision that had unsought consequences.

On 15 April Renat, Marat, Ruslan and Kolya Negmetzhanov awaited us in Karabulak. We parked the caravan in Renat's drive, Traceur in his garden, then went into the house for a big meal of *plof*. By the time we had finished, the fire for our saunas was hot. It was great to sweat out weeks of dirt.

For two days we entered upon a never-ending feast with the extended Negmetzhanov family, until we had eaten and drunk to a standstill. Renat's wife Natalya made *beshparmak*, a traditional Kazakh mutton dish featuring a sheep's head, very filling. I had even eaten a cartilaginous, lanolin-flavoured sheep's ear, traditionally given to an honoured guest and – to satisfy an old curiosity – an eye. We talked about being trucked between Leninogorsk and Ust'Kan, across a rough mountain road, which was reportedly open and would lop six weeks off our journey time. The Negmetzhanovs and neighbour Fedya Ochman had bought lorries when Communism collapsed and were owner-drivers. Business was all right but banditry on the roads a constant risk.

Traceur's mud-encrusted legs had been hosed off and the van manhandled from Renat's drive to the road, preparatory to departure. Eilidh went to fetch the tack from the outhouse, in which I had cleaned it the evening before.

'Where are the reins?' she called.

'They're there.'

'No, they're not.'

'Yes, they are. On top of the saddle with the bridle and traces.'

'No. The breeching's not there either.'

'Of course they are. I left them like I always do.'

'They are NOT THERE.'

Bridle, breeching, reins and traces had gone. Saddle, tug-straps and collar remained. Renat was extremely upset, reluctant to believe someone could have made off with half our saddlery while we were his guests, without alerting the dogs.

In ten minutes the militia had been called. In twenty, a lieutenant-colonel and two plain-clothes policemen were with us. In thirty, the chief of police himself had appeared and a major. The Chief's first question was, 'Why haven't you registered?' (We had, in Almaty.) They set about their work efficiently; I gave them a photograph of Traceur wearing harness and a detailed drawing. When they eventually departed we held our own post-mortem.

It was an unmitigated disaster.

Without harness we were immobilised. Despite police optimism and the forty-one footprints they had found leading into the yard from the back, I did not expect them to achieve anything. I telephoned Annie McMahon in Almaty, told her the tale and asked if she would ring Joël

Moyne, ask him to buy replacement harness from our original supplier, Monsieur Coeur, and have it sent out. Meanwhile, two policemen returned, bringing bridles and a bundle of leather, nylon and webbing strapping, the contents of their long-disused saddle-room cupboard. We appreciated the gesture and using some of it and an old bit we had, we contrived to adapt Traceur's head collar so Eilidh could exercise him.

Renat, Kolya and I spent most of the rest of that day fashioning breeching from the best of the tough military webbing. Used to having to make do, the Tatars saw possibilities that eluded me. By the end of the afternoon, fingers painful from shoving needles through the thick material, we had a functioning though non-adjustable breeching, strong if not stylish. The long nylon straps turned out to be reins and fortunately we had spare traces. Meantime Annie and Joël had done wonders. Within two weeks replacement harness would be on its way. Getting it from Almaty to us might be the problem, for I intended to go on, now we had harness of a sort.

On the airfield north of Taldy-Kurgan, a few score miles from the Chinese frontier, we viewed the mothballed might of former Soviet air-power: dozens of hangars, about 300 Mig-23s, a handful of Mig-21s and Mil-8 helicopters. Clearly not only the West had been perceived as a threat by the Kremlin.

The long haul up the eastern margins of Kazakhstan took us through beautiful country. Spring greened the steppe. Our bird list included exotic species like Isabelline shrike, sandgrouse, mynas and a middle-spotted woodpecker as well as more familiar ones. Lizards were common and snakes not unusual but finding tortoises was a surprise. East of us, always, were mountains, at times reaching almost 10,000 feet. There were wonderful marshes and lakes north of Ucharal, with lots of grass and little habitation till we reached Ajaguz, then grass again till Georgievka. We watched a felt tent being erected, similar to those we should encounter later in Mongolia. Kazakh shepherds use them in summer. Searching for fodder one day, we were invited into one. 'Tchai budish?' asked the kindly shepherd's wife, reaching for her tea-pot. The front half of the tent floor was earthen and served as kitchen and workspace, while the rear was covered in rugs and mats to sit or sleep on. There was a barrel-stove in the middle, a bed near one side of the door and a small cupboard on the other. The walls were hung with carpets and it was cosy. The family were handsome-looking and exceptionally nice, the five children shyly polite.

A shattered Fedya Ochman and co-driver stopped by one evening on their way home to Karabulak. The previous night they had been held up by eight men with automatic weapons, boxed in by a Mercedes and a Lada Zhigouli. Their truck was empty but the robbers relieved them of thirty dollars before letting them go. They were lucky. Others had had their trucks stolen or burned. We poured tea into them, but on discovering it was my birthday, Fedya, who was not driving, produced a bottle, which we drained. When they left, we were the richer for a present of potted meat, jam and *salo*.

Once, we saw several families moving north with huge herds of cattle, including a venerable 2-ox-powered covered wagon. They were going 150 kilometres, taking five days over the journey, a living lesson for the children about transhumance.

Someone told us a joke: A Russian was carrying two sacks, each containing a Kazakh. The police stopped him and asked what was in the sacks. A wolf in each, was the reply. The police asked to see. 'These are people!' they exclaimed.

'Oh!' the man replied. 'Well, they steal horses anyway.'

We had bitter winds and cold rain the day we reached Ajaguz, a military town full of soldiers, with tank parks and a large airfield. We stopped at a big *gai* post and the police took Kate and Eilidh shopping in their jeep, while the boys and I were invited in to get warm. Kate, whose health was no better, was suffering nausea and dizzy spells and was now definitely homebound. She returned from shopping having found that there was a 5 p.m. train to Almaty. Then, by chance, two journalists arrived, who happened to be on their way there. They had a spare seat in their car and would be happy to take Kate. Fifteen minutes to pack and she was gone. She wrote, 'Yet again saying goodbye to the family was awful. I was fated, it seemed, not to be fit enough for this expedition.' It was tough both for her and the children to be apart and I missed her company, but she had become increasingly unwell during the travelling. I hoped that this time when she got back to England the doctors would be able to sort out her problems.

Ten days later we reached Georgievka. The kind, efficient telephone girls there wielded magic plugs and had me connected to Kate in no time. After a protracted trip, she had arrived safely in Britain. From Annie McMahon, I learned that the harness had arrived. Sergei Belousov, a businessman we had met in Andreijevka, had collected it from Almaty to bring north.

Lake Sasykul had given us a feast of birds, including twelve soaring pelicans – 'A wonderful bird is the pelican/ His beak can hold more than his belly can.' My favourites were the flocks of rosy starlings, bright pink with black wing-tips. There were masses of colourful butterflies and moths, and Torcuil saw a grey fox. The country was lovely; nowhere more so than the Monastir mountains, a distinctive triple peak where a Russian monastery once stood. Destroyed by Genghis Khan's men, no trace of it remains. The farmer who told me this also solved a mystery. We had seen many ridden horses with fresh blood on their necks. He said it was a natural phenomenon, occurring in spring, and that horses that do not bleed are prone to foot trouble. It was an extraordinary explanation but I was sure neither maltreatment nor injury was the cause.

Renat and Kolya paid us a surprise visit on their way to Barnaul with a load of biscuits. Another surprise was the unexpected arrival of Simon Jackson, on business in Ust'Kamenogorsk. Unfortunately the harness had been given to Sergei Belousov before Simon knew he was coming.

Two days later we crossed the river Irtysh, whose waters flow into the Ob and thence to the Arctic, and entered Ust'Kamenogorsk ourselves. It was a fine town but we did not linger. Our road northwards left the plains behind as we plunged into beautiful birchwoods and faced a series of small hills. At Sekisovka we committed ourselves to the Altai crossing to Ust'Kan and turned east. We had also spied a sturdy 20-litre plastic jerry in a shop and pounced. Such finds were rare.

The hot, hilly road to Leninogorsk passed through pinewoods, by fast-flowing rivers, and involved several short tows. During stops, Torcuil sewed a rent in his jeans, Eilidh and Fionn went for walks and I made a new Scottish flag, as our original one was falling apart. The temperature soared to 35°C/95°F and biting insects were a daily menace. Three days before we reached Leninogorsk, which was a predominantly Russian town, Vladimir Karmanov, geologist, Green Party activist and official emissary from the town, stopped us on the road. They had heard of us and wanted to help. We were to telephone on arrival. The same day, Viktor Klimov invited us to eat at his restaurant when we got there.

*

Our stay in Leninogorsk began with the best meal we had had since leaving Europe, lunch at Klimov's 'Le Coq d'Or'. We had contacted the *Administratsia* on arrival and deputy mayor Andrei Butrin had taken charge of everything. We were ensconced at a secure, peaceful and verdant base, in the grounds of the television relay station at the top of town. Oats had been brought, our gas-cylinder filled, new studs fitted to horseshoes and the picket welded. We had baths at the Klimovs', and Viktor was organising our tow over the mountains. All we had to do was ask, then sit back and relax. It was easy to enjoy being celebrities!

The following five days had an air of unreality and were one of the best parts of the whole journey. I don't think we met anyone who was not at least mildly eccentric. Vladimir Karmanov brought us copies of his front-page article about us in *Leninogorskaya Pravda*; later he had us carrying placards protesting against the recent Chinese H-bomb test (us, Westerners, in an until recently 'closed area' of the former Soviet Union!) Andrei Butrin was a teetotal vegetarian and had practised as a psychotherapist before becoming deputy mayor. Viktor Klimov, almost as wide as he was tall, resembling in shape the powerful grey Nissan jeep he drove, was in everything from catering to building and slept with a pistol by his bed. There was artist Tamara Kolosova, startlingly good-looking except for coal-black teeth, 'aerobic Tanya', and archaeologist Jura Klassen. Most amazing of all were Vitja and Paulina Laryonovy. Vitja taught palaeontology and Paulina analysed core-samples from the mine, but they were experts on geology, parapsychology, ESP and the paranormal, bio-energy, cosmology and, in Vitja's case, hypnotism. He was dark-haired, with eyes the refulgent deep blue of lapis-lazuli. Normally twinkling, they could exert almost tangible force. I watched him put a girl into a light trance in a split second and, though he failed with me, I *felt* the pull of those eyes. They took us on a tour of old mine-workings and on a fossil-hunt. Engineer Viktor Popov, who was remarkably normal, did our welding and we had a lovely evening at his house. We also met parliamentary deputy Milaslav Kuzmich, who gave me a book about a 1920s' horse-ride to Turkmenistan – and a copy of Burns in Russian.

One evening, as we were finishing supper, a little green Zaparozhets car drove up. Ivan Ribalkin had a parcel for us. THE HARNESS! He had collected it from brother-in-law Sergei Belousov in Ust'Kamenogorsk the previous day. He also had other mail for us, including a parcel from Grant's of Dalvey with saw-blades and bicycle-tyres and another from friends Inge and Douglas Cross containing almost-forgotten tastes of home: oatcakes, Cheddar cheese and Cadbury's chocolate.

Our lotus-eating Leninogorsk days were too short. The complete rest, the chance to see and do new things and the wonderful characters we met had been infinitely refreshing. On Wednesday 15 June we made an early start for the loading bank, to rendezvous with two Kamaz 6×6 trucks. The caravan was embarked on a flatbed, the animals in a van. I had regretted the decision not to be towed but qualms I had about being transported were rapidly dispelled after only a few kilometres. The road was execrable and would have shaken the caravan to pieces. Reaching a river with a washed-out bridge, even the trucks had to feel their way across the fast-flowing waters of the deep ford. Unaided or towed, we should never have made it.

We had passed through recently innovated Kazakh Customs. The Russian post was equally new. Greeted warmly, our papers were quickly processed, a technical squint taken at the caravan and fifty dollars changed for us at the rate of 1900 roubles to one.

*

The Russian Altai is one of the most lovely regions I have ever been in with carpets of flowers of many kinds. Its mix of mountains, rivers, pine and fir woods, small villages and farms is splendidly balanced. There is a wealth of wildlife and, as yet, only limited pollution. The native people, the Altaiets, are of Turkic origin, with their own language and customs, including a shamanistic religion, and live in distinctive wooden houses. We found them dour at first but appreciated their restraint after the inquisitiveness of the Kazakhs, and they were usually helpful and kind. Forestry and deer-farming were major industries, together with herding and some cultivation. The Gorno-Altai Republic has considerable autonomy, its own legislature and even boasts its own flag. This wonderful country gave continuous pleasure every day for the month we were in it, despite the hordes of horseflies, with jaws like sharks and a vampirean thirst and air forces of mosquitoes, which were worse.

On our second morning we had to cross the Koksa river by a wide but swaying wooden suspension bridge. Traceur tackled it happily, ignoring its lateral swing and undulating shape. The first village we came to, Sugash, was entirely populated by Altaiets, timber-built, nestling by a fir wood in an open valley with grassy hills standing away on either side. Wild flowers bloomed in a mass of colour, and we were adding new birds to our list daily: willow tit, redstart, wood sandpiper, a great snipe, huge black woodpeckers and many we did not know. Near Ust'Kan, Fionn discovered fossil plant stems in rocks on our way up to explore some prehistoric cave dwellings. The capacious caves commanded a sweeping view but the story of their one-time inhabitants was a mystery.

One mealtime we were chatting in a general way and the conversation drifted to a day in Leninogorsk when Tamara Kolosova had read the children's palms. She had predicted that Fionn would marry and have three children. 'I'm never going to have a stupid wife or any stupid children!' he snarled. Eilidh was equally unimpressed by her forecast marriage and two. Torcuil, who had refused to proffer his palm, remained disdainfully aloof from the debate.

The Altai was not easy going and we were tired by bedtime. This may have contributed to Torcuil having a lackadaisical spell, barely doing his allotted chores and going about with his brain disengaged. He also began making deliberately annoying remarks to Eilidh and Fionn. One day he was so exasperating I threatened to leave him by the roadside. It upset me that we fell out quite frequently for a time – yet in fairness to the others, and the requirements of the journey, his behaviour could not be ignored. Fortunately the phase soon passed, as such things do, and he regained his equilibrium.

We were free to roam at will but trod lightly on this broad, spacious land. What litter we saw was confined to glass, a few tins, decaying machinery and, alas, the beginnings of Western packaging. Roads, mostly firm unasphalted tracks, were good. Ust'Kan shops stocked Western produce: German boots and chocolate; Italian vodka; the ubiquitous Snickers and Uncle Ben's rice. The latter was much advertised on TV but, as with most Western things thus promoted, nobody could afford it, and wildly expensive things were often jokingly called Uncle Ben's. Junk Western products, plugged by the biggest firms, were gradually being forced into people's consciousness, though seldom into their possession. It seemed axiomatic that the bigger the company, the less scrupulous and less moral its attitude. We had seen this before. In Slovenia John West cigarettes were heavily promoted alongside chocolate wrapped in almost identical packaging, the intent to influence children not even thinly disguised – and, of course, there was no health-warning legislation in place.

The rivers Ursul, Katun and Chuya were all spectacular. The turgid brown of the Chuya merged with the clear glacier-green of the Katun to double its size but cloud its pellucid waters. We had to be towed up a series of passes, the last of which commanded magnificent views. We camped at the top, eagles in an eyrie. As on all summits and at *rodnik,* springs, we found rags tied to trees for luck. Several wishing-wells in Scotland engender the same custom and I speculated on its origin as I tied a strip of an old BBC *Garden Party* T-shirt to a branch. In the meadows, grasshoppers of all shapes and sizes buzzed and chirruped. The biggest ones had wings, though their flying ability was limited and crash-landings the norm. Once a hang-glider descended beside us. The pilot was holidaying nearby and was about to have a cup of tea with us when a pick-up truck – with about twenty other pilots – came to collect him. Another interesting encounter was with ornithologist Yuri Lukyanov and his two Kerry Blue terriers. Yuri was studying the rare Altai snowcock, a huge, grouse-like bird.

We reached the Chuyski steppe and a complete change from forest to plain. High mountains to either side of us rose 3692 metres/13,000 feet, as we strolled gently across the flats. There were spectacular light and sound effects during and after thunderstorms, including once a complete double rainbow. One evening a convoy of four massive Kamaz articulated tankers pulled in beside us. This unusual courier service had brought booklets from Yuri Lukyanov about the Altai snowcock and the Institute of Cytology and Genetics near Gorno-Altai, where he worked.

Next morning we arrived in Kosh-Agach, the last town before the frontier post at Tashanta, fifty kilometres further on. It was imperative we stock up especially well, for we had been warned there was little food in Mongolian shops.

Finding it impossible to change money at the bank, I headed, with Eilidh as translator, for the *Administratsia*, to the director's office.

Director Kidirbaev was welcoming and outstandingly helpful. He not only organised the exchange of a hundred dollars but arranged for our gas-cylinder to be refilled and four sacks of oats to be supplied. I wondered what would have been the result if a Russian or Kazakh turned up at the chief executive's office in, say, Highland Region seeking similar help – but, then, they would not have to. Raking round every shop in town, we amassed most of what we needed. I was rather proud of having found tins of sweet-corn and fish and a jar of jam – in the post office! The boys had seen to watering Traceur and the all-essential jerry filling. We plodded out past the airfield, two of its radar-scanners turning desultorily, with only an occasional red kite to cause a blip on their screens.

We were four days from the frontier. 'This broad, grassy plain, with its fortress ring of mountains, has a spaciousness almost daunting, wonderful and wild, utterly lacking the intimacy of the wooded valleys,' I wrote in my diary. ' Kosh-Agach had been all right. The children did sterling work and we proceed quite well provisioned and very content.' Such complacency proved ill-founded.

A slow uphill slog in humid, showery weather brought us within six kilometres of Tashanta. On the way we had seen petroglyphs, prehistoric carvings of a fine mouflon on one rock and two antlered deer on another. Oh, for a Tardis to visit the sculptors! Instead an Uaz visited us, with a major and captain from the military arm of the KGB aboard. The major took our passport details to give to the duty man, saying he had probably not seen a British passport before.

Setting off smartly at 7.30 a.m. next morning, we

discovered the dogs were missing, and had no clue where they had gone. I was not inclined to wait, with a frontier to tackle. We pressed on, leaving them to come when they chose.

Tashanta was a scruffy hamlet with a few tatty houses, a small shop of sorts, the border post and its barracks. A couple of lorries and a small bus were waiting to be cleared. Several border guards were sitting about. After a short while they apologised for keeping us waiting. Would we like to move Traceur over to some grass till the *nachalnik*, the boss, came? He arrived – and with him the bombshell. This was a limited border. Only Russians, Mongolians and Kazakhs were allowed to cross.

We would not be allowed out of Russia! At least, not this way.

CHAPTER THIRTEEN

≈∞≈

MONGOLIA: JULY–NOVEMBER 1994
THE LAND OF GENGHIS KHAN

Printing their proud hoofs in the receiving earth.
Shakespeare

Retreat from Tashanta was unthinkable. It was now mid-July and rerouting a thousand kilometres north to Novosibirsk, then 1750 east to Irkutsk would take till the end of December; and winter would be too harsh for travelling. While I set about trying to crack the problem, Nin and Tsar sneaked back from whatever excursion they had been on.

I pleaded with the border guards at Tashanta, from corporal to colonel and a visiting four-star general. I made four trips to Kosh-Agach, an uncertain two-way hitch-hike of a hundred kilometres. I had meetings with the KGB, the *Administratsia*, the Vice-president of Gorno-Altai, even with Boris Yeltsin's personal representative, Valentina Viktorovna Linkova, who happened to be visiting. I made two calls to the British Embassy in Moscow. Then three Frenchmen turned up in an ex-military Renault 4×4 panel-van, to face the same problem as us. One, Alexis Suremain, was the son of the French ambassador to Lithuania and telephoned people he knew at the French Embassy in

Moscow. By now we were on tea-drinking terms with the KGB officers, sitting under Dzherzhinsky's portrait in Tashanta barracks, but the impasse continued. It looked like being a very dull winter, even if Fionn recalls with delight the chocolate letters he could buy at the Tashanta shop.

Lieutenant Konstantin Ivanovitch Kosta, Ukrainian and very decent, brought his wife Lena over to take tea in the caravan on our seventh evening in Tashanta. As we sipped, he said casually, 'We are letting you go tomorrow.' Amid wild yells and cheers from everyone, including the French, we switched to vodka in celebration.

At noon on Saturday 23 July, paperwork completed, the big gate in the barbed-wire border fence was swung open and we began the twenty-kilometre trek to the Mongolian border-post.

The track was potholed, rutted and mostly uphill. Marmots squeaked from their burrow entrances, red kites and a distant eagle soared above and a mob of noisy Alpine choughs flew by. The Renault caught us up, tried to tow the caravan up the only steep hill, coughed, spluttered and died. We got a rough ride from a Ural instead, uncoupling just short of the actual frontier, high on bleak Durbet-Dabai, an immense sweep of grassland, with rugged 13,000-foot peaks beyond, where we spent our first night on Mongolian soil.

Our arrival had been expected. Mongolian frontier officials quickly stamped us into the land of legends and Genghis Khan. The road for Tsaganuur was flat and good, and sunshine played pattern games with cloud-shadows on the beautifully shaped green hills, reminiscent of the Scottish Borders. About midday we came to a small lake and a group of three *gers**, traditional circular Mongolian

*The better-known word, *yurt*, is Russian and not used by anyone in Mongolia.

felt tents. I declined an invitation to tea – so the inhabitants, not to be thwarted, brought a rug, bread, butter and *kumiss* out to us. The family, ethnic Kazakh, like the majority of the inhabitants of the western province of Bayan-Olgiy, was charming. After we had eaten, one woman went to milk the mares, which were tethered to picket lines with their foals. The foal whose dam was to be milked was taken off the line, its mother's left forefoot put up into a leather strop, and the foal allowed to nuzzle the teat to ensure the mare let down her milk. The foal was then removed and held by a man while the woman milked about a pint from the mare.

There were clusters of *gers* all along the road. Flocks of goats and sheep and herds of yaks, were spread over the hillsides. Several times we were waylaid and presented with yoghurt or *kumiss*. Eilidh and Fionn, as ever, bludged rides on people's horses at every opportunity. There were ruddy shelduck and young on one lake and two families of bar-headed geese on another. The area appeared prosperous. Each family group was well dressed, had big flocks, horses in excellent condition while a tractor and trailer, lorry and often a motorbike stood outside many *gers*. These strong, well-featured tent-dwellers had the finest white teeth we had ever seen.

Our first day in Mongolia was memorable, but I wondered at the end of it how much yoghurt and *kumiss* I would have to consume before arriving in Ulaanbaatar.

The centre of Tsaganuur comprised a few blocky concrete buildings. Outside the bank, eager money-changers crowded, offering 380 to 400 tugruk to the dollar – but the bank rate was 410! The only edible items in the only shop, amongst an array of clothes, footwear and cigarettes, were Snickers and chewing-gum. We took the northern route, via Ulangom, rather than the more southerly main road because it looked more interesting. Information I had gleaned indicated it was passable.

For two days we picked our way down an increasingly narrow valley; past clusters of tents, stopping frequently to talk to the occupants, often being given cheese, *kumiss* or *arkhi*. *Arkhi*, a distillate of fermented mare's milk, can be mildly alcoholic to very strong, depending on the number of distillations, and has an odd, smoky-milk flavour. In old Mongol culture, no one under the age of forty was supposed to drink alcohol and only the old were permitted the strong stuff. This custom is no longer observed, if it ever was. Most of the people in the valley were Mongolian and well-to-do. Traceur was literally a huge star, three times the size of native horses, and much admired.

The valley opened into a vast empty plain, ringed by distant snow-topped mountains. The sense of space was overwhelming, the mosquitoes indescribable, worse even than in the Altai. Fionn remembers 'going into Mozi Hell Valley. I went inside the caravan and, even though it was quite hot, I put on a raincoat and hat to stop being bitten by what seemed the whole of Mongolia's mosquito population.' A good track led across, with many branches off. We took the most-used track, which meant having to ford the Khar-us, rather than detouring for days via Achit, on poorer track, to a bridge. We came to the ford and found it less deep than expected. There was a steep pull up the far bank, so we unloaded everything before crossing the river to give Traceur the best possible chance at it. Even so we ended up using blocks and tackle, anchored with the picket, to help him. After that came wearisome portaging of gear. We parked on top of the riverbank that night. In the gloaming a massive wild boar came strolling out of the undergrowth, sauntered across the track and disappeared again.

We were off by 7.30 a.m. next day and soon up on the

plain. It was hard, uphill pulling. Torcuil's shoes were falling apart, my feet blistered and my hands were red and black from swatting mosquitoes on Traceur. We had seen no vehicles for two days and now the track got fainter and fainter. Alarmed, I consulted the compass – and found we were heading several points west of north. We stopped and I took Torcuil for a recce. After a ten- or twelve-mile hike we returned with bad news. The track was long, rough, steep in parts and at the top turned *west*. Directly ahead, in a 200-foot-deep gorge, was a fast-flowing river. We were on the wrong road. But how? The suspicion occurred that we had crossed the wrong ford. In any case we must turn back. Mosquitoes and a growing anxiety allowed me little sleep.

I biked ahead to check the only other track off from the ford, which Fionn had said was impassable. It was, but not for a bike. I reached a much wider, deeper river than the one we had crossed. It had to be the Khar-us. We were miles off course.

We essayed the return crossing of the ford without unloading, almost made it but stuck mid-stream. Unloading the back rack and exterior boxes enabled Traceur to pull the caravan out. Back on land we faced another dilemma: to reach the river we had descended a very steep escarpment, which we could not get up again unaided. We stopped at the bottom, beside two interesting cairns surrounded by rings of stones. Graves.

Crossing Mongolia was more akin to crossing the Sahara than anything we had faced before. Taking out the compass sooner would have helped, but nothing had led me to expect such conditions. The tracks were good, apparently clearly marked on the map, and several truck-drivers had said the Ulangom road was all right. However, we had missed the fork to the correct ford and landed all too easily in a potentially dangerous situation. The worn track we had mistaken for the main one led to a disused silver mine. Bitter experience now proved our maps untrustworthy. Shaken by what had occurred, I decided that, if the children agreed, we ought to return to Tsaganuur and take the southern road. The risks of going by Ulangom did not seem justifiable.

Eilidh was despatched to fetch help first thing in the morning. You may dispute the wisdom of sending a twelve-year-old girl alone on a forty-kilometre ride. Why not go myself? First, Eilidh was our best rider, best Russian linguist, riding fit and lightweight. Second, I did not want to leave Traceur on the mosquito-plagued plain. Third, we had met the valley people and knew they were kind. Nevertheless it was not a lightly taken decision. I had an uneasy moment when Traceur's massive behind disappeared over the lip of the escarpment and by afternoon was scanning the plain with binoculars well before a tractor hove into view.

Eilidh returned with Sambu, the tractor's owner, to show him where we were. On the way back she pointed out the Ulangom road. Barely visible, without any marker, it was not surprising we had missed it.

That night we parked across the stream from Sambu's *ger*, after a two-and-a-half-hour tow. With the pervasive smell of sheep and goat wafting around, it was like sleeping in a sheep-fank. We had tea with Sambu in his spacious tent next morning, before continuing to Tsaganuur. The tea came out of a large leather wallet in the form of a block over a foot long and more than half as wide and some was crumbled into the pot. Cheese was drying on the roof. Although covered in branches to keep off birds, one cheeky snowfinch was undeterred and pinched all he wanted.

The caravan was hardly jarred at all during the further tow up the valley and out to the Olgiy road, Sambu was so careful. We were lucky to have encountered this very kind man, typical of the best country Mongols.

*

A herder gave us a note to his brother, who lived in a *ger* five kilometres away, saying we wanted to buy a sheep. The children wanted to go but I stayed behind and baked bread, which became a standard chore every alternate day until we reached Ulaanbaatar. Two brick-like loaves later, dogs and horse fed, the clock approaching 10 p.m., I heard galloping hoofs. Riding double on ponies with two Kazakhs, complete with butchered sheep, came Torcuil, Eilidh and Fionn.

All next day we sat at the foot of a steep ridge, watching fuel-tankers struggle and slide their way up, only just making it. Not till a ten-wheeler double-axle-drive Zil came by at 8.30 p.m. did we get a tow. In ten minutes we reached the top, unhitched and parked in a violent hailstorm.

On 4 August, it was −1.5°C/29°F and ice coated the caravan. A downhill run took us to a wide grassy plain full of purple daisies and small yellow and white flowers. Torpid grasshoppers lay about until the sun warmed them, then suddenly took to life and wing. A friendly tanker-driver took water-jerries to fill at Tsaganuur for us and returned them on his road back. Dry twigs and roots from scrubby low bushes, dry animal dung and a few old survey pegs supplied fine firing. Ahead a stupendous massif rose 7937 metres/12,000 feet or more. It was wondrously bonny in the clear light, the air pure, grasshoppers buzzing and not a soul in sight. Eilidh made dampers – an unleavened flour and water pancake – for lunch, the dogs gnawed mutton bones and Traceur grazed content on the succulent grass.

Bayan-Olgiy was the administrative town for the province. The tidy centre had statues of Lenin and Mongolian hero Sukhebaatar but nothing else remarkable. We bought the last two sacks of oats at the grain store, disturbing a mouse from one. They were the only oats we found before Ulaanbaatar. In the evening an air-force pilot on leave stopped to talk and, learning we needed flour, brought us a 20-kilo sack and another of rice.

There were fifty *gers* – we counted them – on the next plain, which sloped gently south; another seventy or so in a broad valley with a lake beyond. Herds of cattle and flocks of sheep and goats abounded. Riders often galloped up to look at us and marvel at Traceur's size, often bringing us cheese, milk or *kumiss*. We munched our way through the mutton and my baking improved. Lake Tolba, twenty kilometres long and one wide, had gulls and cormorants on it. Rahman, the pilot, brought us fresh cheese, milk and *krt*, curds, welcome additions to our very basic diet.

We bypassed Tolba which, like all Mongolian towns, consisted of a number of administrative buildings and masses of *gers*. Torcuil cycled in, failed to find sugar or eggs but, by some favour of Providence, was given a live culture of yeast. Carefully nurtured, it kept my loaves risen in the months ahead.

The road climbed and the peak of 13,786-foot high Tast appeared. A man and wife were scything grass for hay. Here in the mountains people lived in stone houses during winter, their flocks in large pens; it was the only place in Mongolia where we saw hay being made.

Far ahead, clouds lifted and shifted round the top of the snowy splendour of Tast, as we descended the long, gentle slope to the next valley. Horsemen came up, in groups, until we had an escort of twenty-four. Eilidh and Fionn made off with a roan mare and a pretty skewbald, then Eilidh came cantering back to report a deep ford in front. Fortunately a shallow alternative existed and Traceur went over easily. We stopped soon after and for over an hour talked to people and let them look at the inside of the caravan. This was something we seldom did but we had been a merry company and the children had had long spells on their horses.

Next day on a long hill there was a Zil tanker in the

middle of the road, its driver underneath, the clutch in pieces. The driver, Tchintogtoch, said he was all right for supplies but accepted some milk and *krt*. We continued slowly to the top of the next pass. There we talked to a man who had come up from the other side with a pack-horse. He was a saddle-maker, taking pack-saddles over to sell in the valley we had just come from. They were made with wooden pads and lashings and sold for the price of a sheep, about ten pounds.

Half-way down the south side, Tchintogtoch passed us. A mate with a spare clutch-plate had stopped and together they had reassembled the mechanism. Our good deed in offering help was repaid with invitations to visit his relations' *ger* at the foot of the hill and his house in Hovd. On the way, Traceur stumbled sideways descending a bank, and broke the left-hand shaft.

At the *ger* we were given Mongolian tea. A pan of milk was on the stove. A fresh block of tea was unwrapped from its paper, some was hammered off and the rest put into the customary leather bag. Two handfuls went into the milk pan, along with a dessertspoonful of sugar, a knob of butter and a little salt. I liked it, the others less so, but everyone enjoyed the smoking-hot fried bread-cakes with newly churned butter. A tasty pasta and diced mutton dish followed. Tchintogtoch took the shafts into Hovd, still more than seventy kilometres away, to be welded.

Our enforced stop was an unexpected chance to observe life in a Mongol settlement. Grass was not plentiful at the T-junction of valleys where we were, so the sizeable flocks were driven daily into the mountains to graze and brought back at night. The goats and yaks were milked. At yak-milking, the calves were allowed a short draught, then reattached to their lines, before the mother yak, hind legs tied together above the hock, sometimes forelegs at the fetlock too, was milked. The goats were lined up head to head in groups of between twenty and forty and tied with a single rope run in and out between each head. Everyone, from granny to toddler, then waded in and milked furiously, after which, with one pull on the rope, the animals were loosed.

In one *ger* a woman was distilling *arkhi*. Fermented milk was poured into a wide bowl over the fire and a collecting vessel placed on a tripod standing in the bowl. A slightly tapered cylinder, of almost the same diameter as the bowl, was fitted to the bowl's rim. A sealing cloth was placed round the upper rim of the cylinder and a cone-shaped bowl filled with cold water neatly fitted thereon. The vapour from the heated milk rose, contacted the water-cooled surface of the cone-shaped bowl, condensed and dripped into the collecting pot. Simple but effective.

As we had finished the first sheep I arranged to buy another. It was a smallish wether and I asked our friends to kill, skin and butcher it for us. The Mongol method of slaughter is unusual. Turning the sheep on its back, they make a slit below the breastbone big enough to insert a hand, and sever the aorta. The sheep did not struggle and was dead in seconds, quicker than with throat-slitting. Skinning was neatly done, first the forelegs, then central line, then hind legs. Care was taken to keep everything clean and not break or cut intestines. The tripes were rinsed immediately. Abdominal fat, lungs, liver, kidneys, heart, which was split to remove the blood, and intestines were all placed in a bowl. The intestines were taken outside to be washed for later use in sausage-making. The blood, all of which had been confined in the body cavity, was ladled into a small can. The hindquarters were removed as a unit, splayed at the centre join, the fore-quarters likewise, after the ribs and lower breastbone had been severed. Finally, the head was detached from the skin.

We watched butter being churned in a bag using a froe-stick. Outside cheese was being pressed in a great lump in a sack, by the simple expedient of placing a hefty rock on it. In a barrel sheepskins were being pickled in urine to preserve them. Marmots are sometimes shot and eaten. Wild onions are used, other vegetables almost unknown.

Gers vary almost as much in décor as our houses, although the basic layout is common to all. Construction is of lattice walls surmounted by roof-poles, which fit into an upper central ring of wood. Sometimes the poles are exquisitely painted. Four layers of cladding, including the felt one, are used in summer, six in winter. A layer of white canvas over the felt outer layer is usual nowadays. The wooden doors are often decorated, while the interior walls are hung with materials of widely varying colours, depending on taste. On entry, opposite the door, is a centrally placed rectangular closed stove with chimney. To the left are boots, outer coats, saddlery and guns, if owned; next, the milk-bag or barrel for butter-making, then a bed, a chest-of-drawers and another bed, while finally, to the right of the door, are shelves for kitchen equipment and probably a storage chest. The floor to the rear may be wooden – it usually is in fixed urban *gers* – but is more likely of linoleum or plastic, covered with rugs and skins; around the stove there is usually just trampled earth. Aluminium pots and pans and plastic containers have replaced wooden ones in great measure but in essence *ger* life remains as it was before Genghis Khan's time. There is nearly always an array of family photographs, probably a radio and perhaps a small statuette or picture of the Buddha on the chest-of-drawers. Under the bed might be a smart 'masonite' suitcase – or a cheese. Wealthier people have solar- or wind-charged batteries to power lights or a television set. Ash and other refuse is taken well away from the tent for dumping.

Lavatory arrangements entail a long walk to the rocks; only at the stone-built winter houses did we see an outdoor privy.

Eilidh and Fionn had no trouble amusing themselves as long as they could borrow someone's horse. Torcuil, though, was going through a blue phase. Tired of travel, sick of the diet, he said. But whatever ailed him was inside his own head, for he did not know what to do with himself. I was enjoying learning what I could, roaming around the settlement.

At midday on the second day Tchintogtoch's brother brought back the shafts, expertly welded. We set off at once, wending our way down the valley past many more *gers*. Tsar took off, but we expected he would soon catch up. We reached a river, to find the bridge washed out and the far bank short but steep. A mass of people helped shove us up. I had been offered so much *kumiss* that day it leaked from every pore, but it was difficult to refuse without giving offence.

We stopped short of an immense plain where, we were warned, there were terrible mosquitoes. Our peace was disturbed by a drunk. He was with a sober couple who were unable to control him and at one point he threatened to get out a pistol and shoot everybody. Eventually they all left, to be followed by a tipsy, impertinent man on a motorbike. He climbed on to the caravan, demanded food and refused to leave. I literally booted him off. Only later did we learn that, in Mongol culture, anyone might go to any *ger* and request food and shelter for the night. However, it was not obligatory for the occupants to take them in.

Tsar had not returned. Next morning the children, whose job it was to look after him, tossed a coin to see who should go back for him. Fionn lost. We got him a lift, plus bike, on a passing lorry.

A breeze kept the plain mercifully mosquito-free as the caravan crawled across. I climbed a rocky knoll to photograph it, to show the scale of this huge country, disturbed a fox and photographed him too.

A lorry-driver reported seeing Fionn on the way back – but it was hours before he returned, exhausted. He had found Tsar not two kilometres from where we had started the day before, but the dog had been awkward to lead and twice pulled Fionn off his bike during the eight-hour trek back. A tougher boy would be hard to find. He did not complain at losing the toss, or moan when he returned. He deserved a medal – and got one: my Slovenian army cap badge. He said little, but looked pleased.

At the top of a pass we encountered Michael and Jean Campaign. He was Australian, a Customs adviser with UNCTAD, but Jean was from Paisley. Hearing her Scots voice did us a power of good. Catherine Waridel was in Ulaanbaatar, they told us, having succeeded in crossing China to Xinjiang. She was not the sort to give up.

A day short of Hovd, we were woken at 2 a.m. by a tanker-truck pulling alongside, lights blazing, horn blaring, its three male and one female occupants blind drunk. They would not go, and when at last they tried to, could not start their truck. Hours later the engine fired and they shot off fast. In the morning Traceur's bucket, two jerries and a strap were missing.

The road into Hovd was downhill. Tchintogtoch came to escort us in. There were no houses. Apart from a few blocks of flats, the twenty thousand inhabitants live in *gers*. We parked in the grounds of a large school, stowed everything movable inside the caravan and went to lunch at Tchintogtoch's flat. His wife Oyungtsktsk gave us salt tea, sweet cakes and tasty soup. They had three children, daughter Tsoloh and sons Chang-gal and Nemich-bayargh. We made a major shopping excursion and found Hovd bounteously stocked: cabbage, turnips, carrots and baby apples, spaghetti, cooking oil, batteries, a pair of good Russian army boots and in lieu of lavatory paper, lots of old newspapers. I telephoned Kate, and Oyungtsktsk prepared a lovely supper and before the end of the evening we learned our jerries had been recovered. This was excellent news, because they were vital for the long, dry stretches to come.

In the morning we bought barley for Traceur and sugar and flour for us. At the caravan, a delegation awaited, consisting of the procurator, his assistant and Tchintogtoch's boss, with the jerries. I expressed our gratitude, emphasised that I did not want to make a fuss and hoped the driver would be let off with a warning and not lose his job. They appreciated this, for it saved embarrassment all round.

Tchintogtoch towed us across some soft sand and up out of the Hovd basin. Traceur was glad to be moving, having been pestered by admiring crowds and not left in peace to graze. However, as we headed down a long slope past Lake Khar-us towards the hefty lump of 12,340-foot-high Jargallant, he behaved abominably, trying to trot, fidgeting and refusing to take any of the caravan's weight. I had to haul on the reins and yell at him and the dreary downhill stretch went on and on. It was not often I found the day's travel long, boring and infuriating but that day I could have seen Traceur sold for pet-meat ten times over.

Next morning he had gone AWOL.

Eilidh and a herdsman found him six kilometres away, the only time he was ever more than a short walk from the caravan, though in Mongolia we never tied him up or fenced him in. I was sure he did it to punish me for yelling at him, although the good grass he found might have had something to do with it.

One day we met a man and his wife coming towards us with six camels on which were loaded all their worldly goods. They were kindly folk and brewed tea while telling me they were moving to new pastures forty kilometres off. The camels, carefully loaded, carried about two hundred kilos each and were joined nose to tail with camel-hair ropes. Unusually, they had no children to help so someone else was bringing on their stock. They were a dignified couple and looked sad when telling us this. We were lucky to have seen the old way of moving, as most *gers* are transported by truck nowadays.

That afternoon we failed to find a well that was marked on the map. For the only time ever, we had to make double distance to find water. As if to compensate, we discovered a peaceful place to stop beside an offshoot of the river Shenkher, on level ground with plenty grass. We were close to two *gers* belonging to a friendly man who had met us earlier and I arranged to buy another sheep from him. Exhausted, we went early to bed, the moon bright upon us, a wonderful pallid solidity of hills and mountains all around, the stream glinting and jabbling just below. Not a bad place, Mongolia . . .

I was using the compass a lot to take bearings and calculate our distance run. At Yereg Gol we stuck in the mud. But for an error on the map we should never have been there. A camel was hitched ahead of Traceur and the two big beasts strained and hauled and pulled out the caravan, as bar-headed geese and cranes flew over.

Drunks caused all the serious trouble we had in Mongolia. On one especially nasty occasion, an inebriated man arrived in a jeep, with other people, and started to stone Tsar, who was, as always when we stopped, chained to the caravan. Eilidh happened to be outside and remonstrated, whereupon the man picked up a fist-size stone and threatened to throw it at her. Fortunately his companions removed him before he did. He could have killed her.

*

After being nagged for weeks, I had agreed to buy Eilidh and Fionn a joint birthday present of a Mongolian horse when we reached Bulgan. The head of the village, Dembrel, a pleasant man who was a vet and spoke Russian, said he would help. Together we awaited the arrival of a possible horse-vendor. Eventually a posse approached, leading probably the worst horse in Mongolia. A sad little dun, it was lame, had injuries on three legs and a raw patch behind its left foreleg. Even at a knock-down price, including saddle, bridle and hobbles, he was not for us. Another man said he had an eleven- or twelve-year-old chestnut gelding he might sell. We asked to see it, which entailed him bringing up his herd to catch it, as it had been turned out three weeks previously.

This was fascinating to watch. The owner and another rider fetched the herd. The owner wielded a seventeen-foot-long pole with a noose at the end. The trick was to get the noose over the chestnut's head, not so easy with the thirty- or forty-strong herd milling about, trying to break out of the surrounding circle formed by those on foot. The chestnut knew he had been singled out and did not want to be caught but was nabbed after several failed attempts. Once the noose dropped over him he stood stock-still and was bridled without difficulty.

He was a four-square little horse and apart from some white hairs which suggest that at one time he had had saddle-sores, his only blemish was a slight bump on his left hindquarters, legacy of some old cut or kick, which impeded him not at all. Eilidh mounted and was promptly bucked off as he made a bid for freedom. Caught again, he was brought back sweating, for he was in good condition and tubby. He was not nervous of the caravan and I rather liked his cheeky look. His owner drove a hard bargain, saying 60,000 tugruk was his price. He would not haggle so I paid the equivalent of ninety-six pounds, plus twenty-four to another man for a saddle and hobbles. Fionn and Eilidh were ecstatic.

Mr Chestnut, ridden most of that day by Eilidh, proved docile, comfortable and a shade idle. He walked alongside the caravan without fuss, nor did Traceur mind him being there. The boys rode him a little too. That evening he was given his first job, taking jerries for water, which he did without batting an eyelid. He would be a real asset over the dry miles still between us and Gov'Altai.

Flocks of black-bellied sandgrouse were everywhere now, their whirring wings a common sight. The dogs had fun chasing ground squirrels and we saw several jerboas. A few larks and crows, a white wagtail, a hoopoe and some wheatears made up a scanty bird list.

An ancient Gaz jeep disgorged Englishman Matt Clements, who worked for Nomads, a tour agency based in Ulaanbaatar. We gassed for an hour and swapped paperbacks. Matt said we could use the Nomads address for our mail, which meant I could pass the address to Kate and consequently letters should await us on arrival. When it is so seldom received, mail assumes huge importance.

Fionn officially acquired his half of Mr Chestnut on his tenth birthday. Eilidh fixed a flag with 'Happy Birthday' on it to the bridle. I baked a cake with bread mixture using condensed milk instead of water. It was tastier than I had dared hope, and accompanied by a tin of peaches, positively sumptuous.

It had been getting colder, hovering around freezing on many mornings. The country was arid, with sparse thorn bushes and grass, lots of sandgrouse and little else. North of us 11,739-foot Khasagt Khayrkhan was topped with fresh snow, while south the tail of the Altai still had peaks over eleven thousand feet. We lived on bread or damper, sugar in lieu of jam and mutton accompanied by rice, pasta or potatoes. Milk supplies depended on whether we met any herders. Mr Chestnut, or Chessy as he was known, ferried water if none was close by. Traceur's feed had had to be rationed. He was fine in himself but I worried about how thin he was becoming. Then a passing truck sold us two bags of *kombi korm* and he went back on full rations. So did we, when Matt Clements, returning from a tour, donated us scarce goodies including tins of sausages and fruit, ketchup, mayonnaise and Marmite.

On 13 September we were pulling in to Gov'Altai when Catherine arrived. She was staying in a *ger* belonging to Swiss missionary Walter Bütikofer, in a big yard. There was plenty room for us to park there too. So we did.

It snowed while we were in Gov'Altai and the temperature dropped to −9°C/16°F. Catherine was having trouble with officials who were supposed to help her. She had not completed her ride but had indeed crossed Xinjiang as we had been told. We caught up with her news on the run as we shopped, and arranged another rendezvous in Ulaanbaatar. Now, greatly helped by Walter Bütikofer, we located, bought and loaded horse-feed and hay then left. More than nine hundred kilometres still lay in front of us.

It took another month to reach Bayanhongor, with winter tightening its grip all the time. Traffic density on the main east–west road remained light. Torcuil's census of day-time vehicle numbers never exceeded thirty-eight or fell below three. Our life continued as before. Fuel for the fire became scarce and we resorted to cutting stumps off old telegraph poles left protruding from the ground.

One day we came upon two women and two men felt-making by their *ger*. The women teased out the wool, discarding daggy bits, and the men beat it with long metal rods. Unfortunately we did not see the next phase, which apparently involved horses and water.

Torcuil volunteered to hitch into Bayanhongor to try to buy feed, as Traceur was again running short. By nightfall he had not returned. I was not concerned, because by now we knew our way around and I was sure he would have found shelter. He had, but had a much-disturbed night hearing the couple next to him noisily making love. He returned to great praise, having acquired two sacks of *kombi korm*.

Bayanhongor provided us with limited vegetables and fruit and a call to Kate. The feed-store director kept us waiting and overcharged us hugely but there was nothing to be done about that. At least we had sufficient feed to see us to Arvaiheer, which was another month away.

The terrain became very tough for Traceur. We encountered ridge after rolling ridge, with some slopes steeper than I would have wished and chances of a tow usually slim. Chessy was fine. He had slimmed down but remained in good condition. He shared Trass's feed-bucket, provided pleasure for Eilidh and Fionn and continued to ferry water when required. The two horses were company for one another, which helped Traceur during what was a lean time for him. Luckily I did not have to shoe Chessy, for he was accustomed to go without. Traceur's feet were iron-hard now and when changing shoes I could do no more than minor trimming and rasping of his hoof.

We entered coal-country, and found a small, open-cast pit at Bayanteeg, which solved our fuel problems for a while because the tracksides were littered with lumps of coal that had fallen from lorries. We occasionally found pieces of *torf* and bits of wood too.

Our language was becoming so bad I instituted a swear-box. The fine began as twenty tugruk per offence, double for foreign-language swears but had to be reduced after only a day to ten togruk to avoid all-round bankruptcy. On the first day Torcuil had been fined fifty-seven times, Eilidh seven and Fionn only six; my own sins numbered twenty-seven. By such stratagems did we pass cold hours trudging the ridges.

Daily temperatures were between 0°C and −10°C (32°F and 14°F), but strong winds from west and north often gave a high wind-chill factor. We wrapped up as best we could, Fionn and Eilidh in warm new boots from Gov'Altay, but for Chessy's jockey life could be miserable. One day I found Fionn with tears streaming down his face he was so cold, but as usual he never complained. Even walking beside Traceur could be miserable, the pace slow and the wind always finding gaps to pierce through clothing. On two occasions I saw a ground jay, and black vultures were not uncommon, but small birds were scarce.

On 18 October, an incident occurred that had horrendous repercussions. Eilidh, Fionn and I were having lunch in the caravan, well off the track, with neither a *ger* nor another vehicle in sight, when a Gaz lorry pulled up in front of us. Two passengers got out and went to look at Traceur. This in itself was not unusual; we just left people to pat him, provided they did not mess him about. Mongolians normally respect other people's horses. These two, however, were drunk. One came up to the window and shouted something. Then they began to lead Traceur towards the truck. At this point, afraid they were trying to steal him, I went to the door, told them to let go Traceur and leave. It was windy and I was not wearing spectacles. Their driver was slumped over his steering-wheel, drunk or asleep. They did not go. Because one of them was weaving towards the caravan, I fired warning shots over their heads with the catapult. Torcuil was away on Chessy fetching water and, from experience of earlier incidents, I was apprehensive of drunken Mongolians. The nearest man staggered and fell, then got up. His companion went on annoying Traceur and they still did not go. I twanged stones at the lorry to wake the driver. After a tense twenty minutes or so, to my enormous relief they climbed aboard the truck and drove away.

Two days later, on 21 October, we reached Arvaiheer. I had been considering having Traceur transported the last four hundred kilometres, for he was thinner than ever, despite double rations. Available feed was of poor quality and grass now had little nutritional value. However, if we could get hold of better feed, the remaining road was asphalt and perhaps we could do it. In fact we were able to buy five sacks of cubes, which Traceur adored, plus hay and a horde of things for ourselves too. Arvaiheer shops were better stocked than any yet seen in Mongolia. It was Eilidh's thirteenth birthday. She had been enjoying her half of Mr Chestnut for some time; now fresh provisions meant she could have a good party, too.

It was wintry as we set off, −8°C/18°F with snow showers and a strong, dagger-sharp wind, but knowing it was the last lap gave us inner warmth. Traceur found pulling easier on asphalt and visibly perked up. Near the bridge over the Ongi river we saw a monstrous bird, a lammergeier. New to us and quite magnificent, it was almost four-foot long and had a ten-foot wingspan. The wind pushed us up the hill on the far side and we stopped satisfied that afternoon. Two men, from *gers* about two kilometres off, visited us riding on oxen, which were in superb condition. This was the only time we saw oxen ridden. Horses hereabouts were also in excellent shape; with the onset of winter, they needed to be.

Banshees from the north had howled about us all night, rocking the caravan, and we set off on 26 October in a north-westerly gale, which was blowing snow across everything. It was down to −35°C/−31°F including wind-chill, horizontal visibility often almost nil, yet the sun shone faintly through and it was not snowing. It was like being in a sandstorm, only marginally less gritty. The fine powder snow got into everything, back-box, front-box, tack-box, even my jacket pockets. The horses were iced up like cakes. Hissing serpents of snow snaked across the road. A herd of horses, bums to the wind, looked resigned to endure. Four white-coated camels gave the lie to images of desert and date palms. At a burn, where we watered, a Zil lay on its side, its load of flour awash, the driver curled up, unhurt beside a fire he had made under the culvert over which his truck had plunged. A rider leading a horse materialised out of the blizzard, passed and was swallowed up in the swirling storm. Hundreds of bar-headed geese flew south in honking skeins high above the blast and six swans, white on white, slipped silently by.

The road made a right-angle, taking us face-on to the gale and our third hour was brutal. Sharp snow-crystals streamed towards us in sheets. Handfuls of needles were driven into my eyes, yet I had to open them, as there were jeeps and lorries about. For Traceur, the force of the wind doubled his burden. The children and Chessy took refuge in the lee at the rear of the caravan.

Gradually the storm abated. By stopping time the black ribbon of road was visible to the horizon. Untacking with numb fingers took longer than usual. The horses' water half froze on pouring. While we worked a tractor approached, loaded with oat-straw. Eilidh stopped it and we were able to buy two bales. Providence had provided the horses with a well-deserved treat at the end of a gruelling day.

There were no classically spectacular views in this region, just great swathes of space stretching far and far, dotted here and there with flocks of sheep and herds of camels, horses and cattle. From the top of a col one day, snowy hills lay clear to the horizon, blue upon powder blue, like some Antarctic scene, breathtakingly beautiful. The quality of light and clarity of the air defied description and to have gained moments such as these made all privations and hardships seem as nothing.

In spite of the difficult travel, lessons were not neglected and the children put in several hours most days. We had been learning poetry and even attempting to write some. Torcuil was consistently scoring over 90 per cent on his self-assessment English O-level course.

Our water came from wells, streams or lakes. Often now, we had to break ice to reach it. At one defunct Archimedean-screw type well, we used a rope and bucket instead. The water was 'full of bird-shit and bits of half-eaten mouse'. I was glad we had our bacteria-removing British Berkfeld filter.

Walking along with Traceur I had plenty time for thought, though frequently I simply freed my mind to absorb the superlative sweep of the landscape. Jeeps often stopped and eight or ten Mongols would emerge from on top of a mound of luggage to chat. Or five or six would climb down from the cab of a Zil. Most wore the traditional *del*, a unisex calf-length wraparound sleeved cloak, with sash, often fleece-lined in winter, and long boots with turned-up toes. Some *dels* were elaborately trimmed at the edges with braid and had fine silver buttons. Older men would offer me snuff from traditional stone bottles; some smoked slender, small-bowled, silver-trimmed pipes. Traditional saddles were wooden, with leather flaps and huge round or rectangular stirrups. Four silver roundels fixed on the seat represented hidden wealth and sometimes the leather was finely tooled. Cheaper modern saddles had metal pommels and detachable cushions, with thick rubber flaps replacing leather.

Nearing the capital, we saw a number of ploughed stretches. Voles or hamsters were so numerous they had stripped the ground bare in places. Abandoned spanners and fractured bolts told of motoring mishaps. Bald tyres, gashed tyres, missing tyres or even wheels, slack steering, sagging suspension and faulty brakes were commonplace. The high level of inebriation of some drivers must cause accidents, although we saw only two.

On 6 November we bought our seventh and last sheep, and had a grand evening in the vendor's *ger,* drinking salty tea and telling him and his family as best we could about our journey. Next day, we were in sight of Lün when a Volkswagen van pulled up and out tumbled a troop of Ted Turner's own from CNN. They had spotted us by chance – but would we mind if they came and filmed us in the morning?

At precisely the right moment, as we were about to tack up and put to, the CNN crew arrived. It was a grey day, started calm but with a rising wind spearing out of the north. By the time we were on the road it was a gale and soon it brought horizontally driven snow. I had always been impressed by the quality of CNN's news reports and the crew was as pleasant as I had expected. They worked round us with minimal fuss and quiet professionalism, in increasingly atrocious conditions, letting us get on with our work and filming what we did. The only special shot was when Mike Chinnoy, then CNN's Beijing bureau chief, made his concluding remarks to camera in front of us. The broadcast four-minute piece was the best report we ever saw about ourselves. The crew was not only great to work with but left us peanut butter, raisins, fruit juice, McVitie's Rich Tea biscuits and *sliced bread*!

Elsewhere in the world, the US Democrats took a pounding in mid-term elections. The impending metamorphosis of GATT into the World Trade Organisation* made me pessimistic. It seemed to me the natural world, and remaining tribal peoples dwelling in harmony with it, were doomed to disappear to the crash of cash-registers filling multinational company coffers, as forests were felled, fisheries destroyed and the tundra swamped in oil.

A week from Ulaanbaatar temperatures plunged to −21°C/6°F. Predictably road traffic increased. We caught up with a piece of living history: half a dozen drovers were driving over a hundred yaks, sixty or seventy cows and more than seven hundred sheep to market in the age-old way. It was a magnificent sight. In Scotland droving ceased in the nineteenth century, but harsh though their life was, Scots drovers never had to camp out in the cold these lads were enduring.

We sighted Ulaanbaatar on 14 November and entered it on the fifteenth. The director of the State Circus agreed to accommodate our horses in their stalls and the caravan and dogs in their yard. Catherine Waridel found us and we spent the night at her hotel. It cost 1800 togruk each, with Fionn free and was worth that for the hot showers alone. It was a marvellous feeling to have battled through, for Ulaanbaatar was another of Those Places on the map. If we could find a flat at a reasonable rent, we should be all set for winter.

Next morning, we did.

---

*If anyone should doubt the WTO can have a negative effect, I would cite as example its pronouncement that US conservation regulations, designed to protect turtles, constitute 'a restraint of trade'.

CHAPTER FOURTEEN

~~~~~~

ULAANBAATAR: NOVEMBER 1994–JULY 1995
MONGOLIAN CIRCUS

No light can compare with the light of justice. The establishment of order in the world and the tranquillity of the nations depend upon it.

Bahá'u'lláh

Ulaanbaatar has a population of approximately seven hundred thousand, a third of Mongolia's total. Beautiful, spacious Sukhebaatar Square is the centre. The parliament building fronts its north side; head post office, fledgling stock exchange and trades union buildings on the west; opera house on the east and semi-formal gardens to the south between it and the main street. Other official buildings are within a short distance, along with museums, art galleries and major shops and hotels. Rings of apartment blocks stretch out along the main roads west and to the airport, and a dense suburbia of *gers* beyond them. The whole city lies in a basin surrounded by hills and whenever there is no wind it traps air, including terrible pollution from coal-fired Power Station No. 3, which supplies the whole city. It was on its last legs, and engineers from the Morrison Knudsen Company were endeavouring to prolong its life. Power cuts were frequent but if it ever broke down completely, the city would freeze.

During our first week I dealt with administrative matters

about the flat with our landlady, Altanzaya, and with circus director Batmunkh, about stabling the horses. Rents were high and our two-bedroom, kitchen and bathroom flat, with telephone, cost two hundred dollars per month. The circus stabling was expensive. Batmunkh, a man I never took to, at first demanded a thousand dollars for five months but eventually we settled on $750, including feed.

Foreigners are required to register with the police in Mongolia, I understood within ten days of arrival in Ulaanbaatar. Accordingly I went to do so, only to be told we should have registered within ten days of arriving in Mongolia. No one had mentioned registration before we reached Ulaanbaatar, though we had been checked by the Bayan-Olgiy police. We might be fined, they said; come back tomorrow morning. I enlisted the aid of Catherine's friend Khurelbaatar, who spoke fluent English, and together we trekked across town next morning – to find Police Registration shut. I soon learned that this was typical of Ulaanbaatar.

That afternoon, I received a telephone call from the police. Would I please come to the central police station at four o'clock? The conversation was in broken Russian, they mentioned Khurelbaatar's name and I assumed it was to do with registering. I went – and got a nasty shock. A complaint had been laid against us – or me – by a Mr Bolt. By coincidence the police officer was a Captain Khurelbaatar and by a bizarre twist the police already held David Grant's passport, only, incredibly, another David Grant. The nature of the complaint was not revealed. I was simply told it involved criminal charges and to come back on Thursday with an advocate.

Bolt was one of the drunks who had so alarmed us on 18 October and he was claiming he had been shot and blinded in one eye. This was revealed when, along with

Khurelbaatar as translator and advocate Mrs Taivan, I attended my second meeting with Captain Khurelbaatar. It was explained to me that I was a suspect, subsequently possibly an accused and finally a defendant, should I be charged and put on trial. I made a statement, giving our account of what happened that day in Over-hangai *aimag* (district). We signed it and left.

This affair was to dominate and blight our winter, delay our departure and for a time sour me utterly with most things Mongolian.

Of eight months spent in Ulaanbaatar – or UB, as every Westerner called it – over three were because of my case. The city offered relatively little entertainment but there was a well-developed social round, thankfully not the cocktail-party variety. In addition there were the animals to look after, the caravan to be cleaned and repairs to be done. Our mailing address continued to be Nomads' office, situated in the trades union building. The business was owned by Australian Sean Hinton and the office was a meeting-place, especially for members of the local Baha'i community.

The British Embassy operated a pub! On Friday nights the Steppe Inne, voluntarily staffed, functioned as social hub and safety valve for stressed expatriates, mainly Brits but with a scattering of Americans, Canadians, Australasians and others. Admittance was by invitation. During the run-up to Christmas, Friday evenings became the high point of the week, not for the booze but for the distraction of meeting people. The embassy staff were cheery, and for a few hours I could forget about my case.

During the winter we visited many of Ulaanbaatar's attractions. The Gandang Monastery was active again after years of suppression; many monasteries had been destroyed and monks killed in Mongolia, under Communism. The Bogd Khan Palace, pre-revolutionary home of the country's rulers, was open to the public and contained many splendid things – including a conservationist's nightmare, a *ger* dating from the 1890s covered with 150 rare snow-leopard skins. The main art gallery housed a lot of bad paintings, in garish primary colours; however, we saw lots of good watercolours elsewhere, including many for sale. Mongolia is the site of exciting dinosaur finds and the Natural History Museum had fine examples, though its animal collection was a taxidermic disaster with the most ineptly stuffed specimens I'd ever seen. The Lenin museum displayed a comprehensive geological collection, while the excellent Museum of Mongolian History included good examples of a *ger*, old-style furnishings and agricultural implements. A small building close to the opera house housed an extraordinary collection of interlocking wooden puzzles, ranging from easy four-piecers to complex monsters comprising thousands.

Our flat was comfortable and warm. One night there was a flood, because the people above had gone to bed drunk and left their bath running. Occasionally there would be violent shouting in the street outside. Once the folk below had a real ding-dong and we could hear the furniture being demolished. Finding blood on the stairs, or a drunk curled up by the stair radiator, was not unknown. We used to see drunks lying comatose in the street sometimes, including one, I remember, with blood all over his face.

Pickpockets were common, notably in the state department store ('Harrods' everyone called it), on buses and at markets. They were adept, and not averse to using a razor on anoraks and briefcases.

Buses were the official city transport and private cars doubled as taxis – you simply flagged one going your way. The system worked well and few drivers tried to charge over the odds. The buses were better than in Almaty but we walked a lot. The flat was only five minutes from Sukhebaatar Square and fifty yards from the circus.

We met most people we came to know either at Nomads or the Steppe Inne. Through Nomads we were introduced to Loïs and David Lambert. They kept open house and it was usual to find their small flat full of people, often from far afield. Most were Baha'is working in Mongolia or Mongols who had accepted the Baha'i faith. When I worked for Africar in Lancaster, I had eaten at a restaurant owned by an Iranian Baha'i, so I knew something about it. They were invariably nice people. At the Steppe Inne we met Wilf McKie, a consultant to World Bank projects, while Paul Cooke worked for a Japanese company upgrading the railway system. There was geophysicist Andrew Rybaltowski, whom we had met on the road. He and two colleagues had been held up at gunpoint, by two drunks, while out prospecting. After his return to Canada he sent us excellent maps for the next stage of our journey. Australian Jane Hamilton was assistant to Jan Vegter on the Przewalski's horse scheme. Debbie Atkins, from Kenya, owned five hundred camels and was involved in a UN project surveying wild camels in the Gobi. Nick Honhold, a vet working with the agriculture ministry, normally lived in Edinburgh. There were many others, mostly bankers, accountants or engineers attached to aid schemes.

Reintroduction of Przewalski's horse, or *takhi,* was a co-operative Dutch–Mongolian effort. Jan Vegter was in charge of it. In spring he took us to Hustai Nuruu to see the project in action. Horses collected from zoos and bred from especially for the project were kept at Elspeet in the Netherlands – by coincidence we had driven past their enclosure on our first day on the road. The progeny were flown out in batches, then gradually accustomed to local conditions before release. We saw one group of new arrivals, still being kept close to the laboratory, and another, which had been there longer, in a very much larger enclosure. Best by far was sighting one of the released groups: a stallion, six mares and two foals. It was thrilling to see them roaming free, the first to do so on their native soil for many years. This impressive programme, while centred on the horses, is a holistic one and a comprehensive study of the entire flora and fauna in Hustai Nuruu was being undertaken.

My case ran like poison through our social life, our shopping expeditions to the market, visits to sights and occasional excursions out of town with friends. After the initial questioning in early December, two meetings were arranged at the police station then called off. Our registration problem was solved when a Mongolian we knew, who knew an official, took our passports and brought them back stamped. But concerning the case, nothing. I almost began to wonder if it had been dropped.

Kate was due out on 20 December. She had had treatment for symptoms akin to Ménière's syndrome, which cause attacks of tinnitus and vertigo and '. . . took time and didn't go away for months. I was fitter and flew to be with the family for Christmas, with the thought of travelling across the Gobi with them into China.' On arrival, she looked well and bore the usual heap of luggage containing items from our 'wants' list. She was plunged directly into our mad Mongolian life. The children took her shopping at the Russian Market – so-called because when Russians were the dominant foreigners here, they used it – while I tried to arrange for a fine to be paid to get Khurelbaatar out of jail. He had been breaking up a fight between two youths and been arrested as part of the affray. Three days after she returned Kate had her purse lifted in 'Harrods', though she swore she had had her hand on it at the time.

'Like being in a room full of treacle, trying to pin a jelly on the wall,' was how Nick Honhold described trying to get things done in Ulaanbaatar. Personally I felt as though I was wandering round in a bowl of candy-floss. Whenever the case seemed to make tangible progress it dissolved into a sticky mess. While it lacked the humour of Disney and the tragedy of Kafka, there were elements of both in the convoluted police procedure and quirky judicial processes to which I was subjected. I do not want to inflate the case, which was a very real ordeal at the time, to a position of overly dominant importance in the context of our journey but some account of it may interest, amuse – and serve as awful warning. It received a great deal of press coverage, mainly in the UK but also in Mongolia, and I was even sent a clipping from Indonesia.

New Year came and went. January dragged into February. Apart from brief contact with my lawyer, nothing happened. The Russians reduced Grozny, which our Chechen friends in Kazakhstan had told us was a beautiful city, to rubble. Despite the dire state of their economy, the Russians announced an essential new measure: bread would be wrapped. Five thousand people died in an earthquake in Kobe. And a trader named Leeson bankrupted Baring's Bank in a failed attempt to boost his already large income by gambling in megabucks on the Tokyo stock exchange with other people's money. I got a job, teaching an outline course on British history at the Foreign Languages Institute. My pay was that of Mongolian teachers, equivalent to 80p an hour. Then, on 24 February, Eilidh and I went to the police station, for a confrontation between Bolt and ourselves under the eye of Captain Khurelbaatar.

It was a farce. Mrs Taivan, Khurelbaatar, Eilidh and I were there but there was no sign of Bolt and Captain Khurelbaatar declined to see us. The rearranged meeting the following Monday was worse, as neither Bolt nor

Mrs Taivan were there. Mrs Taivan arrived and told me that if (my) Khurelbaatar – who, though having a heart of pure gold had a severe drink problem – turned up tipsy again she would no longer work with him. (Actually he had been only slightly tipsy. I could always tell: the tighter he got, the more his accent resembled that of the Pink Panther.)

Early on 12 March, Mrs Taivan called me – and gave me a shock. Without telling me she had arranged a meeting with Bolt at our flat that morning. I could not find Khurelbaatar, so asked our neighbour from two flats above, Sara, half Korean, a doctor who spoke excellent English, if she would be kind enough to fill in. Bolt appeared with his advocate, a translator and a journalist, whom I refused to admit. I did not recognise Bolt. He was bigger and coarser-featured than I recalled – but, then, without my specs I had seen a man in a *del*; now, a leather-jacketed fellow wearing tinted glasses confronted me. We talked for a long time, without admitting any of us were responsible for his injury. He did have one – an opaque spot on his left eye. As I had expected, it boiled down to money. Bolt obviously assumed we were loaded. He talked about treatment for his eye in America costing sixty thousand dollars – more than we had started the trip with. I told him insurance companies could be expected to pay about two thousand for a similar injury incurred, say, at work. The meeting ended without agreement but at least we had tried.

Matters stretched out, seemingly for ever, delayed because the police could not locate the lorry-driver. Eventually they discovered he was already imprisoned, accessory to a killing. On 4 April, Kate left for Britain to try to get help and stir up media interest. 'I didn't want to leave at all, especially under the circumstances. Two weeks later David rang to confirm our worst fears so I set to work. The story was picked up quickly by the media and the telephone never stopped ringing. The Foreign Office was very supportive.'

I should mention that, although I felt our position was unassailable, the more so as Bolt's and his companions' accounts of what happened were full of contradictions and discrepancies, one point always disturbed me. The principal of Mrs Taivan's law firm, Bakhdal, had said at the outset that on no account should I admit to using the catapult. Instead I should say Eilidh, concerned about Traceur, had used it because I might face jail but a minor would only be reprimanded. I was never happy with this lie but advice from a seasoned advocate, especially in a foreign land, was not to be dismissed. It says something for our adamancy that eventually even Bolt, who had always maintained I shot, admitted not knowing who had.

At no time was evidence produced that I had damaged Bolt's eye. I always admitted that an accident had been possible. Small, irregularly shaped stones shot from a catapult in high wind are inaccurate, more so in the highly charged atmosphere engendered by the men's threatening behaviour. But the man had been staggering drunk, could have fallen, had a fight or some other accident before he came or after he left. He had helped move a *ger* after leaving us, then waited two more days before attending a hospital in Ulaanbaatar. Yet when interviewed by the BBC he claimed the pain in his eye had been excruciating. If so, why had he not sought medical attention in Arvaiheer, an hour's drive away from where the incident took place?

On twelve occasions Captain Khurelbaatar failed to keep arranged appointments. Twelve times I tensed up for them and twelve times was let down. Then his attitude suddenly changed. Having been not unfriendly, he became overtly hostile. I wondered who was paying him. This may have been unjust but the change in him was marked. When Bolt and I had been examined jointly in front of him, I was sure Bolt had blown his case. He had admitted drinking before visiting us, said the driver was asleep, said the third man did not see what happened and – incredibly – that he was hit on the eyebrow, not in the eye. This was all taken down by Captain Khurelbaatar and signed into the police records.

There was talk of taking me into custody. The driver of the lorry (who had been zonked out the whole time and could not have seen anything) made outrageous statements when I had a 'face to face' with him. I should not have known him from Adam, in or out of his convict garb. He lied in his teeth, in such a confused way that I thought it gave little credence to his tale.

My position deteriorated with seeming inevitability. We met the prosecutor. We consulted the State General Administration of Crime Investigation Office. We lodged a counter-charge against Bolt. The embassy was kept informed and was as helpful and kind as its official position allowed. Unofficial, personal support was enormous. Alarmingly, I was told a 'draft charge' stated that I had injured Bolt intentionally. This was outrageous if true. I had used the catapult as a last resort in self-defence. Unfortunate precedents had shown us drunken Mongolians could be dangerous. Even if it was believed *I* shot the catapult, the opposition evidence could not be interpreted to show I deliberately injured anyone.

Nevertheless Captain Khurelbaatar was hell-bent on pushing it. On 14 April I was formally charged, under Section 90-1 of the Mongolian Penal Code: Deliberate Wounding. Possible sentence: three to eight years' imprisonment.

Emotionally, from then till the case came to court on 3 May, I became a yo-yo. Good news, the matter was being dropped, zoomed me to heights of hope; bad news, nothing had changed, snapped me back into tight knots of despair –

up down up down up down up down till I became ragged and wrung out.

As the trial approached, Khurelbaatar was approached in different fashion. It was suggested he should 'soften' his translation of my evidence . . .

Wilf McKie had been hugely supportive in many ways. Through George Kadis, an American contact of his in the China North Hauler Company we now had an invitation to visit that country. On 7 April, I had presented it at the Chinese Embassy and paid $152 for our visas. Preparations for departure had continued, because I believed Bolt could not win. Brian Young, an Ulsterman whose Sisyphean task in Mongolia was returning garment-manufacturers Temujin Mench to profitability but who also owned pubs in Belfast, bought advertising space on the caravan. As our resources drained, his help – and faith that we should be able to continue – was enormously appreciated.

On 24 April consul George Hodgson saved me from immediate imprisonment. I had lodged papers with the court, then been taken upstairs, where an aggressive woman rattled out something about passport, gold, dollars, which I completely failed to comprehend. I called the embassy, where Munkh, the delightful cheery translator, told me that in lieu of my producing security they wanted to remand me. I was furious, because all I had been told to date was to the contrary. Had I known that the harpy was a senior judge I might have been less truculent. Diary: 'George Hodgson and Munkh arrived on the run, George looking extremely grim. I was sent to wait outside. Later, emerging, George said it was touch and go right till the end whether I was going to be locked up. He and Munkh had had to stand as guarantors that I won't vamoose.' Apparently it was customary to remand people at this point though no one had seen fit to mention it and 'I just do not trust the

bastards, not least because of so many broken promises,'
reads my diary.

Not many pages later I wrote: 'That word: trial.
Frightening in its implications of what a fragile line I am
walking.' I was becoming increasingly uptight and apprehensive. Everything I was told, everything the embassy was
told, kept being reversed. The whole business was unreal
but I plunged on down, as if I was in a falling nightmare.
Having to cook meals, visit the dentist and oversee repairs
to the caravan only heightened the sense of unreality. The
rock-fast support of the children alone kept me from losing
my grip. They appreciated the danger I was in fully, but
apart from being extra-close as a family, they were
remarkably unaffected by it all. Eilidh, of course, knew she
had not used the catapult but went along with the story we
had been advised to tell. The police, however, did not, and
she was never charged.

In Britain, Kate had achieved wonders. As the trial drew
ever closer, I fielded increasing numbers of calls from newspapers, radio, TV – and old friends.

Then the trial was postponed for a week, adding more
stress.

Someone gave me a copy of Amnesty International's just-
published report on conditions in Mongolia's prisons. First
paragraph, third sentence read: 'Any jail sentence in
Mongolia must be regarded as a potential death sentence . . .'
Ninety people had died the previous year from starvation or
starvation-related disease. Most encouraging. Then it was
time to go to court. Diary:

Wednesday 3 May 1995. Court at 10 a.m. Bolt's
advocate absent. 12 o'clock, Bolt's advocate arrives. We
start. There is no jury but a tribunal of three judges. All
three are women. Formalities. I tell our tale. Bolt tells his.

Eilidh is called. Prosecutor has his say. Nothing new. There is a 'citizen's representative' present; he asks a couple of questions. We break after three hours when all is done for the judges to decide their view.

George Hodgson tells me he thinks they must dismiss the case, as there is no evidence. After nearly an hour we go back in.

The presiding judge stands to give the verdict and we all rise. '. . . Mongol Mongol Mongol . . . *to three years in jail . . .*' I lose the translation and feel a blow to the heart like a punch. Behind me I hear the consul's jaw thud into the floor. '. . . reduced to two years suspended under supervision . . .'

Shock still, but immediate relief I am not for jail yet. Can we leave Mongolia? Yes. NO! Bolt is unhappy, no money for him. He will appeal. I cannot leave before it.

Totally shattered, utterly depressed by the thought of more delay and expense, somehow I get to Mrs Taivan's office. She and Khurelbaatar try to explain answers to my questions but I am near snapping point and find the long-winded indirect Mongolian translation too much. I apologise and go home.

Wilf and Paul Cooke invite me to the bridge-club evening at Paul's. I accept gratefully, anything to take my mind off the afternoon's horror. Maybe I shall learn a little more bridge – but it is not to be, for the telephone never stops. The British media are in full cry, all supportive and wanting to talk. Kate had done a tremendous job – and is as shattered as we are.

Batmunkh said the circus animals would be going to pasture for the summer and we must leave. On 5 May Khurelbaatar and I went to see him and appeal for time to find alternative accommodation. He gave a blank refusal. We must leave by

10 a.m. tomorrow. He went on about payment, though failed to mention the two buckets and halter-rope someone had stolen from us. The German ambassador, Herr Metternich, whom we knew slightly, kindly agreed we could put the caravan in their spacious embassy compound as the British one was too small. John Teggart, another Irishman, who worked for contractors Holzmann-Wimpey, who were resurfacing the airport runway, arranged to house the horses and dogs temporarily at their site there.

Next day at the circus there was a scene with director Batmunkh. He demanded payment before we left and wouldn't let the truck in to tow the caravan out. He then insisted on seeing inside it – afraid we were stealing a bear, perhaps? – and demanded a huge sum per bale for hay he'd said we could have for nothing. He seemed to be enjoying himself. The accountant, whom I went to settle with that afternoon, had been horrified at his director's behaviour.

A worse blow was hearing from Kate that the possessions we had left behind, in an acquaintance's outbuilding near Kelty in Fife, had been pillaged. Our pictures, crockery, cutlery, tools and a lifetime of accumulated knick-knacks were gone. These were family things, irreplaceable, their value not great and immaterial anyway. I was greatly distressed, and so was Kate.

The appeals – I had, of course, submitted mine too – were heard in the Cassation Court on 22 May. That they took place so swiftly was in great measure due to continuing pressure by our embassy, boosted by Kate's efforts and the mounting publicity in the UK. A week before, the BBC had sent Andy Webb out with a camcorder to film the story. One of the nicest reporters I have met, he also had high standards of integrity. Although he was with us for days and sympathised with our plight, he rightly would not let us view the footage of his interview with Bolt. Nor did I ask to see it.

This contrasted with a Mongolian newspaper article, highly prejudicial to us, illustrated by a photograph I recognised as one from the police files.

The District Court verdict was overturned, ending my criminal career after exactly three weeks. But I had no time to draw breath for a silent cheer before the judges announced that, because of lack of evidence, they were ordering a complete re-investigation. Diary: 'Back to square one. Incredible. What evidence more can there be? There *were* no witnesses except Bolt's lot and us. I am in total despair and near tears.'

Sustained by the help and kindness of many people, I drew on Taurean reserves of stubbornness and strength. I was particularly buoyed up by the Baha'is and had been having long talks with the Lamberts about the Faith. I found Baha'i beliefs and my own views ran parallel on many topics, including the oneness of humankind, proper treatment of the environment and animals, the equality of men and women, the elimination of prejudice and racism, the need for world peace, the elimination of extremes of wealth and of poverty, the need for truth and justice and the eventual formation of a world government. There had been manifold occasions during our journey when I felt we had been helped by some external power. I had never been an atheist, or even an agnostic, although I had long since rejected the format offered by the Presbyterianism in which I was brought up. I had been fascinated by the extraordinary work of the late T. C. Lethbridge, which demonstrated by dowsing that there is more than one plane of existence, but spiritually I had my own personal bubble and was not – or not consciously – seeking an alternative. I was still not quite ready to accept that man is subservient to one God, a god so infinitely superior as to be unknowable, but I liked the Baha'i concept of progressive revelation, which was new to me, and the openness of this independent world religion. And I did, with considerable difficulty, attempt something I had not done since I was a child. I prayed.

We went racing, invited by the president of the Mongol Horse-Racing Association. Mongol races are run over distances of about twenty-five kilometres, so one only sees the finish. The jockeys are children, aged from five to fifteen. The interest was in the colourful crowds, the side-shows, including wrestling, rather than the few moments it took for the riders to appear over the hill and cross the finishing-line. It was a day out with a difference and a tonic change from courts and cop-shops.

The reinvestigation of the case was continuing. It was suggested to me, by the officer reinvestigating the case, that if I admitted firing the catapult the charge would be reduced . . . Incredulity. Thanks to help from Dr Ken Mickleson, an eye-specialist from New Zealand, I at last got an independent assessment of Bolt's eye damage, and learned there was a world-class Mongolian eye-surgeon in Ulaanbaatar, Dr Baasanhuu, who could perform the necessary operation to repair it. Being tried twice for the same offence – 'double jeopardy' – is illegal under international law and Mongolia was a signatory to the relevant convention that banned it. On 1 June George Hodgson rang to tell me Prime Minister Major had called in the Mongolian ambassador in London to protest. A local diplomatic protest was also made. Stops were being pulled out all round on our behalf and I was very grateful.

In mid-June we endured another heavy blow. Mr Chestnut was stolen. The circumstances were never elucidated but the finger of suspicion pointed at soldiers from a small barracks near the Holzmann site. They were unco-operative when questioned and I have believed since then that Chessy went into their pot. He had been grazing and would never have run off from his big pal Traceur, and I discounted the fantastic suggestion he had gone hundreds of miles 'home' to Bulgan. Police inquiries proved unavailing. We were all sad and further downcast, especially Eilidh and Fionn.

The possibility of another trial, appeal, progress to a higher court, appeal, until finally the matter went before the President, brought me to despair. Consul Hodgson had told the prosecutor-general that if the illegal retrial went ahead there was every likelihood that Britain would take Mongolia to the International Court of Justice. Comforting as it was, that stratospheric prospect brought a quick solution no nearer. Neither did it staunch the haemorrhage from our bank account. Mash-Erdene, a friend of Catherine's, legally trained and fluent in English, had translated on several occasions when Khurelbaatar was 'indisposed'. I suggested the only thing to do now, armed with full knowledge of the extent of Bolt's injury and Dr Baasanhuu's estimate of the cost of operating, was to go and talk to Bolt. Mash thoroughly agreed with this ploy, saying it was the age-old traditional way Mongolian disputes were resolved. Mrs Taivan suggested taking a small gift as evidence of good intent, cigarettes and chocolate.

We met Bolt outside the hospital, where he had had a preliminary operation. He wanted his medical expenses paid – which was what he had always been after. Through Mash I had already offered to pay the cost of his operation in Mongolia. The grey area was whether he would insist on awaiting a necessary second operation before coming to terms. Bizarrely, he invited us to his flat for lunch the following Sunday.

Bolt fetched us in his car. He had brought his wife and daughter with him, which Mash said was a good sign. We talked about everything except business till the meal was over. Bolt was not allowed to drink after his op; I, teetering on the edge of joining the Baha'is, who don't drink, decided not to – so Mash was left to absorb the lot. Maybe it helped his advocacy, because it was effective. Bolt contrived to have me pay his legal costs as well as medical, bringing the bill to $1,700 altogether and in return agreed to drop his complaint against me.

There was no sense of relief, only a numbness, a realisation that Bolt might have had two thousand dollars at our first meeting, that it had cost over four thousand to stay on and fight the case and that it was a pity we could not have come to terms before. If I *had* been the cause of Bolt's injury – which I had always said was possible but which was never demonstrated with any certainty – it had been accidental and stemmed entirely from his drunken behaviour. Nevertheless, I was not comfortable with the thought I might have injured him. In the end Bolt proved rather a simple soul, foolish, maybe, but not bad. It had seemed very different on 18 October.

It was too late and too hot to contemplate the eight-week Gobi crossing to the Chinese border. With Paul Cooke's assistance, we hired railway wagons, a flatbed for the caravan and a boxcar for Traceur, for $540. In terms of world-girdling, the line was due south and therefore 'gained' us far less than we 'lost' in having to divert north from Almaty. The usual hectic rush took place, finalising formalities, thanking innumerable people and saying farewells. We fitted in a visit to the Peace and Friendship Building to see a wonderful display of Lakota Indian flute-playing and hoop-dancing given by Kevin Locke. His daughter Kimimila demonstrated traditional jingle dances. A fine accompanying show was put on by Mongol singers, dancers and Yat'k players. We had met the Lockes, including Kevin's mother Pat, at Loïs Lambert's a few days before. Later, in America, they helped us enormously.

My best memories of Mongolia were and remain the warmth, simple sincerity and decency of most Mongolians, in one of the most beautiful countries I have ever seen. Personally, the high point of our eleven months there was my acceptance of the Baha'i Faith. A recognition rather than a conversion, I declared on 2 July amid much rejoicing – and much to Kate's astonishment when she telephoned and heard about it.

On Saturday 8 July, loaded on to a train, we pulled out of Ulaanbaatar, bound for Zamyn Uud and China.

CHAPTER FIFTEEN

CHINA: JULY AND AUGUST 1995
CHUCKED OUT OF CHINA

One can determine the morals of a nation by the way it treats its animals.

Mahatma Gandhi

I was told the train would take three days to arrive in Zamyn Uud. As we passed out of Ulaanbaatar eastward towards the steppe, we looked forward to the slow chug across the semi-desert. Eilidh was travelling with Traceur and the dogs in the boxcar; the boys and I in the caravan on the flatbed.

The train turned south and breasted a hill. We went to bed. I had just nodded off when fearsome swaying and banging woke me. Our slow train had become a hurtling express. The caravan rocked violently, the motion so alarming I ordered the boys out, afraid they might be flung from their bunks and hurt. We lay on the deck of the truck beneath the caravan, thundering down the line. As sunset faded into dark, we were thankful it was a warm night. The track was old, the rails no longer quite parallel, and looking behind as we bucketed about, streams of sparks could be seen trailing away from the wheels rattling against the lines. I fell into a doze until we stopped at Sainshand, when Torcuil woke me. It was a bleak prospect in dawn light. We transferred to the boxcar, because I fully expected the caravan body to part from its chassis, so viciously was it slamming back and forth.

In daylight we could see how arid, harsh and featureless was the land. Small herds of antelope sprang away from the train's roar. Eight weeks in the fierce July heat would have been a gruelling ordeal for Traceur and I was glad we were not subjecting him to it. After nineteen shattering, shaking, swaying, sleepless hours, including two stops, we arrived in Zamyn Uud at 3.30 p.m. on 9 July. With the caravan intact.

Next morning we were still there. No one had come to unload us. Eilidh and I went to investigate. We were told nothing ever drove across the border. We must go to Erenhot in China before unloading. Another 3540 tugruks . . .

About 6 p.m. we clanked the short distance to the Mongolian border. Our passports were stamped, the border guards gave us two tins of lemonade, one, grinning, made catapulting gestures. Five minutes more and we stopped again. A platoon of slim green-clad soldiers trotted up, taking station at ten-yard intervals on either side of the train. We had arrived in China. After the train was checked came the short haul to Erenhot, where we were uncoupled and shunted into a siding.

Officials from the Plant and Animal Quarantine Station quickly found us. They took the animals' papers and warned us not to let them off. Then I heard a loud 'Ni hao!' China North Hauler, our host company, had sent Mr Liu, together with translator Mrs Deng and a driver, Mr Jiao, to meet us. I hoped their presence would expedite our customs clearance. They brought gifts of watermelon, peaches and bananas in welcome. To us these were succulent rarities and as soon as they left we fell upon them greedily and devoured the lot.

Early next morning we met Guo Yi-miao, a doctor

turned businessman, who was in Erenhot to inspect timber he was importing and was a fluent English speaker. An official arrived to stamp our passports. The North Haulers came – and said there were problems . . .

Before departure in 1990, I had checked horse quarantine requirements for all countries we might pass through. Then China had none – but had since introduced it. The quarantine period was *forty days*.

We languished in Erenhot for sixteen days. Lip service was paid to quarantine when we unloaded, all straw, hay and dung being buried – although Nin pooped immediately his paws touched the ground and no one noticed except us. Then we put to and trekked six kilometres to the Plant and Animal Quarantine Station, where we ensconced ourselves in the yard at the back. There was no grass and no fence, so we had to pen Traceur in. I cleared a garage of rubbish to serve as a stall. Hay was brought and I bought expensive maize, the only available grain.

The quarantine station was not equipped for quarantining any animals, let alone a horse. It was a fiasco. There was no isolation, no provision for disinfection, nothing sterile. Anybody could wander in and out – and did. I contacted the British vice-consul, Sandra Tyler-Haywood, in Beijing, who beavered away to release us from what was pure bureaucracy, with no bearing on veterinary actuality.

The North Haulers gave a feast for us, diplomatically inviting three of the quarantine people and our chum Yi-miao. The meal, in the Boss Hotel, bore as much relation to Chinese restaurant food in Britain as haggis does to honey. Masses of dishes were piled up on a huge glass dumb waiter, including a smoking, hissing-hot dish of beef and onions and a large whole fish. There were 'hundred-year-old eggs' – which tasted disappointingly like any other hard-boiled egg despite their greeny-black colour – liver, beans, chicken, pork, pig's ear and tongue; hot peppers, green leaves, mushrooms and spicy mixes, accompanied by green tea, strawberry shake and pure coconut milk. A rice pudding followed, then, oddly to us, a tureen of soup. After the deprivations of the previous two years it was almost unbelievable.

As we ate, we discussed pandas. 'Ugh! Dirty pandas!' exclaimed Yi-miao, who claimed they have insalubrious habits. This immediately earned him the sobriquet Panda from Eilidh, by which we called him henceforth.

The Chinese railway demanded $111 for bringing us the few miles from the frontier. I refused to pay this outrageous addition.* Traceur became off-colour from too much feed and insufficient exercise. We explored Erenhot on foot and by bicycle-rickshaw. It was wonderful to visit the market just to gaze at rank upon rank of fresh fruit and vegetables. Meat was confined to pork and fowl but absence of mutton, believe me, was no hardship. A policeman came to say we must register and helpfully issued us with an Aliens Travel Permit to ease our passage through road-checks en route.

One day several men arrived and began digging up the yard. The dogs refused to stop barking so I went to see the quarantine director Mr Xiu and find out what was going on. He handed me a fax: we could go as soon as we had been inspected! The digging was to erect four iron posts, to which rope 'sides' were added. This was to contain Traceur so they could take a blood sample. I wasn't sure whether to laugh or cry, when they tried to get Trass to go into their contraption.

Next a wire cage was produced to enable them to inject

---

*I believe North Hauler eventually paid it. I had no conscience about this; they were a state company and it was the state causing us hassle. I paid the 600 yuan quarantine expenses, though.

the dogs. Mrs Deng was very pleasant but I had great
difficulty getting her to ask what they intended injecting the
dogs *for*. Once she did so someone went to fetch the
information while we returned to Traceur. With trembling
hand a white-coated fellow clipped away some hair,
swabbed the spot with iodine, produced an unsterile needle
and prepared to plunge it into Traceur. Aghast, I gave him
one of our big syringes instead. I also conveyed to him that
the dogs had current vaccinations, so Act II of the comedy
was cancelled. Traceur's blood test was clear. An eye-test
they gave him was clear too.

On the eve of departure we invited the North Haulers
and Panda to a restaurant, to thank them for their work.
Without their help we might have been in Erenhot yet. Nor
had I made their task easier. I had been impatient and edgy,
still stressed from the after-effects of the trial.

The next morning at five, to avoid the heat, Traceur
leaned into his collar and we set off south.

The popular image of China is of a bustling land with wall-
to-wall people. But from horizon to horizon it was flat,
green and almost uninhabited. At first the road was a thread
of tar with macadamised verges, then it became just maca-
dam. Traffic was light: a tractor, three-wheeled vans, jeeps
and lorries. Far off, shepherds tended their grazing flocks.
Black-bellied sandgrouse whirred away from us and swallows circled around insect-catching. Squashed hedgehogs
lay on the road and Nin chased a jerboa crazily all the way
to its hole.

It was great to be travelling again. Traceur pulled well
after eight months' lay-off – a tribute to Eilidh's labour with
him over the winter and long Ulaanbaatar summer. The flat
plain was ideal for accustoming him to work once more and
there was a refreshing lack of gogglers stopping to ogle us.

The weather was unsettled but the heavy showers made refreshing breaks from the heat.

In my diary I noted some introductory impressions of China:

There is a hive of activity in Erenhot quite absent in any Mongolian town. Rickshaw-bikes abound, very cheap, easily pedalled along the flat streets. Streets surprisingly clean. Buildings solidly unimaginative. People seem friendly.

Food is cheap. In the market it is best to watch locals and see what they pay, to avoid being diddled. We tested a few tinned meats: they ranged from bad to awful, fatty and sometimes almost all breadcrumbs.

We are stared at and once or twice my bare hairy arms were touched in wonderment, for the Chinese are not hirsute.

I get the impression that if one is prepared to live within the boundaries of the system, life is not too bad. Panda, for example, has his own flat – but no car. Private cars are rare. People seem over-disciplined, 'regulated' might be a better word and do not want to dispute the system. I don't mean dissidents, just tacit acceptance of clogged bureaucracy and really shoddy products. But then, in the UK people are notoriously unwilling to complain either.

There was a police check and toll collection post on the road. The officer in charge had been looking out for us because he had a letter for me from Guo Yi-miao, giving directions for crossing Saihan and finding the Jinning road. Thoughtful Panda. The officer insisted we stayed a night there as his guests.

The policemen were rather idle. Drivers had to get out, pay their five-yuan tolls, then open the flimsy barrier themselves. Their accommodation comprised a big caravan-trailer with a brick hut built on to the end for the kitchen. Water was hauled from the nearby railway station and a generator furnished light and powered the all-important TV. There was a road-menders' camp opposite and we could not think why the roadmen flocked over in the evening – till it dawned they came to watch television. For supper we had *mantou,* a sort of outsized ravioli but much meatier, sago soup and a sort of sauerkraut. Testing my new Baha'i principles, I resisted several offers of beer. Lavatory facilities were apparently basic. We did not even ask. Our host was most attentive and had taken us to meet some Mongolians, in *gers* some miles away, in the afternoon.

Near Saihan we saw a goods train hauled by a steam locomotive. Saihan was one of those towns with a feel-good factor, though rain was bucketing down when we got there. The cleansing department – two enormously fat black pigs – was enthusiastically clearing a mound of rotting refuse in the road. Donkey and mule carts plied the streets. The large vegetable market provided all we needed except, astonishingly in China, rice. Torcuil, guarding the caravan, was besieged by a friendly crowd and delighted I had bought a dozen *mantou*, which we ate on the road out.

Traceur was in excellent health, grazing free most nights. The continuing rain troubled me, lest the track became impassable before we had regained tarmac further south. The BBC announced the province of Heilongjiang, west of us, was suffering its worst flooding this century. The tail-end of the weather system gave a flick in our direction, causing heavy storms. It continued to be boiling hot and we thoroughly enjoyed our pre-dawn starts, travelling in the cool of the day, seeing the sun burst anew every morning over the Earth in a chorus of larksong.

Immediately before entering Juha, we crossed a double

line of ancient earth walls, the two-foot-high remains of a wall which predated the Great Wall and were historically possibly more important in terms of local power struggles. In the town, a bright girl in the only open shop spoke some English. She told us water remained turned off until 8 p.m., so we scrounged a few litres for ourselves and filled horse-jerries later from a stream. This was a region of low hills, with rolling valleys and a richer flora than on the plain. There were lots of birds, many of which we could not identify but hoopoes, swifts, larks and the odd black vulture were familiar.

From the hills we came to another plain – its shape reminded me of Rannoch Moor. Flowers and butterflies added brilliant swatches of colour. The track was muddy with water and a brace of lorries, laden with tatties, struggled through an appalling bumpy stretch, one belching black smoke, the other slithering to a stop, bleeding oil. Two men pushed us up a steep section, after we had tied up the dogs. Many Chinese were afraid of dogs. We had climbed, without realising it, to four thousand feet.

Torrential overnight rain turned the track into quag-mire. Picking our way carefully, we slid along, passing a truck bogged to the axles, which we were unable to assist. Viscous mud nearly brought Traceur down twice as he slipped and skidded, the caravan fishtailing behind him. When we reached firmer going, his stupendous striving was rewarded with a fistful of sugar lumps.

Our pleasant stop that evening was by a lake with ruddy shelduck on it: big orange-chestnut ducks, with honking goose-like voices. We washed clothes and swam with the tadpoles, water-beetles and assorted micro-fauna. Two nearby farms had mud-brick houses, neat vegetable gar-dens, flocks of sheep and little two-bladed wind-generators. Next day we dropped off the plain into a fertile valley – and populous rural China. As we travelled south the countryside became more and more densely populated. We enjoyed being among trees again. I was impressed by the agriculture. Whereas we use one man and a tractor to produce a crop, the Chinese use many people and no tractor. The result is high productivity per acre and, with their low wages, at far less cost.

We reached Agiut on market day. The main street was clogged, with stalls lining either side of the road and down the middle as well. Traceur behaved impeccably as we edged our way slowly through the solid mob of people and bicycles. Miraculously I avoided squashing anyone. A policeman materialised, beckoning me to follow him. Our Aliens Travel Permit proved its worth and we were soon clear and back into chaos. During the hazardous drive through town, we passed stalls with hardware, two shooting galleries, a rubber-bucket stall, a timber yard, a welder's, many produce stalls and numerous mule, cow and donkey carts. At last, after a month in China, we were able to buy rice, and at a bee-keepers' camp, not far from town, we bought a three-litre jar of delicious honey.

Pa-Yin-Ch'a-Ken was busy too. An English teacher told me foreigners were almost unknown there, which explained the curiosity with which we were regarded. The road was asphalt again, the traffic heavier. Small, noisy, single-cylinder flywheel-driven tractors were everywhere; these were too light for cultivation work but pulled trailers. Bicycles swarmed and donkey carts plodded along. Occasionally a truck would pass, and now and then army convoys. Some of the trucks were incredibly battered, many missing lights, a wing and, in one case, all bodywork forward of the bulkhead. Mules ploughed, a shepherd sat with his sheep under trees and once we passed two rake-thin cows struggling to plough a shallow furrow. Women were cutting oats and barley with sickles. People were friendly, their faces breaking into wide grins when we waved.

Far south, ranges of substantial hills poked above the horizon as we approached Jinning, population over 300,000 and our first big town. Its wide streets were easily navigated. Bicycles and mule carts overtook us. The pavements were crowded with small businesses, repairing punctures, welding, selling things. We turned left off the main thoroughfare into another wide street and parked. Eilidh and Fionn went to buy provender while I hunted down a gas-cylinder for the cooker, which entailed buying a new regulator. Neither European nor Russian models fitted the Chinese cylinders.

When I returned to the caravan, two plain-clothes police-men worked through the surrounding crowd and asked to see our passports. There was then a long delay while a uniformed English-speaking officer was sent for. He told us to follow him to the police station to escape the crowds, which seemed sensible. Then the trouble began. Our Aliens Travel Permit was not correct, they said. We might have to stay a few days in Jinning . . .

I telephoned George Kadis at China North Hauler in Baotou. They were our putative hosts and had arranged permission for us to drive through, which was now being queried. He said to leave matters to him and also mentioned he was allowed to drive by himself wherever he liked on business, including on to military airfields.

I had had to go to the post office to telephone, as the police* would not let me use theirs. When I got back, the English-speaking policeman, Tong, announced we must

---

*It is necessary to put in an explanation here. I have used the word police throughout but in reality we had fallen into the clutches of the Public Security Bureau. It equates roughly with the Soviet-era KGB and has an unsavoury reputation with almost everyone we talked to, before,

return to Erenhot. I said that was nonsense and he started to shout. When he calmed down I went to tell George Kadis this latest twist, and also contacted Sandra Tyler-Haywood.

It was ludicrous. We had not broken any laws. I had obtained all the necessary papers and permits. We had endured sixteen days of so-called quarantine – and now this. I recorded in my diary:

> The best we can hope for is to be transported to Tianjin. At first they said train then Tong said truck. I don't trust Tong, he blows hot and cold: one minute saying he wants to help, the next ordering us to go. He did arrange a good parking-place for us.
>
> China has done itself no good by its behaviour towards us today. There is no point being bitter but I am sad about it – and it has been a costly exercise in time and money. We could have gone through Russia for much less than the cost of the train to Erenhot plus quarantine plus truck to Tianjin.
>
> We have had no explanation *why* this is happening. It is plain dumb.

during and since being in China, including journalists and diplomats. I am not sure to what extent the police and the PSB overlap, but I think Tong was PSB. Of the 'Tianjin Ten' in charge of us when we arrived there, four had formed our escort and I am pretty sure three of them were ordinary police, possibly all four. Not that it mattered much; they just seemed nicer. We had had to buy a second set of visas after my Mongolian case was finished because the earlier set had expired, and it is unlikely they would have been issued had that been a factor; nor is it likely our short anti H-bomb protest in Leninogorsk was on file, because at that time we were heading for Russia and Mongolia. We had not knowingly committed any offence on our way from the border to Jinning, for which I was glad, because I had a clear conscience and the ensuing account does not really convey how unpleasant our experience of being in PSB hands was.

I was with Tong in his office next morning, awaiting further contact with his chief in Hohot but this never happened. I telephoned Mr Kadis again but he had been unable to do anything. Tong was being pleasant and I was resigned to going to Tianjin by truck, but had to choke back laughter when told that we would be escorted by Ministry of Public Security men. What are they so afraid of? I wondered.

The weather turned foul, with torrential rain lasting from lunchtime till dark. It matched my mood. 'I couldn't believe it. It seemed so unfair after all we had been through,' was Kate's reaction. 'China was to be the highlight of the expedition, visiting all the famous sites, especially [the Emperor's warriors at] Xian. As it turned out, I had seen more of Beijing [*en route* to Mongolia] than the family would.'

Public Security had insisted we go – but at our own expense ... I had to cash our hard currency emergency reserve. We had plenty money for food till Kate arrived with funds in Beijing in two weeks, but not for truck hire. A long articulated lorry, with eighteen-inch sides, four-foot vertical front end and metal floor was earmarked for us. It would cost $420. A pen would be built on it for Traceur. I demanded a cover for him and pointed out the necessity of putting a deep bed of sand on the floor.

The police organised a loading-bank. It had a roof but the lorry platform was too high so we had to go to the bank at the railway station instead. This entailed driving through the back streets of Jinning, through squalid slums, a facet of China not usually revealed to tourists.

The caravan was loaded and lashed down with fence-wire, tightened by Spanish windlass. Traceur's pen, built of stout poles, was firm and strong. He had to be loaded before it was completed and the last part was constructed around him. No cover had been provided and I refused to go till they arranged one. Eventually the front was covered, but there was no roof or side protection. A big argument about sand for the floor ensued. I again dug in my heels, sand was essential, to stop Trass skidding and probably falling. This entire time hordes of police fussed around, including a couple of plain-clothes men from Public Security. They did not want me taking pictures – but I already had.

At 5.45 p.m. we left. Eilidh and I were on the lorry, a policeman and the two drivers in the cab. Torcuil and Fionn went in the escorting police jeep with two uniformed men and one woman. First stop was a café, to eat. Traceur had no hay, and I had to buy a sack of grass from some locals for three yuan. Before we set off once more, I swapped places with Torcuil. The jeep would take me to the British Embassy in Beijing, to collect the money that I had had to ask Kate to send, so I could pay for the hire of the truck, while the slower truck bypassed the city.

We drove all night, passing the Great Wall about 3 a.m. I had asked if we could stop, however briefly, to see it – but no. Shortly after dawn, at six, we came to a traffic jam. Using the authority conferred by a police jeep, we overtook a line of stopped vehicles several kilometres long. At the head of the jam, the wreckage from a collision was being cleared. We soon continued, snaking down past a big line of oncoming vehicles, which included several heavily laden carts pulled by pathetically thin mules.

By 9 a.m. we were in appalling traffic on the outskirts of Beijing. It was hot and windless, the air polluted. It took the police two hours to find the embassy. Sandra Tyler-Haywood was on the point of leaving for a reception at the ambassador's residence. She told me she would be back at noon. The police didn't like this, but could do nothing about it.

Sandra Tyler-Haywood, already responsible for helping us out of 'quarantine' earlier, could not have been kinder or more helpful. Fionn and I spent over an hour with her, giving her what information we could and collecting two hundred pounds in yuan, which had been wired through to pay the balance of the transport. We were allowed to telephone Kate, which was marvellous. The boost to morale of this all-too-brief interlude, especially seeing a friendly face, was enormous.

The police found their way to the Tianjin road more easily than they had to the embassy. We had seen nothing of Beijing but concrete buildings. A lot of signposts were being erected for the forthcoming UN-sponsored Women's Conference. Thirty thousand delegates were expected, which had freaked Public Security and possibly accounted for our predicament.

The land from Beijing to Tianjin was flat all the way, the maize crop interspersed with numerous lakes, ponds and canals. We were missing little, not having to trek the 140 kilometres, and stopping places might have been hard to find.

Entrance to the Public Security building in Tianjin was through an unprepossessing dirty brown door. We were taken into a wood-panelled room where a woman appeared to tell us categorically we *had* to leave on Monday – by ferry to Japan. It would cost ten thousand yuan, about £825. My vociferous protests about the cost, never mind that we wanted to go to Canada, were met with stony silence or repeated statements that 'There are no ships going to Canada', which was not true.

There was no sign of the truck by 7 p.m. but I was not worried. It would certainly have been delayed by the traffic jam.

The woman was the local Public Security chief.

Astonishingly, she and her number two, an older man in uniform called Hu, took all of us for a meal at a very reasonable restaurant. They put on nicer faces and we had some conversation through Hu, who spoke Russian. I have often wondered why they did this and concluded it was mainly to keep an eye on us – we were not prisoners but not free agents either – and perhaps to see what we knew. Any hopes I harboured that telling them about the trip might alter their attitude, however, were doomed to disappointment.

The truck had still not arrived by the time we had finished eating. Because it had not and it was getting late, and we had nowhere to sleep, they took us to a hotel. I assumed they were paying the 160-yuan per person tariff, but when it became apparent that they were not, I told them it was out of the question. In the end we were taken to a clean room with a shower, but did not register. Presumably the hotel would have been the loser as we were not officially there, but in fact we lived in the caravan, because to my relief, the lorry rolled up just as we were settling in.

My relief became fury when I realised the caravan chimney had been smashed. Torcuil said it had happened five minutes before they arrived, at a low bridge. Both children were ravenous, because, in spite of a promise to the contrary, they had neither stopped to eat, nor had they been allowed to cut grass for Traceur, which greatly upset them. Eilidh and I sallied forth to cut what we could for him in the dark, but it was not really enough.

I rose very early on Saturday, armed with a sickle, to find more grass. The humidity was as high as the temperature and I sweltered, but cut enough to keep Traceur happy for a while before taking a shower in the hotel. Expecting more rain, I fitted a thick piece of rigid plastic over the hole in the roof where the chimney should have been and taped it watertight. Of course we could not use the fire but in the steamy heat we would not need to.

At about 9 a.m. the police arrived, bringing with them a little man of about twenty-five. This was Liu, their English speaker, to whom I took an instant dislike, though was careful not to show it. He repeated that we must leave on Monday's weekly ferry to Japan, although Kate was not due until 1 September with more funds. It was Friday and even through the embassy it would be difficult to obtain the money for our fares over the weekend.

I telephoned the long-suffering Sandra to tell her the bad news: we had not just been banned from driving through China, we were being deported. The verb 'to deport' was never used, presumably because then the Chinese would have had to pay. We were just being asked to leave . . . and when I asked why, Liu said nastily, 'We don't have to tell you,' which was all the explanation ever given to us. I am certain there was no good reason; the authorities had just changed their minds – but to say so to us would entail embarrassing loss of face. The reason why I did not put up greater resistance was the presence of Traceur, the dogs and the caravan. I did not trust the Public Security people and feared that if I refused to co-operate they would put me and the children on the first aeroplane out at their expense, but would almost certainly keep the caravan and our adored animals. I was not prepared to take that chance.

Sandra asked to speak to Liu, the translator. In a much pleasanter tone than he had been using to me, he told her they were treating us well. 'Well' was a relative term. There was a subdued air of menace whenever the police were around, difficult to describe, but I felt we trod a very fine line. Anything they did for us – a meal, accommodation – was because, short of taking us into custody, they had to. As seasoned travellers, we had seen how animals are sometimes treated in other countries but even allowing for cultural differences, I cannot forgive the way all my requests for help in finding fodder were ignored. Worst of all was their refusal to let us unload Traceur. It was hot, the flies were bad, he had no shade, could barely turn round and was standing in sand that was now wet and increasingly smelly. We were parked close to the hotel, but that seemed to make no difference.

We had cut all the grass within walking distance so, when the police went for their lunch, we took a taxi to look for more. In the afternoon, I was taken to the shipping company, China Express Lines, where I received the biggest shock so far. The fare on the *Yanjing* would not be 10,000 yuan but 36,208. Our tickets alone would be 10,000; the caravan, charged as two half-containers, 24,000; 1,749 for Traceur and 459 for the dogs. There followed a lot of talk, including threats to send us back to Erenhot if we could not or would not pay.

Back at the hotel I further messed up Sandra Tyler-Haywood's weekend. We seemed to have no alternative but to comply. By now $4,500 seemed cheap, for escaping from the hands of the Public Security Bureau. Somehow we would get the money.

Later a pleasant, English-speaking Chinese with whom I was chatting told me the *Yanjing* was a very expensive ship.

Kate rang that evening to confirm she would meet us in Japan instead and that arrangements were in hand to transfer enough money to pay for the ferry. This made the police happier – but Traceur was still not allowed off the lorry. A kindly hotel employee, with the one policeman who seemed sympathetic, took us to cut enough grass for the night.

I have scarcely mentioned the children. While I dealt with the police, they had had to amuse themselves as best they might, which was little fun in the heat, with no money and nowhere to spend it even if they had. They willingly tackled the chores, which helped me a lot. On Sunday morning Eilidh, Fionn and I set forth to cut more grass, a Herculean labour, from verges and wasteground, until I had enough to take back for Traceur's breakfast. The children foraged on and filled two more sacks but it was still not enough. We were told to cut sufficient for the two-day sail to Japan. Requests for hay were ignored.

Sandra rang at midday on Sunday to say that the money would not be available before 8.30 a.m. on Monday, when someone with authority to release it would be on duty. Diary: 'The police panicked and held another of their meetings. They seem unable to make decisions that are not the product of collective discussion. I must go with them to Beijing to collect the money – despite the embassy offering to send it down by car. Unfortunately CEL [the shipping company] won't accept an embassy guarantee of payment.'

That evening we moved to the dock area. As the truck pulled out from the hotel yard, the caravan roof was damaged by a branch. To my surprise, the lorry was unloaded and the caravan put aboard *Yanjing*. The hold, reached by a stern-quarter ramp, was roasting hot. I feared for Traceur and we were permitted to keep him with us until morning. When I pointed out that there was no stall for him, one was immediately created, using the poles from the truck. Reluctantly I decided the dogs must stay aboard, as we should have enough to do in coping with Traceur all night.

What really upset me was the duplicity. This had obviously been planned all along. There had never been any intention of unloading us before. Traceur was mighty glad to set his feet on solid ground again and to stretch his legs. He had been on the truck for four days, enduring heat, rain, flies and mosquitoes. I don't think the police would have cared it he had died on it.

With the caravan loaded, the police had to find us accommodation and we were taken to a cheap hotel nearby for the night. The bed-linen was dubious, the lavatories un-usable, but the room had been swept and had a functioning fan. The police now became worried they did not know the way to the embassy and would not get back before the ship sailed. Hu insisted I call Sandra yet again, on his mobile telephone, though I knew there was nothing she could do. We reverted to Plan A: the embassy car would bring the money down.

We sought out a restaurant, taking Traceur with us and hitching him outside. The staff was delightful, letting us visit the kitchen, where we chose a feed of beef, pork and prawns with fried egg and rice. Soup was thrown in free. As always, in China as everywhere else, the ordinary people were great, and we were able to relax for a while.

On the way back to the hotel we met an interesting man, a salesman, one of whose relatives had been a senior officer in Chiang Kai-shek's army. He stayed to talk while I took first watch with Traceur. He though that China would not change much after Deng Zhiao-ping died. Government policy was to focus people's attention on the pursuit of wealth and sports, away from politics, giving them enough freedom to keep them calm. He also told me that since the Tiananmen Square massacre in 1989 there had been tighter controls on foreigners. He had not known that Tibet had been a free country before China's invasion in 1959, or that Greenpeace had unfurled a banner in Tiananmen Square protesting against China's recent H-bomb tests.

Torcuil took second watch and when I came down at first light I found Eilidh on duty. We had to fill five more sacks of grass before 9 a.m., when the police were due.

Luckily there was plenty to be had beside the dock railway.

A personnel van came to take us to the ship. Our faithful hounds went into a frenzy of joy at seeing us, and Traceur walked aboard as if he were one of the crew. The hold, thankfully, was cooler now, and his stall, which was adequate provided no gales blew up at sea, was below a ventilator, which would keep him cool.

It was barely 9.30 when I was hustled back into the van by the police. I was sure that the embassy car would not appear before 10.30 at the motorway toll-booth, fifteen minutes away, which was the rendezvous. They were anxious about traffic and time. I had decided not to accept the money from the embassy official until we were back at the CEL office on the docks. I thought it unlikely that the police would try to steal it, but I thought it wiser to be safe than sorry. After the agonies of the previous few days, I was wary of them.

By 10.29 the police were like hens on a hot griddle. Then, just after the half-hour, Hu's mobile jangled to announce the embassy car's arrival. Andrew Blanch kindly agreed to come to the docks – but Hu would not allow me to travel with him.

At 10.53, I signed for the cash and moments before the eleven o'clock departure I paid it to Mr Tsiao, CEL's shipping manager. Then a demand was made for a twelve-dollar exit tax, which I didn't have, so Mr Blanch paid, saying he could claim it on expenses. I didn't know if that was true but I was grateful to him. We were hustled through passport control and Customs and over to the ship. Our boarding slips were taken and we ascended the gangway. We did not look back.

Crossing the Yellow Sea was a moment out of time. The waters stayed calm. We saw the southernmost South Korean islands, rugged, steep-to, with dense scrub vegetation.

Large petrels skimmed the waves. Fionn spotted sixteen flying fish. The water looked clean, though garbage was strewn across its surface: plastic bottles and bags, bits of rope, a plastic dustpan, foil wrappers.

On the ship meals were extra and expensive, priced in yen. We lived on pot noodles from a vending-machine. Only breakfast and the washing-machines were included in the fare. We filled the latter with foul objects and were amazed to discover crisp T-shirts, socks and pants at the end of the wash. A bold stowaway, a praying mantis, sat out on a stanchion. Our animals were comfortable in the dim but cool hold.

I knew the British Embassy in Beijing was contacting the consulate in Osaka but had no idea whether the Japanese would allow us to land. A nightmare vision of being condemned to shuttle for ever between Kobe and Tianjin, neither China nor Japan willing to allow us ashore, haunted me. For in the throes of expulsion I had made a major blunder: I had forgotten to obtain Chinese export papers for the animals.

We sailed up the Japanese Inland Sea in haze, land and islands to either side, like part of a Japanese painting, exactly as I had imagined it.

As *Yanjing*'s bows thrust ever nearer Kobe, faxes flew between me and the authorities. I spoke to consul Matthew Johnson in Osaka. Good news. We should be allowed to land. The bad news? The cost would be astronomic . . .

CHAPTER SIXTEEN

━━◄◦◦◦►━━

JAPAN: AUGUST TO NOVEMBER 1995
JAPANESE PIZZA

So powerful is the light of unity that it can illuminate the whole earth.

Bahá'u'lláh

A delegation filed into *Yanjing*'s dining saloon: from China Express Lines Kitamura San and Kohara San, from the Animal Quarantine Service Hyase San and Juro Hitomi San, from Sanyo Unyo transport company Taniguchi San, plus Shiraishi San, a brokerage and customs-clearance agent. It was 23 August 1994 and we had just docked in Kobe after being piloted through the busy shipping lanes. On the quayside it was searingly hot and humid.

Japanese import regulations, though rigid, were not insurmountable. Our difficulty, as always now, was money. The cost of twenty-one days' quarantine, including horse-food and transport to Osaka Quarantine Station, was going to be over nine thousand dollars.

The meeting adjourned to CEL's offices, via Immigration. I was shown the account. Studying it, the first thing I read was 'Groom: $3000'. Well, strike that. We'll put Eilidh in instead. And they agreed. Further trimming brought the sum down to six thousand dollars. I gave my word the bill would be paid, though it would take time to have cash wired through and would empty our coffers. We called the consulate and Matthew Johnson, putting his job on the line, said we were good for the money. I got the impression the Japanese were doing all they could to help.

The caravan and animals were unloaded and went, along with Eilidh, to Osaka Quarantine Station. We were lucky there was a space for them at such short notice: the bigger Kobe facility had been damaged by the earthquake in January and was out of commission. Customs clearance was postponed till next day. There was talk of a 2-million-yen bond, refundable on departure, more than we owned in total. However, Kitamura San, to whom I had immediately taken a liking, arranged for the boys and me to have supper and spend the night on the ship, rather than in the caravan on the hot, busy, noisy dockside.

A steward woke us in the morning bearing a tray of breakfast. Afterwards, I walked with Shiraishi San to the Customs office, passing a lot of earthquake damage on the way. A remarkable amount had been cleared and repaired but twisted flyovers, empty buildings and closed roads testified to the scale of the destruction. There was no difficulty with Customs. I just signed a paper promising not to sell the caravan and Traceur in Japan. But we were most upset when they confiscated our huge watermelon. A real beauty, it had cost fifty cents in China but would have been ten dollars in Japan.

When we returned, a little low-loader had arrived for the caravan. It was winched on and secured with bottle-screws. *Yanjing*'s friendly master, Captain Wang, was on the quay and I went over to say goodbye. We had spent time with him on the bridge, being shown the ship's instrumentation, which was surprisingly basic for a modern vessel, with no computerisation.

As we drove through Kobe the obvious remaining signs

of the earthquake were gaps between buildings. Those still standing but damaged were wrapped in blue plastic sheeting or green netting, to prevent masonry falling on pedestrians below while repairs were carried out. One particular office block was a startling sight. The first eight storeys were intact but the ninth had gone. It had been completely flattened, beneath the tenth, eleventh and twelfth storeys, which were also intact – but displaced six feet sideways. The tremor had struck early, while people were making breakfast. Had it been later, many more might have died, caught on their way to work or in their offices. Almost everyone we met knew someone who had been killed, been injured or left without a house. Hutted camps testified to the numbers still homeless.

Between Kobe and Osaka Animal Quarantine Station (AQS) we had a slow drive along congested roads, and over several huge flyovers and bridges. Whole sections of overhead expressway were dangerously buckled or missing, so traffic was forced to use the original road, which lacked sufficient carrying capacity. Having seen the traffic I was heartily glad we should not be driving in Japan. We would have required a special permit to drive but as Traceur had to fulfil export regulations, which stipulated a sixty-day period of isolation from other equines, we did not have time. The cars we saw were all nearly new and clean, trucks spotless and often gleamingly chromed. No battered Kamaz with missing wheels here! Buildings were well maintained, streets litter-free. In the waves by the harbour wind-surfers played. By contrast with China we might have been on another planet. Asian as Japan is, materially we were firmly in the West.

The caravan was parked on the pavement in front of the AQS building under a protruding awning, which gave some shade. High overhead a huge bridge carried double-decked roads across to the sprawling container terminal and industrial centre on man-made Nanku Island. It was noisy but there were public tennis-courts and a small tree-shaded park opposite, and we could use the AQS showers. Soon we were taken to see Eilidh through the netting. She appeared dressed in rubber boots and a blue boiler-suit rather too large for her. Although a 'prisoner', she was more comfortable than we were, having her own room with air-conditioning and TV; bath and washing-machine to hand. Next day she and Traceur would have a zoo-bound hippopotamus and llama as neighbours.

On a first shopping expedition, Fionn and I bought peppers, potatoes, cucumber, tomatoes, bread, noodles, peanut butter, half a cabbage and, as first-night treats, some biscuits, peanuts, crab-pieces and ice-cream. That little lot cost the equivalent of thirty-three dollars. Food alone would cost us a thousand dollars a month in Japan.

My time was taken up with trying to get away again. Horse quarantine normally lasted ten days but because of where he had been and his lack of papers, Traceur had to stay in for twenty. Almost since we left the UK I had been trying without success to establish Canadian import regulations, but on 7 September I received a letter from Agriculture Canada, which stated bluntly: 'We have no import protocol for horses from Japan. Your horse will therefore not be admitted to Canada.' If Traceur was admitted to the USA, however, it would be easy to cross to Canada from there.

In theory importing him to the USA was not difficult. He would have to fulfil the sixty-day isolation requirement immediately preceding departure, then on arrival show negative results to a screed of blood-tests. Choice of destination was limited to New York, Miami, Honolulu or Los Angeles. I was strongly recommended to use one of the import agents on the list supplied. This information came from the aptly named Dr Grow of the US Department of Agriculture, to whom I had written.

I proceeded to search for a shipper, and came up against refusal after refusal. In this technological containerised age, there was no place for animal passengers, let alone humans, aboard a cargo ship.

Ship-search and shortage of cash notwithstanding, we learned something of Japan and its culture. The Japanese don't wear hats – apart from a few old men and regulation safety helmets. The majority wore drab, ill-fitting dark blue, black or occasionally daring olive green suits of poor cloth, with dull ties and polished black shoes. Colour was equally lacking among women, though the brave might flaunt a red kerchief or bright blue scarf. Cars were equally uniform, in black, grey, silver or white. Petty crime was rare. Living close to the docks, we never feared to walk the streets at night. Nor were we molested or pestered by crowds, as had been the norm in the rest of Asia. In town, bicycles shared the pavement with pedestrians and were expected to give way to them. Extravagant packaging was used for everything, but especially for food, whether a snack meal in a box or a full-blown banquet, because appearance was all.

The Osaka–Kobe conurbation of 15 million people occupies a flat plain between a range of tree-covered hills and the north end of the Inland Sea. Juro Hitomi, the vet in charge of Traceur, invited us to his house a few days after we arrived. It was a flat in a four-storey block, twenty-five kilometres away, undamaged by the earthquake. Opposite, two smaller blocks were gone, cleared to the foundations. I was surprised how small the flat was. We greeted Juro's wife Noriko, his sons Ryuta and Tsugumichi, who were twelve and seven respectively, and daughter Yuriko, who was eight. Then we were introduced to Japanese food. Tea was accompanied by *kuzukiri*, strands of clear jelly in lightly flavoured liquids, one orange, one peppermint and one honey. *Sushi* followed: a selection of raw sea-bream, cuttle-fish strips and tuna pieces. *Okonomiaki* – Japanese pizza, Noriko quipped – was a wonderful pancake of squid, shrimps and beef in a rich sauce, cooked on a griddle then turned on to spaghetti and cooked a bit longer and topped with fine slivers of bonito. The delicate subtle flavours took a while to appreciate and the children weren't enthusiastic about any of it but I thought *okonomiaki* excellent, although I still prefer my fish fried. Torcuil played Ryuta at Hashimi Shogi, a board game, and we had a little firework display outside before Juro drove us home.

Next day the boys and I went to Nara by train. It was saturatingly hot and we consumed gallons of drinks. These were easily available from the vending-machines we found everywhere, which dispensed almost everything including packaged meals, alcohol and cigarettes. Most of the journey was through built-up areas but as we came through the Ikomo Mountains the countryside opened out to parkland and small ricefields.

Nara was founded in AD 710 as Japan's first capital, later superseded by Kyoto, and became a Buddhist centre. Emperor Shomu constructed the Todaiji Temple, which houses the Great Statue of the Buddha, the biggest bronze statue ever cast. Burned to the ground during wars in 1180 and 1567, the temple was rebuilt at two-thirds its original size in 1708 and is the largest wooden building in the world. It was most impressive, though as always in Buddhist temples I found the magnificent shrines lacked a surrounding atmosphere of holiness. In the park there were masses of people and almost as many tame sika deer. The fine five-storeyed pagoda of Kotukuji was the first we had seen, not having seen any in China.

This enjoyable day was spoiled when we got back to discover that Traceur had a temperature. His tests, for equine anaemia, piroplasmosis, glanders, dourine, rhino-pneumonacosis, paratyphoid, equine arthritis and even trypanosomiasis, had all been negative. We hoped the cause was heat exhaustion, coupled with a total change of diet and routine.

Another day the boys and I went to Nanku Island, because the map marked a bird sanctuary on one tiny corner of it. Wildlife, like Buddhism, is honoured in Japanese culture, though nowadays often only by token observance. Temporary corrugated-iron screens round a building site were painted with trees, rabbits and birds; sculpted dolphins gambolled in stone waves. Wending our way from the bus-station through forests of concrete, past piers piled with containers and serried ranks of people fishing off break-waters, we eventually found it. Overlooking three artificially created ponds was a vast hexagonal concrete hide, fully equipped with information, videos and viewing-ports. There were lots of birds, for this was an oasis of tranquillity and cover unavailable elsewhere for miles in any direction. Observers had a grand view and the birds were left in peace, which is as it should be.

Kate caught up with us on 2 September. Her air-fare had been paid by the *Sunday Post* in return for an exclusive story and pictures about our reunion. An Air France foul-up meant she arrived at Kansai airport six hours late. I escorted my weary wife on the sweltering two-hour train and tube trip to the caravan, where an ecstatic welcome from the boys awaited her. A chat through the wire with Eilidh followed, before she collapsed into bed exhausted, for her first sleep in twenty-four hours.

Osakoko – Asashiobashi – Bentencho – Kujo – Awaza – Hommachi: metro-station names, burned on to my brain from frequent visits to my 'office' – the British Consulate General on the fourteenth floor of the Seiko Building in downtown Osaka. Matthew Johnson was going beyond the call of duty to help us, greatly easing an uphill struggle, for I was making no progress in finding transport to the USA for Traceur and all the time our money was trickling away.

It transpired that Traceur had contracted Japanese encephalitis, a mosquito-borne disease mainly of pigs. I had been unable to have him vaccinated against it in Mongolia but had been assured that the risk in northern China was small. Undoubtedly the four days standing on the truck in mosquito-ridden Tianjin had done the damage. He came close to death but Juro's ministrations and Eilidh's untiring attention pulled him through. Then I discovered that until his antibody count was normal, he could not begin his export isolation period.

By late September I despaired of ever finding transport for our animals. Then NYK Line told me they had once shipped a circus and said they might agree to ship Traceur. It was my last hope. After several meetings, everything looked good. Then they said they would take Traceur, though possibly not us. Finally I had a meeting with them, at which they denied saying they would take Traceur and added that the caravan would cost $3500, not the $2500 originally quoted. I lost my temper and stormed out, accidentally sending a plant-pot crashing to the floor on my way. If they wanted a way out, I had handed it to them. That night the caravan shook gently. I thought someone was climbing out – or in. However, everyone was snug in bed and there was no sign of nocturnal visitors. The following night it happened again. Days later we learned the tremors had registered over three on the Richter scale.

Traceur and Eilidh came out of quarantine a day earlier than expected, to make way for two Thoroughbred stallions from America. Collectively priced at $15 million – ten thousand times more than Traceur had cost – these fleet-footed creatures were not worth his hoof-parings to us. He was above price, our engine and our dearly loved friend.

AQS offered to house Traceur and the dogs in one of the undamaged Kobe quarantine barns, for his sixty days' isolation. The barns came with an attached one-room apartment, bottled gas and electricity supplied. Tanaguchi took Kate, Eilidh, Fionn and the animals over there, while Torcuil and I remained in Osaka. We moved the caravan a few hundred yards, to a berth alongside the Osaka Municipal Port and Harbour Bureau's tug-boat control centre. Masaki San, secretary to the Bureau, came with a dozen hard-hatted stalwarts and we manhandled it to its new position. We were given keys to the building, so that we could use the lavatory and have showers whenever we wanted. A water-pipe was laid on and we had use of the telephone for incoming calls. Someone gave us fish and Kenji Yamamoto from AQS, who was really a frustrated farmer and spent all his spare time cultivating his tenth-hectare plot somewhere in the hills and whom we all liked immensely, brought us pears. Earlier Juro had given us a big sack of brown rice. We should not starve.

My ignorant, faltering footsteps into the Baha'i Faith had helped to sustain me through our Chinese ordeal and David Lambert had given me a list of Baha'is to contact in Japan, which is how we met Foad Katirai. He was Iranian, his parents having left their country, victims of persecution, when he was three. Torcuil and I ate with him and his parents one Sunday, and subsequently he played a major part in helping us get out of Japan.

We had already attracted some press interest but Foad marshalled bigger forces and we were interviewed by *Yomiuri Shimbun, Kobe Shimbun* and by telephone for the

Japanese Times (English edition). Foad and Suda San, a quiet Japanese Baha'i lady, organised fund-raising for us and yen began to trickle in. In mid-October Asahi Channel 6 filmed us, and the trickle became a stream.

The publicity also produced two new advertisers. First came ARC International, an American–Japanese firm specialising in Earth-friendly business-training techniques. Then we had a telephone call from Peter Liu in Taiwan. He had recently bought Letham Grange Hotel and its golf courses near Arbroath in Scotland and thought advertising in conjunction with a Scottish expedition might help to promote it. He added the offer of a month at Letham Grange on our return, but I thought it unlikely we should take up that generous offer.

During my search for trans-Pacific horse-transport I had been in touch with Japan Airlines (JAL) international public relations director Geoff Tudor. I knew it would be expensive but I had asked him to quote for a one-way air-fare for Traceur. $17,000! A bagatelle in the context of $15-million racehorses, maybe, but slightly out of our price bracket. Now, desperate, I called him again to ask whether JAL might consider giving us a special deal. If nothing else our publicity value had increased.

Contributions continued coming in, from three thousand yen (about thirty dollars) contributed by three school-children to four huge gifts of a hundred thousand. Suda San co-ordinated collection and passed the letters to me with English translations so I could thank the donors. Foad continued to drum up help and support. We attended the One World Festival in Osaka, with a table at the side of the Baha'i tent, and raised almost another hundred thousand yen.

At last the dam broke.

Wilhelmsen Lines' Paul Carlton in Tokyo said they would ship the caravan to Long Beach. For nothing. It would leave from Rokko Island terminal on 25 October aboard their massive MV *Texas*, registered in Tønsberg, once Norway's main whaling-port. Geoff Tudor came back to me with an affordable price for flying Traceur, Tsar, Nin and a groom to Los Angeles. The groom had to be me, as Eilidh was too young.

British tourists do not require visas for the USA but Matthew Johnson advised that, in view of what we were doing, I should talk to the US consular officials. In typically generous American fashion they gave us two-year visas. They must have gazed into a crystal ball, because at that point I expected to be in Canada within months of crossing the Pacific.

Keeping all of us in Japan eating was eating up yen, so the family left for San Francisco on 2 November. My old schoolfriend Ewan Macdonald, who lived in Bolinas, thirty miles north of the city on the coast, found a house they could use pending arrival of the caravan. The animals and I would join them two weeks later.

During our stay we had visited Osaka Castle and Daiwa Bank's Money Museum. Kate, Eilidh and Fionn had been to Kyoto. Torcuil and I had been out on one of the harbour tugs to bring in a container ship. We had ranged the docks – an endless fascination, especially the Russian vessels. They came from Vladivostok with aluminium ingots, and left crammed with second-hand cars, in one case with so many that the front wheels were hanging over the gunwales. The captain of the *Kapitain Lyutikov*, hearing we had been to Russia, gave us lunch on board. We had attended a concert given by two Iranian violinists, talked to the English class at a Japanese school and been to Osaka's enormous aquarium.

The Bosnian war was spluttering to a close. Yitzhak

Rabin was assassinated and the promise of peace in the Middle East vanished.

A simple Buddhist ceremony was held at Kobe AQS to commemorate the animals which had had to be put down because they failed quarantine. I was invited to the sumptuous feast afterwards, in the AQS headquarters building in Sanomiya, wrapped in green plastic, still under repair. The AQS staff presented me with twenty thousand yen from a whip-round they'd had earlier. They had been so kind, had bent many rules to help us, that it was difficult finding words to thank them, especially Kunio Shirai, Juro Hitomi and Hyase San.

That evening, the last difficulty was overcome. Barry Myers of US Equine Inc. telephoned from Los Angeles to say his company would pay Traceur's hefty US import bill. He requested a blood sample be sent to them for pre-testing. The results came back within a few days. Negative. With four days to go, all was set for departure.

Then catastrophe! Traceur's temperature shot up. He exhibited all the old symptoms, and was quite gaga. The vets stuffed him full of antibiotics and the fever abated.

On my last day, I went to Osaka to say farewell and offer completely inadequate thanks to Matthew Johnson and the Katirais. At Foad's office, last-minute donations had come in – 'a further staggering 158,000 yen. The sum raised on our behalf was now within a few yen of the exact amount needed to get us across the Pacific.' The generosity of the Japanese to strangers had been moving and humbling.

AQS Kobe held a farewell party and we exchanged token mementoes. These lovely people had done so much to make our stay enjoyable and enhance our impressions of their fascinating country. Geoff Tudor rang to say it was 'all systems go' at his end. All now depended on Traceur's temperature being normal in the morning.

It was.

I mucked out the stable, tidied and swept the flat. A quick call to Kate in the US to say we were on our way elicited the information that Eilidh and Fionn were out boogie-boarding. Whatever that was.

At Kansai, the dogs were whisked away in boxes. Traceur was loaded directly from the truck to his 'flying stable', an aluminium crate with stalls for three riding horses or two Traceurs. Then he was tugged out to the waiting JAL Boeing 747 cargo aircraft, its nose-cone swung up to reveal the gaping maw of the hold. A lift hoisted him level with it, the crate was slid neatly on to the built-in rail-system, manoeuvred to the desired spot and anchored down with integral catches. Geoff Tudor was coming along for the ride and we boarded by the crew door aft of the cockpit and settled into the only seats, an economy-class bench with first-class leg room, on the starboard side. There was a galley on our left, a double bunk behind. Between us and the cockpit was a large hatch with a small glass port set into it. I could look through this to see Traceur, or open the hatch and go down and talk to him.

We taxied out, cleared for take-off, thundered down the runway and soared aloft. At Tokyo's Narita airport, we should have to change aircraft. The one we were on was bound for New York. Traceur happily nibbled hay and we happily nibbled an airline meal.

We landed at 10 p.m. and were at Tokyo for an hour. The dogs and Traceur were transferred to our next aircraft. Geoff and I stretched our legs, then boarded it too.

Our next stop was Anchorage, Alaska.

CHAPTER SEVENTEEN

~~~~~

THE USA (1): NOVEMBER 1995–SEPTEMBER 1996
BOOGIE-BOARDS AND BEAVER

*Half the misunderstandings between Britain and
America are due to the fact that neither will regard
the other as what it is – a foreign country.*

John Buchan

Alaska. The name evokes images of untainted virgin
land, limitless forests, wild rushing rivers. If the reality
is water polluted by gold-washing, disfigurement by pipe-
line and despoliation by oil spill, this was not apparent from
six miles above the forbidding ice-girt Aleutian Chain in the
first flush of dawn.

At snail's pace the islands slipped by, to be replaced by
a roseate blanket of snow stretching smoothly away and
away north, till rumpled by the thrusting peak of distant
Denali. Descending, toy oil-wells appeared in the sea below
flaring gas, man's puny playthings. Lower now, Kodiak
Island flashed beneath, its dark pines snow-trimmed. Ahead
appeared a tiny strip of black, growing perceptibly as we
sped towards it. 'Fifty feet,' called the tinny automatic pilot.
'Thirty feet. Twenty-six feet – touch-down.' The 747 kissed
the earth, rolled and rumbled down the runway, taxied to
its allotted place and came to a standstill.

I had always yearned to visit Alaska but never imagined
approaching it at dawn, like a stooping eagle, swooping out

of the west. It was cheating, of course. One is not entitled to be delivered, ill-attired in shirt-sleeves, to the world's wild places. Experience of wilderness, as with all worthwhile things in the world, must be earned to be appreciated, reached only with effort. But we were late autumn migrants, alighting briefly to feed; gaining a glimpse of wonders to come back to, and I was content.

I was whisked across to Immigration in a chunky pick-up, tyres crunching in the snow, hardly aware it was −11°C/12°F in the crisp morning air. Passport examined and stamped, with a cheery 'Welcome to the USA,' then back out to the aircraft; fuelled and oiled, brakes de-iced, a fresh crew in the cockpit, ready to go. As I had for landing, I occupied the observer's seat immediately behind the captain for take-off. He was American this time, with Japanese co-pilot and Canadian engineer. Climbing away southwards, the captain pointed out Turn Back Inlet, where Captain Cook had had to do just that. Then cloud swallowed us up.

It was brilliantly sunny, cruising down the coast past Canada, across the border again to Washington and Oregon but dense cloud obscured all sight of earth beneath till California loomed ahead and it cleared. Far east, Crater Lake was visible. Below, the jaggy Sierra Nevadas poked up like three-dimensional models in a geography classroom. Mount Shasta's 14,162 feet stretched to greet us, a startling white cone in a green-brown world. Somewhere down there, near San Francisco Bay, blurred by increasing haze, was my family.

Over Los Angeles in a pall of thin unnatural brown air, the lights of nine aircraft glimmered ahead of us. On the ground, pale ribbons of yellow light were evidence of evening traffic-jams. This city had no visible heart, just block after block of adjoining buildings. Swimming-pools in every garden testified to high incomes. We circled the skies, queuing in the aviation supermarket to reach our turn at the checkout and get permission to land.

●

I spent two days in Los Angeles. Traceur was installed at Jet Pets' extortionately expensive quarantine barn. I was installed at the Hacienda Hotel, at $44 a night the cheapest I could find. I felt no urge to rush out and see Beverly Hills, Hollywood or Disneyland but cranked up my jet-lagged brain enough to find transport for Traceur, the dogs and myself.

The run to San Francisco in Cargill Transport's huge Freightliner was long and uneventful. Driving through LA, everything looked dirty: grime-covered houses, grubby old cars, dull brown skies. By the time we cleared San Francisco it was dark, late and foggy as we wound our way to Bolinas along tortuous narrow roads, arriving about half past one in the morning to find the children looking out for us. Traceur was offloaded at the farm where he was to stay and Kate drove us to the caravan in the Jeep Ewan Macdonald had kindly lent us.

Kate had had the unenviable job of fetching the caravan up from Long Beach a week earlier. She also recalled that 'hitting the States was a real culture shock, especially for the children after being in Asia for so long', and described Fionn as 'liberated, finding all the materialist and 'fun' things he had missed – or thought he had – taking to boogie-boarding, fishing and particularly basketball'.

The USA was certainly different but the natives were friendly. They even spoke English . . . of a sort.

I woke to find a veritable encampment, not just the caravan but a tent and a chemical privy. Port-o-Let, it called itself, and cost $75 a month to hire. Popping off to poo in the bushes was not done, and neither was digging latrines. A flicker, which is related to woodpeckers, white crowned-sparrow, humming-bird and red-tailed hawk were all new to me. Some hungry-looking turkey vultures sat in trees nearby. We were on Burr Heneman's land. An avid naturalist, he had visited us in Orkney years before.

Traceur's accommodation was owned by Aggie Murch, who was English. The name conjured up a little old lady with grey hair and rosy cheeks, dressed in black, living in a rose-entwined cottage. The reality, once she unveiled after collecting honey, was a youthful and vigorous six foot two. Blackberry Farm was a large old weatherboard house set in seven acres, facing towards Bolinas Lagoon and hills beyond. Traceur had a choice of fields or stable; his boarding-fees would be bartered against work around house and grounds. In a huge room above the stables, Aggie's husband Walter was busy editing the Oscar-winning film *The English Patient*.

Bolinas was a small sleepy village at the end of a narrow road over the hills from the east. It had been a timber town long ago, but twenty-five years before had acquired cult status when, to help clean up a major oil-spill, many hippies had arrived. They never left. Pigtailed and beaded, grey-haired and balding, the 1960s lived on, alive and well in Bolinas. A wholefood shop, art gallery, museum, craft shops and studios augmented the bar, garage and general store. The town drunks were accompanied by a variegated collection of ownerless mongrels. The population of about two thousand mainly lived spread out over the Mesa to the north, an extraordinary mix of people with artists, writers, film-makers and musicians in high proportion.

The town's geographical position made it outstandingly beautiful. Perched almost on the San Andreas Fault, it nestled just north of the narrow tidal channel between the Pacific and Bolinas Lagoon, surrounded by tree-clad higher ground. The extensive, shallow lagoon was a magnificent place, protected from the sea by a substantial sand-bar, haunt of many thousands of waterfowl and wading birds, as well as a colony of common seals. US Highway 1 passed along its southern shore through the hamlet of Stinson Beach, before climbing away south to join Highway 101 at the approach to San Francisco. Bolinas beach – and the Pacific – was a short walk west past the tidal inlet. One could walk north towards Point Reyes National Seashore, past eroding cliffs on one side and treacherous tidal Duxbury Reef on the other, doom of more ships than the schooner it was named for. It was a perfect place for us to spend a winter before beginning the trek to the Atlantic. But we soon discovered American culture was less free and open than the wilds of Asia.

The night after I arrived with the animals, I was woken at 2 a.m. by a furious Burr striding down the hill from his house. The dogs, unaccustomed to their surroundings and having been confined almost entirely since we left Jinning, had been barking. Burr's neighbour had complained. 'You call these pets?' he yelled, which I didn't, they were guards, but you don't argue with an apoplectic host in the middle of the night. He put them in his pump-house but they went frantic and broke a pipe, flooding the place. To placate a now speechless Burr, we took the smelly brutes into the caravan for the night.

We had never intended to take the dogs home to endure the barbaric six-month quarantine, which is still required by UK law in spite of modern anti-rabies innoculation. However, I had not foreseen being put in a corner immediately on arrival in the US. Burr refused to let us keep them on his property another night, so we took them to kennels, and with immense reluctance, put Nin up for adoption. Tsar would never have passed the necessary behavioural tests, and when we moved to a new site, we brought him back. I have a lasting bad conscience about what we did to Nin and hope he found the loving home he deserved.

The four months we spent in Bolinas passed quickly. The children, having discovered the joys of abundance, the surrounding country and beach providing ample scope for their energy, were only seen when hungry. Eilidh continued to ride Traceur and any other available mount. Fionn, wrapped in a wet-suit, almost developed flippers he spent so long in the sea boogie-boarding. This, it transpired, was a sort of water-sledge on which one surfed. He also went fishing with new chum Nick Newcomb. Torcuil, always interested in wildlife, became a passionate bird-watcher, encouraged by Keith Hansen, expert ornithologist and highly talented bird artist, who had a studio-shop in town. Kate had time to relax, enjoy the countryside, walk Tsar. I enjoyed the peace after the traumas of the previous year, went birding and walking – and planned the next leg of the journey.

Early in our stay in Bolinas a 'Pot Luck' was held in our honour in the village hall, which resulted in many more invitations. Ananda Brady, joiner and jeweller, had built his own horse-drawn caravan, beautifully finished and decorated, and we came to know him and his family well. At nearby Paradise Valley, the Newcombs provided almost a second home and after we left acted as our mail-box for over a year. Roofing contractor Jazon Wonders provided Eilidh with all the horses she could want, and later the chance to compete at endurance riding. The rest of the story of our time there, the people we met and the places we visited, would require a book to itself.

On four occasions Traceur became listless and went off his feed, with a rise in temperature. These spells lasted only a day or two but he was not right. We took him to the

University of California vet school at Davies for examination. Jazon kindly drove him there and we left him in the care of leading horse veterinarian Dr Gary Carlson. After eight days of exhaustive tests, during which Trass obligingly displayed his symptoms, they found nothing. No disease or infection was present in his blood or serum samples. Dr Carlson confessed to bafflement, surmising only that there might be a slight viral infection of the upper respiratory tract and that the horse might work through these episodes. Almost as though he had been listening, Traceur had no further illness. From then until we left at the beginning of March he was markedly more alert.

We planned to drive to Canada up Highway 1, then turn east. In January Irma O'Brien took us to have a look at it and visit Fort Ross, sixty miles north. *Krepocty Rocc* was the furthest penetration into the Americas by the Russian Empire. It was built in 1812 and given up in 1842. During those thirty years, the Russians almost wiped out seals and sea-otters. This decimation of the fur-bearing animals made hunting unprofitable and, although they had the opportunity to acquire the inland area from the Mexicans, who then controlled it, the Russians left. Had they not done so, how very different the course of world history would have been. And steep, twisting, narrow, busy Highway 1 was quite unsuitable for horse-drawn caravans.

During the winter we had had several media interviews. The publicity was welcome. Our funds were so disastrously reduced that crossing America was going to depend on raising more. Presciently, Ananda Brady said, 'Don't worry about money. It will come.' I twirled the ring he had made for me on my finger, and hoped he was right.

Three days before we left, the Murch family gave a party, enabling us to gather almost everyone we knew in Bolinas under one roof to thank them and say goodbye.

Then, on the morning of 6 March, with a crowd of friends to see us off, we pulled out from our winter quarters, bounced down the dirt track to the tarmac and headed east. It had been a memorable winter, Bolinas a beautiful place, but our feet were itching. It was time to go and see the *real* USA.

Travelling in the USA was very different from anywhere else we had been. In Europe and all across Asia we had usually been able just to pull off and stop. Not in the Land of the Free. Roadsides were fenced, many bearing 'No Trespassing' signs, which meant having to ask – if we could find the owner. A patch of unfenced grass might turn out to be private too. Once, two deputy sheriffs, armed with a brace of pistols apiece, spare magazines, flick-knives, night-sticks and mace, not to mention the pump-action shotguns and high-velocity rifles in their cars, stopped to investigate because someone had reported us. After we explained who we were, they went to mollify the owner, then came back to chat. They wore body-armour in addition to carrying an arsenal and claimed they would be outgunned in any serious confrontation.

We had an easy first few days, travelling up and out of the Coastal Range by Point Reyes Station and east through Novato. From there to Napa and beyond, the roads were busy and at times lacked any shoulder. We had arranged an escort across the narrow, busy and blind Petaluma river bridge on Highway 37 and it was comforting to have burly Terry Sims guarding our rear in his black and white California Highway Patrol car, battery of lights flashing.

The smugness I felt at the superior law-abiding qualities of the British was savagely ripped away on 15 March. DUNBLANE, screamed the headlines. MASSACRE AT SCOTTISH SCHOOL. The news shocked us, deeply and numbingly, for a long time. Such tragedies didn't happen in Scotland and certainly not in sleepy Dunblane. Even today I can hardly believe it did.

The Sacramento valley was wide, cultivated and hot as a cauldron. The delightful back road we took to Elk Creek and on up to Paskenta was cooler, quieter, partly untarred, and passed through a wonderful mix of hills, deciduous trees, pine forest and grazing land. We also had an outrider. Jazon had lent Eilidh Socks, a little chestnut Arabian, for a few weeks. This was useful as well as fun because she was able to scout ahead for water and stopping-places.

Bird-life was prolific. Keith had Torcuil so well taught by the time we left Bolinas, that he could identify almost everything we saw, from Wilson's warblers to bald eagles. Spring flowers were showing, trees almost fully in leaf. From atop Blue Ridge one evening Torcuil and I glimpsed the unmistakable cone of Mount Shasta, far north. Sudden storms could blacken the sky in a minute, turning a sunny day into a deluge. The splendid sight of comet Hyakatake dominated the heavens at night, streaking towards the sun, trailing its diaphanous tail. It was so peaceful plodding up Bear Valley and on to Indian Valley, it was hard to believe that 30 million people lived in California.

We were often stopped for a chat, to be given a pot of honey or a few bucks. Ananda Brady had been right, money was no problem. It kept trickling in, ten dollars here, twenty there, sometimes more. In Suisun Valley we saw our first wild turkeys and some Suisun Indian petroglyphs. We were given breakfast at John Pickerel's Putah Creek Café – and while we often found American cooking too rich and too much, their breakfasts are a magnificent institution. Ham and eggs (over easy – how else?), loads of toast and lashings of coffee, or perhaps a stack of pancakes and maple syrup, or blueberry muffins . . . Once we lunched at Full Belly

Farms, a three-family co-operative on a hundred acres. They grew organic vegetables, using restored old machinery, had two Jersey house-cows, twenty-five sheep, some goats and hens – and employed a Mexican family to wash, pack and deliver the vegetables fresh to nearby cities. In the consumption-crazed US, it was an object lesson in wise use of resources.

One day, Socks came hurtling past the caravan at a full gallop, a hatless Fionn aboard, legs flapping wildly, totally out of control, to disappear over a rise. Moments later, Socks came tearing back without Fionn. I flung Traceur's reins to somebody and set off at a run. Visions of disaster were dispelled when I came up to him. He had managed to slip off and was unharmed – and got a hell of a rocket for not wearing his hard hat.

We followed the back road all the way to the town of Red Bluff. It was peaceful and beautiful, no spectacular mountains, roaring rivers or vast plains but a lovely grassy valley bottom with deciduous woods, streams and pine forest running up the sides. At Elk Creek primary school, 35 per cent of the pupils were Native Americans from two small tribes on the Grindstone Reservation. Californian Indian tribes had always been small. Several were exterminated during the early years of white settlement, deliberately hunted down and wiped out. In Flournoy, Dean Connard, holder of the Californian calf-roping record, shod Traceur. From there, distantly, we could see the 10,000-foot peak of Mount Lassen, glistening white, high in the Sierras. Which we must cross.

In the space of hours we left our quiet minor road and descended into the maelstrom of Red Bluff traffic. Thankfully, American towns have wide streets and there was plenty of room. After spending a small fortune at the local Wal-Mart on clothing, shoes and supplies we crossed the

Sacramento river. Superstores, never my favourite places, had plenty of parking room and we could find most of what we needed at one stop.

Once over the river, we began to climb a series of low rolling ridges. Traceur was pulling well as we approached Payne's Creek, though it was hot and sweaty. We gave him plenty of rests and slowly left the valley behind. The road steepened as we passed a big trout farm. Scrub-covered cliff rose on our left, the creek flowed along the flats below. As we pulled into a turn-out – lay-by – it looked as though we would soon need a tow.

Hardly had the thought crossed my mind when a Jeep arrived, followed by a pick-up from the trout farm. The pick-up was bigger and the driver knew a place we could spend the night. They took us to a field and left a fry of trout. The Jeep driver, Pam Warren, had followed and offered to take us to survey the road ahead. We drove twenty miles, up to Mineral and beyond. Several places on the way looked hard pulling and Pam insisted she would return in the morning to help.

We spent a night at Mineral, 5266 feet up, and woke to snow. It had been over 26°C/80°F in the Sacramento two days before. Now, deep in Lassen National Forest, among giant ponderosa and sugar pines, Douglas firs and red-woods, it was winter again. The sun streamed through the trees, dappling the snow. Mountain chickadees piped busily as they fossicked for food in the trees and Trass's big feet clomped slushily along the road. The Sierras, that great bogey which had haunted me all winter, had been surpassed with ease – and help from Pam Warren's Jeep. Not far south, a great pioneering tragedy was commemorated by the name Donner Pass. Attempting the east–west crossing late in 1846, the Donner party had become trapped by blizzards. Some survived, many died. Tackling tarred

Highway 36 in spring was a very different proposition from taking ox-carts across trackless passes at the onset of winter.

Salmon ran up these clear mountain rivers. Dippers inhabited the streams. A pair of ospreys attempted to build a nest in a most unsuitable scrawny pine. Fionn found a wallet that had lain under the snow for months. It contained no identification, only a hundred dollars. In part of the forest that had been felled, I sat on a stump and counted the rings. The tree had been a seedling during the French Revolution, long before Europeans arrived here. Now, in minutes, a snarling chain-saw had dropped the giant and sent it lifeless to market, for pulping or to form the beams of some instantly erectable kit house. Two hundred years' growing-time is 'not economic' nowadays. The once-vibrant forest would be replaced with regimented rows of even-age plantation, sterile but harvestable every forty years, eminently profitable for the board and shareholders of some big timber company.

Lake Almanor was huge. We stopped beside ground reserved for nesting Canada geese, with yellow-headed blackbirds in bushes beside us, Clark's grebes and common loons on the lake, and a quartet of bald eagles disputing ownership of a dead fish on the shore.

It was barely spring in this high mountain country and short of Westwood it snowed again. In accord with the grey, wintry scene, Kate and I fell out over some triviality and the argument became interminable. I took myself off into the woods in the still-falling snow and walked for an age – and nearly got lost. As I picked my way back, concentrating hard on finding the right direction, I calmed down. Kate was no more adapted to caravan life than she had ever been and she still became physically unwell travelling. She had done wonders in the UK over the Mongolian business, was great at finding all we asked for to bring out with her, but on the road her ill-health seemed to make it impossible for her to settle. I hoped our mutual shock at this explosion of emotions would produce its own balm.

Next day Socks, scared by rustling plastic bags of shopping that Eilidh was carrying back to the caravan from Westwood, dumped her and careered down the road, just as his owner arrived to collect him. Jazon invited Eilidh to return to California with him, to compete in an endurance ride of fifty miles the following Saturday. She had been deprived of a similar chance before we left because Jazon got flu. We knew she wanted to go and consented. She would rejoin us – somewhere! It was our two thousandth day since departure from Britain – and the 250th anniversary of the battle of Culloden.

Days later we made a two-mile curling descent from the 5748-foot Fredonyer Pass into Susanville. We bought a bag of oats for Traceur and continued on, into sage-brush country. A few miles later we stopped at the Schechert Ranch, managed by Virgil Dilts and his wife Sally.

The ranch was situated almost adjacent to the largest prison in the western hemisphere, with twelve thousand inmates. Of these, 1500 were Category 4, the most dangerous. One man was serving a total of 427 years. Virgil told us all this at supper, for as well as managing the ranch, he had a part-time job teaching agricultural skills to prisoners due for release. We spent two days on the ranch, resting Traceur, clogging the Dilts' washing-machine and recuperating after the tough traverse of the Sierras. The land was pallid after winter, the grass more brown than green, the hills treeless, stark and snow-sprinkled, with vast vistas over the open ground south of us. Contemplating this primal magnificence, I thought how desperate and bleak it must appear to a felon, bred in some urban ghetto, unfamiliar with rural landscape, barred up in the forbidding concrete concentration camp next door.

We left Schechert Ranch loaded with food. The Dilts came next day to tow us up a short steep hill on Highway 395 and presented Fionn with a bicycle outgrown by their own family. On top of the well-filled envelope Virgil had thrust upon me as we left, this was more than generous. Another family long to be remembered for their kindness but, above all, for themselves.

In the Sierras a historic marker had indicated the Lassen Pioneer Trail. Now we came to the Noble Trail. I could almost hear the creak of wagons, the snorting of oxen and mules, the rattle of iron-shod wheels against stone and the hoarse cries of the pioneers as they drove their animals on.

We passed a huge, shallow but extensive slick, a seasonal lake. The weather was fickle, one minute sunny and warm, the next snow flurries. We persevered, making miles along the die-straight road, frequently passed by 'snowbirds in RVs' – pensioners in recreational vehicles or motor homes – migrating north after a winter in the sun. Climbing gradually to about five thousand feet, we entered an area of extensive juniper forest, the massive old trees covered in berries, a few blackbirds inhabiting their branches. Then came Termo: population twenty-four, altitude 5300 feet, one fading store. It was the image so often portrayed in American films of a small, dead-end place. Even its name expressed a sort of finality.

Road traffic through this mossy-grey country was light. Occasionally a goods train clanked along the railway that paralleled the road. Ponds and lakes held a wealth of wildfowl, including white-faced ibis. Sandhill cranes were becoming frequent and we saw our first Clark's nutcrackers. Harsh hills lent a rugged air to everything. One day after stopping, Fionn and I climbed 7930-foot McDonald Peak.

Snow lay in patches and the wind whistled round the summit. The view was grand but it was too cold to linger so we scrambled back down to the caravan, over boulders and through tussock grass, to a welcome late supper. We had covered a total of twenty-five miles since breakfast.

At Likely, we had an introduction to Lorraine Flournoy, who not only let us park but fed us. She suggested we should go next day with the local school outing to Lava Beds National Monument.

The lava beds had a labyrinth of subterranean tubes, formed thirty thousand years ago as the flow of lava cooled and finally ceased. Plunging down these was like entering a huge aorta. More interesting was the walk through the place where Kientpoos, or Captain Jack, had led the Modoc Indians in a desperate stand against the US army. It was the old story of indigenous people trying to preserve a remnant of their ancestral lands in the face of massive settlement by outsiders. Sixty Modoc men, with their women and children, held out for five months against 3500 troops. The end could never have been in doubt. Shortage of water caused the Indians to slip away one night and thereafter, rounded up in small groups, they were deported to a reservation in Oklahoma. As the guide to the area stated, 'Walk this trail with reverence. The cultural identity of an entire people was lost here . . . so settlers could graze a few cows.'

We were almost out of California. The caravan was towed up the steep top section of 6305-foot Cedar Pass. For a change, I rode Traceur up, thoroughly enjoying being astride the big fellow as we passed through pines to the summit. The drop to Cedarville was 1600 feet, the view over Middle Alkali Lake and far Goose Lake outstanding. With many days of bush country ahead, we stocked up well, pulled out and parked for our last night in the state at the far side of the Alkali Lake causeway. We spent it skinny-dipping by moonlight in a stream fed by hot springs. The temperature was perfect.

Seven of our nine days in Nevada were on dirt road in uninhabited sage-brush, which the Americans call desert, though it was lush compared with the Sahara. We crossed the Applegate Trail and came to Fortyniner Rock, a marker, named at the time of the great 1849 gold-rush. We could only marvel at the hardships people endured for the faint hope of a fortune. The country east of us was arid, its lakes undrinkably alkaline. We saw wild horses and a few prong-horn antelope. Part of our way lay through the Charles Sheldon National Wildlife Refuge but few creatures crossed our path and even fewer people. The scenery was wild and dramatic, great gullies and huge flat-topped buttes, a far cry from that popular Nevadan image, the gambling hells of Reno and Las Vegas.

Denio, our first town for a week, had a store that didn't open till 11 a.m. and stocked little we needed. The curse of the car meant everyone shopped at Winnemucca, a hundred miles away. We crossed into Oregon marching along the foot of the Pueblo Range, solid lumps of snow-capped mountain 8500 feet high. Ahead was another formidable chunk, 10,000-foot Steen's Mountain but we turned off at Tum Tum Lake to follow Trout Creek into much lower hills.

We climbed on dirt track till we came to an abandoned and ruinous stone house, occupied only by barn swallows. There was a small meadow next to the rushing waters of the creek and we pulled off. A covey of California quail, a yellow warbler, two mourning doves, a couple of western kingbirds and some starlings dwelt among the shady branches of the big old cottonwoods beside the house. We were astonished and delighted later in the day when Pam and Rick Warren drove up, complete with tent, mountains of food and their beautiful dog, Akita-cross-wolf Charlie. They had driven over three hundred miles for a weekend visit because, for some reason, we had touched their hearts and they could not do enough for us.

It took eleven days to cross Oregon, to Jordan Valley on the Idaho border. We lingered to visit the rodeo there. Fionn, who had sported a cowboy hat since Red Bluff, decided he wanted to become a bull-rider. I found the expertise of big-loop roping more to my taste. Two cowboys, whirling riatas – 20-foot-diameter lassos – had to neck-rope a horse. That done, one had to try and put a noose round the animal's forelegs to topple it. They were allowed three throws between them. We watched a winning team catch their horse in about twenty-one seconds but many pairs failed to rope their quarry or ran out of time. I think the Mongolian system was easier.

I discovered that a Mike Hanley had draught horses locally and could probably shoe Traceur for me. I was about to seek him out when he found us, bringing a message from one Bob Davy, who wanted to interview us for radio. Hanley Ranch was almost as much museum as ranch. Mike collected and restored horse-drawn vehicles of all sorts, from a road-coach to a dump-wagon, from buggies to carts. Traceur was induced with difficulty into the farriery crate. This device is fine if the horse is used to it and saves the smith's back – but Traceur was unfamiliar with it, hated it and fought the restraint all the way.

Next day Fionn and I went to a traditional branding at the Lowry ranch. We travelled over in Mike's buggy and pair on a dull grey morning, following an old section of stagecoach route. The cattle arrived just after we did, and were herded into a three-sided corral, where the bulls were cut out and let go. Three branding irons and four cauterising irons were laid into the log fire to heat. Eight mounted men then began roping the calves, working in pairs. One dropped a noose over the neck, the other would catch the hind legs – not infrequently they missed. They brought the calf over to the fire, where the 'ground crew' tipped it on its side, removed the neck rope and replaced it round the forelegs. The cowboys kept the ropes taut, dallied round their saddle-horns, immobilising the calf. One man branded it, another nipped off the horn-buds with a sharp knife and yet another cauterised the stumps. The ears were notched and – something I had never heard of before – a strip of skin over the throat was cut loose and left to heal as a toggle, another form of identification. Finally, before release the calf was given an anti-clostridium injection and, if male, castrated.

We had a filling mid-afternoon meal of 'Sloppy Joe over biscuit', mince on rolls, cooked on a portable wood-stove. Fionn did such good work fetching the hot irons and later some branding that he was given ten dollars and a lasso of his own.

I had been dubious, but local opinion was agreed that we could manage the road to the ghost-town of Silver City. This would cut off a lot of miles and keep us away from the maelstrom of busy highways. We decided to try it and rumbled east, into Idaho.

It was harder than I had expected but the country was interesting so probably only Traceur noticed this. Looking back west we could see so far, it was easy to imagine the Pacific waves crashing on the rocky coast of California. Mountain bluebirds, long my favourites, were so tame they hopped about by the caravan, feeding. The streams were crystal clear and the air pure and clean. We had been expecting Aggie Murch's visit but it was great to see her when she arrived one breakfast-time. She stayed only briefly, for Bolinas was a long drive away, leaving us a stack of mail, bags full of groceries, 'trashy books' and vital replacement carabiners, used to attach the traces to Traceur's collar.

It was interesting to see Silver City, once a thriving mining town, now being revitalised as a tourist attraction, but for me, the outlook from the 7200-foot pass to Sinker Creek and the Snake River Valley miles below better repaid the struggle up. The long hot descent was hard on the brakes; several times we had to stop and wait for them to cool. Lewis's woodpeckers, chukor partridge, lazuli buntings and Cassin's finches graced our road down. When we reached Highway 78, it was sticky-hot, sultry, and the wild country was gone, replaced by cultivation. State licence plates proclaimed the crop: 'Idaho – famous for potatoes.'

Without the Snake and irrigation, south Idaho would be a desert. Near Indian Cove only the river edge was vegetated. The valley walls, topped by short cliffs, were as arid as Mars and reflected heat beat down on us. The fast-flowing turgid grey-green waters did not invite a cooling plunge. We crossed a bridge to the north bank. About two hundred cliff swallows wheeled out from under it, filling the air with their cheerful screams. A lugubrious American pelican flap-glided down river, three big double-crested cormorants perched ridiculously on a slender tree and a Bullock's oriole flashed brilliant orange as it dived into the bushes. The road bent round to wider, greener pastures, irrigation pipes squirting, with Interstate 84 and the Union Pacific railway visible to the north.

Near Bliss was the spectacular 140-foot-deep Malad Gorge and the roiling Devil's Washtub, the Hagerman Fossil Beds and Thousand Springs, where water gushes forth from cliffs above the Snake. It was here the pioneer

John Fremont reported meeting many Paiute and Bannock Indians fishing for salmon, but the Snake today has been so altered by dams and irrigation works that no salmon can get upriver.

As we crossed more open dry country, moorland almost, the Bennett Range stood off north of us, with the Soldier Mountains beyond, 10,000-foot Smokey Dome showing faint but clear. Gooding – 'a neat little town' – was friendly. In the park where we stopped, Torcuil and I witnessed an encounter between two crows and a half-grown red squirrel. The crows chased the squirrel across the grass, diving at it. The squirrel leaped on to the trunk of a tree only to be knocked to the ground by a crow. It ran to another tree but the crows dislodged it twice more before it finally made its escape into a third tree. We obtained a tyre for Fionn's bike here and an axle for the Muddy Fox, both urgently needed.

That evening, stopped by the Little Wood Canal, Fred and Judy Brossy and their son Cooper brought us fresh chives, mint, parsley and oregano and invited us to stay at their place next day. We stayed four in the end. Traceur was due for a rest and Bryant Ranch, which Fred managed, was ideal. There was lots of good grass and big trees offered shade from temperatures in the mid-90s Fahrenheit. We helped round up cattle, the boys went river-rafting and Judy took us into the town of Twin Falls. The Shoshone Falls, though far less massive than Niagara, drop four feet further. It was here that Evel Knievel tried and spectacularly failed to jump the Snake Canyon on a motorcycle. Bob Davy, the radio journalist who had contacted me at Jordan Valley, came to interview us. When we left, Fionn stayed behind to go rafting from Jackpot downriver to Nevada.

We were never far from the Oregon Trail. It had been the easiest route for draught animals, and the Snake provided water in a region of desperate aridity. We saw some fox cubs and a screech owl. We encountered prosperous and friendly Mormon farmers, with prolific families. The Minidoka County Museum in Rupert was excellent, with fine displays of domestic items, farm implements, even a complete railway station. I was particularly interested to see the sheep-wagons, in which shepherds lived on the range in summer. They resembled gypsy bow-tops but were more compact, the design elegant and sparing.

On 17 June we parked for the night by the banks of the Snake, just short of American Falls, eagerly awaiting the arrival of the Newcomb family. They came bringing our accumulated mail – and Eilidh. It was a noisy, joyful reunion.

Next morning, I was tacking up Traceur from the right side because it was windy and he was busy eating in the lee of the caravan. His head and the feed-bucket blocked my view of the collar-fastening so I moved round behind him to fasten it from the left side. Suddenly a great blow to the head felled me, knocking me half unconscious. As I struggled up I realised it had been the collar which had hit me and thought, I hope it's not broken. When Traceur put his face down to feed, the unfastened collar must have slid down and hit his ears, whereupon he flung up his head, sending the 20-pound collar hurtling skywards. I was bleeding from a gash on the forehead and went to hospital in American Falls. Sixteen stitches, for which the bill was $380.32. Removing them was free. I did it myself.

This was our second large medical bill. Days after we left Bolinas, a tick bit Kate and the puncture became infected. Because of the danger of Lyme disease, she had seen a doctor. An antibiotic injection and a course of pills had cost $140. Our combined medical and dental expenses totalled over five hundred dollars and we had a long way yet to go.

The Newcombs stayed five days. Together we visited

Pocatello, explored the replica of Fort Hall and attended a rodeo. They left us on the Portneuf road, which would take us by the flattest way to Wyoming. This time, they took with them not only Eilidh but Fionn as well, both to be returned – somehow – in late July.

The Bannock Highway was roly-poly but attractive, its bushes, streams and small fields a welcome change from endless acres of potatoes and pinto beans. We continued to be well received by people as Wyoming drew ever closer. Old Bud Bullock drove a horse and cart, met us on the road and let us park in one of his shady paddocks. Steve Gravis was mowing his lawn when we stopped to ask for water. We stayed the night, were fed by his wife Kenna and listened to Steve accompanying his own hilarious comic songs on guitar – and had a deadly argument about US gun laws. They became firm friends and visited us several times before we drew out of their range.

Lava Hot Springs really were hot. We bathed for hours in the dusk in the fuming water. In Montpelier, astonishingly, someone told us Kate's sister Lesley had been looking for us. We could hardly believe this but it was true. She and a friend had flown to Florida and driven half across the US as a surprise – but they never found us.

On 1 July we crossed into Wyoming. 'Like No Place On Earth,' proclaimed the sign at Border, a hamlet of two houses, a garage and a shack selling fireworks. It was hot as hell as we climbed a rolling shoulder of hill. A massive semi-trailer thundered past with 'Trucking for Jesus' written boldly across its rear. Pronghorn antelope bounded away over the fields and man-eating mosquitoes rose in dense clouds around us.

We paused at Fossil Butte National Monument, which protects some of the world's finest fossil plants and animals, preserved in the ancient lake sediments known as the Green

River Formation. At Kemmerer we passed the biggest open-cast coal-mine in the world and J. C. Penney's original store. Next day, below Round Mountain, we were at 7570 feet. A panoply of dark, rolling land spread before us, unfolding infinite vistas of inspiring immensity.

Fontenelle was a shop and garage on the Green river, a few trailer homes set about it, its trade coming mainly from anglers. We parked a mile on, across the river. A sheep-wagon was visible on top of the escarpment ahead. I determined to visit it and see what life in one was like. Namou, an old Navajo in his seventies, was dragging up a dry branch for the fire on which his coffee-pot bubbled. His wagon was immaculately clean and tidy, a commissariat wagon parked neatly behind, his dogs in the shade beneath it, his horse tied to it, munching hay. This was Namou's last season shepherding, he told me, as we drank coffee and shared an excellent flat loaf he had baked. He had land and animals at home in New Mexico and that would be enough for him. His quiet, dignified and courteous character was not unlike that of shepherds everywhere, who live alone in remote places.

I returned to the caravan and we had the most extraordinary encounter of the journey, when Dr Anatoly Shimansky knocked on our door. He was Russian, a geneticist, and was travelling across the USA in a horse-drawn covered wagon. To have met him at all was chance enough but, in fact, he had been travelling with the two men described in the article we had been given on our first day in Kazakhstan three years before. They had completed their original venture and were now headed east–west across the States. Shimansky had fallen out with them over money and was pursuing a solo journey to the Pacific coast. He would not stop beside us for the night, so we walked back to Fontenelle with him to see Vanya, the Belgian gelding he had bought from the Amish. His cart came from Belarus and contained only his clothes, sleeping-bag and scrap-books. Two water-jerries were slung outside. There was no stove or table. After a long chat, we waved him off into the sinking sun.

In mid-July we crossed the Continental Divide at 7525 feet and gazed towards the old pioneer crossing at South Pass. The modern road swung north, crossed the Sweet-water river and began an uphill slog. Kate, who had again been feeling unwell, announced that she intended returning to the UK at the first opportunity: 'I felt terrible but was eating a healthy diet and couldn't understand why I felt so lacklustre. My memory failed me, my hair was falling out and I was puffy-faced, dry-skinned and constipated. I needed a body transplant, fast.' She was obviously struggling to keep going. However, we were still at least ten days from the nearest town of size, Casper, but it was on our road and had an airport. Fortunately it was delightfully hot and we had interesting American pioneer sites ahead to see, which I hoped would cheer her.

Red Canyon was a deep spectacular gash in the dry green country of the Shoshone and Arapaho. We often went for walks after stopping and among much else saw a beaver and a Hammond's flycatcher. Torcuil almost stood on a rattlesnake, which shook its tail in warning at him.

The five-mile haul up Beaver Divide would have posed no difficulty had not the polished road-surface caused Traceur to slip and slide. The sweeping landscape dwarfed us as we plugged our way to the top, resting frequently, then dropped gently down to Jeffrey City, barely a hamlet now, though once a uranium-mining town. We telephoned Wiki Newcomb and heard that Ewan Macdonald had taken Fionn and Nick fishing in his boat – and the boys had each caught their first salmon.

Wagon-train history was all around us. At Ice Slough, slow-seeping water, percolating through peat, froze hard. The insulating property of the peat kept it frozen till midsummer, providing welcome coolth for the pioneer wagontrains. Split Rock was prominent for miles, a major landmark for them and for Indians long before that. Buffalo Bill Cody and other riders of the Pony Express had galloped this road. At the Sun Ranch the Sweetwater carved its way through the narrow gap of Devil's Gate. A bit further east was Independence Rock, called 'the great register of the west' by Father de Smet. An estimated three to five hundred thousand westbound pioneers stopped at it, many leaving names or initials incised into the mile-round, whale-backed outcrop. It was extraordinarily evocative: each journey represented such stupendous effort by ordinary people seeking a better life. Our own exploits, cushioned by tarred roads and shops, seemed like luxury travel in comparison. As backdrop to all this striving stands a range of granite hills. *They* have been there for fourteen million years.

At the end of July we were still in sage-brush, not far short of Casper. Pam and Rick, who were on holiday, brought Eilidh and Fionn back but Eilidh did not stay long. She cajoled Kate and me into letting her return to Bolinas yet again and left with the Warrens two days later. She was beginning to make a name for herself at endurance riding and it would have been unfair to deny her the chance to continue, but we missed her.

Reconstructed Fort Casper gave an excellent idea of what cavalry life had been like in earlier times. In Casper, the Whitneys joined the Warrens, Brossys and Gravises on our list of star families. Jack drove oversized loads all over the US, sometimes accompanied by daughter Venessa as escort driver, while Carol ran their hundred-acre farm. Not only were they very hospitable but when we left they towed the caravan up the steep approach to old Highway 87.

Days later they paid a surprise visit – and Kate went back to Casper with them. She was not at all well: 'I was so desperate, after month upon month of feeling miserable, that Carol suggested I really should see a doctor. I did but they didn't find the cause and the prospect of further expense left no choice but to fly back – something I definitely didn't want to have to do yet again.'

The boys and I soldiered on, crossing the Bozeman Trail, notorious cause of bloodshed between Indians and Europeans, on past Pumpkin Buttes, through oil-producing country towards Gillette. One day after we stopped, Traceur showed symptoms similar to those he had had in Kazakhstan, lip-twitching, with almost a rigor in his neck. Once again I was sure he had eaten something poisonous because next day he was fine.

We stopped for water at 'T&G Guns and Ammo', a gunshop and firing range. The place was an arsenal, but the genial owner kindly offered the boys a shooting lesson. They cycled back in the evening for it and scored well for beginners, with shotguns, rifles and pistols.

On 16 August we sighted Devil's Tower. We had wanted to see it, partly because it featured in the film *Close Encounters of the Third Kind* but mainly because of its spiritual significance in Indian culture. The name is a mistranslation, for it is sacred to many Indian tribes and far from devilish. We had heard it referred to as Grey Horn Butte but I prefer Mahto Tipi, Bear's Lodge. The story goes that several young children were surprised by a huge bear in the forest, which chased them. They ran as fast as they could until they reached a large rock and scrambled up it. The rock, alas, was too low to save them from the rapidly approaching bear. In desperation, they prayed to Wakan Tankah, the Great Spirit, to save them. The rock grew larger and larger, higher and higher. The bear hurled itself at the rock in rage and frustration as it tried to reach the children, repeatedly gouging great claw-marks in the stone, until at last, realising its efforts were futile, it lumbered away.

We walked sunwise round it in proper Celtic fashion, awestruck. No other word can truly express what I felt about this majestic and undoubtedly spiritual place. Wrangles about the name, desecration by climbers, exploitation by traders, all were diminished by the rock itself to petty squabbles, above which it towered and which it would outlast. I wanted to stay on and on but we had to go down.

As we reached the park entrance, Carol Whitney and Kate arrived. They had been to Yellowstone and seen both bear and moose. Our joint meal was the last before Kate flew out from Denver in three days' time.

About the time she took off, the boys and I crossed into South Dakota, having shopped at Aladdin's hundred-year-old store on the way out of Wyoming. Two mule deer seemed to be making heavy weather of jumping a roadside fence ahead of us on the left. Torcuil, who was behind, said, 'Have you seen the elk?'

'They're mule deer,' I replied.

'The one on the right, I mean.'

I looked round. Behind us was this *massive* beast. My 'mule deer' were elk calves and this was their anxious mother.

On our first night in South Dakota, we took a short dirt road and parked beside a Minuteman missile silo. Its lid was off, the missile gone, conforming to US–Russian treaty terms. The firm tracks to these sites were very convenient although there was a frightening number of them. We used them several times while crossing the Great Plains.

Faith was built on the edge of the Cheyenne River and

Standing Rock Indian Reservations. The Locke family, of
whom we had met Kevin, his mother Pat and daughter
Kimimila in Ulaanbaatar, lived on the latter. I telephoned
Kevin to let him know we were in the area. He said he was
going to the Eagle Butte Pow Wow the following day and
would meet us on the way.

The day began messily: Fionn sat on my breakfast. We
scraped jam, marge and mashed toast off his bum, gave Tsar
this unexpected treat and jogged on. Dean and Mavis
Schrempp had stopped to talk and invited us to stay when
we reached their ranch, which was less than a day's drive
from Eagle Butte. As we approached it, a battered red
Datsun of uncertain vintage pulled up and out stepped
Kevin. We arrived at the Schrempps', then rudely rushed off
with Kevin to the pow wow, perhaps our only opportunity
to see Indian culture on display.

Tents, tipis, a few dented campers and many cars surrounded the arena. Nearly everyone was Indian and Kevin
seemed to know them all. We ate the excellent picnic lunch
his mother had put up, then wandered about chatting till
Kevin went to change for dancing. The entrance parade
formed up. The elders and dignitaries led it off, followed by
Vietnam veterans, male and female dancers. Drums beat a
rhythm and all spiralled slowly round, till everyone was in
place. The veterans fired a ragged volley, then dancing
displays and competitions began.

The costumes were magnificent and colourful. Men
wore headdresses of porcupine hair set in deer's tail, topped
with eagle feathers. Some had 'fans' of tail-feathers, too,
sometimes with a central picture of an eagle's head.
Wristlets and moccasins were of beadwork, with whatever
design the owner fancied – Kevin's had nine-pointed Baha'i
stars worked into them. Many dancers had anklets of bells.
The women were less gaudy, in jingle-dresses with little

cones of metal dangling from them and a headband with an eagle feather.

Different drum-groups, five or six drummers to each drum, played in turn and kept up a constant, hypnotic percussion. Dancers of all ages, from seventy-eight-year old Joe Flying By to tots of four or five, circled, whirled and stamped. The hungry and thirsty could visit stalls set around outside the arena, where there were games to play and bric-à-brac to buy. The atmosphere reminded me of Highland games.

At the Schrempps' afterwards, we were fed a mighty stew, then Kevin left. Dean, who was running for the state legislature as a Democrat, was one of six brothers of German ancestry. He and Mavis, a skilled artist, had lived in the area all their lives and had eight children, of whom their five sons all ranched close by.

I was taken 'pasture flying' in Dean's 1959 vintage Cessna 150, a marvellous way to see the undulating grass-land of the Great Plains. Flying at three hundred feet, we checked out the cattle, then took a look at some of the surrounding area, including Eagle Butte. Dean was an excellent pilot and in an hour we did what would take a day in a pick-up or a week on a horse. The aircraft ran on motor-fuel and apart from its annual certificate of air-worthiness, cost nothing. Torcuil went up too but Fionn elected to stay earthbound. He was blissfully happy driving the Yamaha ATV* around the ranch all by himself.

We had had such a good time we did not want to leave next morning – and couldn't, at first, because thick mist

---

*In the UK these are called quad bikes, but as they were unknown when we left, we always think of them by their US terminology of ATV – All Terrain Vehicles.

enclosed the ranch. We drank coffee and ate toast, waiting till it cleared.

We shopped in Eagle Butte, finding Indian-owned store prices lower. A representative of the Tribal Council, Madonna Thunder Hawk, presented us with skip-caps and souvenir mugs. A plague of grasshoppers swarmed from the roadsides. Multitudes were squashed by vehicles, many were blown into the caravan by the stiff breeze that had arisen. In the evenings, friendly and welcoming Indians visited, with interesting and often sad tales of life on the reservations. I was beginning to realise how those living today were still being affected by the destruction of their whole way of life, which culminated in final defeat at the end of last century. The discovery that they may operate casinos legally on reservation land has brought a new prosperity to some tribes, because Americans love to gamble. While it is a nice irony the Indians are getting a bit of their own back this way, gambling holds its own dangers – and by no means all tribes benefit.

We had crossed the Big Owl or Moreau river and were about a day short of Timberlake. It had been extremely wet and cold till mid-afternoon, as we tramped across gently rolling grass plain on the arrow-straight road. On our way we met Cathy Smith, who had been responsible for costuming on the film *Dances With Wolves*, and later Milo Yellow Hair, vice-president of the Oglala Lakota Tribe.* Traceur had been tending to drift right, which I thought was because of the rain and wind. However, he became almost uncontrollable when I tried to turn him left to our selected stopping-place. Once fenced in he walked in circles, quite gaga.

*Lakota is the name the Indians prefer rather than Sioux, a French corruption of an Ojibway word meaning enemy.

He was still not right next morning. We had to move. It was immediately apparent when we moved off that he was far from well. Two miles down the road we found shady trees, with a ranch-house a half-mile away. We parked. Traceur's temperature was 104°F, his breathing shallow, and he was barging about so violently we had to chain him to a tree. I went for help.

Helen and Louis Keller owned the Keller Ranch. Mercifully they were at home and immediately offered barn-space for our horse. It was 7 September. By the evening of the tenth, Traceur was no better and he had stopped drinking. Louis offered to trailer him the fifty miles to Mobridge's Oahe Veterinary Hospital. If nothing was done, Traceur would surely die.

The next few days were a nightmare. Trass was still alive but gravely ill. His white blood-cell count was up from a normal 12,000 to an incredible 80,000. On the fourteenth, as antibiotics combined with his own immune system to beat whatever was devouring him, he was a little better. His medicine cost forty-eight dollars a day but Tami Schanzenbach, veterinary assistant at the hospital, performed the first of several financial miracles and obtained a free supply from the manufacturer, Upjohns. We hated being so far away from him, until Kevin, whose house at Wakpala was five miles west of Mobridge, lent us the old red Datsun. We visited Trass on the eighteenth. He looked haggard, gaunt and miserable, but his eye was a shade brighter, his demeanour a trifle less listless. Then Dr Jason Mez gave me terrible news.

Traceur had tested positive for equine protozoal myeloencephalitis (EPM) and would require treatment for several months. Sixty per cent of cases recovered, but relapses were not unknown. The normal life-cycle of the protozoan parasite that causes this disease takes place between opossums, which are the primary host, and scavenging birds. Horses, however, can contract it from feed contaminated by opossum excreta and the parasite lodges on their brain-stem. Untreated, it is invariably fatal. We would give Traceur the best chance we could. Whatever it cost.

We were still parked at the long-suffering and incredibly kind Kellers'. They fed us frequently and helped maintain morale at least one degree above total misery. The loan of the Datsun meant we could shop in Timberlake, as well as go to Mobridge. Most days hung heavy but I accompanied Kevin and some visiting Baha'i educationalists to Sitting Bull College at Fort Yates and another day I co-drove for him when he was performing at Pine Ridge. On the way we visited the haunting, tragic monument at Wounded Knee, commemorating the massacre there of Big Foot and his people in 1890, which marked the end of Indian resistance to European settlement. On the way home we stopped at the Badlands, an area in the middle of the South Dakota prairies, now a National Park, where wind, rain and frost have carved out canyons, gullies, knobs and spires. It gained its name from early European settlers, for whom it represented a bar to both settlement and onward travel. When Kevin and some cousins performed for Eureka's 'Schmeckfest', we all went along. The town is inhabited almost entirely by descendants of Germans, who had lived in Russia until the early 1900s, and this was their annual feast. It took our minds off Trassy for a while.

It was only the middle of September. However, we should not be able to travel again before winter, nor could we remain much longer at the Kellers'. The caravan was not suitable accommodation for a Plains winter. Yet again Kevin came to our rescue. He rented a flat in Mobridge that he would not be using for at least a month. It was ours if it would help.

Kate had been kept in touch with frequent calls, and if news of Traceur was bad, her own was better. 'After returning [from America] with symptoms worse than ever, the verdict from my tests came through: myxoedema, a very under-active thyroid. I should have known, as it runs in my family. I took my thyroxine daily and gradually felt better.' Once we were settled she would be coming out for the winter.

Franz Welz, whose large advertisement we had carried since Almaty, did not pay their final instalment of £1200, which added to our woes. Tsar was another worry, because he could not live in the flat. I introduced him to Twyla Fritz, who had boarding kennels. She liked him and agreed to keep him for a week while she tried to find someone to give him a home.

On 29 September we loaded the contents of the caravan into Louis Keller's capacious pick-up and drove through to Mobridge. Our second American winter looked like being long – and difficult.

CHAPTER EIGHTEEN

~~~⧼⧽~~~

THE USA (2): OCTOBER 1996–APRIL 1997
SITTING BULL AND SNOW

America has been sick for some time. It got sick when the first Indian treaty was broken.

Vine Deloria Jr

No sooner had we unloaded our gear at 102 Brown Palace Apartments than it was time to drive over to Winona Flying Earth's house at Wakpala, where we had been invited to attend a traditional Lakota 'maiden ceremony'. We dropped Tsar off at Twyla Fritz's kennels on the way.

The ceremony was being held for sisters She-who-steps-first and Little Owl Black Cloud to mark their passage to womanhood. Their mother, Donna, a Pima-Maricopa Indian from Arizona, had chosen four older women, Pat Locke, Winona Flying Earth, Imogen Taken Alive and Dolores Taken Alive, to be their advisers or godmothers. Before the ceremony began, the girls' father, Edward 'Luigi' Black Cloud, formally requested the help of Stanley Looking Horse, the elder who was to oversee it, and gave him an offering of tobacco.

Only the four women and girls participated in the first part of the ceremony. Dressed in pretty print dresses made for the occasion by their mother, wearing gorgeous moccasins beautifully ornamented with beadwork, their hair centrally parted and the parting painted vermilion, the sisters and their advisers entered the tipi Kevin Locke had erected that morning. There, in private, advice was given to them concerning their role as Lakota women and their path into the future, their hair was combed with new combs and they were ritually washed.

Outside, Luigi had erected a small sacred circle of sage on the grass. Four choke-cherry branches bearing flags of the sacred colours marked the four directions: red for south; black for west; white for north; yellow for east. To the beat of a small drum, Stanley Looking Horse chanted as his son Ivan filled the sacred Pipe. He also purified the branches and area of the sacred circle with sweet-grass smoke. Before the girls emerged, Stanley's wife, Cecilia Looking Horse, laid a path of sacred sage from the tipi to the circle, placing more in the centre of the circle. The girls came out, followed by the four older women, and walked to the circle, stopping thrice briefly on the way. Stanley stood behind, holding the Pipe unlit between them. Ivan, kneeling, drummed and sang while each of the four directions was saluted in turn. The girls faced south, the Pipe was lit and they took a token puff apiece, concluding the ceremony. The participants then stepped out of the circle and we all filed past, relatives of the girls hugging them, the rest of us clasping hands. It had been very moving, enhanced by the backdrop of early evening light on the waters of the Missouri, the sacred sage and choke-cherry branches, the tipi and the quiet dignity with which the ceremony was held. It had been a privilege to be present at this ancient rite.

We discovered that more and more native Americans are taking up their old rituals. The tragedy of Wounded Knee in 1890 marked the end of effective Indian resistance to conquest by Europeans. Since then, tribes all over America have lived in a state of humiliation. Children were taken from their parents, sent to special white-run schools, clothed like European children and, worst of all, forbidden to speak their language. The people, unable to pursue their normal way of life, were herded like beasts onto reservations. Deprived of the work required to obtain the necessities of life – hunting, gathering, fishing and limited farming – they became idle, many took to drink, their morale broken and all but destroyed. Once-proud nations began to disintegrate. This decline has not been entirely stopped yet and will take longer to reverse but there is a new awareness abroad. The people themselves are taking action to educate the youth, rehabilitate substance abusers and restore a sense of pride and worth, which has been missing or dormant for nearly a century. There is little help forthcoming from national government. The USA made 367 different treaties with Indians ratified by Congress and three more (in the 1790s) signed by the President and broke the lot. The attitude today is not much different. By and large Americans believe Indians live the life of Reilly on reservations, on government handouts. Most have never been on a reservation, don't know and don't want to know about Indians, wish they were not there. The facts are that the 'handouts' are agreed treaty-payments for land or assets taken, usually assessed at a fraction of true value, that substance abuse problems are disproportionately high, that enormous domestic problems follow from this, that violence is often rife . . . The list of dreadfulness is long and shameful, and cries out for redress.

Traceur, weak, with a long convalescence ahead, was discharged from the Oahe Veterinary Hospital and taken two miles to Julie and Gene Turner's, where we had arranged accommodation for him. With great generosity, his bill was rendered at cost. Tami Schanzenbach persuaded the Mortar & Pestle Pharmacy to donate his supply of medicine, saving us a huge sum. Everyone was on Traceur's side and doing all they could for him.

This encouraging news was swiftly counterbalanced. Tsar made an unprovoked attack on Twyla Fritz as she was taking water into his kennel. She escaped unscathed, tried again, and again he lunged at her. On previous days he had allowed her to befriend him, play with him and tease out his matted coat. When tied to the caravan, guarding, he had nipped several people and bitten a couple but then he had been doing his job. However, he had clearly developed an uncertain, dangerous streak and I was not prepared to take the chance of him mauling someone severely. Before I could change my mind, I took the woolly monster to the vet. Holding him in my arms, tears in my eyes, pentathol did its lethal work. I buried him at the foot of an old tree in a field by the clinic. The boys were stunned and upset when I told them, but realised it had been a hard, unavoidable decision.

Traceur was proving difficult to keep apart from the Turners' horses. We moved him to June and Bill Imberis', to a paddock next to their cow, a convenient mile from the flat. He continued to improve, till only his right eye, rolled forward and unseeing, was evidence of his disease.

Fionn went fishing with Louis Keller in his boat and caught a good-sized walleye. Torcuil almost daily added to his local bird list. We made a trip to the Little Owl river and saw a herd of buffalo. The fall colours were spectacular, the bright yellow leaves on the trees shimmering in the sunshine. From Chief Sitting Bull's monument, we had grand views across the Missouri to Mobridge on the opposite bank; KELO-land TV interviewed us and we attended the Mobridge high school pow wow, surprisingly the first ever held in the multiracial school. We fetched a winter's supply of hay, donated by our guardian angel Tami, who also wheedled a half-ton of feed out of the Purina salesman.

On 21 October United Airlines' twenty-seater Beech-craft 1900 feeder-flight from Denver touched down on time at Pierre, capital of South Dakota. Out stepped a sun-tanned, fit-looking Eilidh. It was her fifteenth birthday.

We had to quit the flat. Regulations stipulated that tenants' visitors could stay only three weeks. Debbie End of Horn helped us obtain the tenancy of 520 2nd Av.E. It was a tiny free-standing clapboard house, consisting of sitting room, kitchen and bedroom and was owned by ninety-three-year-old Mrs Wiegam. There was a large porch, plenty cupboard space, gas heating and the rent was very reasonable. We moved in on 27 October as the first geese flew over and the temperature dropped close to freezing. That winter we lived like regular householders. We joined the library and I was lent an old IBM computer to begin work on this book.

I attended several *inipi,* sweat-lodge ceremonies, at Kevin's, once taking Torcuil. The ceremony is for purifica-tion, a sauna with spiritual overtones, and at Kevin's adapted to the Baha'i Faith. The lodge is a frame of wooden hoops covered traditionally with buffalo hides but more likely with old carpets today. In the centre is a small pit filled with glowing hot stones from a fire outside. Participants enter the lodge, and to the accompaniment of ancient sacred singing, water is poured over the stones, causing steam to form and quickly heat the air. A prayer or chant accom-panies each procedure. The water-vessel is handed to each participant, who may choose to say a prayer, make a state-ment or remain silent, before pouring a little on the rocks and passing it on. It is womb-like in the small, pitch-dark lodge and very intense. The sacred Pipe, filled earlier to the accompaniment of the Pipe-filling song, is lit and makes a round. The water makes another circuit. When the final hiss of steam came from the rocks and the ceremony ended, I always felt thoroughly cleansed and spiritually refreshed.

Irma O'Brien, whom we had met in Bolinas, telephoned, inviting us to her house in Poulsbo, Washington State. She came to collect Torcuil, Fionn and me in early November. Eilidh, having spent all summer away, remained to look after Traceur. The drive over was via the Badlands, Custer National Park, Wind Cave National Park, the half-finished Crazy Horse monument being carved out of a mountainside and Mahto Tipi. In Montana we visited the site of the famous Indian victory over the 7th US Cavalry at the Little Bighorn river – 'Custer's Last Stand' – and went on through Idaho and into Washington where we visited the Grand Coulee Dam before descending in thick mist to Seattle and the Poulsbo ferry.

Our three weeks with Irma, her husband Dan and their nineteen-year-old twin daughters, Alison and Sarah, passed quickly. Dan, once a schoolteacher, had his own salmon-fishing boat in Alaska; Irma had run a shore-based netting station there and they had many tales to tell. We explored the Poulsbo and Puget Sound area, travelled along the south shore of the Straits of Juan de Fuca as far as Cape Flattery on the Makah Indian reservation, visited the grave of Chief Sealth, after whom Seattle is named, and saw the Suquamish museum. We spent a day in Seattle to see the aquarium, Pipe Street market and 'The Old Curiosity Shop' and went kayaking in Puget Sound. Torcuil spent hours behind his binoculars. I was delighted to see harlequin duck and over-joyed when we found another species of duck, dainty hooded mergansers, which I had wanted to see since I first saw a picture in a bird-book. We even saw a black bear, trundling across the road ahead of us near Cape Flattery. A Greyhound bus brought us back, a thirty-hour haul via Bismarck in North Dakota, to find Mobridge covered in deep snow.

Snow fell again on 24 November and the temperature dropped to −19°C/−3°F. Another skiff fell overnight on St Andrew's Day, and on 2 December there was more. Then the temperature rocketed to −8°C/18°F and luckily the snow stopped before the fourth. That day I had to drive a hundred miles to Bismarck airport to meet Kate.

On my way out I went to feed Traceur and found he had had a relapse. He was turning in tight circles, blundering about, his lip was quivering, and he had a marked head-tilt. He knew my voice but was not interested in his feed. In a state of sinking despair I returned to the house and called the vet, though there was nothing more they could do.

Northwest Airlines expected no weather delays to Bismarck arrivals. Taking the main highway north via Bear Soldier (McLaughlin), rather than the prettier Highway 24 along the west bank of the Missouri, because of the snow, I found the roads clear but ran into patches of light fog. Kate's DC9 flight flopped down seventy-five minutes late and disgorged a seemingly impossible number of people. I was beginning to wonder if she was aboard when she appeared, looking tired and pale but with a smashing new haircut.

The fog had thickened, I missed the turning for Highway 6 and we ended up almost in New Salem, adding eighty minutes and as many miles to the return journey. Fortunately Kate was able to doze in the back seat until we reached the house. Torcuil and Fionn had waited up and there was a frantic half-hour before exhaustion claimed its victim.

The day after Kate arrived Traceur was a shade better. I had a long telephone conversation with Scott, one of Mortar & Pestle's pharmacists, who told me it was normal for horses to have symptoms such as Traceur was showing during treatment. They indicated that his body was expelling dead cystic material. This was reassuring, though my fears were not entirely allayed.

December 6 was bright and cold. Eilidh returned early from giving Traceur his morning medicine and feed. She came in through the porch, still padded in many layers of clothing topped by her old purple anorak, a bright red woollen scarf over her head like a balaclava, to find Kate and me still in our bed in the sitting room. Eilidh, who never cried, had tears streaming down her face as she uttered the awful words 'Trassy's dead.'

Diary: Friday 6 December.
Mobridge.
Crisp sunny morning. About 6–8°F.
Our beloved *Traceur is dead*. There is nothing else to say on this sad day, except that we shall all miss the big brave fellow, perhaps Eilidh and I most of all. I cannot conceive of driving along with another horse, he was almost part of me. I had so hoped he would finish the journey with us and enjoy a long and happy retirement. We had done so much together, all of us. I cannot write more now. Too many memories are overwhelming me.

He is surely now in a better world.

It was not EPM that had killed Traceur. He had had a cholesteatoma, a growth the size of a small tangerine, located deep in his brain beside his pituitary gland. It would have been inoperable, even if it had been found while he was still alive.

A terrible pall hung over the rest of winter.

In mid-December there was a massive dump of snow. Bill Imberi gave the boys a job shovelling it off his roof, and after that, other people needing their roofs cleared employed them. I was amazed that the local lads were not out in droves doing the same thing because householders willingly paid our boys ten to fifteen dollars each for their work.

On 16 December we had a blizzard and by the eighteenth the temperature was hitting –9°C/–40°F, with wind-chill.

On Christmas Eve we went to the Lockes', but on Christmas Day we had a quiet time on our own. Eilidh earned pocket-money 'granny-sitting' Mrs Weigam when her companion had a night off. I continued trying to convert my diaries into readable form. We became librarian Ione Styles's best customers, often visited Evie Rice, who had lent the computer, and her family and went sledging.

The Schrempps invited us for New Year, so on 31 December we drove the eighty miles there in another snowstorm. The local buffalo herd was standing close by the road, encrusted in snow. Near Timberlake, about three hundred pheasants were crouched down in the shelter of a hedge. Despite having to battle the worst winter in South Dakota in living memory, Dean and Mavis were in good form. Their cattle were in-bye, their losses few. Some ranchers lost half their herds, trapped in deep drifts.

Early January brought freezing rain, more snow and high winds. The Persil-white countryside looked starkly beautiful but as barren of life as the Moon. All but the hardiest creatures had fled south. We were getting cabin fever from lack of exercise and began working out at the Mobridge Wellness Centre. Even well wrapped, going for a walk was no pleasure in these conditions.

Our sponsor, Sir Patrick Grant of Dalvey, visited us for four days, and we visited local places of interest with him. I gave talks to the American Association of Retired People, Rotary, the Lutherans and the Baha'i community in

Bismarck. Usually the family was invited, and we were always well fed and sometimes given a donation.

About finding another horse I did nothing. I could not. I had no will to replace the irreplaceable. We had to go on but I, who usually looked forward to the spring and the road, almost dreaded it.

Dean Schrempp had been victorious at the elections and was now Democratic Member of the House of Representatives for District 28A in the State of South Dakota. He invited us to Pierre to see the legislature at work. South Dakota's State Capitol, built in modified Greek Ionic style and completed in 1908 at a cost of just under a million dollars, was majestic. The interior featured Greek and Roman designs and stencilling and held some remarkable murals and paintings. However it was seeing American democracy at work that was most interesting. We were introduced to and welcomed by the Democratic Caucus. I had to say a few words, managed to raise a laugh and we fielded some questions about the journey. Then the representatives began their business, while we became flies on the wall. Later they moved to the floor of the House and we trooped into the Visitors' Gallery. The House was oak-panelled, with white-plastered walls and pillars, and the gallery ran the whole way round. The representatives sat at individual roll-top desks, set in rows facing the speaker. Proceedings were brisk. At some point we all stood up and Dean introduced us. Mavis then took us for a peek at the Senate, whose members were not sitting, before we went to the cafeteria for lunch.

On our way home we took Eilidh to the airport. California and endurance riding called.

On 1 February I set off at 5.30 a.m. on a horse hunt. From legions of telephone calls, I had whittled down the list of potentially suitable animals to four. Unfortunately all

were in the south-eastern part of the state. I returned home
well after midnight, my neck stiff and sore, having driven a
gruelling 714 miles via Ipswich, Stickney, Mitchell, almost
into Sioux Falls, Dell Rapids and back by Madison and
Winfred. But we had a horse. If she passed the vet.

Bertha was a six-year-old seventeen-hand chestnut
Belgian mare, weighing around 1800 pounds. She was
trained to harness but had never been shod or ridden. She
drove well but was inexperienced in traffic and had almost
certainly never been hitched single. Bill Imberi made
makeshift shafts for an ancient flatbed trailer he had, which
was heavy and about the size of the caravan. With this,
usually with one of the boys and occasionally Kate, Bertha
and I cruised the roads and streets round Mobridge,
training.

Farrier Brad Stolsmark was young, strong, tall and
patient. I had worked on Bertha's feet, picking them up and
tapping them, to get her used to the idea. When he put her
first-ever shoes on, he took nearly two hours but had almost
no trouble from her. As he banged in the last nail, he told
me he had never shod a heavy horse before. He did a
beautiful job and refused payment, saying it was his contribution to the journey.

Canada geese were flying north, mountain bluebirds
were passing through and a herd of thirty mule-deer
appeared on the edge of town. Spring was coming and it
was time for Torcuil and me to fetch the caravan. It was
none the worse for having stood out all winter on the Keller
Ranch and we pulled it out of the remains of the snow and
on to the level ground at our old site for the night. Then we
went to have coffee with Louis and Helen and to thank them
again for their tremendous help.

All that night it blew a gale. Next morning Bertha put to
as though she had been pulling the caravan all her life. She

went like that for fifty miles, all the way to Mobridge. We were lucky to have found such an easy horse to educate, with excellent temperament.

The splendour of comet Hale-Bopp's twin tails adorned the clear night skies during our trip. A Lakota woman we met told us it is known in their legends as 'The Old Man', who sweeps through the heavens gathering up spirits which have not managed to cross to the next world. As the comet last appeared around 4000 BC, this was astonishing information.

At the last moment Eilidh telephoned – to say she was not coming back. I was furious, because this inconvenienced a number of people and was very thoughtless and selfish. She may have thought we should have baulked at letting her stay longer, if she had asked, but Jazon Wonders rang later and said he had taken her to the airport and she had flatly refused to board the aircraft. It was impossible to rearrange her return before we left, so we packed her stuff into a large box and shipped it off to her.

I had planned to leave on 4 April. We had had the usual pre-departure scramble but everything was ready. Next-door neighbours Helmut and Lucylle Eisenbeisz had given us supper the night before. Everyone in the Mobridge area who had helped us had been seen, telephoned or written to and thanked. I went to fetch Bertha in crisp clear sun.

'Don't go,' said Bill Imberi. 'The forecast is terrible.'

I might have been inclined to disregard his advice but even as we stood chatting, it began rapidly clouding over, with fog rolling in from the west on a rising wind. And it began to rain. Hard.

All afternoon and all night freezing rain fell, coating everything with a thick layer of ice. Next day it turned to sleet and by evening to tiny crystals of snow. During the second night the temperature was −9°C/16°F, the wind gusting to 60 m.p.h., blowing the snow into vast drifts. We camped in the house as best we could with no furniture; warm, though at times without electricity. Evie and Richard Rice fed us during a power cut, cooking over a camping-stove. On the seventh it dawned sunny but was a chill −12°C/10°F. The roads were only just being ploughed and many had icy stretches.

The eighth was even colder, only −15°C/5°F but the roads were clear and we had to go.

An hour later, looking back, Mobridge was already just a darker patch in a white world, attached to us only by the black ribbon of road. Soon it would pass out of sight altogether.

Our last year of travel had begun.

CHAPTER NINETEEN

―――――≈ళ≈――――

CANADA: APRIL–NOVEMBER 1997
HALIFAX – AND HOME

*Children begin by loving their parents; as they grow
older they judge them; sometimes they forgive them.*
Oscar Wilde

Our last year on the road began in conditions as wintry
as those we had encountered in Kazakhstan. During
the first week temperatures never rose above freezing. The
flat plains of eastern South Dakota, once magnificent tall-
grass prairie, had long been ploughed up. Corn-stubble
poked through the snow. The skies were lowering and
leaden and the birds we saw underlined the bleak winter
scene – Lapland buntings, snow buntings and a magnificent
snowy owl.

As we trudged east, spring tentatively replaced winter.
Migrant birds, delayed by the late blizzard, began streaming
northwards. On 16 April I wrote: 'Tonight the sky belonged
to geese. For hours, skein after skein of snow, white-fronted
and Canada geese poured north. We did not, could not even
try to, count them. More than 10,000 . . . more than 20,000
. . . perhaps hundreds of thousands. They just came on and
on, like great wisps of smoke, from horizon to horizon,
honking and gabbling from high overhead, a magnificent
sight, a privilege to see. Now and then a feather drifted to

earth from the blue above and as the sun sank below the western rim and the last faint honk was heard, nothing but the feathers remained to remind us of the wonderful spectacle we had been watching.'

The melting of winter's accumulated snows and fresh spring rain caused flooding. The thirty-yard width of the Elm river, a tributary of the James, had expanded to two miles. Fortunately the road was embanked and remained about three feet above the water. As we approached the Minnesota border, flat plain gave way to the hillier *coteau* country. Bertha was fit and pulling famously.

Every day we had visitors. Often we were invited to dine. Sometimes friends found us, including the Eisenbeiszs, Rices and Kevin. We stopped at Brad and Penny Stolsmarks' and put studs into Bertha's spare shoes. In Groton, at an old people's home, we spoke to a woman of ninety-eight, with a mind as sharp as a needle. 'It is not often one meets someone from the last century nowadays,' I noted. On Lake Sisseton Traverse Indian reservation we talked to the children of Tiospa Zina, a happy school with pleasant staff. They presented us with a traditional star quilt, complementing the gorgeous one the Locke family had honoured us with before we left Mobridge.

The welcoming kindness with which we were greeted along the road was heart-warming. Sometimes it was almost too much for us, at the end of a hard day's travel, to have to put on sociable faces, emerge from the caravan and for the umpteenth time answer the same old questions. We did it, because people were supportive and interested and it would have been ungracious not to. Rudeness was rare but once, while shoving and sweating up a tough slope, a pick-up stopped behind us. Great, I thought, extra push. Not a bit.

'If ya just pull up Ah'll take a coupla pictures.'

More characteristic was the two bales of hay, bucket of

oats and groceries brought to us one evening – though the glamorous donor, Miss Rodeo South Dakota 1997, Jennifer Denkinger, was anything but a typical farm-hand.

Our last night in South Dakota was spent on top of a hill, with Minnesota laid out in a spectacular panorama before us, eight hundred feet below. It still looked winter brown. Next morning we crossed a half-washed-out bridge and almost immediately reached the North–South Continental Divide, where waters from Lake Traverse flow north to Hudson Bay and those from Big Stone Lake south to the Gulf of Mexico. The flat, low-lying, monotonous maize-producing country was severely affected by flooding. We were fortunate not to be impeded by it and only once had to make a diversion.

April gave a last wintry kick, with an overnight temperature of –1°C/28.5°F on the thirtieth. We were lucky to be there to experience it. The day before a semi-trailer loaded with grain had overtaken us on the verge *on the inside*, causing Bertha to shy into the middle of the road, almost flattening Fionn in the process.

Trees became more frequent. At Glenwood we saw Foster's terns, wood duck, blue herons and uncommon purple martins. In the UK general election, the Tories were swept from power, ignominiously left without a single seat in Scotland.

The Interpretative Center on the outskirts of Sauk Center contained memorabilia of Sinclair Lewis, one of America's foremost authors, plus items of local interest, including the story of the Viking Altar Rock. Did Norwegian Vikings really penetrate into Minnesota? Evidence comes mainly in the form of mooring stones and medieval Scandinavian implements unearthed along the supposed route. It was an intriguing idea.

We collected a load of mail from the Sauk post office.

The Schrempps had sent us a parcel, *Trailer Life* had accepted an article and our entry in the *Guinness Book of Records* had been confirmed. All this and my birthday too . . .

On 9 May we reached the Mississippi on the southern outskirts of Little Falls, with houses all along the banks. The river was broad and bonny in the sun. Charles Lindbergh spent his boyhood there. His parents' house, next to a display-centre about his life, is preserved as a historical site. None of us was aware that besides his world-famous aviation achievements, he had been a pioneering supporter of Robert Goddard's rocket research, inventor of an apparatus for growing cultures and, latterly, a keen conservationist. He stated he would prefer birds to aeroplanes if he had to choose – but, then, who wouldn't?

There was a mêlée of traffic as we left Little Falls. I was holding well to the right and noticed a car signalling to turn left. The following driver did not. There was a tremendous *bang*. Bertha, badly scared, jumped sideways, towing us off the road before I could stop her. Had there been more than a slight slope, we should have been wrecked. Three vehicles had shunted expensively into each other but no one was hurt.

Mille Lacs Lake was so big we could not see across it. Then came Isle, the model for Garrison Keiller's Lake Woebegon, according to a lady who knew him. For us it was anything but woebegone, for we were again overwhelmed by American generosity and given a hundred-dollar donation and lunch by the staff of the *Mille Lacs Messenger*, and a hundred dollars-worth of food by the Supervalu store manager. Fionn went fishing and stayed overnight with journalist Coleen Ziwicki and her family.

Two days later, the right-hand swingle-tree hook sheared, abruptly leaving me driving a horse with no caravan attached.* Understandably startled, Bertha pulled the reins from my hands and made off down the mercifully empty road. Fionn had the presence of mind to brake the caravan and prevent it rolling into the ditch, while Torcuil, ahead birding, retrieved Bertha. I detached the swingle-tree and hitched back to the LeCocq Ranch, where we had dined the previous evening. Their efficient welding job soon had us mobile again.

In Hinckley, local journalist Tim Burkhardt invited us to sup with his family and Fionn enjoyed the chance to 'shoot a few hoops'. He was now devoted to basketball and most days Bertha's clip-clopping hoofs were accompanied by the thumping of his ball on the road behind.

With more trees and less barren ploughland, birds were numerous, including red-breasted grosbeaks, northern cardinals and Baltimore orioles. A ruby-throated humming-bird went away disappointed when it found the red-and-yellow lion rampant badge on the caravan was not an exotic flower overflowing with nectar. Our biggest thrill was seeing pileated woodpeckers. Mainly black, with white and red markings, they were *huge*, crow-sized, the most spectacular woodpeckers we'd ever seen.

Ticks were a constant problem. The ever-present possibility of Lyme disease kept us on our guard but it was difficult to keep Bertha free of them. Once we parked in woodland and by morning she was infested. For the next two days, whenever we stopped we spent time removing them from her with tweezers. Not since Tsar became ill from tick bites in Kiev had I seen so many but fortunately they seemed to do Bertha no harm.

In late May we descended a hill and crossed the St Croix

---

*The swingle-tree is a pivoting bar on the caravan, to which the horse is attached by means of the traces, which attach to the horse's collar.

river to Wisconsin. The land was flat, and travelling through pine forests and past lakes, we rarely had much view. It remained like this for the two weeks it took to reach Michigan – and the Eastern Time Zone. The combination of horse and children seemed to appeal to people's sense of adventure and we continued to receive unsought but welcome donations. Very few *really* wanted to do what we were doing, whatever they might say, but by donating a few dollars they acquired a share in our enterprise and could feel part of it.

Meeting Scots who had emigrated, or people of Scots descent, was commonplace in the States and one roadside encounter was a little different from usual. From the boot of his car, Bill Fyvie took out his pipes to serenade us, but I think his astonishment was the greater when I played him a tune myself. As a result we later spent a pleasant weekend with him and his family.

On 9 June we found a tree-lined track by an old railway, not ideal but shady in the 28°C/82°F heat and with adequate browsing for Bertha. We were comfortably settled in when a woman appeared, bearing cakes and an invitation to her house round the corner for a hamburger supper. She was Ann Lequia and with husband Tim and sons Matthew and Dusten lived in a lovely spot overlooking the Escanaba river. Their boys and Fionn had a great time churning up and down in a pedal-boat and took Bertha for a cooling bathe. Fionn and Matthew got on so well that Fionn was invited to stay, so the next morning we left without him.

At Marquette, Ann's brother, Calvin Honkala, took us flying in his father's 1948 Ryan 'Navion 255' low-wing monoplane. It looked brand-new, it was so well kept. Marquette airfield was 'Unicom', which meant without air-traffic control but pilots called up so that other aircraft knew where they were. We took off and flew over the colossal Empire open-cast iron-ore mine, with its acres of tailings and settling ponds; across Marquette; across the shore and over Lake Superior. Down at four hundred feet we cruised along the coast for a while, seeing nothing but pine forest stretching for ever in one direction and the waters of Lake Superior in the other. An orbit over the caravan completed our tour.

Torcuil went bird-watching next day with Louis Taccolini, a contact he had made through the American Birdwatching Association, to try to see the rare Kirtland's warbler, of which only seven hundred pairs are known to exist. Fionn was staying a bit longer at the Lequias, so Kate and I took Bertha on. For the first time in seven years, though only for a few hours, we were travelling without the children. Louis and Torcuil found us at Cherry Creek, where we had stopped, having seen the warbler, and we were all driven into Marquette to have supper with the Taccolinis.

At one point we turned inland on a back road, to avoid hills on Highway 28. It was a rough track in thick, mixed woodland, very bumpy but comfortably cool. Most of the time we were close to the shores of Superior, in the chilly waters of which Torcuil, Bertha and I swam. Ann Lequia paid us numerous visits, sometimes with Fionn, sometimes without, as we worked our way across the lengthy Upper Peninsula of Michigan. The predominant settlers in this area had been Finns and many still spoke Finnish better than English. The 'Seney Stretch' ran arrow-straight for twenty-five miles through pine plantation. Fortunately there were patches of grass here and there to keep Bertha in grazing. The heat was barely tolerable, the horse-flies horrendous.

At the northern edge of the Seney Wildlife Refuge, Torcuil saw a black bear. That afternoon Cal Honkala brought Fionn back and drove us round the refuge. We saw trumpeter swans, bald eagles and beaver, and had a wonderful view of a snapping turtle. *If* Cal and his family were going to visit an aunt in Canada in July and could return him to us, Fionn was going to stay with the Lequias again. If that were the case, Ann would fetch him in a few days' time.

Bertha would need a fresh health certificate for Canada. I knew it might take several days to acquire so I telephoned Sault Sainte Marie tourist office from Seney and asked if they could help. 'Give us a day or two,' they said. We sweated on.

Two or three days later, as we were packing up, Fionn said, 'Where's the hammer?' and I remembered . . . I had taken our precious splitter-cum-sledge-hammer out the evening before and not put it back. Fionn saved me a long bike ride by volunteering to fetch it; a woman from the house next to the field we were in drove him back to find it. That evening he got his wish and was whisked away to the Lequias for a month.

Sault Sainte Marie, 'The Soo', a nickname applied to both the US and Canadian towns of that name, had a very active chamber of commerce. My request had been passed to executive director Bud Mansfield and when I called I found he had arranged both parking and a vet to check Bertha for us. In addition we were asked to lead off the annual International Bridge Walk on the following Saturday, 28 June, when up to six thousand people would walk to Canada across the bridge spanning the St Mary's Rapids.

The morning of the twenty-eighth was bright, clear and promised to become hot. A big crowd had assembled on the university campus by the time we drove in with Emily and Harley Boone, on whose farm we had been staying. Over the public-address system, Bud Mansfield welcomed us.

Bertha gathered a fan club, including small children who assiduously fed her grass and buns. At 9.30 we lined up behind a police-car and the parade started.

The long, narrow International Bridge had only one lane running each way and no pavement. There were two steep sections on the bridge but many willing hands pushed and Bertha never even paused. Half-way over we passed the flagstaffs marking the US–Canadian border and from there it was all downhill. Walkers are normally banned on the bridge. We should have had to hire a truck for Bertha and a tow for the caravan had not our arrival in the Soo coincidentally enabled us to walk across on the one day in the year when it is possible to do so.

I had wanted to visit Canada for most of my life. At one time I had almost joined the Hudson's Bay Company and had many Canadian relations. Kate had relatives there, too, and an ancestor of hers had founded the town of Hamilton, Ontario. It was satisfying to have our passports stamped, pick up Bertha's papers, say a fond farewell to the kind Boones and head off through the Canadian Soo after twenty amazing and enjoyable months in America.

It was stiflingly hot and Bertha flagged, till we gave her a drink. Traffic was heavy and the fumes, coupled with 34°C/94°F and no wind, made us glad to reach Highway 17 and find a stopping place in richly flowered pasture. The caravan temporarily bore a 'Wanted' poster for fourteen-year-old Kristen King. She had been missing for two weeks and we had been asked to help the search by advertising it. Happily, we subsequently heard she turned up, safe and well.

We crossed an Ojibway reservation and it was at once apparent that Canadian Indians had an air of prosperity and a better standard of housing than American ones, whatever other problems they might have. Canada had never made war on Indians in the way the US government did, which probably accounts for their better conditions today.

Quieter than Americans, Canadians were no less welcoming and hospitable. On our first weekend, which coincided with Canada Day on 1 July, we went for a boat trip on Lake Huron's North Channel with Charlie and Marie Egglesfield. The iron-grey waters were calm under thin stratus cloud as we wove between pine-covered islands, passing an osprey's nest. Stone from this area had been exported years ago in sailing ships to pave the streets of Chicago and the old pier and quarries could still be seen. Next day, in Bruce Mines, we watched the Canada Day parade, featuring several teams of horses as well as the local fire engine, floats and clowns.

In my ignorance, I had thought the stirringly named Trans-Canada Highway must be a mighty four-lane affair. Planning our route, I had worried whether there would be side roads on which to travel. The reality was twisting, mainly two-lane Highway 17, often with soft shoulder, sometimes no shoulder, on which phalanxes of enormous semi-trailers raced by. I did not dare keep the caravan on the tar because some of the drivers were manic. Yet the shoulder, especially on hills, was soft enough to make exceedingly heavy hauling for Bertha. It was not pleasant travelling and when we entered pine forest we lost even the compensation of good views.

The temperature again soared over 32°C/90°F in Espanola, where there was a huge paper-mill. Sudbury bypass was new, a ghastly steep hill with deep ditches and nowhere to pull off. In Wahnapitae we had a ferocious thunderstorm with marble-sized hailstones, which *hurt*.

We had often been complimented on how well our horse looked. The caravan was quite heavy but a regimen of good feed, plenty of stops and tows on steep hills, coupled with a moderate daily distance, had kept Offy, Traceur and now Bertha in good condition. And they were much loved and petted too. Thus it was a shock one damp afternoon when a woman from the Society for Prevention of Cruelty to Animals arrived at the farm on which we were parked. Her opening words were 'Don't you think that is a big load for one horse?' which set the tone for what followed.

Agent McAllister was quite properly investigating a complaint the SPCA had received. She brought with her a Mr Jim Rockie, whom she said owned Appaloosas, but who had no official status, to advise her 'Because I don't know much about horses.' We went to look at Bertha, who was grazing happily. Mr Rockie pronounced that she had a bruised frog and cracked left hind hoof and that the shoe was not only loose but that there was insufficient hoof remaining for it to be shod. This was all nonsense (except the loose shoe, of which I was aware) but Miss McAllister lapped it up.

Agent McAllister returned in the evening with a vet and I was delighted when the vet turned to Miss McAllister saying, 'This horse is in excellent condition.' She could hardly have done otherwise, for Bertha glowed with health. The incident was unpleasant, not because of the anonymous complaint which Miss McAllister was duty-bound to investigate but because of her aggressive determination to find something wrong. Her reliance on an outsider's opinion, inability to see Bertha was fine and subsequent summoning of a vet after hours must have cost the SPCA several hundred unnecessary dollars. I demanded and got a paper from the vet, attesting Bertha was fit, in case . . .

The Shell Station and Restaurant in Warren gave us lunch on the house and a free fill of propane for the cooker's gas-cylinder. After we had stopped for that night, a big yellow Chevrolet station wagon, with a smiling Cal Honkala at the wheel, rolled up and disgorged seemingly endless numbers of children – he and his wife had nine and she was expecting another. Among them was Fionn. It was good to have him back, full of tales about a camp he had attended with Matthew, places he had been and things he had done.

We had encountered a number of hardy cyclists while crossing North America. Renaud Laflamme and Eric Archambaud, whom we met in the straggling village of Verner, had been to the Grand Canyon and were returning to Québec. We gave them a couple of our postcards and Renaud gave me his address in Le Bic, with an invitation to call when we got there.

In North Bay on 21 July, we stopped for water. I was chatting to Sergeant Stefan Naylor of the Anishnabek Police, who had pulled up to have a look at us, when an SPCA man arrived. Someone had complained about 'a small horse pulling a house'. I flourished the quittance I had been given four days before and that was the end of that. Stefan Naylor, who was Ojibway and exceptionally nice, helped to find us a place to park and bought us all 'subs', sandwiches in French bread named for their submarine-like shape. In the evening, off-duty, he returned with his girlfriend Cecille, a load of Anishnabek Police badges and insisted we accept a donation.

We were becoming tired of endless conifer plantation and hills so it was a relief when at the end of July we eventually arrived at flatter ground in the lower Ottawa valley, passed Petawawa and reached Pembroke. Three days later, Bertha went lame.

She was still lame early next morning when Shirley McLeese stopped to offer us a place to stay but neither Shirley nor we anticipated an eleven-day visit. She and her husband Ronald could not have been more helpful towards their unexpected guests. They were gradually modernising their ancestral stone house and by way of thanks, with the boys' help, I cleared the jungle in front of it for them with a scythe. We had rested Bertha, thinking it was muscle-strain, but she had not improved and it took a course of antibiotics to combat what was probably a small foot abscess before she was ready to go on.

On 16 August, we crossed the Ottawa river into Québec at Portage-de-Fort. There was no sign of Frenchness apart from the village name and it stayed like that all the way downriver. We passed Ottawa, on the far bank, in a downpour, sorry not to be seeing it, glad not to be driving through it. Aylmer and Hull had been urban enough.

It was still wet when we crossed the Gatineau – and, with startling suddenness, were in Francophone Canada. This was the Québec we had heard about, shop names and street signs all in French, fleur-de-lys flags everywhere, not even token bilingualism. And the police stopped us. It was very dangerous, they said (which was poppycock, it had wide, empty four-lane streets and shoulder too) and insisted on escorting us through.

Retired dairy-farmer Colin McNamara, as Irish as his name, found us and insisted we stay. Given our bedraggled state, we were only too glad of the prospect of warm baths and a hot meal cooked by someone else. His daughter Kathy was as welcoming as her father and we not only spent the night there but were taken to Ottawa the following day. We saw the changing of the guard on Parliament Hill, complete with pipe-band, had a tour of the parliament buildings and a short walk round some of the nearby shops. After a quick lunch at the Market, we drove out past the prime minister and governor-general's residences to the aviation museum. It was excellent, with many examples of early and unusual aircraft. At the McNamaras', a corn-roast had been laid on for us and we munched on freshly roasted cobs and chatted to guests till bedtime.

August 29 started badly. Bertha, who was tied up, broke her head-collar and got away. Recaught and retied, both Torcuil and Fionn refused to stand behind her ready to give her a whack if she tried it again – which she did. Successfully. I was too angry to speak. Not only was the head-collar smashed, but Bertha had learned she could get away with breaking it. I was tired before we pulled on to the road and actually sat on board during the first hour, drained of energy. Then Kate said she had a headache, her second in three days, and went into the caravan to lie down.

Everyone was trip-weary. The previous evening Fionn had told me I was not a fun father – and he was right, for I was acutely aware I lacked the energy to play basketball with him, or anything else, these days. Bertha had *required* a lesson in the morning and would require a harder one now, having got away with it. You cannot simply tell a horse 'Please don't break your head-collar and run off,' because they don't understand. Mostly Bertha was a delight to be with and easy to handle but not on this occasion. The humid weather, flies, mosquitoes and prospect of another two months on the road did not help.

A blow-up often clears the air and so it proved. We passed through Laurentides, birthplace of Sir William Laurier, first French-Canadian prime minister. Dana Whittle and Claude Méthé, of Québecois folk-group Dent-de-lion visited and played for us. In Berthierville we saw the Gilles Villeneuve Museum of Motor-racing. The delightful Lincourt family had us to stay on their dairy farm. I found Québecois French hard to follow and its country version almost impossible.

Traversing Trois Rivières the police stopped us. Did we have permission to drive through the town? No, didn't know it was required. And why hadn't we picked up Bertha's droppings? Well, we'll pick them up when you stop vehicles emitting toxic gases. Silence. Faint grins. We were allowed to proceed.

We were alongside the St Lawrence river now and saw ships from faraway places: *Federal Rhine* from Barbados, *Bataafgracht* from Amsterdam and, astonishingly, little *Balaton* from Hungary. It was a beautiful day, the weather perfect as we drove past small farms, neat houses, woodlands, fields of corn and always the shining river, with sandy or rocky shallows by the shore where ducks swam and gulls wheeled. Traffic was light and the verge tarred. We basked happily in the sun.

The high cantilever Québec Bridge over the St Lawrence and newer Pierre-Laporte suspension bridge next to it was reminiscent of the Forth bridges. The guiding hand that enabled us to walk across the International Bridge into Canada now ensured we had a safe walk across the Québec Bridge to the south bank of the St Lawrence. The right-hand lane was coned off for roadworks that had barely started, so we used it, leaving motor traffic unimpeded. I had a quick glimpse of Québec itself and cliffs that were presumably the Heights of Abraham but driving required all my attention.

Scotland voted overwhelmingly to establish a devolved assembly. Being in Québec, with its substantial minority in favour of separating from Canada, we began to be looked on as representatives of a similar-thinking people. It was hard to convince Québecois that their Provincial Parliament *already* had far more power than Scotland was gaining – or rather regaining – especially as I could see no purpose in a separate Québec, which was a founding province of Canada but never a sovereign state, and neither the English-speaking, nor the Indian and Inuit populations wanted or would be likely to accept separation.

The banks of the St Lawrence were encrusted with ribbon development. There was no wild country, only a shading of small farms into villages, into the odd town and back to farms again. Nevertheless it was beautiful plodding along peacefully in the September sun. Gradually the waters became tidal and the smell of seaweed filled our nostrils. It was an unmistakable Atlantic smell, quite different from the Pacific, and its odour bore memories of home. We hurried on impatiently.

From quaintly-named Trois Pistoles, I telephoned Eilidh, to learn that she had won the Virginia City hundred-mile endurance ride, youngest rider ever to do so, and had gained 'best condition' for her horse Gyani as well. Even our laid-back lassie could not help sounding thrilled when she told me.

It took us two months to travel the almost seven hundred miles from Verner, where we had met Renaud Laflamme and Eric Archambaud, to Le Bic. We had two glorious days there with Renaud's parents. The village commanded a magnificent outlook over Le Bic Bay and its islands, to the river and the north bank beyond. Guy and Agathe fed us and later Renaud arrived from his digs in nearby Rimouski. We heard details and saw pictures of the tough 7,000-mile cycle journey. I did not envy them the thirty-odd punctures they had had. Next day Guy helped us accomplish a list of essential tasks before we took our leave.

By the shore east of Rimouski was a marker commemorating the 1,012 people who perished when the *Empress of Ireland* sank off Pointe-au-Père on 29 May 1914, after a collision. Eider duck swam near the spot where she had gone down.

At Mont Joli we turned inland and south, climbing hard to the Matapedia Valley, which lies at the western end of Monts Chic-Chocs on the Gaspé Peninsula. October began wet but once it faired the trees in the valley revealed the fabled Canadian fall colours in all their glorious shades of red, yellow and brown. The Matapedia was hard travelling, with many hills, no doubt accounting for the following in my diary: 'Torcuil was ultra-rude to me this morning because I had had to use a water-jerry off the rack for Bertha and did not tell him. Kate had not ensured adequate bread-supplies for 2–3 days with no shops and Fionn has been stroppy most of the day. The tensions and strains are really telling now. Probably this has been one year too much travelling . . .'

We crossed into New Brunswick on 7 October, though with names like Glencoe, Glenlivet, Campbelton and Dalhousie, it seemed more Celtic than Teutonic. In Dalhousie we were hospitably looked after by the director of parks and recreation, Gary Archbald, parking at five-star Inch Arran camp-site, going on a boat-trip round Chaleur Bay and swimming in the new pool opposite the camp-site.

Hurrying on, Torcuil at last found me boreal chickadees, lovely birds, resembling larger Siberian tits, with which I was familiar. The same day we saw a porcupine in a tree. The first overnight frost was recorded on 13 October and that day I really felt we had reached the Atlantic when a gannet cruised leisurely past close inshore. Lobster boats, drawn up out of the water for winter, seemed to be parked behind every house, especially in Acadia, as parts of this area were known historically. All were similar in design, about forty-foot long with wide flared bows, forward wheelhouses, spacious well-decks and square sterns. The Acadian flag, a French tricolour with gold star added, flew in many places. The British had expelled many French people from here during colonial wars. They went to Louisiana, became known as Cajuns and gave the world their unique lively music and spicy foods.

Nova Scotia bore great resemblance to Auld Scotia the day we crossed the border – it was cold, wet and foggy. However, it brightened and by the time we reached Pugwash it was sunny. The town was the venue for the famous series of Pugwash Conferences, attended by such luminaries as Einstein and Bertrand Russell. Our approach took us around the mirror-calm harbour basin, where only a solitary female scaup disturbed the waters. It was a surprise to find the street-names bilingual – in Gaelic.

Near Truro we had a rest-day at Milferns Farm. A raccoon climbed on to the caravan front board, hissed at us when we dislodged him with a pole, lumbered away and climbed into the nearest tree. Perhaps he thought he would get a taste of the grand roast-beef supper we had just had. Joe Miller and Pam Pauley, who had Clydesdale horses, came visiting. They were to prove instrumental in easing our way into Halifax and provided accommodation for Bertha afterwards. Without their help, arranging our Atlantic crossing would have been even more problematic than it was.

We skirted Truro, passed the Millbrook Micmac reservation and were caught on the road for an interview by freelance journalist Laurie Papineau. She offered us accommodation, but had she known she was letting herself in for five weeks of the Grant family, might never have done so . . . Just short of Halifax we encountered Marni Gent, animal-welfare activist and Air Canada stewardess, who also played an important part in helping us cross the Atlantic.

Day tried to dawn on Sunday 9 November but had a hard struggle against drizzle and fog. We set off at 7.30, five minutes after Laurie arrived to act as escort-car along the busy road to Halifax past the south shore of Bedford Basin. At the end of the second hour, the police decided to give us a more formal escort. In the dank, dim weather this was welcome, for traffic was heavy. CBC-TV, ATV and Global TV, who had been alerted, were waiting for us as we hauled into the city limits. Approaching the Citadel, the fortress that dominates Halifax, Joe Miller swung ahead of us with his light cart pulled by hefty Clydesdale-Belgian cross, Nick, to lead us in procession for our last mile.

There were no cheering crowds or fanfares as we slogged the last yards wearily through the foggy town, only queues of irate motorists wondering what was holding them up. We passed the Armoury, coasted by the great mound of the Citadel and halted, fittingly, by the Junior Bengal Lancers Riding Club. A tired Bertha was untacked for the last time and allowed a welcome graze and a good roll.

In an all-too-appropriate Scotch mist, after 2570 days and 12,360 miles, our long land journey had come to an end.

After seven years, we should soon be home.

AFTERWORD

*I like to meet the man who, at the age of fifty-three,
says he doesn't quite know what he is to be in life.*

A. S. Neill

It took five weeks, chasing around Halifax and on the telephone, before everything was organised for crossing the Atlantic. Instead of the hoped-for return to the UK *en famille*, we went back in batches. Kate went first on 22 November, because Grandpa was ill. Eilidh, having missed the finish, arrived on the twenty-fourth from California. There was no likelihood of a sea-passage for us, so she and Fionn left by air on 5 December, to save money and probably Laurie Papineau's sanity.

I faced similar problems to those encountered in Japan: finding passage for caravan and horse. Irene, in Atlantic Container Line's office, persuaded her bosses to ship the caravan to Liverpool at token cost. Marni Gent talked Air Canada into flying Bertha to London Heathrow gratis. Bertha, meanwhile, was fulfilling pre-export isolation requirements on a farm opposite Joe Miller, who was feeding her. She awaited transport to Toronto; there were no equine cargo flights out of Halifax. Marni also organised air-tickets for Torcuil and myself. The caravan was eventually shipped on the morning of 12 December and that evening Torcuil and I boarded an Air Canada Boeing 767 for London.

We were in the cockpit as dawn broke over England and we descended to land. I knew we were back in Britain when I saw graffiti on the tail of a British Airways jet – though while we waited for an onward flight to Scotland I discovered it was supposed to be art.

We were all reunited at Letham Grange Hotel that evening. I had never expected we should need to take up Dong Guang (Peter) Liu's invitation to stay there but it proved to be our salvation. With no home of our own, it gave us time to organise ourselves and try to find our way back into mainstream life once more.

In the end we decided to sell Bertha in Canada. Heathrow handling charges, vets' fees and transport to Scotland were going to cost over a thousand pounds we didn't have. Besides, we had nowhere suitable to keep her, long-term. Marni Gent found her a suitable home where she is much loved, and though it caused us a lot of heartache, and our friends in Nova Scotia considerable bother, in the end to no purpose, it was the right decision.

I had hoped to drive for a few miles from wherever we docked in the UK but was frustrated in this because of the impossibility of Bertha, the caravan and us making the Atlantic passage together. However, we eventually did drive in Scotland, though not until the end of February 1998. The occasion was filming of an item for the BBC's *Blue Peter*. With Barney, a borrowed Clydesdale, we re-enacted life on the road for the camera around the by-ways of Angus.

We spent seven years of our lives – and our house – on the journey. We home-educated our family, saw a lot of the world and endured some hardships. Considerable stress was put on Kate's and my relationship at times but our marriage survived. Sadly, we returned without any of our much-loved animals. Over a year later, our lives are only now beginning to regain a semblance of equilibrium again. So – was it all worth it? Unequivocally, yes! and I hope at least an indication of why I think so has shown through in our story. But in case there was a chance of our becoming big-headed, the sole contribution to a suggestions box at Letham Grange for what we should do next read: 'Go back to the Orkneys and contact the DHSS and Job Centre – what you have done is stupidity personified. Anon.' Ah, well . . .

Fionn opted to return to school and is at Webster High School in Kirriemuir. Unsure in which class to place him, they gave him an assessment – and said it was the best they'd ever had. He laments the limited opportunities to fulfil his passion for basketball, but is doing very well in class. Torcuil attended a catch-up course at Angus College during the summer, was accepted for their HNC course in applied ecology and hopes to go on to university. Eilidh's plans for returning to California have been frustrated by the unexpected refusal of a US visa. She has instead been working at Henry Candy's racing stables near Wantage in Oxfordshire. The question 'What about your exams, Eilidh?' elicited the fierce reply, 'I don't need exams for what I want to do and if I do I'll do them.' Among many other qualities, our journey fostered determination and independent thought in all three children. Kate has returned to the workplace, undergoing retraining on computers. Me? Once this book is with the publishers, it will be time to organise the next expedition. But I may have to paddle my own canoe . . .

ACKNOWLEDGEMENTS

To my agent Maggie Hanbury for having the courage to take on a then still-unwritten book by an unknown author, to Helen Gummer for commissioning it and to her, Ingrid Connell and to the entire team at Simon & Schuster, my grateful thanks for their patience and hard work.

We could never have completed the journey unaided. Apart from sponsors in cash and kind, large and small, it was shared with countless people who welcomed us and helped us along the way. Some gave us outstanding help and their special parts in our story – and I hope our gratitude to them – feature large in the text. In the countries of the former Soviet Union we should have starved for want of food to buy, while in Japan and North America we should have starved for want of money to buy food. So many people helped in ways that never ceased to amaze and humble us that I had intended to list all our helpers by country. However, by the time we got to Slovenia the list was already a page long and I began to realise it would be impossible to include everyone. Not only that but I should almost certainly have forgotten a few names and there were all the anonymous helpers whose names we never knew. All I can say is, on behalf of us all, *you* know who you are and because we could not have succeeded without your help, this trip was partly yours. Please therefore accept our love and grateful thanks for making it possible.

SPONSORS, in cash
Grants of Dalvey, Alness, Easter Ross, IV17 0XT, Scotland
Letham Grange Hotel, by Arbroath, Angus, Scotland
ARC International, 32 Kowa Bldg 7F, 5-2-32 Minami-Azabu, Tokyo, Japan
Franz Welz, Bachstrasse 75, Salzburg, Austria (part paid)

SPONSORS, in kind
Wilhelmsen Lines a/b, Oslo, Norway: transport of caravan, Kobe–Los Angeles
Japan Airlines, Tokyo, Japan: reduced fare to fly Traceur from Osaka to LA
US Equine Inc., California, USA: cost of importing Traceur to the USA
ACL, Halifax, Canada: transport of caravan, Halifax–Liverpool
Air Canada: flight for Bertha, Toronto–London (not taken up)

The following firms donated products or gave us a discount
Products
Bartholomew: maps; Beecham Health Care: medicaments; The Body Shop: shampoos and soaps; Burton's biscuits: shortbread; Crown Consultants: 'Alert' alarm-system; Fairey Industrial Ceramics Ltd: British Berkefeld water filter; Forbo-Nairn Ltd: linoleum; James Keiller & Son Ltd: butterscotch; Kangol: berets; Munster-Simms Engineering Ltd: Whale Mark IV foot/electrical pump; Thetford Aqua: 'Porta Potti 265'; World Book: 1989 *World Book Encyclopaedia*; Paterson Zochonis plc: Cusson's soap.

Discounts

Burton McCall Ltd: tent, sleeping-bags, rucksacks, etc.; Camping Gaz (GB) Ltd: Optimus cooker, solar torches, etc.; Exide Batteries Ltd: storage battery; Gardner Portable Showers: shower; Marlec Engineering Co. Ltd: aerogenerator; Muddy Fox: bicycles; Musto Limited: jackets and thermal clothing; North Sea Ferries: Hull–Rotterdam fare; P&O Scottish Ferries: Stromness–Scrabster fare; Safariquip: assorted useful items; Smith Wellstood Esse: 'Diamond Esse' stove.

Personal cash donations were received before the journey began from: the late Captain George Cochrane MN; the late Winifred 'Mitch' Doyle; Rob and Harriet Forrest; Ian Hamilton/Kytra Ltd, and A. Boyd Tunnock/Thomas Tunnock Ltd. Many people gave us donations during the journey, far too many to list. Whether modest or substantial, we were very grateful to all these generous people.

Mail forwarding and other vital communication services were performed for us by:
in the UK: Sir Ian Macdonald of Sleat, Bt/Thorpe Hall Estate Office, Sir Patrick Grant of Dalvey, Bt and Peter Bullick/Taits, WS, of Kelso
in Switzerland: Heidi Keller and Charly Iseli/ISKAverlag AG and *Achenbach* magazine, to whom especial thanks for looking after all my films safely for so long
in the USA: Louisa 'Wiki' Newcomb and family.

Very special thanks to Christine and Alison Little-Lüthi, for providing me with a lair in Switzerland in which to write the draft of this book.

The author would be pleased to answer serious enquiries about aspects of caravan construction, horse-management, saddlery and other equipment used on the expedition.

FURTHER READING

This represents only a small selection of books that were useful in preparing for the journey or subsequently.

Bawden, C. R., *The Modern History of Mongolia* (second edition, Kegan Paul International, 1989). Covers from the time of Genghis Khan to 1988, the best compact history.

Hitches, M. W., *Man and Action* (published by the author, 1991). Extraordinary horse-caravan journey to Romania while it was still Communist.

Olcott, Martha Brill, *The Kazakhs* (second edition, Hoover Institution Press, California, 1995). Excellent – and one of the few books available on the country.

Oliver, Marjorie Mary and Eva Ducat: *Ponies and Caravans* (Country Life, 1941). Family holiday travel with horses and caravans in the UK.

Tschiffeley, A. F. *Tschiffely's Ride* (Heinemann, 1935). One of the earliest long-distance rides, from Buenos Aires to New York.

Ward-Jackson, C. H. & Denis E. Harvey, *The English*

Gypsy Caravan: Its Origins, Builders, Technology & *Conservation*, second edition (David & Charles, 1986). This is *the* authority, very comprehensive and readable.

Wickert, Erwin, *The Middle Kingdom: Inside China Today* (Harvill Press, London, 1983). Brilliant account by a man who was there in 1936, from 1939 to 1945 and from 1976 to 1980.

INDEX

Au = Austria; Bg = Belgium;
Ch = China; Cn = Canada;
Fr = France; Hg = Hungary;
It = Italy; Jn = Japan;
Ky = Kyrghizia
Kz = Kazakhstan;
Mg = Mongolia;
Nl = Netherlands; Rs = Russia;
Sl = Slovenia; Uk = Ukraine

Abdurahmanov family 204
Abonyi, Imre 112
Acadia (Cn) 374
agriculture
    China 286
    factory farming 10-11
    Hungary 106, 108
    Slovenian forestry 79-80
    Ukraine 139, 148
Aguit (Ch) 286
Ahmed Yasawi 203-4
Ainigazov, Aleg and family 194-5
Aitmyxanov, Bulat 176
Ajaguz (Kz) 224, 225

Aktyoobinsk (Kz) 185
Alaska (USA) 312-13
Alga (Kz) 185-6
Alma-Ata (Kz) 153, 167, 199,
    216, 217-21
Almanor, Lake (USA) 323
Almaty river (Kz) 216
Altai region (Rs) 229-31, 250
Altanzaya (landlady) 260
Amnesty International 270
Amsterdam (Nl) 5-6
Amur Darya river (Kz) 193
Anatoly, Sasha, Peotr and Franz
    141
Andrusinis (old couple) 60, 62
Animal Quarantine Service (Jn)
    299, 307, 310 bis
Ansambel Slovenija 95-6, 99
Aral Sea 191, 193
Aralkum (Kz) 194
Aralsk (Kz) 192-3
Arataou mountains (Kz) 211
Arbuthnot, Julia 46
ARC International 308

Archambaud, Eric 369, 373
Archbald, Gary 374
Ardennes (Bg) 18
Arma di Taggio (It) 52
Arnoldstein (Au) 68
Arvaiheer (Mg) 254
Atkins, Debbie 263
Austria 67-72 (notably 71-2)
Avignon (Fr) 35, 40

Baasanhuu, Dr 274
Badlands National Park (USA)
    343
bagpipes 19, 49, 81, 95-6, 97,
    125, 363
Baha'i faith 261, 263, 273-4,
    277, 284, 307, 349
    Bahá'u'lláh quoted x, 259, 299
Baikonur Cosmodrome (Kz) 198-
    9, 200
Baimuradov family 172
Baja (Hg) 111-12
Bakhdal (lawyer) 267
Balaton, Lake (Hg) 105-6
Baldisseri, Terese and Ivo 62, 64
Balog, Paul and Miraslava 126
Ballantrae (Scotland) xii-xv
Bannock Highway (USA) 333
Baranja, Miško 100
Barham, Rev: The Jackdaw of
    Rheims 31
Basharivka (Uk) 140
Batmunkh (circus director) 260,
    271-2
Bayan-Olgiy (Mg) 240
Bayanhongor (Mg) 251-2
Bayanteeg (Mg) 252
BBC xxii-xxiii, 81-2, 86, 87-8,
    139, 187, 267, 272, 378
Beduschi, Emilio 61
Beijing (Ch) 289, 290, 291
Bekkers, Vincent 20, 25
Belgium 17-26 (notably 19, 20-21)

Belousov, Sergei 225, 228
Belovodsk (Uk) 155
Beltinška Banda 100
Berezin, Igor/Anna 199, 215,
    218, 219, 221
Bertha (mare)
    bought 355-6
    complaints to SPCA 368, 369
    on journey 361-2, 365-6, 369-
        70, 371
    retired 376, 377-8
Bešlagič, Nađa and Muris 103-4
Big Stone Lake (USA) 360
Bishkek (Ky) 212, 213
Blanch, Andrew 297
Blue Peter (TV) 378
Bolinas (USA) 309, 314-19
Bolt, Mr 260-61, 265-76 passim
Boone, Emily and Harley 365
Bormida river (It) 55
Borovitskiyi, Anatoly 159-60
Bosnia 187, 214
Boucan, Jean-Pierre 49
Bozeman Trail (USA) 337
Brady, Ananda 317, 318, 320
branding calves (USA) 328-9
Brody (Uk) 140
Brossy, Fred and Judy 331
Brown, Mick xviii, xxi
Budapest (Hg) 97, 117-18, 122
Buddhism 304, 305, 310
Bugac (Hg) 112-13
Bulgan (Mg) 249
Bullock, Bud 333
Burkhardt, Tim 362
Burlet family 22-4
Bussana Vecchio (It) 52
Bütikofer, Walter 251
Butrin, Andrei 227

Cadibona (It) 47, 53
Cajuns 374
Callian (Fr) 45-6

camels 174, 188, 190, 191, 247-8, 248 (*bis*)
Campaign, Michael and Jean 246
Canada 302, 366-76
Candy, Henry 379
caravan and equipment
  brakes 21, 27, 33, 54, 67-8, 99
  buying and fitting xv-xxiii, 3-4
  chimney smashed 292-3
  layout 21
  harness stolen 222-3, 225
  Irish caravans xix
  lighting 53
  shafts 41, 242, 245
  stove 9
  suspension 4, 7, 60, 61, 121
    bis
  swingle-tree 361-2
  transport by sea 294, 295,
    308-9
  transport by train 276-7, 278-9
  turntable 57
  tyres 7, 53, 135, 136 *bis*, 138,
    151-2
Carlson, Dr Gary 318
Caroline, Princess 49
Carpathians (Uk) 126, 127, 134
Carville, Daniel Gaultier de 186
Casper (USA) 335, 336-7
Cedar Pass (USA) 326-7
Cehner, Max 84, 91-2
Cehner, Moica 80
Celtic exhibition (Venice) 63
Centre Hippique St Georges 49
Centro Ippico La Marcella 54
Četniks 96
Chapaev (Kz) 180
Charles Sheldon National
  Wildlife Refuge (USA) 327
Chechnya/Chechens 172, 212,
  213, 265
Chelkar (Kz) 189, 190, 191

Cherenko, Vassily 151
Chernobyl (Uk) 146-7
Cheyenne river (USA) 339
China 219, 227, 246, 269, 278-98 (*notably* 282-3, 296)
China Express Lines 294, 299
Chinnoy, Mike 257
Chinodyevo (Uk) 129
Christmas 41-2, 98, 208-10, 353
Chu (Kz) 215
Chumish (Kz) 194
Chunkunov, Daulet 220
Chuya river (Rs) 231
Chyr river (Rs) 160, 161
Clark, Adam 118
Clements, Matt 250, 251
Clough, David 46
CNN 257-8
Cody, Buffalo Bill 336
Coeur, Paul 41, 223
Coia, Paul xxiii
Connard, Dean 321
Connolly, Kevin 187
Continental Divide (USA) 335,
  360
Cooke, Paul 263, 271, 276
Čop (Uk) 125, 131
Cossacks 160
Cremona (It) 56, 58, 60
Črneče (Sl) 83, 90-91
Croatia 81-2, 87-9, 96, 97-8,
  103, 107
Cross, Inge and Douglas 228
Crupet (Bg) 24
Cunningham, Gemma 46-7, 49,
  50
Customs
  Austria 68, 73
  China 279-80
  France 26-7
  Hungary 104, 124
  Italy 48, 50-51
  Japan 299-300

(Customs cont.)
  Mongolia 235
  Netherlands 1-2
  Russia 157-8, 233, 234-5
  Slovenia 73, 104
  Ukraine 124-5
Cuttini, Michele 65-6, 72-3

Daele, Didier de 25-6
Dalhousie (Cn) 374
Danube river (Hg) 109-10, 110-11
Davy, Bob 328, 331
Debbie End of Horn 349
Dembrel (village head) 249
Deng, Mrs (translator) 279, 282
Denio (USA) 327
Denkinger, Jennifer 360
Devil's Tower (USA) 337-8
Dewez, Joseph and family 22-4
Dilts, Virgil and Sally 324-5
Dina (stable girl) 220
Dinant (Bg) 24-5
Dishoeck, Nella van 1-3, 6
Dnepr river (Uk) 146-7
Doboj (Sl) 103-4
Dobrovnik v Prekmurje (Sl) 100, 101
Dodewaard (Nl) 13
Dolores Taken Alive 345
Don river (Rs) 163-4
Donna (Native American) 345
Donner, Anton and Digena 12
Donner Pass (USA) 322-3
Dosaev, Director 217
Drava (Drau) river (Au/Sl) 71-2, 73, 75, 77, 88, 91, 98, 109
Drávafok (Hg) 107-8
Dravograd (Sl) 74, 76-100
  passim
Dubrovnik (Croatia) 97-8
Dufey, Dr 25-6
Dunaev (Uk) 140

Dunblane (Scotland) 319-20
Durance river (Fr) 45
Durbet-Dabai (Mg) 235
Dzhamboul (Kz) 210-11
Dzha, Consul 219
Dzhambetoo (Kz) 180, 182-3

Eagle Butte (USA) 340-41
Edelbiyev, Ruslan and family
  212-13, 215
Edward 'Luigi' Black Cloud 345, 346
Eger (Hg) 120-21
Egglesfield, Charlie and Marie
  367
Eisenbeisz, Helmut and Lucylle
  356
El Basiev, Saken and Zhannat
  205-7
Elm river (USA) 359
Emba (Kz) 187-8
Empress of Ireland (ship) 373
Entraigues-sur-Sorgues (Fr) 35-6, 37, 41-2
equipment see caravan and
  equipment
Erdene, Mash 275-6
Erenhot (Ch) 279-82, 283

Faith (USA) 339
Finns in Michigan 364
Fliert, Jan and Ancka 10
Flournoy, Lorraine 326
fog 19
Fontanelle (USA) 334, 335
Fort Casper (USA) 336
Fort Ross (USA) 318
Fortyniner Rock (USA) 327
Fossil Butte (USA) 334
Foster, Colin 109
France
  northern 26-36 (notably 27-8)
  southern 37-47

Fremont, John 331
Fritz, Twyla 344, 345, 348
Frkowitsch, Sissy and Hannes 93, 97
Fyvie, Bill 363

Gagarin, Yuri 199, 200
Gál, Jenő 107-8
Galambos, István 121 *bis*
Galič, Jože and Cita 95-6, 99
Gallipoli (Turkey) 28-9
Gandang Monastery (Mg) 261
Gankovica (Uk) 131
Garini, Dr Fausto 58
Garzó, György 'Georgie' 112-13
Gauld, George xxi, 41
Geetbets (Bg) 19
Gemona-del-Friuli (It) 64-5
Genghis Khan 34, 189, 226, 235
Gent, Marni 375, 377, 378
Georgievka (Kz) 225
Germany 98
gers (felt tents) 224, 235-6, 241, 244, 248, 251-2, 262
Gooding (USA) 331
Gorchkova, Galena 217-18
Gorno-Altai Republic 229
Gov'Altai (Mg) 251
Grant children
  education ix, xxii, 7, 11, 16, 18-19, 30, 69-70, 95, 256
  reactions xxi, 8, 177-8
  see also separately Eilidh; Fionn; Torcuil
Grant, David (author)
  Baha'i faith 273-4, 277, 284, 307
  begins this book 349
  early married life xi-xiii
  early work xii, xxii
  horse collar accident 332
  pilot 90
  preparations for journey xiv-
  xxiv
  sued for assault 253-4, 260-61, 264, 265-76
  teaches history 265
  tensions of journey 177-8, 207
Grant, Eilidh
  arrested 120
  birth xii
  birthdays 193, 249-50, 254, 349
  breaks ankle 61, 62, 63-4
  breaks wrist 153-4, 161, 162
  competition riding 317 *bis*, 320, 324, 336, 354, 356, 373, 377
  and court case 270
  finds money 215
  future 379
  helps on journey 174-5, 239
  love of horses 11
  tensions on journey 39-40, 177, 197
  and Traceur 299-300, 302, 306 *bis*, 350, 352
Grant, Fionn
  birth xii
  birthdays 97, 181, 249-50
  confronts drunk 129
  excursions alone 198, 245-6
  home interlude 102, 103
  and palmist 229-30
  present schooling 379
  reactions to journey 11, 54-5, 253
  riding accident 96-7
  run over 6
  on runaway horse 321
  sickness 174-5, 176-7
  in USA 317, 331-6 *passim*, 362-9 *passim*
Grant, Kate
  beginnings xiii-xxiv
  Canadian relatives 366

(Grant, Kate, cont.)
  cares for father 166-7, 220
  departures and returns 39-40,
    42-3, 43-4, 61, 69-71, 101-
    2, 103, 225, 264
  early married life xi-xiii
  early stresses 7-8, 16, 20, 24,
    27, 30
  friendships formed 80, 93, 97
  future 378-9, 379
  helps with court case 266-7,
    270, 271, 272, 305
  illness 332-3, 335, 337, 344
  last days of journey 351, 364,
    377
  sister Lesley 333
  tasks on journey 11, 95, 134,
    162-3
  in USA 309, 314, 317, 323-4
Grant, Lt L.R. 28-9
Grant, Sir Patrick 353-4
  Grant's of Dalvey xii-xxiii, 228
Grant, Torcuil
  appendicitis 57-61
  bird-watching 317, 364
  birth xii
  and Dina 220
  emotional reactions 47, 184,
    230, 245, 374
  future 379
  nasty encounter 197
  and runaway horse 38-9
  sickness 174-5, 176-7
  shoes 192
Grasse (Fr) 48
Gravis, Steve and Kenna 333
Grozny (Chechnya) 212, 265
Gruchkov, Consul 145
Gubaev, Zhenis 176
Guinness Book of Records 361
Gulf War 43
Guo Yi-miao, Dr 279-81, 283
gypsies 51, 62, 100, 107, 115,
    125, 161, 227

Hajdú, Mátyás 115-16
Hale-Bopp comet 356
Halifax (Cn) 375-6, 377
Hamilton (Cn) 366
Hamilton, Jane 263
Hamont (Bg) 17
Hanley, Mike 328
Hansen, Keith 317
Harkàny (Hg) 108
Hàromfa (Hg) 107
Heel, Willem Dudok van 1
Heilongjiang (Ch) 284
Heneman, Burr 315, 316
Hidden Village (Nl) 6
Hinton, Sean 261
Hitomi, Juro and family 299,
    303-4, 306, 307, 310
Hodgson, Consul George 269,
    271, 274, 275
Hollingworth, Larry 139
Honhold, Nick 263, 264-5
Honkala, Calvin 363-4, 364-5,
    368-9
Horol (Uk) 150-51
horses
  see also Bertha; Offy; Traceur
  Barney 378
  Chessy 249-51, 252, 274-5
  cruel transport 104
  harness systems 127, 151
  horse meat and milk 220, 236,
    237
  Lippizaner 99, 121
  Mongol races 274
  Petite 35-6
  Przewalski's 8, 263-4
  puszta riders 112-13
  shoeing 106, 112, 153, 328
  Socks 320, 321, 324
  spontaneous bleeding 226
  studs 156, 211-12

Hortobagy National Park (Hg) 114
Hovd (Mg) 246-7
Howe, Sir Geoffrey 26
Hu (official) 292, 296, 297
Hungary 97, 100-101, 104, 105-23 (notably 106, 122-3), 126
hunting 5, 78
Huron, Lake(Cn/USA) 367
Hustai Nuruu (Mg) 263-4
Hyakatake comet 320
Hyase San 299, 310

Ice Slough (USA) 336
Idaho (USA) 328, 329-33
Ilya (policeman) 155-6
Imberi, Bill 352-3, 355, 356
Imberi, June 348
Imogen Taken Alive 345
In memoriam Achenbach magazine 43
Independence Rock (USA) 336
International Bridge (Cn/USA) 365-6
Ireland xviii-xx
Irgiz (Kz) 190
Irtysh river (Kz) 226
Italy 48-66, 104

Jack and Pat (house owners) xvi-xvii
Jackson, Simon 218-19, 220, 226
JAL (Japanese Airlines) 308, 311
Jampol (Uk) 141
Japan 299-311 (notably 303)
Jargallant mountain (Mg) 247
Jelky, Andris 112
Jerman, Barbara 95
Jinning (Ch) 287, 289
JLA (Yugoslav People's Army) 89
Joe Flying By 340
Johnson, Matthew 298, 300, 309, 310

Juha (Ch) 285
Kadis, George 269, 287-8, 289
Kapele (Sl) 101-3
Kapitain Lyutikov (ship) 309
Karabulak (Kz) 221
Karmanov, Vladimir 226, 227
Katchmer, Dr Oleg 137, 138
Katirai, Foad 307-8 (bis), 310
Katun river (Rs) 231
Kazakhstan 145, 153, 172, 173-228 (notably 182, 188-9, 192, 201, 204-5, 223-5), 236
Kazakhstan International Bank 219
Kaztalovka (Kz) 177
Keiller, Garrison: Lake Woebegon Days 361
Keller, Helen and Louis 342, 343, 344, 348, 355
Kemmerer (USA) 334
Kenny, Mary 109
Khar-us, Lake (Mg) 247
Khar-us river (Mg) 237, 238
Khasagt Khayrkhan mountain (Mg) 250
Khurelbaatar (friend) 260, 264, 266, 271, 275
Khurelbaatar, Captain (police) 260-61, 265, 267-8
Kientpoos, 'Captain Jack' 326
Kiev (Uk) 143-4, 146
Kidirbaev, Director 232
King, Kristen 366
Kisdobron (Uk) 126
Kitamura San 299, 300
Klagenfurt (Au) 70-71
Klassen, Jura 227
Klimov, Viktor 226-7
Kljajič, Inspector Žjelko 94
Kobe (Jn) 300-301, 303, 310
Kodiak Island (USA) 312

Koksa river (Rs) 229
Kolenbrand, Boris 79
Kolosova, Tamara 227, 229-30
Komintern (Kz) 183
Kompressornoe (Kz) 189
Konečnik, Anton 77
Konjeniški Klub 74, 94, 101
Kosh-Agach (Rs) 231-2, 234
Kosta, Konstantin and Lena 235
Kovacs, Mária 116
Kozova (Uk) 135
Kravchuk, President Leonid 130
Kremenec (Uk) 140
Krepocty Rocc (USA) 318
Kreslin, Vlado 100
Krivoruchko, Anatoly 154
Kroos, Herr 5
Krpač, Rado 77-91 passim, 94, 99, 101
Kučan, Milan 82-3
Kulan (Kz) 212
Kurds 204
Kuzmich, Milaslav 228
Kyrghyzstan 212, 213, 215
Kyzl-Orda (Kz) 201

Lady (dog) xxiii-xxiv, 1, 41, 44
Laflamme, Renaud 369, 373
Laflamme, Guy and Agathe 373
Lambert, Loïs and David 263, 276-7, 307
Laryonovy, Vitja and Paulina 227-8
Lassen, Mount (USA) 321
Lassen National Forest (USA) 322-3
Latica river (Uk) 130-31, 131 (bis)
Laurentides (Cn) 371
Lava Beds National Monument (USA) 326
Lava Hot Springs (USA) 333
Lavamünd (Au) 72, 92-3, 97

Le Bic (Cn) 373
Lees, J.J. xxii-xxiii
Lendova (Sl) 101, 103 bis, 104
Leningorsk (Rs) 226-8
Leninsk (Kz) 198-9
Lequia, Ann and Tim 363, 364
Letham Grange Hotel 308, 378, 379
Lethbridge, T.C. 273
Lewis, Sinclair 360
Libeliče (Sl) 91
Linkova, Valentina Viktorovna 234
Little, Christine and Stephen 42
Little Bighorn river (USA) 350
Little Falls (USA) 361
Little Owl Black Cloud 345-6
Liu (translator) 293
Liu, Peter 308, 378
Ljubljana (Sl) 85, 96, 97
Locke, Kevin and family 276-7, 339-49 passim, 353, 359 bis
Los Angeles (USA) 309, 313-14
Lukimya (Uk) 150
Lukyanov, Yuri 231
L'vov (Uk) 136-8

Maas river (Nl) 14
McAllister, Agent (SPCA) 368
Macdonald, Ewan 309, 314, 336
Macdonald, Ian and Juliet xxiii
McDonald Peak 326
McKie, Wilf 263, 269, 271
McLeese, Shirley and Ronald 369-70
McMahon, Annie 218-19, 220, 222-3, 225
McNamara, Colin and Kathy 370-71
MacTaggart, Sir William xiv
McTiernan, Steven 218
Madonna Thunder Hawk 341
Magdeev, Rakhim 189, 191

Mainardi, Ferdi 57, 60-61
Major, John 214, 274
Mansfield, Bud 365
Marengo (It) 55
Maribor (Sl) 77-8, 86
Marković, Ante 81-2
Marquette (USA) 363-4
Martin, David xxii
Masaki San 307
Massera, Giovanni and Anna 56-62, 114
Matapedia valley (Cn) 373-4
Melovoe (Uk) 156
Metternich, Ambassador 272
Meuse river (Bg/Fr) 24, 27
Mez, Dr Jason 342
Mezőkövesd (Hg) 113, 114-15, 118-19, 121
Michigan (USA) 363, 364
Mickleson, Dr Ken 274
Milan, Roberto 65
Mille Lacs Lake (USA) 361
Mille Lacs Messenger 361
Miller, Joe 375, 376, 377
Milo Yellow Hair 341
Milošović, Slobodan 98
Minidoka County Museum (USA) 332
Minnesota (USA) 360-62
Miskolc (Hg) 117
Mislinja valley (Sl) 86, 90
Mississippi river (USA) 361
Mobridge (USA) 342, 343-4, 351, 355, 356, 357
Mohács (Hg) 109-11
Moj Drugi Dom (song) 95-6, 125
Monaco 49, 50
Monastir mountains (Kz) 225-6
Mongol hordes 189
Mongolia 219, 224, 234-77 (notably 235-6, 242-5)
Mormons 332

Morrison Knudsen Company 259
Mortar & Pestle Pharmacy 348, 351-2
Moyne, Christiane 37, 38, 42
Moyne, Joël 35, 37-8, 40, 42, 222-3
Mugodzharskoe (Kz) 188
Munkh (translator) 269
Mura river (Hg) 107
Murch, Aggie and Walter 315, 318-19, 330
Mykačevo (Uk) 128

Nagy, Imre 123
Namou (old Navajo) 334
Nanku Island (Jn) 302, 305
Nara (Jn) 304
Native Americans
   Canadian Indians 366-7
   ceremonies 339-40, 345-6
   history 321, 326, 343, 350
   life on reservations 341, 346-7, 359
   myths 337-8, 356
   Navajo shepherd 334
Naylor, Sgt Stefan 369
Negmetzhanov family 221-3, 226
Nemesnádudvar (Hg) 112
Netherlands xxii, 1-16 (notably 13-14)
Nevada (USA) 327
New Brunswick (Cn) 374
Newcomb, Wiki and family 317, 332, 333, 336
Nice (Fr) 49
Nikolaevsk (Rs) 170
Nin (dog) 203, 233, 234, 281-2, 316-17
Nyéki, Zsuzsana, and father 119
Noble Trail (USA) 325
Norsea (ship) xxiii-xxiv
Nova Scotia (Cn) 375-6

Novostoilivka (Uk) 156
Nurgalyev, Dr Gabit, and Goolya 192-3
Nyeste, József and Manszi 115
NYK Line 306

Oahe Veterinary Hospital 342, 347
O'Brien, Irma and Dan 318, 350
Ochman, Fedya 221-2, 224
Odyoot, Latsi and Nina 129-30
Offereins, Dr 4-5, 20
Offy (horse)
  bought 4-5, 8
  feeding 16
  on journey 12-13, 18-34 passim
  retired 34
Oktyabirsk (Kz) 186
Olyesko (Uk) 140
One World Festival (Osaka) 308
Ootegenov, Dr Amangeldy and family 173
Ooteshkalyev, Marat and Armin 171-2
Opheusden (Nl) 12-13
Oregon (USA) 327-8, 332
Orkney xvi-xviii, xxii-xxiii, xxiv, 31
Orsay (Fr) 27, 33, 34
Osaka (Jn) 309
  Quarantine Station 299-300, 301-2, 306
Ostachersee (Au) 70
Ottawa (Cn) 370
Ottocella, Giovanni 55

Pa-Yin-Ch'a-Ken (Ch) 286-7
Pallasovka (Rs) 171
Papineau, Laurie 375-6
Parád (Hg) 121
Paris (Fr) 33, 34-5
Pauley, Pam 375

Peelen, Jan and Wis 14
Perevica (Uk) 148-9
Person, Paule 27, 34
Petaluma river (USA) 319
Petrovich, Paulov and Ljuba 148-9
Piana Crixia (It) 54
Pierre (USA) 354
Pivka river (Sl) 94-5
Platica river (Uk) 128
Plochke (Uk) 140
Poberžnik, Berta 81, 95
Pochaev (Uk) 140
Podpolozya (Uk) 132-3
Podzolli, M. 41
Pogner, Dr Melitta 72
Pólik, István 119, 121, 122
Pólik, Klára 113, 115, 119, 122
Poltava (Uk) 152
Popov, Viktor 228
Po river (It) 56
Postojna caves (Sl) 94-5
Praper, Otokar and family 74-5, 77, 78, 88-9, 92, 93, 101
Prekmurje region (Sl) 99-100
Pucher, Anita and Gernot 72, 92
Pugwash (Cn) 375

Quarnan, Monte (It) 65
Québec (Cn) 370-74

Radio Alma-Ata 198
Radio Murski Val 100
Radio Riviera 46-7
Radio Slovenija 83
Radio Slovenj Gradec 82
Radiviliv (Uk) 140
Ragosa, Viktor and Svetka 168-70
Rahman (pilot) 240-41
Raymaekers, Dane and Ria 19
Red Bluff (USA) 321-2
Red Canyon (USA) 335

Rédics (Hg) 105
Reims (Fr) 30-32
Rhine river (Nl) 12
Rians (Fr) 45
Ribalkin, Ivan 228
Rice, Evie and Richard 353, 357, 359
Rimouski (Cn) 373
Rishko, Lev 136 *bis*
Risorb (Kz) 215
Rockie, Jim 368
Rostov (Rs) 157, 162
Rotterdam (Nl) 1, 3
RTV 96
Russia 96, 101, 117, 118, 157-72, 214, 228-33, 234-5, 265
  Russian ships 309
Rybaltowski, Andrew 263

Sabine (groom) 54
saiga (antelopes) 194, 203
Saihan (Ch) 284
St Lawrence river (Cn) 372-3
Saint Sauveur (Fr) 35-6, 43, 45
Saksaoulskyi (Kz) 192
Sambu (Mongolian) 239
San Francisco (USA) 309, 314
San Remo (It) 51-2
Sanyo Unyo transport company 299
Sara (neighbour) 266
Sarikiylik (Kz) 178
Sariozek (Kz) 221
Sarsenby, Director 178-80
Sársomlói hill (Hg) 108-9
Sasykul, Lake (Kg) 225
Satz, Joseph and family 68-9
Sauk Center (USA) 360
Sault Sainte Marie (USA/Cn) 365-6
Savona (It) 53
Schanzenbach, Tami 342, 347-8, 348-9

Schechert Ranch (USA) 324-5
Schrempp, Dean and Mavis 339, 340, 353, 354, 361
Schueren, Alain van der 23, 24, 33
Scotland/Scots xiii, 56, 63, 87, 97, 363, 372, 375, 378
Scotsman 88, 96, 122-3
Seattle (USA) 350
Sekisovka (Kz) 226
Seney Wildlife Refuge (USA) 364
Serafini, Elisabeta and family 64
Serbia 78
Šetinc, Igor and family 100, 101, 103
Severin, Tim: *Crusader* 67
She-who-steps-first 345-6
sheep slaughter (Mg) 243
Shenkher river (Mg) 248
Shilikti (Kz) 191
Shimansky, Dr Anatoly 334-5
Shirai, Kunio 310
Shiraishi San 299, 300
Sholokhov, Mikhail 160
Shortie Cottage (Orkney) xvii-xviii, xxiii
Sierra Nevadas (USA) 313, 322
Siklós (Hg) 108
Szilvásvárad (Hg) 121
Silver City (USA) 329-30
Skrap, Rok 99
Skye, Isle of xi-xii, xiii, xiv
Slattery, David xvi, xviii-xx
Slovenia 72-92, 94-104
  independence 78-9, 81-92, 98
Slovenj Gradec 96-7, 99
Smith, Cathy 341
Snake river (USA) 330-31, 332
snow and ice
  Asia 134-5, 195-6, 200-201, 213-14, 214-15, 253, 255
  Canada 356-7, 358-9
Solodushino (Rs) 168-9

Somerset, Bill 144
Sospiro (It) 57, 58, 61-2
South Dakota (USA) 338-60
    (*notably* 354)
Sovyetskaya (Rs) 161
SPCA (Cn) 368, 369
Srebrenica (Bosnia) 139
Stalingrad (Rs) 165-6
Stanley Looking Horse and
    family 345, 346
Stashensky, Wyacheslav 137
Stepnoe (Kz) 215
steppe 173, 175, 180-81, 183-4,
    195-6, 221, 223-4, 231
Stevenson, Robert Louis xv
Stolsmark, Brad and Penny 355,
    359
Stoves, Margaret 218
Stradivarius 56
Style, Ione 353
Suda San 307-8 *(bis)*
Sugash (Rs) 229
Sullam, Jean-Michel 34
Summeren, Theo van 14-15
Superior, Lake (Cn/USA) 364
Suremain, Alexis 234-5
Svalyava (Uk) 130
Švarc, Miran 97, 105
Switzerland 42
Sylvie (stable girl) 35-6
Syr Darya river (Kz) 193, 201
Szerdahelyi, Lajos and Éva 111
Szolnok (Hg) 113

Taccolini, Louis 364
Taivan, Mrs (advocate) 261,
    265-6, 267, 271, 275
Taldy-Kurgan airfield (Kz) 223
Tamburlane the Great 203
Tamdi river (Kz) 183-4
Taniguchi San 299, 307
Tarjányi (farrier) 112
Tarvisio (It) 66, 67

Tashanta (Rs) 231, 232, 233,
    234-5
Tast mountain (Mg) 241
Tatarstan/Tatars 189, 221, 223
Tchainikova, Irina 217, 220
Tchimkent (Kz) 204, 205, 206
Tchintogtoch and family 241-2,
    245, 246-7
Terenkul (Kz) 176
Termo (USA) 325
Texas, MV 308-9
Thatcher, Margaret 26, 33
Thine, Catherine de 22-3
Thomas, Amy 116-17
Tianjin (Ch) 289, 291, 306
Tibor (blacksmith) 106
Tien Shan mountians (Kz) 207,
    208, 214-15
Timberlake (USA) 353
Tiospa Zina school (USA) 359
Tisza river (Hg) 114, 124
Tito, Marshal 73, 78
Todaiji Temple (Jn) 304
Toguz (Kz) 196
Tolba (Mg) 241
Tong (policeman) 287-9
Tooziak, Dr Andrew 137, 138, 144
Traceur (horse)
    bought 35, 37-9, 44, 46
    in China 279-82, 284, 289-90,
        294-7
    in Europe/Asia 56-7, 110, 138-
        9, 149, 150, 214, 247, 254
    health 76-8, 79, 80-81, 83, 92-
        3, 173, 175-6, 177-8, 186,
        197-8, 201, 206-7, 208-9,
        210-11
    in Japan 299-300, 302-3, 305,
        306-7
    in USA 309, 311, 314, 315,
        317-18, 332
    in USA – last days 337, 341-3,
        347-8, 351-32

Trailer Life 361
Trans-Canada Highway 367
Trapečar, Dr Borut 77-8
Traverse, Lake (USA) 360
Triglav, Mount (Sl) 103
Trois Rivières (Cn) 371-2
Tsaganuur (Mg) 235, 236-7,
    239, 240
Tsar (dog)
    bought 122
    on journey 164, 176, 233, 234,
        245-6
    in USA 344, 345, 348
Tudor, Geoff 308, 309, 310, 311
Turkestan town (Kz) 202, 203-4
Turkey 109, 203
Turner, Julie and Gene 347
Twin Falls (USA) 331
Tyler-Haywood, Sandra 280,
    288, 290-91, 293, 294, 295,
    296

Ukraine 117-18, 119, 124-56
    (*notably* 137, 140, 147-8)
Ulaanbaatar (Mg) 240, 258, 259-
    77 (*notably* 259, 261-3)
Ulangom (Mg) 236-7, 238-9
United Kingdom 98, 101,116,
    316, 360
United States of America 101,
    302-3, 309, 312-57 (*notably*
    319)
    Peace Corps 116-17
    see also Native Americans
Ural river (Kz) 180
Uralsk (Kz) 180, 181
Urquhart, Donald 97
Ursul river (Rs) 231
US Equine Inc. 310
Ust' Kamenogorsk (Kz) 226
Ust' Kan (Rs) 229, 230

Večer newspaper 83

Vegter, Jan 263
Veliki Lučki (Uk) 127
Venice (It) 62-3
Ventimiglia (It) 50-51
Verchne Siniovedne (Uk) 135
Verhoef, Dries 2-3, 7
Veshenskaya (Rs) 160
Vič (Sl) 86, 91, 92
Vierhouten (Nl) 3, 5
Viking Altar Rock (USA) 360
Villach (Au) 69-70
Villány (Hg) 109
Ville-Juste (Fr) 34
Visscher, Isobel and Eric de 19-
    20
Volga river (Rs) 166, 168, 189
Volga-Don canal (Rs) 164-5
Volgograd (Rs) 165-6
Volzhskiyi (Rs) 168
Vukovar (Croatia) 98

Waaldijk (Nl) 13-14
Wang, Captain 300
Waridel, Catherine 195, 202,
    220, 251, 258
Warren, Pam and Rick 322, 328,
    336
Webb, Andy 272
Welz, Franz 344
Whitney, Jack and family 336-7,
    338
Wiegam, Mrs 349, 353
Wilhelmsen Lines 308
William of Rubruck 220
Winkler, Dieter 92, 93
Winona Flying Earth 345
Wisconsin (USA) 363
wolves 192, 196, 215
Wonders, Jazon 317, 318, 320,
    356
World War One 28-9, 31, 33
World War Two 6, 150, 165-6
Wounded Knee (USA) 343, 346-7

Wouter, Jannecke and Otto
　　(children) 15
Wyoming (USA) 333-8

yaks 236, 242-3, 258
Yamamoto, Kenji 307
Yanjing (ship) 294, 295, 297-8,
　　299, 300
Yaseniv (Uk) 140
Yeltsin, Boris 96, 170, 187
Young, Brian 269
Yugoslavia 73, 78-9, 81-2, 88
Yuri, Nora, Ivan I and Ivan II
　　127-8

Záhony (Hg) 124
Zamyn Uud (Mg) 278, 279
Zaporozhe nuclear plant (Uk)
　　151
Zaritov, Khambal 189-91
Zdravo! (TV) 95
Zeeland (Nl) 15
Zharokova (Kz) 174
Zhitomir (Uk) 142-3
Zhurin (Kz) 186
Ziwicki, Coleen and family 361
Zwaan, Jan de 23

TOUCHSTONE

SIMON &
SCHUSTER

ONE RIVER
SCIENCE, ADVENTURE AND
HALLUCINOGENICS IN THE AMAZON BASIN
WADE DAVIS

A stunning account of adventure and discovery,
betrayal and destruction, *One River* is a story of
two generations of explorers drawn together by the
transcendent knowledge of Indian peoples and the
extraordinary plants that sustain all life in a forest
that once stood immense and inviolable.

'This is an eloquent and complex book, filled with
superb evocations of the Latin American
landscape . . . Davis is a remarkably good writer'
SUNDAY TIMES

'Davis is a fine writer . . . He has passion on his side
– one of the greatest assets a writer can have'
TELEGRAPH

'Further evidence that the rainforests of the world
hold something of vital importance to mankind . . .
read this book'
STING

ISBN: 0 684 81764 0
Price: £7.99

POCKET
B O O K S

REAL CHINA
From cannibalism to karaoke
John Gittings

REAL CHINA is a revealing journey through the
heart of China, far away from Beijing, exploring
the realities of life in the villages and towns.
Beyond the 'economic miracle' much praised
abroad, there is a widening gap between rich and
poor. Urban squalor persists alongside a new
generation of 'Get Rich First' entrepreneurs. The
popular press revels in crime and sex but cannot
discuss politics. And no one knows where China
is headed after the death of Deng Xiaoping.
John Gittings brings the real China – and the
truth behind the hype – vividly to life.

'*Real China* is as splendid, horrifying and delightful
as the real China is . . . It is, quite simply, excellent'
John Simpson, *Dail Mail*

ISBN: 0 671 51651 5
Price: £7.99

POCKET
B O O K S

THE WINNERS' ENCLOSURE

ANNIE CAULFIELD

'Most Irish families are the descendants of Kings.
Most Irish families have no particular proof of this,
but it is nonetheless so. For those who are not the
descendants of Kings, there are Earldoms, Dukedoms,
the fortunes of an ingenious inventor, sharp
entrepreneur or plain hard-grafter back along the
family line. No one is just what they seem.'

So begins a comical and idiosyncratic odyssey to unravel
fact from fiction in a well-spun family tale. On her
travels Annie Caulfield finds the real, bittersweet
Australia in a series of bizarre encounters with larger
than life characters. Not always pretty, but full of dayglo
local colour, the individuals she meets give a startling 3D
snapshot of modern Australia, and shed light on a past
full of contradictions and complexities. Wry, funny,
touching, and sometimes tragic, Annie Caulfield's quest
to find her Irish connection to Australia uncovers much
more than she bargained for.

ISBN: 0 671 01801 9
Price: £7.99
Published August 2000

**SIMON &
SCHUSTER**

This book and other **Simon & Schuster** titles are available from your book shop or can be ordered direct from the publisher.

☐ 0 671 01801 9   **The Winners' Enclosure**   £6.99
                        Annie Caulfield
☐ 0 684 81764 0   **One River**   £7.99
                        Wade Davis
☐ 0 671 51651 5   **Real China**   £7.99
                        John Gittings
☐ 0 684 85181 4   **China Through the Sliding Doors**   £7.99
                        John Gittings

Please send cheque or postal order for the value of the book, free postage and packing within the UK; OVERSEAS including Republic of Ireland £1 per book.

OR: Please debit this amount from my:

VISA/ACCESS/MASTERCARD ....

CARD NO: ....

EXPIRY DATE ....

AMOUNT £..

NAME ....

ADDRESS ....

....

SIGNATURE ....

Send orders to SIMON & SCHUSTER CASH SALES
PO Box 29, Douglas, Isle of Man, IM99 1BQ
Tel: 01624 675137, Fax: 01624 670923
www.bookpost.co.uk
Please allow 14 days for delivery. Prices and availability subject to change without notice.